Y0-EEK-300

R.L.Y. Peyton
An American Journey

Tom A. Rafiner

Cover Design by Jackie Polsgrove-Roberts

R.L.Y. Peyton
An American Journey

Published by
Burnt District Press
Burnt District of MO, LLC
Harrisonville, MO 64701
BDPress@ymail.com

Printed in the United States of America

R.L.Y. "Lud" Peyton

Acknowledgments

Jackie Roberts, the co-owner of The Burnt District Press, but more importantly a steadfast friend, deserves my undying thanks for her constant support and encouragement. Whenever my research hit a dead-end, Jackie plied her miraculous research skills to uncover new avenues. Quite frankly this biography would not have been possible without her assistance. So often a project of this type requires connecting the dots – Jackie *helped locate* the dots!

Diane Magness's support and assistance cannot be appreciated enough. Diane provided research material and consented to read and edit manuscript drafts. Her sincere interest and gracious encouragement often kept me moving forward.

Brian Hawkins's artistic skills continue to astound me. His attention to historic detail and accuracy turns a drawing into a photograph. Brian's illustration of Lud's speech on the Jefferson City Bluffs literally pulls you into that moment, May 9, 1861!

Valerie Elliott was unbelievable! The Manager of the Smith Library of Regional History in Oxford, Ohio, Valerie went above and beyond in providing information and research. I can't adequately thank her.

Mary B. Fishback never seemed to tire of my annoying e-mails. Mary guides research at the Thomas Balch Library in Leesburg, Va. Her assistance on Loudoun County and the early Peyton's was invaluable.

Dolores Rush shares my passion for western Missouri history. Dolores's unrelenting search for the history of Martin White often shed light on Lud Peyton's life. She kept me constantly in mind and shared unselfishly.

Andy Dolan's guidance and expertise resulted in over 20 maps. His wonderful maps illustrate Peyton's journeys and glue his life to the land.

I owe special thanks to John L. Peyton, Warner Lewis and Robert Sloan. These three gentlemen personally knew and revered Lud. Each wrote a biographical sketch of R.L.Y. Peyton, hoping to solidify Lud's memory and legacy. Their words and memories provided the touchstone for my research.

Finally, and most important, I give my unending thanks to my wife Nancy. At every turn over the past 16 years, she provided constant encouragement allowing my research trips to interrupt her life. Her patience in diligently proof reading hundreds of drafts elevates her to saint status.

Introduction

I first encountered Robert Ludwell Yates Peyton, or as he was known, "Lud Peyton," in my early research for *Caught Between Three Fires*. An edition of the *Liberty Tribune*, January 8, 1864, contained a very brief announcement of Lud's death. The article identified Peyton as a former Cass County resident. I was diligently compiling an inventory of all 1860 Cass County residents - but Peyton's name was a mystery. Copying the announcement I began a search. When I next visited the Cass County historical society asking about Peyton the staff drew a blank – they had never heard of him. At the time, little did I realize that recovering Lud's life would become an all-consuming passion for the next 16-years.

Lud Peyton would have needed no introduction in western Missouri between 1844 and 1865. From his arrival at Harrisonville in 1844 until the beginning of the Civil War, Lud practiced frontier law in Missouri's Sixth Judicial District Circuit; his law practice included the counties of Jackson, Cass, Bates, Johnson, Lafayette, Pettis, and Saline. He also worked in Vernon, Henry, and Cedar counties. A Southern firebrand during the ante-bellum years, Lud was well known to western Missouri residents. During the golden age of oratory, he was an orator of the highest order, brilliant and electric.

Voters sent Peyton to Missouri's Senate in 1858. In 1861, as a member of Gov. C.F. Jackson's inner circle Lud helped orchestrate Missouri's secession. He recruited and led the Missouri State Guard's 3rd Cavalry Regiment. From early 1862 until his death in September 1863, he represented Missouri in the Confederate Senate at Richmond, Virginia.

Lud's brief life is representative of our country's, and Missouri's, complex ante-bellum history. Born among an early generation of natural born Americans, Lud's journey from Virginia to Ohio to

Missouri mirrors that of thousands of immigrants moving west as the country expanded.

Lud Peyton never doubted slavery's legal, moral, and economic legitimacy. A dedicated Southerner he unfailingly defended slavery and states' rights against the moderate positions of friends and community.

Civil War and the holocaust of General Thomas Ewing, Jr.'s General Order No. 11 obliterated western Missouri's ante-bellum history. Accompanying Lud Peyton on his life journey deepens an understanding of Missouri's western frontier as well as furthering our knowledge about the political winds raging through the state during the 1850s.

How is it that no one has heard of Lud Peyton? A series of contributing factors drove Peyton's disappearance from Missouri's historical record.

Less than two years after his death the Civil War ended, and in the decades following, Lud's presence and influence in Missouri history slipped into oblivion. Frustratingly, as my research progressed it became clear that very few people, including local and state historians, recognized his name.

Lud's personal life left no clues and little documentation. A bachelor, no surviving wife or children lived to memorialize his life. No personal letters or correspondence of any kind survived. Malaria killed Lud in 1863 at Bladon Springs, Alabama, he was just 39.

Lud's political life, although explosive and soaring at a critical point in our history, was overshadowed by his age. His youth relegated him to "the next generation" of statewide political leaders.

He was often referred to as a "rising star." Additionally, Lud was a Southern fire-eater. His radical position alienated him from much of Missouri's moderate electorate.

Peyton commanded a cavalry regiment of Missouri State Guard. In 1861, as Colonel of the MSG's 3rd Cavalry he fought at Carthage, Wilson's Creek, Drywood Creek and Lexington. Lud's military service, although laudable, was too brief to achieve battlefield fame.

The Civil War's total destruction of western Missouri did much to erase his memory. Many of the towns and villages where Lud practiced law and campaigned were destroyed, along with their local newspapers. Thousands of refugees, neighbors and friends, who would have remembered and documented Lud's life fled, never returning. These refugees carried, in their hearts and heads, western Missouri's ante-bellum history.

Ironically, Lud's death occurred during the exact 15-day period Union troops were enforcing General Orders No. 11. As Lud lay dying in Alabama Union troops were torching 2,200 square miles of western Missouri while driving out all of the remaining civilian population.

Peyton's lost legacy is also due in no small part to the fact the Confederacy lost the war. Northern immigrants, many of whom had fought for the Union, largely resettled Missouri's burnt district. They had no memory of Peyton or the area's ante-bellum history and no motivation to resurrect it.

Folks who personally knew or heard Lud Peyton never forgot him as both a human being and impassioned leader. After the turn of the century, 1904, a friend and admirer of Peyton, Warner Lewis wrote an article about "Senator Robert L.Y. Peyton."[1] Lewis's article, was triggered by the death of George G. Vest, considered by many to be Missouri's greatest orator. Lewis reminded Missourians that Vest paled in comparison to Missouri's greatest ante-bellum orator, R.L.Y. Peyton. A.B. Boone, a Clinton, Mo., attorney and Peyton contemporary, had earlier advanced the same opinion in 1899.

So, why read the biography of a man who left few personal footprints and has fallen from memory? Lud Peyton's life captures and personifies the tapestry of Missouri's ante-bellum journey.

- Lud was born in Loudoun County, Va. to a historic and prominent family with ties to George Washington and Thomas Jefferson.
- Lud's birthplace is on the National Register of Historic Places.
- Lud's father moved the family to Oxford, Ohio during the great Virginia exodus of the 1830s.
- The Peyton family trek on the National Road mirrors the experience of thousands of Americans in the move west.
- Educated at Miami University and the University of Virginia Lud experienced, first hand, early abolitionist debates and he knew the Beecher family.
- Lud Peyton moved to the primitive Missouri frontier when white settlers and Indians mingled, cohabitating Missouri's western border.
- Lud practiced frontier law in the raucous Sixth Judicial District from 1844 to 1861, relishing the high drama of murder trials.

[1] *The Montgomery Standard.* August 24,1904.

- Lud Peyton was elected to the Missouri Senate representing the border counties during the height of conflict between Missouri and the Kansas Territory.
- Lud's oratorical brilliance lifted him to the top of Missouri's ante-bellum Southern political movement where he shared the public platform with two U.S. Senators.
- Before serving in the Confederate Senate, Lud, as a member of Governor Claiborne F. Jackson's inner circle, helped orchestrate Missouri's secession.
- In 1861, Colonel Peyton commanded a cavalry regiment of the Missouri State Guard.
- Lud played a key leadership role in the Governor Jackson's "Extraordinary Legislative Session" at Neosho.
- Lud represented Missouri in the Confederate Senate from 1861 to 1863. He was literally an eye witness to history.
- Lud became a member of Jefferson Davis's household during the Civil War. His sister Fanny married Joseph R. Davis, a favored nephew of Confederate President Jefferson Davis.

For years known as Harrisonville's "lovable eccentric," the frontier attorney leapt into the ante-bellum political fracas becoming one of Missouri's rising stars.

Lud's life is significant because it is our history and heritage. I hope you enjoy accompanying Lud on his journey – a life unique, eccentric, yet universal – an American journey.

Tom A. Rafiner
September 20, 2019

TABLE OF CONTENTS

MAPS

Chapter One
The Virginia Peytons

Robert Ludwell Yates Peyton, R.L.Y. Peyton, hereafter Lud Peyton, entered the world a Virginia Cavalier, grew to manhood in Oxford, Ohio, achieved public prominence in western Missouri, legislated in Jefferson City, Missouri, rebelled in Richmond, Virginia, and died in Choctaw County, Alabama. Lud's journey was uniquely American. Lud Peyton's brief life left few tangible footprints. Peyton never married. Peyton never accumulated substantial property. Although a Southerner both by birth and political persuasion, Peyton never owned slaves. Although an accomplished cavalry officer, Peyton never achieved military renown.

Peyton however played a pivotal role in western Missouri history and during his lifetime, achieved, throughout Missouri, an unmatched reputation for oratorical fire. Lud Peyton's journey from frontier lawyer to Confederate Senator encapsulates the dramatic events that shaped Missouri and national history. Within a generation of the Civil War, Lud Peyton's presence and influence, as a frontier lawyer, fiery western Missouri border leader, and Missouri State Senator evaporated.

---------- The Cavalier Virginians ----------

Lud's life journey began in Virginia, the Old Dominion. Like many of his generation who left the state, regardless of the distance from his birth place, he identified as a Virginian. To understand Lud's cultural core it is necessary to revisit early 19th century Virginia.

Virginia Circa 1824

By 1824, Lud's birth year, Virginia had supplied four of the first five United State Presidents. These four Virginian Presidents had held the nation's highest office for 31 of the country's 35 years. Virginia delegates, representing one of the original 13 colonies, had signed the Declaration of Independence. Virginia's already rich heritage boasted, Jamestown, one of England's first colonial settlements in the New World. Virginian, Thomas Jefferson, had in 1803, doubled the country's land mass. From Jefferson's Louisiana Purchase, Missouri, Lud's eventual destination and destiny, emerged to statehood in 1821.

Virginia's name itself bespoke English nobility, reflecting the prestige and power of the English crown. Queen Elizabeth I, the Virgin Queen, planted the state's early settlements. Virginia's first 200 years were crafted and controlled by English families of noble descent who first settled the Chesapeake Bay area. These cavalier families transported traditional English mores and values. The social and political culture was hierarchical, male dominated. Status carried weight and authority. Virginia's culture differed dramatically from that of New England's English Puritans. Indeed, New England's Puritans had been driven from England by the same beliefs and authority exercised by Virginia's cavalier immigrants. These two adversarial cultures later faced off along the Missouri – Kansas Territorial border in the 1850s.

Lud Peyton's ancestors stepped ashore in Virginia among the flood of "cavalier" immigrants. This initial wave of Royalist immigrants arrived between 1642 and 1675. "Shortly after Oliver Cromwell established the Protectorate in 1653, Henry Peyton (1590 – 1656) of Lincoln's Inn, London, who rode with the 'Cavaliers', sent four of his sons to Virginia and they settled in what was then Westmoreland County. Two of Henry's sons, Colonel Valentine Peyton (1627 – 1665) and Henry Peyton (1631 – 1659) settled permanently in Virginia."[2] Their descendants, the Virginia Peyton's are listed among the Commonwealth's prominent and ruling families of the sixteenth, seventeenth, and early eighteenth centuries. Lud Peyton descended from Henry Peyton. Lud's forefathers were:

- Valentine Peyton: Valentine Peyton was a son of Henry Peyton, one of the original Peyton immigrants. Lud's great grandfather, Valentine served in a number of civic positions in Prince William County, Virginia.

- Francis Peyton: Lud's grandfather settled in and developed Loudoun County, Virginia. Francis fought in the American Revolution and served in the House of Burgesses. Francis counted George Washington and Thomas Jefferson among his associates.

- Townshend Dade Peyton: Lud's father continued Francis's civic and business endeavors in Loudon County. Townshend in the early 1830s made the difficult decision to uproot the family and move to Oxford, Ohio.

Lud Peyton's birth, 1824, came 170 years after Henry Peyton first set foot on Virginia soil. The Virginia culture and social milieu enveloping Lud Peyton placed him, by birth, within Virginia's ruling, prominent families. The commonwealth of Virginia, from its very beginning, adhered to an unbending hierarchical structure. Early immigrants had been recruited from among England's royalist cavalier caste. Through two centuries these cavalier immigrants

[2] *The Peyton's of Virginia, II.* Vol. I. Page 18.

anchored the Commonwealth's political, social, and economic foundation. "Of 152 Virginians who held top offices in the late seventeenth and early eighteenth century, at least sixteen were connected to aristocratic families, and 101 were the sons of baronets, knights, and the rural gentry of England."[3] The Peyton family fell within this strong, influential landed gentry class in early Virginia.

North Virginia Counties circa 1824

Lud Peyton, throughout his life, identified, foremost as, a "Virginian." Lud's lifelong Virginia identity was typical of the thousands of Virginians who left the Old Dominion while retaining, and esteeming, their Virginia roots. When Townshend Peyton moved the family to Ohio, they re-settled in an area where transplanted Virginians composed the population's majority. When, in the 1840s, Lud moved to Missouri, he again floated on the Virginia tide. "Missouri in 1850 was home to 40,777 native white Virginians. Outside Virginia, only four states had more native Virginians. By 1860 only one state had more – Ohio."[4] Lud Peyton, like his fellow immigrant Virginians, embodied and transported the Old Dominion's culture and values.

[3] Fischer. Page 216.
[4] Fischer and Kelly. Page 180.

Virginia's political and cultural system rested upon a stratified, class-conscious society. For two centuries, the twenty-five most powerful families dominated Virginia politics from the county level up through the House of Burgesses. This imported English culture naturally segregated people into two distinct classes, the "gentle folk" and the "common folk." These class divisions were reinforced at every intersection of wealth, dress, land ownership, education, sport, literacy, and marriage. Extended families and "blood lines," carried tremendous weight in Virginia's patriarchal society.

Virginia's ruling class, men of the "gentle folk" lived atop the social, political hierarchy, atop God's logical order. These men were expected to exhibit "honor;" honor as in valor and honor as in virtue. Young boys were shaped to exhibit "strong wills while developing boisterous emotions."[5] This explosive persona was to be nurtured, by and within, "formal rules of conduct."

These rules of conduct, memorized by children, included such guidance as: (1) Fear God, (2) Honour the King (3) Reverence thy Parents (4) Submit to superiors (5) Despise not thy inferiors.[6] The logical extension of this process led to the practice of hegemonic liberty; liberty anchored in aristocratic privilege whereby a few men ruled the lives of man. "A gentleman of Virginia was trained to be, like Addison's Cato, 'severely bent against himself.' He was taught to believe that a truly free man must be the master of all his acts and thoughts. The ideal itself was pursued for many generations. At its best, it created a true nobility of character in Virginia gentlemen such as George Washington, Robert E. Lee and George Marshall."[7]

Formal education was required for the men of Virginia's leading families. Beyond educational advantages, social boundaries were wider for males. Men exercised and expected more freedom in gender and sexual relationships than women.

---

[5] Fischer. Page 312.
[6] Fischer. Page 314.
[7] Fischer. Page 416.

Outside the home, men enjoyed a broad scope of entertainment. Virginia law codified gambling and gaming – both were legal and guided by statute. Hunting and a variety of "blood sports" fueled life when there was time to kill.

In application these cultural directives created men quite unique. Although tethered to an unbending moral and ethical code young men were also given long leashes. Held to high belief standards, they were also encouraged to enjoy and learn from the often wild pursuits of hunting, gaming, gambling, smoking, drinking and womanizing. A disciplined work ethic often fell by the wayside. Over time, outside of Virginia and the South, young Southern men were feared as being "bad influences."

Lud Peyton's formative, early years shaped him in the mold of his Virginian forefathers.

---------- Virginia and Slavery ----------

Slavery supported and permeated the Virginia culture. "The development of slavery in Virginia was a complex process – one that cannot be explained simply by an economic imperative."[8] The Commonwealth's ruling elite required slavery as a means of sustaining the hierarchical class structure. "In short, slavery in Virginia had a cultural imperative. Bertram Wyatt-Brown writes, '…the South was not founded to create slavery; slavery was recruited to perpetuate the South.'"[9]

Strong delineations defined slave roles and relationships on Virginia plantations. Slaves fell into two classes, "house" slaves and "field" slaves. Full time hard work in the fields, in the mills, and in the barns defined the field slaves' world. Field slaves were banned from entering the plantation's main house on pain of severe punishment. The field slaves' living quarters were separate from the house slaves. Field slaves lived under the close daily supervision and control of an overseer.

---

[8] Fischer. Page 388.
[9] Fischer. Page 388.

House slaves lived in the plantation's main house, working under the supervision of the master's wife. "Masters and house servants lived close together – often sleeping in the same room."[10]
Inside the masters' homes relationships and roles were defined but blurred. The hard distinction between owner and slave softened with daily contact and shared living quarters. Household jobs such as cooking, cleaning, and caring for the children moved the house slave into the family.

Male masters and female slaves living in the same household, under the same roof, weakened barriers. Predatory sex pervaded in Virginia's culture and naturally entered the master-slave relationship. Mary Boykin Chestnut wrote, "'…our men live in one house with their wives and their concubines, and the mulattoes one sees in every family exactly resemble the white children.' "[11]

The Peyton's Loudoun County plantation shared the ugly dynamic Mary Chestnut described. The relationships created deep, lasting personal attachments. When Townshend moved his family to Ohio, the house slaves and their children also made the journey. Once in Ohio these slaves were freed, but the familial attachments continued.

The Peyton's field slaves did not make the journey to Ohio. Defined as property assets, attached to the plantation, these enslaved people were sold to new owners.

Lud's grandfather, Francis Peyton's slave ownership was typical of Virginia's landed gentry. As Francis's wealth increased so did the number of slaves. In 1757 Francis owned four slaves, Phill, Suca, Sampson, and Florah. Thirty years later the number of slaves on his estate had increased to 19.[12] By 1799 the number stood at 17. In 1810 Francis owned 24. At Francis's death in 1815, the slaves, a major part of his property estate, were passed to Lud's father, Townshend.[13]

---

[10] Fischer. Page 278.
[11] Fischer. Page 304.
[12] Sheel. Page 26.
[13] NRHPRF. Oakham Farm. Section 8. Page 16-17.

Townshend and his wife, Harriet, owned slaves throughout their lives in Virginia. In 1799, shortly after their marriage, the couple owned seven slaves. By 1811, their slave holdings increased to eleven. When Francis died in 1815, Townsend inherited all of his father's slaves.[14] Among these slaves were Joe, Charles, David, and Joshen. An enslaved family, Jude, Esther and their children also came to Townsend.[15]

Townshend proved susceptible to the sexual temptations present in his female house slaves. Shortly after the turn of the century, and shortly after his marriage, he fathered a daughter by one of the slaves. Townshend's slave mulatto daughter later married and bore a son, Beverly Tyler. Beverly Tyler accompanied the Peyton family to Oxford, Ohio. Beverly and Lud, the same age, played and grew to manhood together - playmates forever linked. Throughout his life Beverly lived in Oxford, Ohio, eventually becoming the caregiver for Lud's mother.

---------- Loudoun County, Va. ----------

Lud Peyton was born, 1824, in Loudoun County, Virginia. Loudoun County already swam in rich historical waters – waters in which he was soon baptized. Established in 1757, Loudoun County's organization predated the American Revolution. When the revolution ignited, the county's men fought for Independence. The War of 1812 flowed through and around the county. At Lud's birth a sitting President, James Monroe lived nearby. Succeeding county generations absorbed the significance, the importance of the county's deep heritage and tradition.

Loudoun County occupies the extreme northeast tip of Virginia. The Blue Ridge Mountains define the county's western and northern borders. In the north, Harper's Ferry, West Virginia (in 1824 still part of Virginia), dominated Loudoun County, beckoning immigrants westward. The Potomac River outlines Loudoun County in the north and courses the county's eastern border.

[14] NRHPRF. Oakham Farm. Section 8. Page 16-17.
[15] NRHPRF. Oakham Farm. Section 8. Page 17.

Loudoun County, Virginia Circa 1824

Peyton Plantation, Loudoun County, Virginia Circa 1824

Fauquier County and Prince William County abut Loudoun's southwest border while Fairfax County defines the southeast line.

Loudoun County's landscape rolls while climbing steadily up to the Blue Ridge Mountains. Lush, wooded ridges and hills watch over lowlands and meadows valued by generations as perfect "horse country." From every prominence, looking north and west, the Blue Ridge Mountains dominate the horizon.

Loudoun County Landscape Photo Credit Tom A. Rafiner

An overabundance of stone challenges the plow. Loudoun County's paths and roads are lined with wonderfully constructed stone walls. Stone walls provide much of the county's rural personality and character. During Lud's boyhood these neighborhood stone walls etched themselves into his memories.

----------- Francis Peyton ----------

From 1757 to 1832 the histories of the Peyton family and Loudoun County intertwined and melded, a 75 year bond. Francis Peyton, Lud's grandfather, played an active civic role in both neighborhood and county government from the county's organization in 1757 until his death in 1815. Lud's father, Townshend, from his birth in 1766 until emigrating to Ohio in 1832, a period of sixty-six years, raised his family, prospered economically, and exercised civic responsibility in Loudoun County.

Francis, born in 1733, in Prince William County, Va. was the son of Valentine and Frances (Linton) Peyton. Francis's life closely paralleled George Washington's. Francis was born the year after

Washington. On Virginia's frontier both became surveyors as civilization pushed westward. During the revolutionary period they became comrades in arms. When Washington died in 1799, Francis could still look forward to another 16 years of active productivity.

On April 24, 1755, Francis, 22, married Frances Dade in St. Paul's Parish of Stafford County, Va. Frances was the daughter of Henry Dade. The newlyweds moved north to the Virginia frontier and set up house in what became, in 1757, Loudoun County. For the next 58 years, Francis Peyton followed a prosperous and politically active life.[16] He bought land on Loudoun County's extreme southern border; in fact, the Peyton farm was so near the county line that it often was incorrectly included in adjacent Fauquier County records.

The Peyton's built their home 50 yards north of the pulsing Ashby Gap Turnpike, just two miles west of the Little River. The Ashby Gap Turnpike constantly hummed with traffic. A major Virginia thoroughfare, the turnpike carried regular stages, produce wagons, and herds of noisy livestock headed to Alexandria and Washington D.C. The Little River flowed into Loudoun County from Fauquier County. The stream eventually linked with Goose Creek; Goose Creek moved east through the county before entering the Potomac River just south of Leesburg, the county seat.

Commensurate with Francis's social standing he early on assumed an active place in county affairs. May 4, 1757, just twenty-four years old, Francis became a member of Loudoun County's first county court.[17] The following year, still on the county court, he served as the county surveyor.[18] In addition to his county court duties, Francis also took an oath to serve as one of two county Under-Sheriffs.

Leesburg, ten miles northeast of the Peyton farm, became the Loudoun County, county seat in 1758. Leesburg took its name

---

[16] *National Register of Historic Places Registration Form*. Oakham Farm. Section 8. Page 16.
[17] Williams. Page 102.
[18] Sheel. Page 11.

from Thomas Lee, whose son, Francis Lightfoot Lee, named the town.[19]

Francis Peyton's active leadership in Loudoun County resulted in his elevation to Virginia's colonial government. From 1769 to 1775 he served in Virginia's House of Burgesses. His time in the House of Burgesses corresponded to the years when the colonies moved from unrest to revolution against England– Francis positioned himself in the center of the fray.

Early in 1774, the English Parliament passed what became known in the colonies as the Intolerable Acts. These laws, in response to the Boston Tea Party, severely punished the American colonies, restricting freedoms and imposing financial reimbursement. Although directed specifically at Boston and the Massachusetts colony, the acts resulted in the 13 colonies bonding together, igniting the anger that ultimately led to revolution.

Debate over the Intolerable Acts erupted in Virginia's House of Burgesses. Peyton, present and engaged in the heated debates returned to Leesburg, both as messenger and lightning rod. June 14, 1774, Loudoun County citizens gathered at the Leesburg courthouse. Francis chaired the meeting educating the crowd as to the extent of the acts and the resistance endorsed by the House of Burgesses. Loudoun County's citizens supported the government's course. Tensions continued to rise throughout the colonies.

Eighty years later, Lud Peyton, Francis's grandson, stood on courthouse steps. In his speech, from the courthouse steps in Harrisonville, Missouri, Lud advocated armed resistance against a rising threat.

Francis, six weeks later, along with Thomson Mason, again represented Loudoun County at Williamsburg. The assembly session's purpose was "to take the sense of this Colony at large on the subject of the preceding resolves."[20] Virginia elected to join the

[19] Sheel. *Discovered*. Page 17.
[20] Sheel. Page 18.

other 12 colonies against perceived English tyranny. Later, in 1776 Francis was a member of the Virginia Convention. When the Revolutionary War erupted, Francis set aside family and local civic duties to fight, joining the Continental Army.[21] He counted among his comrades George Washington, Thomas Jefferson, Patrick Henry and other "spirits of the revolution."[22]

Francis's leadership during Virginia's revolt included both military and civic service. In May 1779 with the war continuing, Peyton and his friend Leven Powell were elected to represent the county in the assembly at Williamsburg.[23] Thomas Jefferson, now Virginia's Governor increased Francis's responsibilities appointing him State Land Commissioner.[24]

---------- Francis's Plantation ----------

By the close of 1764, the first mill had been constructed on the Little River, just two miles east of the Peyton farm. In its early decades Loudoun County's numerous waterways provided perfect settings for mills. Milling emerged as a primary local industry and they became the county's lifeblood. The construction of the first Little River mill at the river's intersection with the Ashby Gap Turnpike attracted businesses. Homes soon appeared and a small village, Aldie, surrounded the mill.

By 1854, 77 mills dotted the county. It had begun "in 1777, (Leven) Powell built a large three story mill on the banks of the Little River," initiating the surge in mill construction.[25] Not long after, Francis purchased the Powell Mill. A significant revenue stream to Francis's growing wealth and early prosperity flowed from the Aldie Mill. This Little River mill fueled the Peyton family income for four decades.

[21] NRHPRF. Oakham Farm. Section 8. Page 16.
[22] *The National Cyclopaedia*. Page 158.
[23] Sheel. Page 19.
[24] Sheel. Page 19.
[25] NRHPRF. Oakham Farm. Section 8. Page 19.

In addition to his business and civic activities Francis devoted the majority of his time and energy toward improving and expanding the farm. Eventually, the Peyton's humble homestead and farm grew to over 500 acres.

Most large and expanding plantations required overseers and in 1786 Francis hired one. The demands of the mill, coupled to his civic responsibilities, over taxed his time and attention. He hired Enos Cooper to supervise all the plantation's activities. Cooper's job carried broad duties. The scope of Enos's responsibilities included fencing, planting, harvesting and managing the plantation's livestock. Francis's livestock now included nine horses and a herd of twenty-two cattle.[26] Cooper also managed and controlled Peyton's field slaves.

Leven Powell, from whom Francis had purchased the Little River Mill, wielded considerable wealth and influence in southern Loudoun County. Over time the two men became close friends and business associates. Powell plotted a village, Middleburg, in 1787; this new community lay a bit over a mile west of the Peyton plantation. Middleburg derived its name from the fact it was exactly halfway between Alexandria and Winchester.[27] When Powell selected trustees for Middleburg, he included Francis. "Of the seven trustees picked by Leven Powell, four knew the area and lived within five miles of town. They were named in the act. Francis Peyton, the former legislator, was Powell's close friend and lived east of town."[28] With Middleburg's presence, the Peyton plantation stood strategically placed about halfway between Middleburg and Aldie.

---------- Townshend Dade Peyton ----------

Francis and Frances lived in a house he had built when they first arrived on the farm. Following standard Virginia architecture, the home "was a square two story, one room block."[29] A large exterior

[26] Sheel. Page 26.
[27] Sheel. Page 22.
[28] Williams. Page 22.
[29] NRHPRF. Oakham Farm. Section 7. Page 5.

stone chimney provided warmth and light. The kitchen was in a detached building near the main house as were other quarters and buildings. The nearby living quarters served the plantation overseer and house slaves.

Children soon noisily ran the farm. Four daughters and two sons kept Frances, and her house slaves, busy. The four girls, Ann, Elizabeth, Mary, and Emily, helped Frances. As the girls grew they learned household skills, spinning, cooking, and weaving. The two sons, Townshend and Francis, followed the traditional Virginia male path.

Townshend Dade Peyton (Lud's father) was born in 1774. Townshend's name communicates his lineage and documents his place in Virginia's social register. With Virginians, there was a "naming-custom in that culture - the use of surnames as forenames to reinforce connections between families and strengthen the solidarity of the elite.[30] Townshend's mother, a member of the Dade family, gifted him with the surnames of her great grandparents, Frances Townshend and Francis Dade. Also, two prominent Dade family men already carried the name Townshend Dade," well known to Virginians.

Townshend personified Virginia's landed gentry following in his father's footsteps. The Peyton plantation provided Townshend's occupation and social base. Through his early life he assumed a growing share of the management of the farm and his father's Aldie Mill operation. After Townshend married, he remained on the plantation and raised his family.

Townshend's brother, Francis, received his father's name, and thus, presumably according to the Virginia naming process, was the second son.[31] Francis chose a career path much different from Townshend's, deciding to pursue a medical degree. He studied medicine at the University of Edinburgh. In the early-1790s

[30] Fischer. Page 308.
[31] **Note**: Townshend's date of birth was recorded as 1774. Francis's date of birth has not been documented.

Francis set off for Scotland, where he received his medical degree September 12, 1796.

Peyton Main House - Photo Credit Tom A. Rafiner

After five years in Europe, Francis was back in Loudoun County beginning his practice. Soon after his return, George Washington noted in a letter, "Dr. Peyton, son of a very worthy man and brother to two of the best officers in Lees Company of horse during the revolutionary war, has applied for a berth in the medical line. Dr. Peyton is but lately returned after an absence of five years in Europe, I believe in the study of physic."[32]

Francis married Mrs. Frances Ball, George Washington's niece, April 7, 1802. Frances, a widow, was the daughter of Charles Washington, a younger brother of George's. The Peyton family, through Francis's marriage, now enjoyed a direct link to the country's founder. Because "the gentry of Virginia studied one another's genealogies as closely as a stockman would scrutinize his stud books," the marriage elevated the Peyton's into Virginia's higher social echelon.[33]

[32] Hayden. Page 507
[33] Fischer. Page 305.

The newlyweds settled in Loudoun County where Dr. Peyton continued his medical practice. On December 5, 1808, he was riding north toward Leesburg when he was brutally ambushed by a local by the name of Littlejohn. A fight ensued during which Dr. Peyton was mortally wounded.[34] His death a tragic loss for both his family and the Leesburg community.

Townshend's eighteenth birthday, 1792, triggered his enlistment in the state militia. Virginia had been among the first states to require military service. "All able bodied male citizens over the age of eighteen were required to enroll in the militia."[35] Townshend served in the Virginia militia from 1792 through 1820. In 1793 he became an ensign, later rising to lieutenant in the First Battalion of the 57th Regiment. Militia duty required attendance at all regimental musters and drills; the drills and musters occurred several times each year. For three decades, Townshend, like all other Virginia men, incorporated militia duties into his daily life. Townshend's militia service continued the military tradition begun by his father, Francis. Later, Townshend's eldest son, Richard entered the militia on his 18th birthday.[36] Lud followed his father and half-brother's military service during the Missouri–Kansas Territory border conflict and then in the Civil War.

Townshend's father was 65 years old when Townshend and Harriet Beale married in 1798. After the marriage, through the next 17 years, Townshend increasingly assumed more responsibility in the family businesses, the plantation and the milling operation. Townshend himself "was like his father, a country gentleman of the old school, and the owner of many African slaves, some of whom had been acquired by inheritance, others by purchase."[37] Friends and family attributed to Townshend "unexceptional morals, clear head, sound judgment, and political energy."[38]

[34] Hayden. Page 507.
[35] Blincoe. Introduction. Page 1.
[36] Blincoe. Page 267.
[37] *The National Cyclopaedia of American Biography*. Page 158.
[38] Peyton. "Sketch." Page 395.

Townshend's social network, friends and acquaintances, included many notable and historic men. Henry Clay and John Crittenden were said to be friends as well as Thomas Corwin, Daniel Webster, Robert C. Winthrop and William C, Rives. Politically, Townshend was "a Whig of the old school," although it was noted "…the Whig principles of the father were not transmitted to the son (R.L.Y. Peyton)."[39]

Townshend married Harriet Colston Beale, March 13, 1798. The next year, Townshend's father gifted the couple 450 acres of his estate.[40] Here Townshend built the couple's first humble home. The house had wood construction, stood one and a half stories tall. Steep stairs led to an upstairs loft and bedroom. A separate detached summer kitchen stood away from the house.[41] Forty-eight years later, 1847, new owners converted the Peyton home into a school.

Original home of Townsend and Harriet – Photo Credit Tom. Rafiner

At some point after 1798, as their family grew, Townshend, Harriet and the children moved into the main house with his parents. During the Civil War, the main house served as the cavalry headquarters for the famous Confederate General, J.E.B. Stuart. In

[39] Peyton. "Sketch." Page 395.
[40] NRHPRF. Oakham Farm. Section 8. Page 16.
[41] NRHPRF. Oakham Farm. Section 8. Page 17.

the home's parlor, Stuart commissioned John Mosby to begin enlisting a Partisan Ranger Regiment later known as Mosby's Rangers.[42] The Peyton's home and estate, just off the turnpike proved strategically placed. Situated halfway between Middleburg and Winchester the Peyton's plantation afforded fast access to the turnpike. Additionally, the Peyton's estate, near the Potomac River and Maryland, became a primary staging point for forays into the north.

---------- Townshend and Harriet's Children ----------

During the 23 years of Townshend and Harriet's marriage they had nine children. Two of the children, Robert and Alice, died in their youth. Robert, according to the family oral history, died from an accidental gunshot wound. A childhood disease claimed Alice. The other seven children, Lud's half-brothers and half-sisters, survived to adulthood. Following Harriet's death in the early 1820s, Townshend remarried; Lud was the second born in this second marriage. Harriet's seven surviving children, to varying degrees, all influenced and shaped Lud's life.

Harriet and Townshend's first born was a daughter, Emily. Emily arrived shortly before 1800. At Lud's birth, December 1824, Emily had married and left the Peyton household. She had married Captain Peyton Noland around 1815. A daughter, Maria Louisa, was born in March 1817 followed by a son, William. Captain Noland died after William's birth, and Emily, now a widow with two young children returned home to her parents. For almost a decade, during the 1820s, Emily and her two children lived with Townshend. During Lud's early childhood, Aunt Emily and her two children were constant participants in his life.

Emily remarried October 14, 1830. She and Lt. Thomas S. Hamersley were married at Middleburg, Va. with her entire family in attendance. Lt. Hamersley was a member of the U.S. Navy and the family evidently moved away from Loudoun County. Their marriage was short lived. Thomas died and Emily again found

[42] NRHPRF. Oakham Farm. Section 8. Page 19.

herself a widow. In 1850, still a widow at 52, Emily lived with her sister Lucy, and Lucy's family, in Richmond County, Virginia.

Richard F. Peyton, Lud's oldest half-brother, was 24 when Lud was born, easily old enough to have been Lud's father. Richard grew to maturity on the Peyton plantation. He soon became involved in the family's milling business, moving to nearby Aldie. As a young man, Richard, like his father, served in Loudoun County's militia. In 1825 he married Virlinda Yates. Richard led the family migration to Ohio. He and Virlinda moved around 1830 but Virlinda died soon after. Richard married Virlinda's sister, Ann.

Tragically, Richard and his second wife, Ann M. Yates, died within weeks of each other. Richard died April 4, 1842 in Oxford, Ohio and Ann died May 16, 1842. Ann had been born in King George County, Va. At the time of their deaths they were living in Oxford's Mansion House hotel. Richard's obituary described him as "urbane and polite without flippancy and with discriminating judgment."[43] Two children, Harriet J. and Howard B. survived. Until they reached majority, a family friend, Peter Sutton was the young Peyton's' guardian.

Townshend and Harriet's second daughter, Lucy Beale arrived in 1804. Lucy survived all of her siblings, living to 83, dying in 1887. Lucy married Albert G. McCarty in Loudoun County on October 10, 1823. Lucy and Albert then settled in Richmond County, Va. where Albert, a slave owner, farmed. In 1850 seven slaves were working the McCarty farm. In addition to farming, Albert also worked on the Potomac River as a Lightboat Captain. During the Civil War the family sought a safe haven in Fredericksburg, Va. Lucy lost Albert a year after the war ended and then settled in Falmouth, Stafford County, Va. just across the Rappahannock River from Fredericksburg.

Townshend and Harriet's third daughter, Maria Antoinette, was born around 1805. Maria married the Rev. Henry F. Luckett, a minister of the Methodist Epistle Church, South. The Luckett's

[43] *Hamilton Ohio Intelligencer.* April 15, 1842.

abandoned Virginia and moved to the far west - Illinois. In 1835 Rev. Luckett was preaching in Logan County, Illinois, just north of Springfield. By 1840 Rev. Luckett had moved the family to Springfield. While in central Illinois, he made the acquaintance of a then unknown lawyer, Abraham Lincoln; during the Civil War, Lincoln saved Luckett's life.

The Lucketts left Illinois settling in St. Charles, St. Charles County, Missouri. In St. Charles Rev. Luckett led a Methodist South congregation. Luckett's southern beliefs and his ownership of 12 slaves put him at odds with the surrounding community when the Civil War began. He and Maria fled finding a safe haven with a daughter in Memphis, Tennessee. In 1863, after Union troops captured Memphis, Rev. Luckett was incarcerated for attempting to smuggle ammunition to Confederate troops. July 24, 1863, a military commission sentenced Luckett to death by hanging.[44] Abraham Lincoln, on appeal from Luckett's family, pardoned him.

Townshend and Harriet's second son, Francis H. Peyton, was born around 1810 in Loudoun County. Francis, 14 years old at Lud's birth, followed in Townshend and Richard's business footsteps. Francis became a merchant. He moved with the family to Oxford, Ohio. In 1839, at Oxford, Francis married Harriet A. Luke. Harriet, Francis's junior by 16 years, was an English immigrant. Francis left Oxford in the early 1850s moving his family to Illinois. While in Illinois Harriet gave birth to three children, Alice, Fannie and William. Harriet died in Illinois, perhaps of childbirth complications, and Francis returned to Oxford. Francis outlived Lud by thirteen years, dying in 1876 at Oxford.

Townshend and Harriet's fourth daughter, Ann Elizabeth was born in 1811. Ann married William B. Vinson in June 1823 and the couple moved to Montgomery County, Maryland. For the remainder of their lives, Ann and William farmed outside Poolesville. Poolesville sits just east of the Potomac River and a few miles northwest of Washington, D.C. Montgomery County

[44] NARA. Record Group 153. Office of the Judge Advocate (Army). E18, Court Martial Files.

experienced more than its share of action during the Civil War. J.E.B. Stuart's raid out of Virginia into Maryland ended with a retreat south right through Poolesville itself. Stuart was back in Montgomery County the next summer stealing horses and supplies. The summer of 1864 General Bradley Johnson and General Jubal Early led forays into the county.[45] Ann survived the Civil War dying in 1872.

Townshend and Harriet's third son, Alfred Beale Peyton, was born in Loudoun County in 1815. Alfred accompanied the family to Oxford, Ohio. He and his brother Francis became business partners at Oxford. Townshend provided the initial capital to fund their mercantile business, F.H. Peyton & Co. A business and/or family dispute split their partnership. Alfred fled Oxford and moved to Logan County, Illinois, evidently following his sister, Maria Luckett. He soon left Logan County settling near the Luckett's in St. Charles, Mo. In St. Charles, October 29, 1853 Alfred married Laura S. Baswise. Alfred was 38 years old and Laura was 19. She was the daughter of Thomas H. Baswise, a wealthy Cincinnati merchant, who had moved his family to St. Charles. Alfred remained in St. Charles County, Missouri until his death May 18, 1876.

---------- Harriet's Death ----------

Harriet died, circa 1821, of now unknown causes. Wife, mother, and grandmother, she left a large vacuum. Harriet was buried in the Peyton family cemetery on the south end of the plantation, joining two of her children and Townshend's parents. Her death, after 23 years of marriage, left Townshend to manage their large household. Children, ranging in age from seven to 20, remained on the plantation. Grandchildren expanded and energized the house. Townshend, now a 47-year old widower faced the unwelcome task of filling the void created by Harriet's death.

[45] Farquhar. Page 30.

Chapter Two
Robert Ludwell Yates Peyton

Harriet Peyton likely died in Leesburg. Townshend had moved the family to Leesburg where he operated a manufacturing business. An overseer managed their plantation. The Peyton's Leesburg household contained twenty-eight people, including 15 slaves. Until her death, Harriet managed this large group with the assistance of two daughters, Lucy and Emily. Emily, now a widow, had moved back home with her two young children, Louisa and William. In addition to the day-to-day household management Harriet also controlled their busy social calendar. The family matriarch occupied the central position in the family's heart and daily lives, her untimely death created a profound void.

Harriet was buried in the family cemetery on the plantation. There she joined Townshend's parents and two of her children, Alice and Robert. Present at the graveside were her adult children, teenage children, grandchildren, and her husband of over twenty years. She and Townshend had celebrated nine births and suffered the loss of two children. During their married life the couple built a large prosperous family and assumed a prominent position in the Loudoun County community.

Townshend Peyton, 46, now a widower, faced the unenviable, difficult search for a wife while he and the family grieved Harriet's loss. Social convention and the practicality of his situation necessitated the painful undertaking. The Peyton household was large, diverse, and complex.

Harriet's responsibilities had encompassed raising the children, directing the house slaves, managing the household's food and clothing needs, and coordinating the calendar. Although Townshend and the family felt Harriet impossible to replace, reality dictated he search for a wife.

Townshend's situation was not uncommon. All too often, early 19th century husbands and fathers found themselves widowed as disease and childbirth claimed spouses. Necessity normally forced widowers to quickly remarry. Need overshadowed romance. Friends, family and community, both experienced and knowledgeable assisted in the matchmaking process.

The Peyton clan's extended family provided Townshend's second wife. Family ties pulled him back to King George County. Townshend's mother, Frances and her sister, Elizabeth were from King George County, St. Paul's Parish. The sisters, daughters of Henry Dade, both had married in the 1750's. Elizabeth, Townshend's aunt, married first, February 17, 1750. She married a member of the local landed gentry, Robert Yates. Elizabeth and Robert remained in St. George County throughout their lives. The couple's oldest son, Robert Jr., married Jane Dade in 1777. Jane and Robert, Jr, had eight children, and one of them, a daughter, Sarah M., "Sally" would become Townshend's second wife.

Elizabeth's sister, Frances, married Francis Peyton on April 24, 1755. Although the young couple left King George County moving to the Virginia frontier in Loudoun County, family connections remained tight and lasting.

When Townshend Dade Peyton began his search the journey naturally led back to the Yates family and possible matches in King George County. Although Townshend's Aunt Elizabeth, as well as Robert, Jr. and Jane Yates were deceased, a strong family network remained. Personal relationships survived through the years. The two families remained close.

---------- The Yates Family ----------

During their lifetimes, Robert, Jr. and Jane Yates, had accumulated a considerable estate. They built a large, attractive plantation on the west bank of the Potomac River. The plantation included extensive lands passed from Elizabeth's father, Henry Dade, to her and then to Robert.[46]

[46] King George County, Virginia. *Deed Book 8*. Page 292.

Family Ties
Peyton-Dade-Yates

PEYTON, FRANCIS		**YATES, Robert, Sr.**
DADE, Frances	*--Sisters--*	**DADE, Elizabeth**
(April 24, 1755)	*by Henry DADE*	**(Feb. 17, 1750)**

PEYTON, Townshend D.	**YATES, Robert Jr.**
#1. BEALE, Harriett C.	**DADE,, Jane**
(April, 13, 1798)	**(April 11, 1777)**
CHILDREN:	***CHILDREN:***
Emily	**Robert Ludwell**
Robert	**Theophilus J..**
Richard F.	**Jane R.**
Alice	**Frances I.D**
Lucy B.	**Virlinda J.**
Maria A.	**Ann M.**
Francis H.	**Nancy M.**
Ann E.	*** Sarah *"Sally"* M.**
Alfred	

PEYTON, Townshend D
#2.*YATES, Sarah *"Sally"* M.
(Dec. 22, 1822)

CHILDREN:
Frances H.D.
Robert Ludwell Yates or R.L.Y or *"Lud"*
Alexander McGonigle

A neighbor, John H. Washington, had long entertained designs on the Yates's plantation. When Robert and Jane died, leaving the estate to their children, Washington began aggressive overtures to buy. Over a period of seven years from 1816 to 1823, the Yates's children one-by-one each sold inherited plantation parcels to

Washington. Of the eight children, only the eldest, Robert Ludwell, retained his inheritance and lived on a portion of the family property.

In 1820 Robert Ludwell Yates lived on his plantation in King George County. Robert's younger brother, Theophilus had accepted a commission in the U.S. Navy. Theophilus's naval career soon carried him away from King George County. A younger sister, Jane, had married in 1816 and moved to the far western frontier in Butler County, Ohio. Robert's five other sisters, all single, had left King George County, moving into Alexandria.

Sarah, "Sally," the oldest of the five sisters, headed the transplanted Yates's household in Alexandria, District of Columbia. Living with Sally were sisters, Nancy, Ann M., Virlinda J. and Frances. The five women had all sold their inherited land in King George County and were now living on the proceeds. Their Alexandria household included three female house slaves.[47] Townshend's search brought him to the Yates's Alexandria residence.

Related and already familiar, Townshend and Sally were a natural union. The short timeframe between Harriet's death and the match, indicates an uncomplicated, rapid agreement. Townshend's marriage offer was accepted.

Sally Yates fulfilled all the social requirements Townshend Peyton sought in a second wife. Elizabeth (Dade) Yates's granddaughter, the daughter of Robert and Jane Yates,[48] Sally was 26 years old and single. Sally was a member of Virginia's landed gentry. She came from a respected old Virginia family, accustomed to the manner of living and cognizant of the social responsibilities. The Yates family fluidly moved within Virginia's cavalier society. Additionally, Sally brought financial resources to the partnership.

The match benefitted Sally and her sisters. Sally had reached an age when marriage possibilities narrowed. For her, Townshend's

[47] 1820 Federal Census. Alexandria. District of Columbia.
[48] King George County, Virginia. *Deed Book 14*. Page 262.

marriage proposal provided a secure future maintaining a commensurate life style. Additionally, Sally's sisters were now afforded the opportunity to leave Alexandria and accompany the couple to Loudoun County.

December 21, 1822, Townshend, 48, and Sally, 26, married in King George County. Their age discrepancy, 22 years, although large was not, due to the circumstances and the period, unusual. If their wedding was typical, they had two ceremonies. One ceremony in the church and a second outside the church, where the couple "jumped the broom." Although theirs was a marriage of convenience, it would last 30 years, and produce a second family for Townshend.

Townshend and Sally's marriage cemented a permanent bond between three families, the Peyton's, the Yates, and the McGonigle's. The marriage naturally tied the Peyton and Yates families. The knot between the two families tightened two years later when Townshend's eldest son, Richard, married Sally's sister, Virlinda. The third family tied into the Peyton-Yates knot was the McGonigle family. Sally's sister Jane had married John McGonigle in 1816. The couple, had immediately settled in Oxford, Butler County, Ohio to be near John's family. When Townshend began considering leaving Virginia, Sally and Jane's tight bond pulled the Peyton's to Oxford.

After their wedding Sally and Townshend returned to Loudoun County. Sally inherited Townshend's large diverse family. The house was filled with his children: Lucy (19), Maria (17), Francis (12), Ann (10) and Alfred (7). Additionally, Townshend's widowed daughter, Emily and her two children had returned home. Richard Peyton, the oldest son, a bachelor and very nearly Sally's age, rotated in and out of the house.

In all likelihood, Sally's unmarried sisters became permanent household members. Virginia's culture defined family as anyone, related or not, staying in the home. They would have assimilated quickly into the daily chaos and been a help to Sally.

Sally assumed a challenging role. Townshend's daughters, nearly Sally's peers in age, were courting. As step-mother, she had to manage the courting process while delicately mentoring "daughters" nearly her age. To the youngsters, Francis, Ann, and Alfred, Sally faced the difficulty of becoming a mother to still grieving children.

Managing the daily household came more easily. Sally had supervised the Alexandria house. She brought experience in handling the house slaves, planning meals and clothing while juggling the schedule. That said, the size and complexity of Townshend's household presented a more daunting job than Alexandria.

Townshend's life spun. Events and circumstances were changing and unsettling. He had lost Harriet. He soon married a woman young enough to be his daughter. Townshend was both a father and a grandfather. Three of his daughters and a son were eligible and courting. More unsettling, Virginia's economy continued to decline. Townshend struggled to reverse the steady deterioration of his agricultural, milling and manufacturing businesses. Slavery's troublesome presence triggered a political debate about emancipation but the debate bogged down in the cultural morass.

---------- Loudoun County in 1824 ----------

By 1824 the American frontier had pushed west, over the mountains, well beyond Loudoun County. Well established towns and villages dotted the Loudoun County countryside. Stonewalls encircled fields and lined many of the roads. With the land cleared, farms and plantations now focused on planting and harvesting. Loudoun County mills provided the county's primary commerce. The county comfortably assumed Virginia's stratified society and culture. South Loudoun County, the Peyton's' neighborhood, was now sandwiched between two thriving communities, Middleburg and Aldie.

West of the Peyton's, Middleburg's population grew to 360 inhabitants. "Two hundred and eight of the 360 were white, 146 were slave – there were six free negroes."[49] The community now supported a school, an academy. The town had also become a regular stop for stagecoaches. Scheduled stagecoaches rolled on the Ashby Gap Turnpike running through Middleburg, past the Peyton plantation, and on through Aldie. Noble Beveridge's large Middleburg tavern and livery served as the stage stop and local watering hole.

To the east of the Peyton's, Aldie's population of 248, over half of which were slaves, rivaled Middleburg.[50] The village, at the intersection of the Little River and the Ashby Gap Turnpike, thrived on its mill. The three-story Aldie Mill, constructed in 1804, attracted "…a store, miller's house, 'mansion home,' and 'spinning house.'"[51] A post office had arrived in 1811. By 1813 a stone bridge spanned the Little River and the population grew.

Leesburg, the Loudoun County seat, had grown into its role as the county's commerce center and seat of local government. It had moved far beyond the rural, outpost county seat of 1758. Leesburg's population now exceeded 1,000.[52] A thriving trade in Potomac Marble, actually a limestone based stone, fueled both the Leesburg and county commerce. The county had provided the Potomac Marble used in the construction of the nation's capital. During the War of 1812 federal government documents had been transferred and stored for safe keeping in the town.[53]

In 1817 Loudoun County achieved national attention. A Loudoun County resident, James Monroe, was elected President of the United States. Monroe had inherited his Loudoun County estate in 1808 and took up residence. During his first Presidential term, Monroe began the construction of a mansion, Oak Hill. Oak Hill was completed in 1823 while President Monroe still served as President. Monroe's estate lay just a few miles north of the Peyton

[49] Sheel. Page 38.
[50] Sheel. *Discovered.* Page 11.
[51] Sheel. *Discovered.* Page 11.
[52] Sheel. *Discovered.* Page 17.
[53] Sheel. *Discovered.* Page 17.

plantation. When traveling to Leesburg, the Peyton's frequently passed Monroe's estate.

It is no little irony that the most "important (and ominous)" and far-reaching domestic issue of the Monroe presidency, debated within miles of the Peyton plantation, would in many ways orchestrate Lud Peyton's life and fate.[54] Monroe presided over the contentious debate swirling around Missouri's admission to the Union and slavery's expansion; the debate eventually resulting in the Missouri Compromise. "He (Monroe) actively participated in the 1820 compromise, whereby Missouri and the free state of Maine were admitted simultaneously (thus preserving sectional equilibrium in the Senate) and a line was drawn in the remaining territory of the Louisiana Purchase indicating where slavery could exist and where it would be banned."[55]

Three years before Lud's birth, within a few miles of his home, the wheels were set in motion. Missouri awaited history's unfolding and Lud Peyton's arrival.

---------- Marquis de La Fayette ----------

1824, the year of Lud's birth, the Marquis de La Fayette, now 47, began his American farewell tour. La Fayette's tour proved historic for Loudoun County, and western Missouri. Although Lud would remember none of it, he would throughout his life, always be attached to and reminded of La Fayette's visit. In August, 1824, the Marquis de La Fayette arrived in New York. For the next year La Fayette's tour dominated national news as he visited friends and dignitaries. His tour moved through many cities, including St. Louis on the country's distant western frontier.

Once in Virginia, La Fayette traveled to Monticello where Thomas Jefferson, now 81, welcomed him. Loudoun County, Leesburg and Oak Hill were also on La Fayette's itinerary. In the middle of the

[54] McPherson. Page 47.
[55] McPherson. Page 47.

Marquis' tour, Robert Ludwell Yates Peyton was born just a few miles south of President Monroe's Oak Hill estate.

August 9, 1825, the Marquis de La Fayette accompanied by President John Quincy Adams, visited, now former President, James Monroe at Oak Hill. La Fayette, riding in a carriage drawn by four white horses, was escorted from Leesburg to Oak Hill by six companies of cavalry militia. Loudoun County turned out in force for this historic visit as "multitudes of people lined the road and crowded forward to behold the veteran apostle of Liberty."[56] It is not a giant step to envision Sally Peyton, sitting in a carriage beside the road to Leesburg, holding aloft, eight month old Lud to "behold the apostle of Liberty."

Leaving Monroe's estate, La Fayette and the dignitaries returned to Leesburg. A banquet was held in the courthouse square, filled with the county's leading citizens and gentry. Townshend and Sally undoubtedly among the guests.

This would be a night never forgotten. The Marquis de La Fayette addressed his adoring audience. Over 50 individual toasts were given. President John Quincy Adam's toast one the most memorable in local history. President Adams, glass raised, wished, "Leesburg, may its future prosperity correspond with the splendid revolutionary services of the family from which it derives its name."[57]

Later during the tour, La Fayette visited St. Louis. At St. Louis, Missouri's State Assembly, then in session, honored him by renaming a western Missouri county in his honor. Lafayette County, Missouri would play heavily in Lud Peyton's life. In Lafayette County, Peyton, practiced law, enjoyed friendships, and eventually led his cavalry regiment into battle.

From 1861 to 1863, Senator Peyton legislated beneath La Fayette's marble bust in the Confederate capital in Richmond, Virginia.

[56] Ward. Page 104.
[57] Ward. Page 104.

Under La Fayette's countenance, Lud Peyton worked and conversed.[58] La Fayette's constant presence a reminder of Lud's odyssey from Loudoun County to western Missouri to Richmond, Va.

---------- Frances ----------

Sally and Townshend's first born was a daughter. She was given the name Frances H.D. Peyton.[59] Frances's name reflected her lineage. Her given name came from her grandmother. Her two middle names, Harriet and Dade, honored her father's first wife and the Dade family. Throughout her life she was known as Fanny. Fanny grew to young adulthood in Oxford, Ohio. She married a University of Miami student, Joseph R. "Joe" Davis in August 1842. Davis, Jefferson Davis's nephew, hailed from Madison County, Mississippi. Following their marriage, and Joseph's graduation, the couple moved to Canton, Mississippi.

Fanny and Joe lived outside Canton, Mississippi from their marriage until the start of the Civil War. In 1860 they lived on a large plantation with Joe's mother Susan. They were wealthy. Joe's real estate holdings assessed at $48,000 and his mother's at $27,000. Their personal property worth, mostly in slaves, totaled $89,000 for Joe and $54,500 for Susan. Joe owned 39 slaves in 1850 and by 1860 the number grew to 65. Other members of the Davis household owned an additional 55 slaves. In 1860, 120 slaves labored and lived on their Canton plantation.

In the late 1850's as national tensions escalated, Joe Davis served in the Mississippi State Senate, while his brother-in-law, Lud Peyton

[58] **Note**: The Marquis La Fayette's bust still (2017) adorns the rotunda of the Virginia Capital. The bust is extensively cleaned every two years. The Marquis's nose was broken from the bust when it was initially transported from Paris; the fracture line must be cleaned extensively periodically in order to remain invisible. This background shared with the author by the Chief Conservator, Mr. Scott W. Nolley in May 2017.

[59] **Note**: The identity of Frances's mother is not documented. After extensive research and consideration, the author believes Sally was her mother. There are significant unknown facts regarding her life: (1) the exact date and circumstances of Harriet's death are undocumented (2) Frances's exact date of birth is undocumented.

served in Missouri's State Senate. Joe Davis was a secessionist Democrat. In April 1861 he became Lt. Colonel of the 10th Mississippi Infantry. Later, in Richmond, the summer of 1861 Joe served as an aide-de-camp to Confederacy President, and uncle, Jefferson Davis. Fanny accompanied Joe to Richmond and became a frequent visitor of Varina Davis, Jefferson's wife.

Joe was promoted to Brigadier General in September 1862. He "served with distinction at the Battle of Gettysburg in 1863 and in the Wilderness, at Spotsylvania, and at Cold Harbor in 1864. He surrendered at Appomattox and was paroled in April 1865."[60]

Fannie and Joe were childless and following a separation of several years, they divorced in 1878. Fanny died July 8, 1885 in Canton Mississippi.

---------- Lud's Birth ----------

Sally Peyton gave birth to Robert Ludwell Yates Peyton in December 1824. Deferring from Virginia's established naming pattern, Townshend and Sally's son was given the name of her older brother, Robert Ludwell Yates. Robert had attended their wedding, in December 1822.

Just nine months, almost to the day, from Sally's marriage, Robert Ludwell Yates, was suddenly and accidentally killed. Robert was working on his estate when a horse kicked him in the head. The force of the blow crushed his skull and he died shortly after. His death was reported in the Alexandria newspapers.[61] Early in 1824, just months after Robert's death, Sally became pregnant. The two life changing events, a death so quickly followed by a birth, blended, and in a seamless transition Robert Ludwell Yates lived on through his nephew.

---

[60] *Biographical Sketches of the Confederacy*. Page 163.

[61] *Marriage and Death Notices from Alexandria, Va. Newspapers, Vol. I, 1784 to 1838*. Page 453.

The nephew, Robert Ludwell Yates Peyton, shortened his formal name to R.L.Y. Peyton but throughout his life was known to friends and family as Lud Peyton.
A second son, Alexander McGonigle Peyton followed Lud. The son's middle name, McGonigle, affirmed Sally's tie to the McGonigle family. Jane (Yates) McGonigle, Sally's sister, remained close. Young Alexander McGonigle, the last of Townshend's children, proved to be the most trying.

---------- Lud's Childhood ----------

Lud's early Loudoun County world resonated with the sights and sounds of a 19th century Virginia plantation. Townshend was 50 when Lud was born. Occupied with the plantation, the mills, and civic duties Townshend played a minor role in Lud's infant years. Sally also carried other responsibilities.

Lud's first eight years rushed by in a blur of activity and people. His life populated with parents, siblings, cousins, extended family members and slaves – not to mention the confusing number of half-brothers and half-sisters. As an infant, Lud, although enjoying Sally's love and attention, received daily care and training from house slaves. During the first few years of his life, the nurturing, caring face he most often saw was black. The daily feeding, rocking to sleep, and diaper changing came from the hands of the house slaves. This was the norm.

Lud's playmates included his brother Alfred, his sister Frances, cousins, Louisa and William. Alfred, nine years older than Lud spent more time out of the house but became a strong childhood role model. Frances and Lud, just a year apart, nonetheless went different directions as they grew. Lud's life gravitated to the outside world and male activities. Frances moved inside to women's duties and responsibilities. Louisa and William, both older than Lud, were regular companions.

The play group also included Beverly Tyler. Beverly, Townshend's mulatto grandson, lived in the "big" house with his mother. Beverly's family history later recorded, the young "illegitimate mulatto child removed from the Negro quarters to the Payton home, and reared as a member of the Payton household."[62] The same age as Lud, the two played naturally. Beverly and Lud shared and shadowed each other's lives for the next 39 years; separated by color and circumstance but tied by blood and family. Beverly and his family later became Sally's caregivers.

The adults in Lud's early life embodied the importance Virginia society placed on the extended family. Inside the home, Townshend and Sally presided but Lud's older half-brothers and sisters, as well as Sally's sisters, constantly moved in and out of his focus. Affluent and active, the Peyton household provided fertile opportunity for Lud to observe and absorb Virginia culture.

As Lud grew from infant, to toddler, to adolescent, his world expanded beyond the main house to the plantation and then beyond into the larger Loudoun County community. Traffic on the Ashby Gap Turnpike passed by just 40 yards south of the Peyton home. Turnpike passer-byes, at the Peyton plantation, shuffled between Middleburg, two miles to the west, and Aldie, two miles to the east.

Young Lud Peyton stood at the plantation entrance absorbing the sights and sounds. The turnpike's regular high traffic of neighbors, merchants, and travelers, as well as the scheduled stage, provided a continuing, vibrant link to the world outside the plantation. Frequent visitors turned off the turnpike exposing Lud to multiple personalities and entertainments.

The entertainments Lud enjoyed certainly included music. Thirty-five years after his death a Chicago newspaper applauded his exceptional talent with the violin, lauding him a natural musician. Lud's talents and love for the fiddle were first inspired in Loudoun County. Virginians held fiddling in high regard.[63] "Fiddle music, dancing, feasts, balls, and attendant frolics were part of everyday life."[64] It was well known that Thomas Jefferson and his brother

[62] *Tyler Family History*. Page 9.
[63] Marshall. Page 2.
[64] Marshall. Page 54.

Randolph played their violins for dances and soirees.[65] Living in a large family and surrounded by house slaves, fiddle music became natural. Lud picked-up basic fiddling from the house slaves because they "in particular were given a musical education."[66]

View from house to Ashby Turnpike- photo credit Tom A. Rafiner

---------- Education ----------

Lud's formal education began at an early age. Virginia's culture required that young men, especially those of the landed gentry, be well educated. By the time Lud reached school age, Middleburg supported an educational academy. "The Middleburg Academy taught everything – at least according the ad, '3 R's, bookkeeping, rhetoric, elocution, painting and drawing, music, poetry, chemistry, logic and ethics, natural philosophy, Latin, Greek, and others."[67]

The academy's curriculum, supplemented by a tutor, introduced Lud to the rigors he would later face at Ohio's Miami University.

Outside the classroom, Lud's cultural education came through his normal, daily immersion in family and plantation life. From cradle

[65] Marshall. Page 5.
[66] Marshall. Page 55.
[67] Sheel. Page 39.

to adolescence the interaction between the people around him informed his status and place in the world. Observing the dynamics between his mother and father, his aunts and uncles, and others, Lud instinctively acquired the expected Virginia culture's male role.

The main house operated with white family members and slaves. The differences between the two groups, the behaviors, and sense of class became normal. For Lud, the presence of slaves and the manner of interaction became second nature.

Lud was immersed in slavery from birth to the family's migration to Oxford, Ohio. Slavery shaped the foundation of his evolving worldview. Slaves lived in the Peyton household and nurtured Lud as he grew.

Field slaves provided all the plantation's labor. Accompanying his father and brothers on the plantation Lud absorbed, without instruction, slave owner – slave relationships.

Lud's relatives, the McCarty's, the Luckett's, the Vinson's, and Richard's family all owned slaves. When these relatives came to visit, slaves accompanied them. Lud internalized and accepted, without question, slavery.

Lud's trips to Aldie with Townshend introduced the expanded commercial world of his father's milling business. The Aldie mills drew men from throughout the south Loudoun County locale. Interacting with these farmers, listening to the conversations, Lud noted the deference and status Townshend received. Also, Richard, Lud's half-brother, lived and worked in Aldie managing the mill day-to-day. Lud watched Richard. Following Richard, spending time with Richard and soaking-in Richard's work added an additional perspective to Lud's development.

Trips to Middleburg provided a different type of education. The larger of the two towns, Middleburg bustled, with energy. Lud's grandfather, Francis, had been one of the town's founding trustees –

literally a founding father. Lud came to appreciate his ties, and his place in Middleburg history hearing stories about his grandfather.

Aldie Mill- Photo Credit Tom A. Rafiner

Noble Beveridge owned and operated the Middleburg Tavern. The tavern, a four story, stone building also served as the stagecoach stop. The Peyton's frequented the tavern. Young Lud absorbed the tavern's energy and noise. When the stagecoaches stopped, passengers filled the tavern.

The tobacco smoke, the laughing, the bustle, the music and the loud conversation was an education. Three decades later, during the Civil War, the Middleburg Tavern temporarily served as Confederated General, J.E.B. Stuart's headquarters.

Lud also accompanied Townshend to William Dishman's Middleburg home. Dishman's home, an impressive two-story structure, dominated the Ashby Gap Turnpike. Being welcome and known in this home, Lud, without knowing it, became comfortable with the affluent.

Middleburg Tavern Photo Credit Tom A. Rafiner

Dishman Home Photo Credit Tom A.Rafiner

Trips to Middleburg always included stops at the post office where Lud met the locals. His personality and easy manner enabled him to relate to everyone. Already, the young boy displayed the courtesy and empathy known throughout his life.

Middleburg Post Office Photo Credit Tom Rafiner

During his early, developmental years in Virginia, Lud acquired a deep sense of self-identity. He was a Virginian, but he was a Virginian of the "gentle" class. Everywhere Lud traveled in Loudoun County he bumped into the presence and the contributions of his grandfather, from the Revolutionary War to the growth of the county. In Aldie, the mills had long provided income to the Peyton family and Francis had early on owned and operated one of the Little River mills. In Middleburg, Francis had served as a founding trustee, his fingerprints all over the town's history. In Leesburg, Francis had led one of the earlier resistances against the English King. Young Lud heard the stories, absorbing the legacy. He also observed and absorbed the relationships Townshend had with the community. The presence and the influence Townshend radiated transferred to his son.

--------- The Cousins ---------

Lud Peyton had two distant "cousins," Balie Peyton and John Lewis Peyton whose lives paralleled and intersected his. All three men became lawyers. All three men led active political lives. All three men played significant roles during the Civil War although in different camps. Although the three cousins shared a common great, great-grandfather, Henry Peyton, they occupied different limbs of the Peyton family tree, and followed vastly different paths to and through the war.[68]

Bailie Peyton
1803-1878

Balie and Lud Peyton shared a great great-grandfather, Henry Peyton. Two of Henry's sons, Valentine and John, by staying in Virginia originated strong branches of the Virginia Peyton's. But Balie's father, John, migrated to Tennessee.

Although a cousin, Balie Peyton was Lud's senior by 20 years. When Lud reached adulthood Balie was already a Congressman and national figure. Throughout Lud's life, private and public, Balie's prominent persona served as measuring stick and sounding board for Lud's beliefs.

November 26, 1803 Balie was born to John and Margaret. Throughout his life, Balie identified with Tennessee. His love of thoroughbred racehorses and politics defined his life. Like Lud, Balie developed a reputation for fiery oratory. Twenty-one years Lud's senior, Balie served in the U.S.House of Representatives during the 1830's. Balie's national reputation and influence changed the political landscape during Lud's formative years. Various times in his political career, Balie served the Whig Party, the Know-Nothing Party, and eventually helped, in 1860, establish the Constitutional Union Party.

Balie Peyton's political associates included a host of national leaders. Balie lived near Andrew Jackson and although they enjoyed a contentious political relationship, a shared love of horses

[68] **Note**: See the Appendix for an abbreviated Family Tree.

cemented their friendship. Henry Clay was a friend and fellow Whig. Balie played an instrumental role in the election of President Zachary Taylor. Following Taylor's election, Peyton accompanied the President Elect to Washington, D.C.

From 1849 to 1853 Balie served as the U.S. Minister Plenipotentiary to Chile. From Chile, Balie moved to California. After several years in California, he returned to the east coast. Balie, a political ally of John Bell, urged Bell to run for President in 1860 under the Constitutional Unionist banner. During the Civil War, Balie remained a Unionist, although he lost a son to the Confederate cause in January 1862.

John Lewis Peyton
1824-1896

Lud's other cousin; John Lewis Peyton was born into a very notable Virginia family. His grandfather, John Rowzee Peyton, fought for seven years during the Revolutionary War. John Lewis's father, John Howe Peyton, played a meaningful role in Virginia government throughout his life. John Howe's circle of associates included Senator Henry Clay, Senator Daniel Webster, Senator Thomas Hart Benton, President Thomas Jefferson, Gov. Thomas Mann Randolph and others.[69] The family home, Montgomery Hall located at Staunton in western Virginia, often hosted government officials as they traveled westward. Educated at Princeton University, John Howe served as a member of the Bar at Staunton from 1808 to 1846. From 1839 until 1845, he sat in the Virginia Senate.

Lud and his cousin were the same age and friends. John Lewis was born at Montgomery Hall in Staunton. He obtained a law degree from the University of Virginia where he and Lud first met. Prior

[69] **Note**: Most Peyton family papers and letters, both public and private, were destroyed in 1861 when Federal Troops burned John Lewis Peyton's Virginia estate on the Jackson's River.

to attending the University of Virginia's School of Law, John attended the Virginia Military Institute (VMI) at Lexington.

During the 1850's John Lewis became Stephen Douglas's personal friend, advisor, and political ally. In 1855, when Douglas defended his "popular sovereignty" policy in Chicago, John Lewis sat on the podium immediately behind Douglas. Although opposing secession, John ultimately served the Confederacy. North Carolina appointed him its special ambassador to Europe in 1861. John remained in Europe until 1876 when he returned to Virginia. Throughout his life John was a prolific writer. Twenty-five years after the Civil War, John authored a hagiographical tribute to his cousin Robert Ludwell Yates Peyton.

The Peyton "Cousins"

Henry Peyton

Valentine Peyton (Brothers) John Peyton

Robert Peyton (Brothers) Col. Francis Peyton John Rowzee Peyton
(??? – 1795) (Circa 1733 – 1815)

John Peyton *Townsend Dade Peyton* John Howe Peyton
(1755 – 1833) (1774 -1852)

Balie Peyton *R. L.Y. Peyton* John Lewis Peyton
(1803 – 1878) (1824 – 1863) (1824- 1896)

Chapter Three
Oxford, Ohio

Early in the 1830s Townshend Peyton uprooted his family, heading west over the Blue Ridge Mountains, seeking better opportunities in Ohio, and following a route and destination previously marked by Sally's sister, Jane and her husband, John McGonigle. Townshend's adult sons, Richard, Francis, and Alfred, as well as his son-in-law the Rev. Henry F. Luckett accompanied Townshend. It was not unusual for an entire extended family to leave together. "Virginians tended to move west in family groups. Family ties and family purposes were strong in the westward movement."[70] While Townshend and his sons settled in Butler County, Ohio, Rev. Luckett and Maria continued westward beyond Ohio, through Indian landing in central Illinois. The Peyton's joined the flood of Virginians abandoning the Old Dominion. Hard times underscored by increasingly troublesome slavery issues drove thousands out of Virginia and into the western frontier.

Forced by necessity and financial desperation, the Peyton's' collective decision to emigrate carried loss. They left much behind. Six decades of daily dedication to their plantation, the mill, and businesses fell behind. They left family - daughters Lucy, Ann, and Emily remained in Virginia and Maryland with their families. They abandoned their heritage. The Peyton family cemetery held parents, grandparents, brothers and children. Like so many of their friends and neighbors, the Peyton's packed and left.

The Virginian exodus, initially a trickle, became by 1830, a torrent of families leaving the Old Dominion. Between 1830 and 1840, 375,000 Virginians fled the state.[71] When migration came to a close, a million Virginians had left in hope of better lives elsewhere. Western destinations, Ohio and Missouri, welcomed the highest number of immigrants. In 1850, Ohio embraced more Virginians than any other state, and Missouri ranked 5th. By 1860,

[70] Fischer. *Bound* Away. Page 216
[71] Fischer. *Bound Away*. Page 211

Missouri, with a Virginian population exceeding 40,000 ranked second behind only Ohio.[72]

The decades long Virginian exodus owed its causes to plummeting land values, and a lagging infrastructure, both issues intertwined with slavery. The Peyton family, like all other Virginians, suffered under deescalating land values. Between 1817 and 1829 the State's land values dropped from $207 million to $90 million.[73] Economic prosperity plummeted, closely following the drop in land values; families at all levels struggled to maintain or improve their standard of living. "For many the only option was to leave the state."[74]

---------- Slavery and Nat Turner's Rebellion ----------

Slavery exacerbated the problem. Many Virginians had come to identify slavery as the prime cause of the economic quagmire but struggled to agree on a solution. Slave revolts had long frightened Virginians, the fear fueling a persistent, lingering uneasiness. In a heartbeat, Nat Turner's 1831 rebellion, transformed the fear into a tangible threat. In every Southern county, in every village, on every farm "a spasm of fear pulsed through Virginia and the South."[75]

From slavery's introduction, southern white families, outnumbered by thousands of slaves, feared slave uprisings and bloody violence. Nat Turner's slave rebellion erupted in Southampton County, Va. Historian, David F. Allmendinger's description of the events succinctly hits home:

> "Starting on Sunday night, 21 August, and continuing all day on Monday he and his men followed a winding route across St. Luke's Parish, stopping at sixteen chosen houses, putting to death every white man (twelve total), women (nineteen), and child (twenty-four) they found at their various destinations. They headed generally east-northeast from Cabin Pond to Jerusalem, the county seat (thirteen miles as the crow flies), but first moved south,

[72] Fischer. *Bound Away*. Page 180.
[73] Fischer. *Bound Away*. Page 202.
[74] Fischer. *Albion*. Page 203.
[75] Fischer. *Albion*. Page 208.

> then west-southwest, east, southeast, and north, before turning definitely east, toward the town. They seldom turned without purpose or stopped by chance. Turner later would claim that when they reached a point three miles south of the courthouse his men numbered 'fifty or sixty, all mounted and armed with guns, axes, swords and clubs."[76]

Although Turner would be captured and executed for the attacks, terror spread throughout Virginia, and bled into the deeper slaveholding south. Long after the Turner episode became history, fear remained, an ever-constant companion to slave holders. Townshend Peyton "accepted slavery as an established institution until startled by" Turner's rebellion.[77] He along with others advocated abolition. "Among the prominent men of the day who advocated abolition were James McDowell, afterward Governor of Virginia: Charles James Faulkner, late minister plenipotentiary to France; Thomas Jefferson Randolph and Townshend Dade Peyton."[78]

When no emancipation directive came from the Virginia general assembly, slavery continued. Those slave owners becoming uncomfortable, opposing the institution were faced with the difficult step of emancipating their slaves and absorbing huge financial losses. A biographical sketch written after Townshend's death said, "Mr. Peyton, with great pecuniary loss, liberated his slaves and immigrated in 1832 to Oxford, Ohio."[79] In fact, Townshend sold his field slaves to the new owner of the plantation, Hamilton Rogers.[80] Like the "Man of Humanity," Mr. Shelby, in *Uncle Tom's Cabin,* Townshend sacrificed his slaves, favoring financial gain. He did however take the house slaves to Ohio where they were emancipated upon arrival.

---

[76] Allmendinger. Introduction.
[77] *National Cyclopaedia of American Biography*. Pages 158-9.
[78] *National Cyclopaedia of American Biography*. Pages 158-9.
[79] *National Cyclopaedia of American Biography*. Pages 158-9.
[80] NRHPRF. Oakham Farm. Section 8. Page 18.

A posthumous biography of Lud Peyton attributes the family's Virginia exodus to Nat Turner's slave rebellion.[81] The murders were horrific, many occurring at night, under the cover of darkness, after the families had gone to bed. Children were the most numerous victims. Nat Turner had been caught, tried, and executed in November 1831. Townshend Peyton's clan abandoned Virginia the following year.

Lud was seven when Turner's uprising reverberated through every Virginia household. If the event unsettled Townshend and Sally, it terrified Lud. Surrounded by black faces that up until then had been sources of security and safety, seeds of doubt and fear took root. Now immersed in shaken adult conversation about the rebellion, sensing visceral real fear, Lud forged permanent opinions and prejudices. Turner's rebellion, in timing and brutality crystallized the psyche of a seven year-old Virginia boy.[82] This terror and the lingering fear became the hard, pro-slavery core around which later experiences layered, creating a southern fire-eater.

---------- Ohio and Oxford ----------

Townshend turned 58 in 1829. The same year a fire destroyed a considerable portion of the plantation's farm buildings. The damage dropped the value of Townshend's structural property by 30%.[83] The financial hit was significant contributing yet another reason to leave Virginia.

The road west literally passed within a few miles of the Peyton plantation. By the time the Peyton family made the decision to move, the National Road had already transported thousands to the frontier. The road's completion opened the floodgates. Construction made travel from the eastern seaside to Ohio, Indiana,

[81] Wakelyn. *Biographical Dictionary of the Confederacy*. Page 345.
[82] **Note**: Nat Turner led a slave rebellion in August 1831 in South Hampton County, Virginia. Turner was captured October 31, 1831. Turner was executed November 11, 1831.
[83] NRHPRF. Oakham Farm. Section 8. Page 17.

Illinois and Missouri feasible for thousands. Western markets opened, commerce expanded and business opportunities beckoned.

Ohio was the primary destination for emigrating Virginians. A large section in southwest Ohio "between the Scioto and Little Miami rivers" had been set aside "as land which Virginia would compensate its Revolutionary War veterans for their enlistment bounties or as pay for their wartime services."[84] The area became known as the Virginia Military District. The Little Miami River marked the district's western boundary. Cincinnati in Hamilton County, thrived just outside the district's eastern border, where the Little Miami and Ohio rivers joined. The Peyton family settled in Butler County at Oxford. Butler County abuts Hamilton County to the northwest and Oxford rests a convenient 26 miles from the Cincinnati riverfront.

Southwest, Ohio Circa 1832

84 Fischer. *Albion*. Page 171.

The Peyton clan moved to Oxford enticed by recommendations from the McGonigle's. Jane, Sally's sister, and John had moved to Butler County immediately after their marriage in December 1816. Initially the newlyweds settled in eastern Butler County in Liberty Township. John's two brothers, James and Phillip, lived nearby. Jane and Sally's correspondence, as well as ongoing contact between the families, introduced Oxford's emerging business opportunities.

---------- The McGonigle Family ----------

In 1805, all the McGonigle brothers, accompanying their parents, arrived in Hamilton, Ohio. The family relocated from Staunton, Virginia. Phillip and John purchased land and later partnered in businesses. During the War of 1812, Phillip enlisted and fought with the American army, returning safely home when hostilities ended.

Prior to the Peyton's' arrival a canal had been completed, in 1825, linking Dayton and Cincinnati. The canal, the Miami – Erie Canal, later expanded to Toledo. When construction first began, Phillip McGonigle won a sub-contract to build a portion of the Miami Canal.[85] The brothers were deeply established in eastern Butler County, to the point a village, McGonigle, took their name.

By the mid-1820s John and Jane (Yates) McGonigle had settled in Oxford. John immediately joined Oxford's burgeoning commercial community. He helped design the village center as it moved to provide "a place in which to exchange the produce brought in from the surrounding districts, a place where town and county might meet their mutual financial benefit and comfort."[86] John in partnership with other merchants planned and built the Market House on the city square.

[85] *History of Butler County, Ohio*. Page 136.
[86] Harcourt. Page 71.

By 1830, he and Jane were proprietors of the Oxford Hotel. Hotel advertisements described a full service stop for merchants, travelers, and students:

John McGonigle respectfully informs his friends and thepublic generally, that he has opened a house of entertainment in Oxford, Butler County, Ohio. This house situated on High Street, near the center of town, commanding a full view of the college yard and buildings of the Miami University. The house is large and convenient, with stabling and out-buildings nearly new, and in excellent repair. His bar is amply supplied with choice liquors; his larder will be well furnished and care taken to make the table acceptable. Every attention will be given to render the traveler or visitor comfortable who may favor him with a call. Carriages and hacks for parties wishing to visit the Bath Springs or other places in the neighborhood will be at all times available.[87]

Oxford Hotel
Courtesy Images of America

The Oxford Hotel was in full operation when the Peyton's arrived in 1832. John and Jane jointly were joint proprietors until John's untimely death in 1834. She then assumed full responsibility. Jane's hotel accommodations welcomed the Peyton entourage when they arrived at Oxford.

The McGonigle clan provided the Peyton's with an established network of friends and business associates. For three decades, the McGonigle's had been active Butler County residents. They provided the initial business introductions when Townshend, Richard, Francis and Alfred arrived.

[87] *Biographical Cyclopaedia of Butler Co., Ohio.* 1882.

---------- Preparation ----------

Spurred by the general decline in the Virginia economy, the Nat Turner rebellion, and the plantation fire, Townshend and his sons decided to head west. Around 1830 preparations began for the move. Lud Peyton's education now took an exciting, transformative step.

The winter and spring of 1832, move preparations started. Each Peyton family began divesting themselves of Loudoun County property holdings. Townshend's daughter, Maria, and her husband Henry sold their Loudoun County farm on January 19, 1832. Just 60 days later, March 23, Townshend's eldest son, Richard sold his 128-acre farm. After the move to Ohio Richard purchased land in Oxford the following October. Townshend finally, after the move, sold the mill to Asa Rogers in 1833.[88] Two years later, the Peyton farm in Loudoun County, including the field slaves, was sold to Hamilton Rogers for $16,586.[89] The families were on the move west. Townshend, Sally, Frances, Lud, and McGonigle joined the adult sons in the exodus to Ohio.

Loudoun County rests on the south side of the Potomac River, just 36 miles upstream from Washington, D.C.'s town center. Ohio, in 1832, westward over the Alleghany mountains was "the frontier west." Just six years earlier the opening of the Erie Canal in upstate New York connected New York City with the country's heartland. The Erie Canal opened the northern floodgates as immigrants and commercial goods flowed into the Midwest. The canal's opening followed the completion of the Cumberland Road from Washington, D.C. to Wheeling, Va. on the Ohio River.

Emigrants in 1832 had limited routes to the Ohio frontier. Thousands moved west on the National Road from the Mid-Atlantic States. New England emigrants floated the Erie Canal to the Great Lakes. Some disembarked at Cleveland then moving overland,

---

[88] NRHPRF. Section 8. Page 19.
[89] NRHPRF. Section 8. Page 18.

south toward Cincinnati. Others continued on Lake Erie to Toledo where the Miami – Erie Canal ran south to Cincinnati.

The Way West-National Road 1825-1860

The move from Loudoun County to Oxford, Ohio was a significant change – leaving the urbane eastern society for the American frontier. But many Virginians chose southwest Ohio as their new home, transporting Virginian culture and values. As a result, although hundreds of miles from Aldie and Middleburg, the Peyton's found themselves settling in a welcoming, familiar Virginia environment. Lud's nativity and core identity, as a "Virginian," comfortably fit.

But as Lud would find later, the world was changing. Included among the 1832 New England immigrants was Rev. Lyman Beecher's large family. The Beecher's settled in Cincinnati, just 26 miles from Oxford. Two of Lyman's children, Harriet and Henry, were to play monumental roles in the slavery debate. Harriet's 1852 novel, *Uncle Tom's Cabin* effectively and devastatingly stereotyped Southerners and slave owners. Her novel's impact ripped through Missouri. Her brother Henry, although a man of the cloth, in 1855 shipped Sharp's rifles to Lawrence, Kansas. In the mid-1850s Harriet's novel and Henry's guns moved them squarely into Lud's stinging oratorical crosshairs.

Oxford's selection as the Peyton's' new home made sense. Although then a frontier village, it was nicely positioned north of Cincinnati and south of the National Road. Just inside Ohio, Oxford also served nearby Indiana markets. Business prospects were good. The town's focus and commercial interests revolved around Miami University, an educational destination for Lud and McGonigle. Equally important, Oxford's distance from Cincinnati offered a healthier environment, one avoiding the cholera epidemics that often ravaged the river town.

---------- The National Road ----------

The migration from Loudoun County to Oxford required two coordinated trips. Handling the first effort, Richard, Alfred, and Francis, early in 1832 moved the farm equipment, family furniture, and livestock. Lud accompanied his brothers on their overland trip using the National Road. Later, Richard returned to Loudoun County and escorted his father, the women, young children and house slaves to Ohio. This second trip followed a different route. Richard and his entourage, following a wagon trip to Brownsville, Pa. boarded a riverboat for Cincinnati.

For eight-year-old Lud the move to Oxford was the biggest adventure of his short life. The weeks and days prior to the move were filled with fantasies of the frontier and adventure. Dreams filled with imagined sights of the Cumberland Road's traffic and thousands of people like them moving west. Excitement overcame fear of the unknown. Lud would be going with the men, and expected to work.

Early spring 1832, excitement surged when the Conestoga wagons first rolled off the Ashby Gap Turnpike and onto the plantation. Each wagon required six huge oxen. Each of the Peyton families endured the process of loading wagons. The wagons' capacity was limited requiring painful decisions. Each piece of furniture had to be individually selected for size, utility and emotional attachment. The women determined what would go and what would stay. Final decisions were made the night before departure, the last pieces loaded into the wagons.

Finally the moment arrived to start. The women waved good-bye. For the next several weeks they stayed with relatives and friends.

The roughly 500-mile trip from Middleburg to Oxford was direct but hardly flat and filled with challenges. The livestock and men would walk the entire 500 miles; the wagons were filled, leaving little room for passengers. A steersman rode the left rear ox while Lud and his brothers walked along side. The trip's first 124 miles followed the Potomac upstream past Harper's Ferry to Cumberland, Maryland. At Cumberland, the group would enter the National Road, and then move 100 miles to Wheeling. At Wheeling, travelers either ferried across the Ohio River, continuing west on the National Road or boarded steamboats for the trip down the river and to points beyond.

Conestoga wagon

Beginning at Middleburg the Peyton wagons followed the Potomac River from Loudoun County to Cumberland, Maryland, 124 miles. The road to Cumberland steadily and steeply climbed the Alleghany Mountain's eastern slopes.

Harper's Ferry was little more than a day's trip from Middleburg. As he walked, Lud could not have imagined that Harper's Ferry would become a national icon of slavery abolitionists and that John Brown; a western Missouri adversary would find martyrdom there. In 1832 when Lud reached Harper Ferry's heights, he turned and looked back to the east, stunned by the view. He stood at the Potomac River's headwaters renowned "for its scenic beauty." Thomas Jefferson declared Harper's Ferry "worthy of a voyage across the Atlantic." "The river at this point passes through the mountains. The mountains rise on either side of the current almost like a wall."[90]

Passing through Harper's Ferry, Lud and family continued the steep ascent to Cumberland, 100 miles to the west. Mountain scenery encased the road's chaotic, crowded multitude. The eight-day journey became a wonder. Lud's reality flooded with new sights and sounds. The road gradually filled with hundreds of people and thousands animals heading west. This westward flood was met by a continual flow of wagons, people and livestock headed east out of the mountains to Baltimore and Washington, D.C.

For several years, young Lud had watched the flood of people and wagons passing by the plantation on the Ashby Gap Turnpike, wondering about their destinations? He was now on the road. Lud in wonder, absorbed the multitude of sights, sounds, and experiences. The long days and seemingly endless ascents challenged his stamina but as evening approached he reenergized. "At night, along the roadway, gypsy fires flickered in the darkness, where minstrels and jugglers crept to show their art, while in the background crowded traders, hucksters, peddlers, soldiery, showmen and beggars – all picturesque pilgrims" educated young Lud.[91]

Reaching Cumberland the Peyton's first set foot on the Old National Road. Commissioned by Congress in 1805 the National Road stretched 830 miles from Cumberland, Maryland to Vandalia, Illinois. The interstate road, after reaching Wheeling, Va., traversed Ohio, then two new states, Indiana, and Illinois, carries thousands of families west.

In the early 19th century, the National Road stood a marvel of engineering and vision. Congress dictated the road would be 4 rods wide (64 feet), wide enough to allow traffic moving in both directions. The road was macadamized – three layers of stone, each

[90] Peyton. *Over*. Page 14.
[91] Hulbert. Page 408.

layer composed of a specific stone size and then compacted with rollers. Culverts lined the arched road's edges, channeling overflow water during rainstorms. America's first interstate highway, the National Road opened immigration floodgates to the western frontier.

National Road Cumberland to Wheeling

At Cumberland, provisioned and rested, the Peyton's began again, joining the torrent of travelers and hundreds of wagons. The 100-mile trip form Cumberland to Wheeling was mountainous and grueling, filled with many, many streams and rivers to traverse. "Some of the scenery on this route is grand, all of it diversified, romantic and beautiful. The mountains were heavily timbered with oak, pine, and cedar. The underwood was generally thick," and "the woods were in many places impenetrable."[92] Along this

[92] Peyton. *Over.* Page 21.

section, Lud encountered rattlesnakes by the bucket; he did not venture far off the trail. One author wrote, here in Pennsylvania, the rattlesnakes "exist in such numbers that it is next to impossible to shoot in the mountains during the summer."[93]

This section of the Cumberland Road, a grueling test of ascents and descents, also contained an endless series of "grog shops" where travelers could stop, rest, drink, and visit. Mile markers regularly allowed everyone to celebrate their progress while lamenting the distance yet to go. About every 10 to 12 miles, an inn invited the emigrants to stop and rest. Stagecoaches stopped at the inns changing teams and allowing passengers to stretch their legs. Fast moving, spring-less carriages called "gut busters" or "shake guts" carried rushing businessmen.[94] Lud, like the other walkers, had to be attentive or be run over.

In addition to the gut busters whipping in and out of traffic, Lud needed to stay alert for "mountain ships," massive freight wagons also moving faster than the pedestrian traffic. These large wagons clipped along at ten miles per hour, pushed on by the driver's frequent use of their "Loudoun County blacksnake whips."[95] A population in and of themselves, the hardened freighters stopped frequently at "wagon houses," every mile or so.[96] The wagon houses provided for the exclusive needs of the freighters.

As eight year old Lud walked, the road's cacophony of sound set his tempo. The crack of the Loudoun County blacksnake whips elicited yelps and the beat of hooves on the stone road. The horse's warning bells clanged relentlessly. Wagon wheels ground their way into the hard road bed. Yelling men, bleating sheep and oinking hogs joined the chorus. A sponge, Lud absorbed every clink and shout.

At this early stage in the trip Lud's fear ratcheted up a bit. He overheard stories about the "Shades of Death!"[97] The National

[93] Peyton. *Over.* Page 21.
[94] Hulbert. Page 407.
[95] Hulbert. Page 468.
[96] Hulbert. Page 467.
[97] Schneider. Page 129.

Road climbed up and then into thick forest. Here, in the shade, in the forest's tunnel, travelers were robbed and murdered. Each mile Lud covered brought him closer to peril. He safely escaped the "Shades of Death" and the Peyton party paused "west of Gobbler's Knob." Having survived, the travelers celebrated, for at Gobbler's Knob horse races and cock fights beckoned.[98]

National Road Inn- Author's Collection

Sixteen years after Townshend's family walked the road, Lud's cousin, John Lewis Peyton followed. Through John Lewis's eyes, a firsthand account of the sights and sounds still resonates:

> I have said the national road was much frequented by travelers. This was true of both man and beast. Particularly of that class of migratory persons, who are called, in common with the hosts who annually arrive from Europe, emigrants. Many of these were wending their way across the mountains from the older States to the flat lands that extend beyond. The groups were generally made up of families, who travelled on foot, accompanying a light wagon drawn by two horses, and bearing a load of bedding, utensils, provisions, and children. Sometimes a cow or two accompanied the party, and comprised their

[98] Schneider. Page 129.

> entire fortune and stock in trade. The wagon was always covered, sometimes with a white cotton sheet or a blanket, which protected the load from the weather, and furnished a snug place for sleeping at night. If the family was too large to sleep in the wagon, a small tent was pitched alongside, by bending down the tops of four saplings, and throwing a sheet over them. Sometimes a poorer class of emigrants conveyed their entire effects in a one-horse cart, called "a carry-all" – still poorer ones, on the back of a pack horse, and I not unfrequently saw a sturdy fellow bearing his worldly goods upon his whole back, and followed by a wife and children with naked feet, these were the poorest in lucre, but rich in spirit and firm in their faith in the West.[99]

Fifteen miles beyond Cumberland the migration had to climb Negro Mountain, the highest mountain between Cumberland and Wheeling. The oxen struggled pulling wagons up the 2,200 foot climb. Following two descents and two ascents the route arrived at Petersburg, Pa. At Petersburg, Lud saw his first miracle of modern engineering, where the road crossed the Youghiogheny River via "a handsome stone bridge three hundred and seventy-five feet in length, with three symmetrical arches."[100] Engineers had constructed bridges over the deepest and most threatening creeks and streams.

The next interim stop, Brownsville, beckoned 26 miles beyond Petersburg. The National Road crossed the Monongahela River at Brownsville. Brownsville provided the first opportunity for some travelers to leave the road and take to the river, boarding steamboats for Pittsburgh and all points west. The town itself was "a wretched village of about 1,000 listless and thriftless inhabitants," according to John Peyton.[101] Nonetheless, at Brownsville the confluence of river and road triggered traffic jams, confusion, and chaos. The road noise intensified.

---

[99] Peyton. *Over.* Page 26.
[100] Day. Page 19.
[101] Peyton. *Over.* Page 28.

At Brownsville, Lud saw his first western steamboat. The Peyton's ferried the Monongahela River and continued westward. Leaving Brownsville, the travelers began to feel the closing distance and magnetic pull of Wheeling, Va., Ohio neared. Coal mining thrived along the entire 125 mile route from Cumberland to Wheeling adding a new element to the journey. Coal dust and coal wagons clogged the air and road. Five days after crossing the Monongahela River they arrived at Wheeling.

Wheeling straddled the Ohio River surrounded by coal country. Already in 1832, Wheeling was a "flourishing manufacturing town," becoming, as John Lewis Peyton would later describe, "...the place is very dirty, and, as its manufacturing importance increases, destined to become more so."[102] In addition to coal and manufacturing, Wheeling also depended on the economic boost from the westward movement. The National Road funneled thousands of west bound immigrants through it.

The intersection of the Cumberland Road and the Ohio River at Wheeling made it a vital confluence. "The National Road was a great asset, turning Wheeling into a bustling hub of the West. Through linkage of the road and river, the city handled such large shipments that it became a port of entry by Act of Congress in 1831."[103]

Wheeling Circa 1832

From Wheeling steamboats headed south on the Ohio River while land travelers followed roads radiating west toward Cleveland,

[102] Peyton. *Over.* Page 41.
[103] Ainsworth. Page 14.

Zanesville, Columbus, Cincinnati, and points further west in Indiana and Illinois.

Although a suspension bridge later spanned the Ohio River, there was no operational bridge when the Peyton's arrived in Wheeling. A large mid-river island commanded the Virginia and Ohio banks. Ferries carried wagons and livestock across the river. The congested Ohio River far exceeded anything Lud had previously experienced. The lines of wagons waiting to ferry the river coupled to yelling travelers and scared livestock provided yet another lesson for Lud in surviving chaos.

Once across the Ohio River, the third and final stage of the trek to Oxford began. The wagons moved toward Zanesville, 74 miles west, and then to Columbus 56 miles beyond. Another 76 miles brought them to Springfield. Dayton, their final destination on the National Road, was just 32 miles further. At Dayton the National Road passed over the Miami – Erie Canal and here the Peyton wagons turned southwest off the road and rolled toward Oxford, now just 35 miles away.

Ohio locals called the National Road the "Old Pike." Traffic did not diminish once the Peyton's entered Ohio. The terrain flattened but the road's traffic increased, fueled by a high number of stages. "The wagons were so numerous that the leaders of one team had their noses in the trough at the end of the next wagon ahead; and the coaches were drawn by four or six horses."[104]

Stagecoaches raced through, around, and past the slower moving immigrants. The stagecoaches were brightly colored, the names of the lines boldly painted on the sides, "The June Bug Line," the "Good Intent line," and the "Landlords" line.[105] Older stages, spring-less, contained three benches travelers had to climb over to

[104] *History of Clark County, Ohio*. W.H. Beers & Company. Chicago, Illinois. 1881. Page 281.
[105] *History of Clark County, Ohio*. W.H. Beers & Company. Chicago, Illinois. 1881. Page 281.

get a seat while the newer Troy stages, all brightly colored sported lamps and silk upholstered insides.[106]

Ohio's "Old Pike" supported numerous taverns and inns along the route, although travelers called them "wagon stands." The taverns' primary purpose was "to water both man and beast. Beer as we know it was unknown. Ale was sold only in limited quantities. Whiskey was the leading beverage."[107] Live entertainment thrived and those taverns with it drew the largest crowds. Landlords playing fiddles to hoe-downs were common. Lud's attention to his evening chores often wavered, distracted by the "wandering minstrels, jugglers, hucksters, showmen and beggars."[108] Already proficient with his fiddle, Lud joined the gaiety.

Once off the National Road at Dayton the trip changed. The crowded National Road gave way to travel with few competing wagons. But the roadway, now dirt, was pitted and bumpy. Riding in a wagon, never fun, now lost all of its appeal. Each mile of the 35-mile trip to Oxford increased the anticipation and thrill of seeing their new home. The men and wagons arrived in Oxford and unloaded. Once settled, Richard started back to Loudoun County to retrieve the ladies and Townshend.

The ladies' itinerary from Loudoun County to Oxford followed a different route as well as a different mode of travel. Leaving home in Virginia, they traveled by wagon to Cumberland and then to Brownsville, Pa. Brownsville was the starting point for "a river emptying its waters into the Gulf of Mexico, two thousand miles distant."[109] So, at Brownsville on the Monongahela River, they gratefully abandoned wagons for the "comfort" and excitement of a western riverboat.

Brownsville was the "head of steam-boat navigation" to the west and the trans-Mississippi. The first leg of the journey was the 147-

---

106 Schneider. Page 134.
107 Day. Page 28.
108 Day. Page 27.
109 Peyton. *Over.* Page 28.

mile float to Pittsburgh and from there to Wheeling. The direct trip interrupted on by brief stops for wood.

In 1832, Pittsburgh was already well on its way to earning the title, the "*Birmingham of America*." The abundance of coal, heavy manufacturing, and immigrant traffic melded to produce a town of commercial importance and energy. The Alleghany River joined the Monongahela, and at the confluence, Pittsburgh rose – unfortunately it stank! Pittsburgh's stench continued and overcame John L. Peyton when he briefly stopped for a couple of nights in 1848. Peyton commented the locals were too busy to notice the smell. Pittsburgh's energy and reputation grew from the river, as riverboats and river people defined the culture.

Sally, and the other Peyton travelers transferred to a second riverboat at Pittsburgh and floated down river to Wheeling. From the river, Sally and Townshend marveled at the iron and nail mill being constructed on the hill. The unfinished construction already overshadowed the town and wharfs. Finished in 1833, the mill, known as the Wheeling Iron and Nail Company, was of the largest in the United States. At Wheeling the immigrants again transferred boats beginning their downriver trip to Cincinnati aboard the steamboat *Emigrant*.

Vintage 1832 steamboats were not luxurious. The craft had two decks, one at the water line, the main deck, and one above. The space below the main deck, the hold, contained freight. The lower, main deck, was crowded and noisy. One passenger wrote, "On the lower deck just above the water line is the boiler, toward the bow, and just behind it is the engine with cylinder, pistons, condenser, and pump."[110] This deck, intended for economy travelers, was packed with families, freight, cows, horses, and all manner of livestock. A cacophony of engine, mooing, neighing, yelling and talking overpowered the silence. Here passengers cooked their own food on a stove bolted to the boat's stern.[111] Deck class passengers, unprotected, endured all of nature's elements – during the summer

[110] Gilliespie. *Come Hell or High Water*. Page 151.
[111] Gilliespie. *Come Hell or High Water*. Page 152.

heavy downpours drenched them and then later a blazing sun baked them. During Spring and Autumn, travelers were often frozen by the breeze and water.

Townshend and Sally purchased "cabin class" tickets rather than the economy "deck class" tickets. Cabin class passengers had meals provided on the upper deck. The *Emigrant* had accommodations for 28 passengers, 20 men and eight women. Berths were provided, each with a window and a privacy curtain. Men and women were segregated. Men ate together at a single table while the ladies dined separately behind a curtain.

Eighty-three miles downriver from Wheeling the riverboat turned in for supplies at Marietta. Moving again, it "passed Blannerhasset's Island, the celebrated spot where Aaron Burr and his co-conspirators met to organize their schemes of usurping supreme authority over the Western States."[112]

As the boat steamed further downriver, the westward character of the land and population slowly changed. The travelers had now entered the "frontier." Even 16 years later John L. Peyton noted the change in the people.

> "I observed that the character of the people was rapidly changing, and that a new type appeared. These were the men of the West par excellence, those silent gloomy men who have so often attracted the notice of the observant foreigner."[113] He further noted, "They care little for the courtesies of life, and are only intent upon their pursuits, which they follow with industry, intelligence, and self-confidence, and in which they rarely fail. Though unprepossessing social habits, with little education, they preserve a manly dignity in their character and conduct, which cannot fail to elicit our respect. Unquestionably, they are a little uncouth in their manners and appearance,

[112] Peyton. *Over.* Page 60.
[113] Peyton. *Over.* Page 61.

> but they have the spirit and enterprise necessary to subdue a new country."[114]

After stopping briefly at Maysville, on the Kentucky side of the river, to load wood, the *Emigrant* pressed on to Cincinnati.
By 1830, Cincinnati had reached a population of 25,000. Three years earlier, gas lighting had been installed. That same year, the Miami Canal had opened connecting Cincinnati to Dayton and all points in between. A Swiss immigrant, Joseph Suppiger, described the city in 1833 – "Cincinnati could well become the second largest city in the United States behind New York. It already has the advantage of becoming the largest in the interior. Many steamboats are being built here, and there are numerous other industries."[115]

Already well on its way to becoming the whiskey and pork capital of the west, Cincinnati sported a nickname, Porkopolis." Hoping to satisfy the frontier thirst, "there were scores of enormous distilleries of spirits in which this fiery liquor was manufactured in fabulous quantities from Indian corn, wheat, rye, and almost every species of grain, and at the absurdly low price of ten-pence per gallon."[116]

The slop from the distilleries was fed to the hogs. "Thus hog killing, for you never hear the word pig in Cincinnati, became the great business of the place. The conveniences for carrying it on were so great, that pigs from all parts of the States of Ohio, Indiana, and Kentucky, were driven to Cincinnati, and were there killed."[117]
Cincinnati became the commercial center of the Ohio River valley and by 1850 grew to a population of 60,000.

When Richard, Townshend, Sally, and Virlinda disembarked the riverboat, Lud, Francis, and Alfred welcomed them. The son Sally hugged had changed. Lud's trip to Oxford had been a transformative, rite of passage. He was a veteran of the Cumberland and National roads. The journey had instilled deeper, permanent character traits and buoyed his confidence. Now

[114] Peyton. *Over.* Page 61.
[115] Gilliespie. *Come Hell or High Water.* Page 150.
[116] Peyton. *Over.* Page 78.
[117] Peyton. *Over.* Page 79.

stronger, a bit hardened, Lud carried a deepened knowledge, an education beyond the classroom. In frontier vernacular, he had "been to town to see the elephant." The road's taverns, masses of humanity, cock fights, horse races, long days, sweat and pain educated.

---------- Oxford, Ohio ----------

Oxford owed its existence, purpose and prosperity to Miami University. The university predated the village proper. February 17, 1809, Ohio's legislature chartered Miami University and eventually selected Oxford Township in Butler County as the university's location. Subsequent to this, surveyor James Heaton, plotted Oxford. Oxford's connection to Miami University was more than symbolic. The village contained 128 "in-lots". By charter, these "in-lots" were "subject to a quit-rent of six percent annually on the amount of the purchase money, payable annually forever" to the university.[118] The rents assured the university a consistent financial funding.

John and Jane McGonigle lived in the "in-lot" addition while operating the Oxford Hotel. Townshend and Sally purchased an "in-lot" near the university and town center.

The symbiotic relationship between Miami University and Oxford created quite a unique social and cultural milieu in the village's formative days. An early university professor who first arrived in 1828 remembered

> "a strong prejudice in the minds of the emigrants of means, who were able to purchase their lands in fee simple, against holding them on the tenure of a mere lease, liable at the end of any year to forfeiture and sale without redemption, in case the rent or tax was not paid within three months after due" to purchase land outside the village limits. As a result, the

[118] *A History and Biographical Cyclopaedia of Butler County, Ohio*. Page 59.

> township became populated "with a poor, and in too many cases not very honest population."[119]

The early village and surrounding environs were frontier primitive. In 1828, four years after the first classes convened at Miami University, Oxford was rustic and minimal. The village was representative of a western, frontier community with the additional caveat that it was married to the university. Oxford contained six dwelling houses and "a commodious brick building for the district school house."[120] The commercial buildings reflected the burgeoning growth of both a university and the frontier. The town already sported a printing press, a weekly newspaper, and a book-bindery. The two tailor shops and two hatter's shops met the clothing needs of citizens and students alike. Three blacksmiths operated in Oxford. Three cabinetmakers and a clock maker kept up with the residential growth.[121]

Not to be overlooked, three taverns supplied sustenance for the village's (and the school's) libation needs. A sole tobacconist kept the smoke rising and the spittoon filled. Several religious denominations met varying spiritual needs. The Oxford Female High School opened its doors in 1830 and offered two semesters of instruction.

Through the early 1830's, Oxford continued to expand. In 1830 as with towns and villages throughout the American west, brick construction marked a community's transition from frontier to civilization

> "The Mansion House" was built in the center of the village. This impressive, three-story brick hotel would dominate the village, serving both locals and visitors, for decades. By 1835, "the number of brick houses in the town had increased so that there were almost twice

[119] *A History and Biographical Cyclopaedia of Butler County, Ohio*. Page 59.
[120] Harcourt. Page 67.
[121] Harcourt. Page 67.

as many of them as there were log houses: log houses numbered thirteen and brick houses twenty-five"[122]

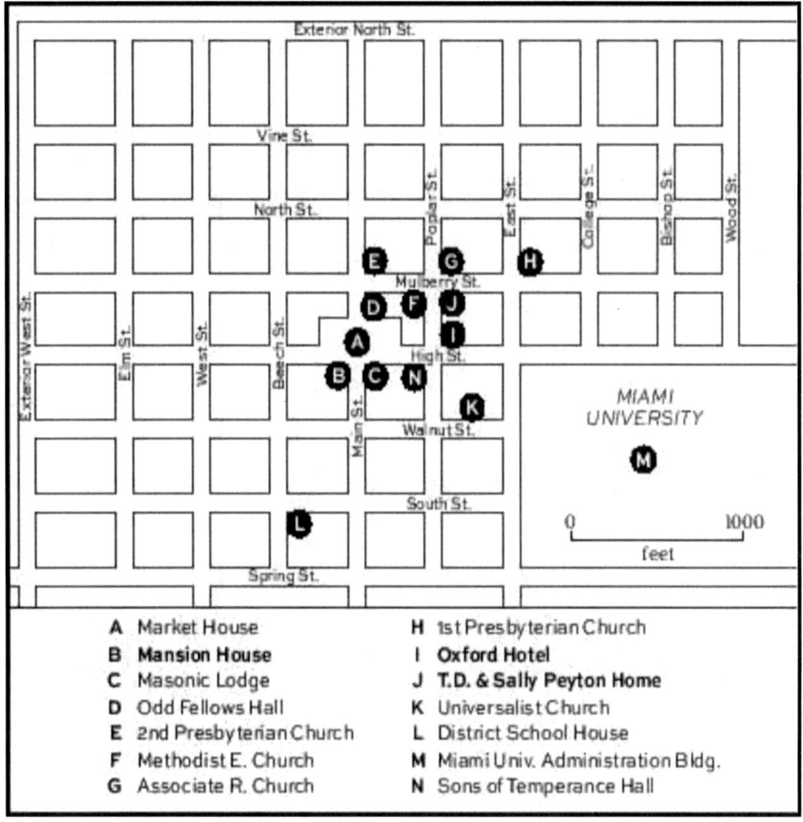

Oxford, Ohio Circa 1840

122 Harcourt. Page 92.

The Mansion House Circa 1851

---------- The Peyton's in Oxford ----------

Jane and John McGonigle welcomed Sally, Townshend and other family members in 1832. The family, finally united and safely arrived, began the process of unpacking and assimilating. The entourage adjusted to a new environment. The biggest change affecting the slaves who had accompanied the family.

The Peyton's house slaves were all emancipated upon arrival – Ohio had outlawed slavery. Now free, the former slaves set about building new lives. They remained in Oxford, finding homes and establishing occupations. The former slaves and the Peyton family remained tied. Beverly Tyler, for the first time in his life, moved away from Townshend.

Townshend and Sally settled into a home in Oxford's "in-lot" addition. Their household, now smaller than on the plantation, was noticeably younger. Alfred, now a teenager, lived with them while working with Francis and Richard. Frances was nine. Lud was eight, followed by his younger brother, McGonigle.

Richard, his wife Ann, and daughter Harriet settled into the Mansion House. Virlinda, Richard's first wife had died, and he had soon thereafter married Ann M. Yates – another of Sally's sisters. Richard immediately entered business with John McGonigle becoming an active member of the Oxford business community.

With assistance from John McGonigle, Richard, Francis and Alfred were soon established in business. Unfortunately, John and Richard's business association was short lived. In August 1832, just a few months after the Peyton's arrived, John fell seriously ill. He soon died. By September 1834, Jane was operating the Oxford Hotel by herself. As John's estate was adjudicated, Richard was forced to file a claim for $100 to settle a business obligation.[123]

Lud Peyton's first documented, public record was registered in 1834 by Oxford village officials. It seems a boy's typical love of guns got Lud in trouble. Although it had been illegal to "fire pistols inside the limits of the in lots" since March 23, 1831, young Peyton violated the ordinance. Lud, 10-years old, fired his pistol against regulations and was fined $2.00 for the offense on March 10, 1834.[124]

The same year 10 year old Lud was fined, John Howe Peyton, his distant uncle and John Lewis's father, met one of Missouri's Senators Thomas Hart Benton. Uncle Peyton wrote he met Benton and Benton's wife, Mrs. Peyton's distant cousin. The Peyton's had "spent time with them pleasantly – they will pay us a visit in October."[125] Exactly 20 years later, Lud and Sen. Benton found themselves squarely on opposite sides when the Missouri – Kansas Territory border conflict began.

Attending school tempered Lud's excitement over the move to Oxford. His education continued. In 1836, he began studies at Miami University. His initial classes, in Miami's preparatory Grammar School, demanded rigorous work. Fluency in Latin and Greek was required before admission to the advanced curriculum.

---

[123] Butler County, Ohio. Probate Court. File 0986.
[124] Harcourt. Page 89.
[125] Peyton, John Lewis. *Memoirs of John Howe Peyton*. A.B. Blackburn and Co. Staunton, Va. 1894. Page 104.

Although, Lud had studied both languages at the Middleburg Academy, his proficiency lagged university entrance standards.

Townshend and Sally settled into the Oxford community becoming involved citizens. Townshend became "for many years one of the more influential residents of Oxford."[126] Their adult sons followed suit.

Francis Peyton became an Oxford Township officer on April 3, 1837. He served on the township board with George White and William Roberts. This group became known as "The Fence-viewers."[127] Francis continued his public service, in 1849 and 1850, serving as an Oxford Township Trustee.

Richard Peyton's participation in the community's civic and commercial arenas was short lived due to his untimely death the spring of 1842. However, before his death, Richard was civic minded serving as a township juror in1839. His commercial pursuits carried him outside Butler County into Preble County.

Alfred and Francis became partners in a mercantile business. Townshend supplied the capital for "F.H. Peyton & Co.," and although the company carried Francis's name the brothers were equal partners.[128] From its start in the late 1830s, and into the 1840s, the enterprise maintained business ties with Miami University. It appears the brothers had a falling out because "F.H. Peyton & Co." was out of business by the time Townshend died in 1852. Francis, however, remained in the mercantile business in Oxford and at the time of his death, was still a "dealer in groceries and hardware."[129] Alfred had left Oxford for Illinois and later moved to Missouri.

Throughout the remainder of their lives, Townshend and Sally continued to rely on African-American servants and caregivers. Although slavery was illegal in Ohio, indentured contracts were

[126] Harcourt. Page 169.
[127] Harcourt. Page 104.
[128] Probate Records & Will of Townshend Peyton
[129] Probate Records of F.H. Peyton. Butler County, Ohio. No. 03601.

common. July 1, 1836, Thomas Bushard, a fourteen year old "mullattoe boy" was indentured to Townshend for six years or until the age of 21. The same day a ten-year old Negro girl, Margaret Gilmore, was indentured to Townshend. Margaret would serve until 18 years old. Both contracts provided that "at the expiration of their terms Mr. Peyton was to provide them with a new Bible and at least two suits of wearing apparel each."[130]

"The practice of 'bind out' children was one generally used in good repute. The usual reason for the indenture was, of course, to train a child in a trade and the process filled the need of a trade school. Between 1832 and 1839, some sixteen persons were bound out by parents or guardians or bound themselves voluntarily for a period of years for the purpose of being taught a trade."[131]
Youngsters abounded in Oxford during Lud's early years. The village was yet small enough that the children played together, forming friendships and acquaintances – when the Civil War erupted, a few childhood associations took unforeseen paths.

Two years after the Peyton's arrived in Oxford, Dr. Robert Moon arrived with his family from Virginia. Wealthy, the Moons were strong Southerners. Lud, a neighbor and similar in age, was probably acquainted with the Moons. During the Civil War, two Moon daughters, Charlotte and Virginia became southern spies and mail runners, frequently passing through Union lines. Virginia, "Ginny," carried messages for Missouri Confederate General Sterling Price. As war raged, either Ginny or Charlotte may have carried letters from Lud to his mother.

Another Butler County youngster figured in Lud's western Missouri life but in unfortunate ways. John Burris was born in 1828 in Butler County. John spent his first eleven years in Ohio and in all likelihood crossed paths in Oxford with young Lud. In 1860, now in Kansas, Burris was a member of the Wyandotte Constitutional convention, later serving in the Kansas territorial legislature. Early in 1861, Burris joined James H. Lane's Frontier

[130] Harcourt. Page 108.
[131] Harcourt. Page 108.

Guards, traveling to Washington, D.C. in April. Burris "was detailed to guard Lincoln until the arrival of regular troops."[132] Soon after, in 1862, Burris as a Union commander orchestrated the wanton destruction of Lud's Missouri community. But in 1836, in Oxford, Ohio, the two youngsters may have crossed paths in play and friendship.

---------- 1842 ----------

Eighteen hundred forty-two proved consequential for the entire Peyton family. In the spring, Lud neared graduation from the University of Virginia Law School. He had graduated from Miami University in August 1841. On April 15, Lud's brother Richard died. Almost exactly a month later, May 16, Richard's wife, Ann died. Disease took them both. Richard's obituary described him as being "urbane and polite without flippancy and possessing a discriminating judgment."[133] Both Richard and Ann died at Oxford's Mansion House Hotel. Their children, Harriet and Howard became the legal wards of a "guardian," Peter Sutton.

Offsetting the tragedy, the family celebrated two marriages. Sally's widowed sister; Jane McGonigle married William C. Anderson. For eight years, following John's death in 1834, Jane had continued as the Oxford Hotel's sole proprietor. Through the years, she had become one of Oxford's leading citizens.

In August, Lud's sister, Fannie, married a Miami University student, Joseph R. Davis. The marriage brought Lud into a family destined to play a historic role in American history. Joe Davis had come to Oxford from his home in Madison County, Mississippi. Joe's uncle, Jefferson Davis, following the Mexican War and years in Congress, became the President of the Confederacy. Joe served as President Davis's aide-de-camp, later becoming a General. Fannie and Joe, following his graduation, moved his home in Madison County.

[132] *History of Johnson County, Kansas*. Page 231.
[133] *The Intelligencer*. April 15, 1842.

Chapter Four
Miami University

Lud Peyton's formal education at Miami University began in 1836. He graduated in August 1841, just shy of his seventeenth birthday. During the years Lud attended Miami University, the school "became the storm center of two great controversies which rocked the national church."[134] His years at the University, during the most formative period in any young man's life, coincided perfectly with the most contentious period in the school's first fifty years. Two debates, the first, the Presbyterian split over "new school" vs. "old school" doctrine, and the second, the slavery abolition debate, embroiled and dominated the University. The two discussions increasingly involved the University, the village, and all of southwest Ohio. The increasingly contentious dialogue permanently molded, fired, and hardened Lud's ideology.

---------- Town & Gown ----------

Oxford's founders, adhering to lofty aspirations, named the village after England's historic seat of academia. In the decades following its founding, Oxford met the founders' hopes. Preceding the Civil War, in addition to Miami University, Oxford became home to a theological seminary and three female educational institutions. Miami University, chartered in 1809, welcomed its first students November 1, 1824. The quality of education rapidly gained notoriety.

> "It might be observed that the grade of scholarship for a diploma was set high (the full curriculum was patterned very much after that of Yale); and in its palmiest days, which were from 1830 till near 1840, when its number of students rose some years to near two hundred and fifty, it obtained from its alumni, patrons, and friends, the soubriquet of 'the Yale of the West.'"[135]

[134] Rodabaugh. "Miami University, Calvinism, and the Anti-Slavery Movement." Page 73.
[135] *A History of Butler County, Ohio.* Page 67.

A strong symbiotic relationship tied the village and the university. Locals described the community and the culture as being "gown and town."[136] Ohio's state assembly chartered the university, selected the site, and the village followed. Land granted to the university contained home lots, called "in-lots;" the university received rent income from these lots and the system continues to this day. Lots outside the university limits were deemed "out-lots." The business ties between "town and gown" benefited both.

The Peyton's were representative of the close ties between "the gown" and "the town." Townshend, Sally, Fanny and the boys lived on "in-lot No. 21." Townshend lived in the house until his death in 1852 and Sally remained in the home until her death in 1864. Although Francis lived in "the out-lots," his mercantile business furnished the university and students with basic school supplies, such as ink and paper.

---------- Lud's Preparation ----------

Given Lud's innate intelligence, and the proximity of the University, his enrollment was a natural step. Attending a university in the pursuit of a formal education was however, a departure from the career paths followed by his father and half-brothers. Richard upon reaching maturity had stepped immediately into the mill business in Loudoun County. After the move to Oxford he continued in business. Francis also seamlessly moved into business without attending a university. An industrious self-starter, Francis opened a mercantile business in Oxford that continued in operation until his death. Alfred, before moving to Illinois, partnered with Francis.

There was however some precedent for a formal education. Lud's uncle, Francis, had pursued a professional career. He earned a medical degree and graduated from Scotland's Edinburgh University; Francis's study provided a precedent and role model. Sally's grandfather, Robert Yates, briefly attended William and Mary College in the 1760s. Sally and Townshend envisioned both

[136] Upham. Page 43.

sons, Lud and Alexander, pursuing formal educations, both attended Miami.

If John McGonigle, Lud's uncle, is an example, the family, although lacking formal education, was well read and solidly self-educated. When John died his sizeable library contained books covering a broad array of subjects. Although not a university graduate, his library included Greek and Latin grammar readers, as well as the works of Ovid, Virgil, and Cicero. Other volumes covered botany, geography, mathematics, history, and religion. Novels, including *Gil Blas*, lined his bookshelves.

Notably, John had a copy of *Captain Riley's Narrative*; Abraham Lincoln attributed *Captain Riley's Narrative* as being one of the three books influential in shaping his views on slavery.[137] This autobiographical adventure told of Riley's capture, enslavement, and eventual escape from African Arabs. Jane McGonigle, industrious and well read, shared John's passion for reading and knowledge.[138] Lud's exposure to the McGonigle's coupled to his literary home life created the initial literary appetite enjoyed throughout his life.

---------- Faculty and Mentors ----------

"Miami University's President, Faculty, and staff although comprised of a relatively small number of men reflected deep academic and religious credentials."[139] During Lud's undergraduate studies, Dr. Robert H. Bishop, D.D., was President of Miami University. A Presbyterian minister, Dr. Bishop previously had taught at Transylvania University from 1803 until his appointment at Miami. Miami University's small faculty,

---

[137] **Note**: Captain James Riley was a Connecticut sea captain. Captured by Arabs and forced into African slavery, Riley last escaped and wrote his memoir. His account of the experience became a national best seller in the early 19th century.

[138] Heiser, Alta. "A Printer's Troubles, Oxford, Ohio During the Eighteen-thirties." *Ohio History Journal*. Volume 47. Page 55.

[139] Rodabaugh. Page 9.

Presbyterians and educators, juggled educational efforts with denominational fights and the slavery debate.

Rev. R.H. Bishop
Author's Collection

Rev. Robert H. Bishop served as Miami University President from 1824 until his forced resignation in 1841. During the entire 17-year term, Bishop taught History, Political Science, Logic, and Moral Philosophy. The first ten years of Bishop's tenure he was able to focus his energy on the university and his teaching responsibilities, but that changed in 1834. Two issues soon dominated his time and attention.

Presbyterian denominational tensions resulted in the church splitting in 1838. As an ordained Presbyterian minister and University President, Bishop could not stand on the sidelines. Secondly, the anti-slavery, abolitionist movement increasingly dominated administrative discussions and challenged his leadership. Bishop's moderate abolitionism eventually cost him his job.

Lud, throughout his student days at Miami, attended Rev. Bishop's classes. Bishop was an engaging educator. Although imposing as an administrator, as a teacher Bishop connected. "Over his high cheek bones twinkled a pair of friendly eyes, which spoke to every boy who penetrated the outer circle of administrative chill, and told of sympathy and understanding."[140] His students were devoted to him. "The very lads whose unchecked pranks spelled disaster to his administration were readiest to defend and uphold him in time of need."[141]

Lud was 12 years old when he entered the university's Grammar School. The Grammar School instructor was James G. Birney, Jr.

140 Upham. Page 27.
141 Upham. Page 28.

the son of James G. Birney, an ardent abolitionist and a U.S. Presidential candidate in 1840 and 1844. James, Jr. led the abolitionist organization on the campus and incited off-campus demonstrations. Birney, like the other instructors, infused abolitionist doctrine into his Latin and Greek studies. From day one Lud stepped into the debate destined to define his life.

Most students did not arrive on the university campus fluent in Latin and Greek. Because the University classes were conducted orally, entirely in Latin and Greek, fluency in both languages was a requirement. Thus, as the name implied, the Grammar School curriculum focused entirely classical language grammar. Only after mastering both languages was the student admitted to the university curriculum. Lud, although he has studied both languages in Middleburg, was not proficient. He successfully passed the Grammar School and was admitted to the University.

William T. McGuffey
Author's Collection

William H. McGuffey taught General Literature from 1826 until 1836. Professor McGuffey and the Peyton family were Oxford neighbors from 1832 until McGuffey left in 1836. During his years in Oxford McGuffey studied children and their learning habits. He invited a class "of village children into his house and directed personally every step of their training up from a, b, c; he was keeping notes of all their blunders and tangles and retailing lessons to fit their growing minds."[142] McGuffey's work with the Oxford village children largely resulted in "McGuffey's Readers," the first standardized school textbooks in the United States.
McGuffey and Lud overlapped in Oxford and then, for a year, at the university. Although a supposition, Lud's age and familiarity with

[142] Upham. Page 28.

McGuffey would have qualified him to be one of McGuffey's village students.

McGuffey, unsettled by the abolitionist movement and the intense heat of the slavery debate, left Oxford. He was a quiet supporter of slavery. After McGuffey left Oxford a student wrote, "'Perhaps he will be an abolitionist when the community in which he lives requires him to be one.'"[143]He eventually landed permanently at the University of Virginia.

Albert T. Bledsoe-
Author's Collection

"Another Miami professor, Albert T. Bledsoe, McGuffey's warm friend and colleague in the struggle against President Bishop, was an ardent proslavery man."[144] Bledsoe had attended West Point with Jefferson Davis. Although a Professor of Mathematics, Bledsoe artfully blended lectures on state's rights with his math lectures.[145] After leaving Miami University, Bledsoe moved to Springfield, Illinois where he became Abraham Lincoln's friend. At one point, Bledsoe agreed to be Lincoln's second in an ill-fated duel. Leaving Springfield, Bledsoe moved to the University of Mississippi where he and Jefferson Davis renewed their West Point friendship. During the Civil War, Lud and Bledsoe were reunited in Richmond, Virginia.

Lud's other teachers at Miami were not immune to the swirling Presbyterian and slavery issues. Lud's instructors Samuel McCracken, Chauncey N. Olds, and John McArthur clashed with Rev. Bishop over Presbyterian doctrine. These three teachers were "rigid Presbyterians" of the "old school."[146] Both Olds and

[143] Rodabaugh. Page 6.
[144] Rodabaugh. Page 6.
[145] Rodabaugh. Page 6.
[146] Rodabaugh. Page 14.

McCracken resigned in 1840 creating the opening for the Board of Trustees to replace Bishop.

Lud attended classes throughout the University's entire fractious period. Tensions tied to Presbyterian doctrine, slavery, and personal animosities bled into the classroom. No student was immune, participation in the class meant participation in controversy. For five years, Lud observed and absorbed the conflict

There is no evidence Lud ever became deeply involved in the Presbyterian debate, but the complete lack of any indication he ever joined, or attended, a church after Miami may attest to his reaction. Lud's Missouri political career strongly attests to the influence the anti-slavery debates had in cementing his allegiance to the Southern cause.

---------- Campus Life ----------

Miami University contained just three buildings, two of which were dormitories, when Lud enrolled in 1836. The third building, initially called the Center Building, later renamed Franklin Hall, had been completed in 1818. Franklin Hall was 100 feet long and 40 feet high, three full stories. This multi-purpose structure contained a chapel, a library, recitations rooms as well as meeting halls for the literary societies.[147] Near Franklin Hall, and completing the Miami campus were the two student dormitories "The North Dormitory" and "The South Dormitory."

Dormitory living conditions in the late 1830s and early 1840s can only be described as Spartan. The buildings were sweltering in the summer and frigid in winter. Winter tested the mettle of all dormitory residents. Cold permeated every square inch and corner of the dormitories. When writing parents and friends, students often complained of the frigid conditions. It was not uncommon for ink to freeze in the bottles. The bottles then required thawing near fires before any writing could be attempted. Dormitory fees did not include firewood, necessitating students cut their own firewood.

[147] Elliott, Valerie. *Images of America: Oxford.* Page 10.

Meals were not provided. The students took their meals, normally two per day, at local boarding houses.

Miami Campus
Author's Collection

Fraternization between the dormitory residents was strictly controlled; visiting another student's room was permitted only during specified hours. Although Lud's family lived in Oxford's environs it is most likely he lived in one of the dormitories due to the University's strict regulations and structure.[148] Additionally, the students' rigid (and long) daily schedules virtually demanded campus living.

Rigorous discipline and structure controlled the daily pace of student life; the dictates of an agricultural, frontier community defined the school year. During autumn, the university took a "harvest break" allowing students to return home and help with the family harvest. During the second semester, a "spring planting" break allowed the students to help with the spring planting.

While classes were in session, the University demanded and adhered to a very tight, structured schedule, weekly and daily. Every Sunday was devoted exclusively to religious activities.

[148] Stuckey Interview Notes.

During the school week, Monday through Friday, students arose by 6:00 a.m. Each class day began and ended with Chapel. During Chapel, scripture reading, praise, and prayer sought to instill a religious foundation. Every Miami student carried a university supplied Bible.

Classroom instruction followed morning Chapel. These instructional periods were called "recitations." The class day contained three classroom recitations. The recitation periods lasted a minimum of one hour. Because Rev. Bishop considered a bell to be an extravagance a bugle announced the beginning and end of class.[149]

Miami University's curriculum provided a classical education; this meant the use of classical language and a total reliance on oral dialogue. Classroom lectures and discussion were conducted in either Latin or Greek. Student examinations were conducted orally in Latin or Greek – no written examinations. English was permitted only in mathematics and the sciences. Textbooks were not used in any of the classes. All students were required to take Ethics and Theology. The curriculum encompassed: Ethics, Theology, Rhetoric, Mental Science, Natural Philosophy, Chemistry, and Ancient Languages.

Years following his graduation from Miami University, friends and colleagues commented on Lud's relatively small legal library and his reliance on oral argument in the courtroom and on "the stump." The foundations for this trait obviously were laid at Miami University where reliance on oratory and mental dexterity trumped books and documented legal arguments.

---------- The Student Body ----------

As 1840 approached, Miami's all male student body stabilized around 250 students. The 250 students represented a broad geographic distribution. Regional differences, cultural and social, set the stage for potentially volatile interaction. This generation of

[149] Upham. Page 31.

young men was called "Young American" students. Although they came from different geographic locations, and different socio-economic backgrounds, they shared the common threads of youth – energy and exuberance.

Miami University contained a high number of southern students. Northern parents worried about the unfavorable influence the southern students brought. There was concern the southern young men carried "'the southern influence' of 'honor and spirit' which often led to dueling, gambling, and other dangerous hobbies that could easily corrupt" impressionable boys.[150] Harriet Beecher Stowe worried about her son Fred being adversely influenced. Harriet wrote, "there are some southern boys here, all dash who are very captivating, inspiring restless desires for pistols & cigars - & breathing an atmosphere of Devil may care."[151]

A bit unusual was the "surprising number of Mississippians enrolled at Miami University. Twenty-two of them had graduated from Miami by 1845, and for four years – the session's 1835 to 1839 – Mississippi provided the largest out-of-state enrollment.[152] Generally through this period Mississippi provided 14 to 19 students each year. Some Southerners feared that educational institutions in the older states (New England) offered a "foreign" education and feared "indoctrination with anti-Southern" values; Southern students, however, continued to enroll and attend northern schools.[153]

One Mississippi student became a permanent member of the Peyton family. An 1836 Miami graduate, William Holmes, moved to Canton, Mississippi and began teaching. One of Holmes's Canton students, Joseph R. ("Joe") Davis, a nephew of Jefferson Davis, decided to follow Holmes's path and enrolled at Miami University. Joe Davis began his Miami studies in 1838.[154] While in Oxford, Davis became enamored with a local young woman, Fanny Peyton.

---

[150] Applegate. Page 73.
[151] Hedrick. Page 255.
[152] Warren. Page 131.
[153] Warren. Page 131.
[154] Warren. Page 132.

Fanny, Lud's sister, returned Joe's affection and the couple married in August 1842.[155] Following Joe's graduation the couple returned to Canton.

Oxford village provided ample opportunity for the students to escape the university's rigid discipline. Several "groceries" in the village were in fact "low grog shops."[156] Students congregated in the groceries where the mix of alcohol and fists, dirks, and pistols led to fights.[157] "Bad spirits in the groceries, rash spirits in the student body; no wonder there were so many fisticuffs and special sessions of the faculty."[158] The faculty punished student behavior infractions with the penalties publically announced in the morning chapel sessions.

During Lud's later years at Miami University stringent rules were enacted to curb outside activities. Weapons and dueling were specifically outlawed. Gambling, evidently a common pastime was also banned. Other less violent but financially damaging activities also fell outside accepted entertainment; attending horse races and the theatre were punished![159] It seems doubtful, however, the southern students were solely responsible for the university's crackdown.

Lud enjoyed these outside activities for life. Gambling and horse racing were easily available and there is ample evidence he participated. Once in western Missouri, Lud's fondness for cigars and whiskey fit well.

Other of Lud's fellow students influenced him in different ways. John M. Junkin was a member of Lud's graduating class. Junkin was also the son of George Junkin, the university's President following Rev. Bishop. The Junkin's, strong southerners, shared none of Bishop's abolitionist beliefs. Charles Hardin, another

[155] Butler County Marriage Records. Ohio Marriage Records Index. Record No. 2-142.
[156] Upham. Page 38.
[157] Upham. Page 38.
[158] Upham. Page 38.
[159] Upham. Page 41.

member of Lud's graduating class, from Columbia, Mo., remained an associate through Missouri's early Civil War. Hardin would join Peyton, and other rebels, in Neosho, Mo. when Gov. Jackson called a special session of Missouri's legislature. Following the Civil War Hardin became Gov. of Missouri.

---------- The Erodelphian Society ----------

A major contributing influence in Lud's Miami education and development was his membership and participation in the Erodelphian Society. This "literary society" organized in 1825 began meeting on the third floor of Franklin Hall. The Erodelphians were one of two literary societies on campus. Society membership and leadership was exclusively limited to students. The Ohio State Assembly granted the society a charter in 1831. "The Erodelphian Society of Miami University was incorporated by an act passed by the Legislature of the State of Ohio, on the third day of February 1831."[160] The Erodelphian Society, by virtue of the charter, although drawing membership from the student body and using university facilities, considered itself autonomous from the administration. This independent attitude became a point of ongoing contention.

Autonomy and independence from the faculty and administration enabled society leaders to manage the literary agenda without interference. The society, in essence, was a debating society. The topics of discussion and debate, regardless of their sensitivity or provocative nature were the venue of the society, not the school administration.

The society regularly invited off-campus speakers to address the membership – the public was invited. These speakers, often controversial, were not always welcomed by the school's administration or the trustees because the literary societies "eagerly debated the controversies stirring the country."[161] President Bishop

[160] *A History of Butler County, Ohio*. Page 74.
[161] Rodabaugh. Page 20.

encouraged open debate but often got caught between his policy and the inflammatory subjects.

The Erodelphian Society occupied a large room on Franklin Hall's third floor. The room was carpeted, fully furnished, with an elevated stand for society officers and debates. Opposite the elevated stand were bookcases separated by columns.[162] The society's influence and importance to Lud's development cannot be overstated. Lud was an Erodelphian Society member during his undergraduate years, 1836 to 1841. It was as a member of society that he sharpened his oratorical and debate skills. These same skills would thrust him to leadership prominence in western Missouri politics and the border conflict.

Miami University.

There will be an Exhibition of the Erodelphian Society of the Miami University, on Tuesday evening the 5th of March next. At which time Orations will be delivered by the following gentlemen, members of the Society: John G. Lowe, Thomas Millikin, Gilbert Kennedy, Milton A. Sackett, John S. Williams, Virgil M. [illegible].

The patrons of Literature, and the public generally are respectfully invited to attend.

M. C. RYAN,
F. D. R[illegible]DON,
R. C. SAUNDERS,
Committee of Arrangements.

Feb. 15.

Literary.

There will be an examination of the Union Literary Society of Miami University, on Monday evening the 5th of March next, on which occasion there will be several speeches delivered by members of the society.

All friendly to the cause of Literature are respectfully invited to attend.

J. R. KNOX,
S. T. MARSHALL,
W. M. TAYLOR,
Com. of Arrangements.

Oxford, Feb. [illegible]

Literary Invitation
Hamilton Intelligencer- February 15, 1838

---

[162] *A History of Butler County, Ohio.* Page 74.

The literary societies supplemented academic studies, further developing talents and beliefs. As a student organization, student officers managed its rules, structure, and administration. The society met twice daily, at 2:00 p.m. in the afternoon and later at 6:30 in the evening. Members were expected to obey society rules and regulations, among which were:[163]

- Attend meetings
- No reading during meetings
- No feet on the furniture
- No leaning on the mantel
- Do not disrupt the meetings
- Participate in debate
- Do not leave while meetings in session

Fines were levied against members for rule infractions.

Erodelphian Society debates were taken seriously. Fines were levied against members for "non-performance."[164] The society's President determined all debate winners. The society entertained debate topics from among the multitude of issues faced by a new and emerging nation.

Government Indian Policy

- Was Georgia justifiable in extending her jurisdiction over the Indian Territory? (January 22, 1838)
- Were the English and other nations of Europe justifiable in taking possession of America in defiance of the claims of Indian Tribes? (October 19, 1838)
- Were any of the principles of justice violated by our forefathers in depriving the Indians of land? (May 11, 18390

[163] Literary Societies: Erodelphian Literary Society Materials, 1826-1895. Box 1. 4A-F-4A.
[164] Literary Societies: Erodelphian Literary Society Materials, 1826-1895. Box 1. 4A-F-4A.

Slavery

- Should slavery be a valid objection for the admission of any territory into the Union? (December 14, 1838)
- Is the representation of slaves in Congress just? (May 10, 1839)

Government

- Did the evil effects of the French Revolution counterbalance the good effects? (July 5, 1838)
- Should Congress have enacted the Alien Law during the administration of John Adams? (November 23, 1838)
- Is Party spirit productive of more evil than good? (November 11, 1839)
- Should the military academy at West Point be continued? (January 18, 1839)
- Would it be politic for Congress to pass a law curtailing the power of the President? (June 1, 1839)
- Does a monarchy tend more than a republican form of government to engender a spirit of "mobocracy/" (June 8, 1839)
- Do the evil effects of the federal system over balance the good effects? (January 8, 1841)

International Policy

- Would the British government be justified in declaring war against the United States on account of the conduct of the latter in regard to the Canadian rebellion? (July 20, 1838)
- Was the United States justifiable in refusing to assist the French in their last war with Great Britain? (November 16, 1838)
- Were the allied powers of Europe justifiable in banishing Napoleon to St. Helena? (May 24, 1839)

Social Issues

- Have statesmen done more for the mental refinement and cultivation of society than Divines? (January 15, 1835)
- Should females have equal training with males? (May 3, 1839)

- Should divorce be granted in any case? (November 11, 1839)
- Should literary institutions be supported by the patronage of government or individuals? (February 1, 1839)
- Does commerce tend more to national prosperity than agriculture? (February 15, 1839)
- Can the orator wield a greater influence at the present time than the writer? (April 12, 1839)
- Which has had the greatest influence on society, the American or French revolution? (April 18, 1839)

The preceding lengthy inventory illustrates the depth and scope of the debate. Debaters were forced by circumstance to think fast on their feet while articulating substantive arguments. Debate forced participants to take a position. Arguing both sides of a question demanded a thoughtful examination of the issue.

Debating's critical by-product was the crystallization of individual beliefs and opinions. While participation was key in developing the confidence for public speaking, advocating ideas with peers steeled strength. The sideline peer discussion and criticism continually challenged the young men. The effort to handle cutting peer criticism built character.

Lud gained membership in the Erodelphian Society as soon as he entered the University as an undergraduate student. Society minutes reveal him displaying all the behaviors expected and common to his age. At the March 1, 1839 society meeting Lud was twice fined for disorderly conduct. He later was fined for being "out a second time without leave of the President." Society records report Lud coming and going from meetings and debates, as he felt, regardless of the rules. A pattern emerges of Lud consistently inserting "disorder" in the meetings. Throughout the winter of 1838-39 he was fined on numerous occasions for "disorder."

As graduation neared the spring of 1841 Lud's attendance and participation in the Erodelphian Society waned. The organization's minutes of April 30, 1841 report him to have been absent from the last three meetings. The May 21, 1841 minutes reflect five absences. With graduation just weeks away, many seniors spent time planning next steps, probably in the Oxford groceries.

Erodelphian Society membership had no small impact on Lud's oratorical skills, political ideology and leadership. His electric oratorical skills, lauded fifty years after his death, initially were honed in the standup Erodelphian Society debates.

---------- The Beecher Family ----------

Lyman Beecher
Courtesy Library of Congress

In 1832, Lyman Beecher and his family arrived in Cincinnati the same year the Peyton's settled in nearby Oxford. Lyman brought the family to Cincinnati from New England intending to save the American west from Catholicism and various moral threats. Accompanying Lyman, two children, Henry and Harriet, became Lud's lifelong adversaries. Lyman soon established the Lane Seminary, a religious institution of higher learning and hired Calvin Stowe as a teacher.

Lyman Beecher and Harriet's eventual husband, Rev. Calvin Stowe, became close associates of Miami University President, Rev. Robert H. Bishop. The trio were linked by religion and a shared belief that slavery should be gradually abolished and the slaves colonized back to Africa.[165] For a period of time in the 1830s, Rev. Bishop published articles in the *Cincinnati Journal and Western Luminary*, edited briefly by Henry Ward Beecher.[166]

Henry Ward Beecher, after the border troubles flared along Missouri's western border, ignited a national firestorm when he led the effort to ship Sharp's rifles to abolitionists in Lawrence, Kansas. These Sharps rifles became known as "Beecher's Bibles." In 1859,

165 Rodabaugh. Page 9.
166 Rodabaugh. Page 9.

Lud's fiery oratory repeatedly singled out and attacked Henry Beecher.

Henry's sister, Harriet Beecher Stowe published *Uncle Tom's Cabin* in 1852. Her novel not only catapulted her into national fame and riches, it demonized Southerners, cemented negative stereotypes and invoked a "higher law," excusing violence and a movement away from civil law. Her work ignited and justified violence along Missouri's western border.

Henry Ward Beecher and sister Harriet Beecher Stowe
Courtesy Library of Congress

Lyman Beecher's Lane Seminary directly influenced Miami University and its student body, including Lud Peyton. In 1833 Lane Seminary students organized a three-day slavery debate. The publicized debate inflamed Cincinnati's anti-abolitionists and triggered violence. The debate residuals absorbed Miami University, located just 30 miles northwest of Lane Seminary. June 12, 1834, the Miami University Anti-Slavery Society was formed and for the next 10 years, the university's facility, student body, and trustees waded in the debates current – the debate years corresponded precisely to Lud's student years at the university.

---------- "Old School" vs. "New School" ----------

Miami University was a Presbyterian stronghold during its first 50 years.[167] The school's classical curriculum, its rigorous daily schedule revolving around the chapel, and the ordained faculty created a religious institution with a secular charter. These elements entangled the University in the Presbyterian split of "old school" and "new school" during the 1830s.[168]

"Old school" theology, anchored in pure Calvinism, "taught that because of Adam's original sin, all men, except the elect who had been foreordained to salvation by divine decree, were inherently evil and damned to a fiery hell by an angry God."[169] The movement away from pure Calvinism to "a new freedom of the spirit became inevitable." The democratic thinking of the American West challenged the old doctrine. The Beecher's, Lyman and Henry Ward, became strong proponents of the "new school" liberalism. This movement, largely attitudinal, opened doors to individual salvation, encouraging good behaviors, offering optimism.

Miami University's administration and faculty contained proponents of each school. President Bishop aligned with the new school of thought. Bishop first invited Lyman Beecher to address students in September 1835 and Beecher spoke to the Union Literary Society celebrating its tenth anniversary. This address elicited no adverse reaction but such was not the case the next time he was invited.

Lud experienced Beecher's next contentious appearance. In 1839 all students assembled in the university chapel for Beecher's address. Once again, President Bishop had invited Lyman but the welcome was not universal. "A group of students prompted by (faculty members) MacCracken and McArthur, tried to break up the

167 Rodabaugh. "Calvinism." Page 66.
168 Rodabaugh. "Calvinism." Page 67.
169 Rodabaugh. "Calvinism." Page 67.

meeting."[170] The raucous protest, inside the chapel, impacting all the students, eventually was settled, Beecher continuing with his message of "tolerance and freedom."[171] Beecher remained in Oxford for two weeks meeting with students.

Lud was fifteen. The riotous confrontation between Lyman Beecher and the "old school" disciples validated a personal knowledge of the Beecher's. It undoubtedly was not forgotten. Later in life, Lud would be able to say with credibility, he had met the elder Beecher. There is strong possibility he also brushed against Henry Ward Beecher and the Rev. Calvin Stowe at Oxford.

---------- The Slavery Debate ----------

Southwest Ohio, during Lud Peyton's impressionable, formative years, became the western epicenter of the increasingly volatile slavery debate. Populated largely by transplanted Virginians, the area largely espoused southern values.

Slave emancipation dominated Virginia's political and economic dialogue while the Peyton's were still living in Loudoun County. When the family moved to Oxford they emancipated the house slaves who had accompanied them – Ohio had abolished slavery.

In the early stages of Ohio's discussion, two common positions generally surfaced, one supported slavery, the other favored gradual emancipation. Those favoring gradual emancipation also often supported re-colonization. Abolitionists, especially those favoring slavery's immediate abolition were few in number, and considered extremists. During the 1830s the abolitionist movement gained momentum and converts, especially among the colleges, and universities. Those favoring gradual emancipation suddenly found themselves caught in the middle, attacked by pro-slavers and abolitionists alike.

[170] Havighurst. Page 57.
[171] Havighurst. Page 57.

Cincinnati was predominately a Southern city in 1832; the slavery debate soon unsettled the city. Lyman Beecher's Lane Seminary triggered the upheaval in 1833 when it hosted a three-day symposium dedicated to a discussion of slavery. Discussion moved to heated debate and the debate ended in resolutions to abolish slavery. The entire event unsettled the town and violence ensued. Lyman Beecher, a moderate emancipationist, was caught in the fray.

June 12, 1834 a group of Miami students organized the Miami University Anti-Slavery Society.[172] Within a week the organization had drawn-up and adopted a constitution. The avowed purpose of the organization was to impress the citizens in non-slaveholding states the importance of abolishing slavery – "to make them feel that it is their duty not to look on as unconcerned and silent spectators, but to be up and doing; to cry aloud and spare not."[173]

Oxford, both town and gown, swam in volatile waters. Miami University unavoidably entered the confrontation. President Bishop nurtured free speech and encouraged active debate on all current issues – slavery not excluded. The university's literary societies, independent, autonomous, and often rebellious, debated slavery, inviting outside speakers regardless of administration approval.

The Presbyterian denomination grappled with slavery; strong proponents, for and against, interjected slavery into doctrinal debates. Miami University, by charter secular but in reality Presbyterian, battled the same demons. Slavery became imbedded in all facets of University and town life.

The pro-slavery, emancipationist, and abolitionist debate raged throughout the University, Oxford, and Cincinnati enveloping southwest Ohio. Lud's presence in the debate's epicenter, during his formative years, challenged his thinking, shaped, molded and hardened his views. Although Ohio eventually became viewed as a northern, Union state during the Civil War, the state, particularly its

---

[172] Rodabaugh. Chapter 5. Page 4.
[173] Rodabaugh. Chapter 5. Page 5.

southwest corner, was decidedly southern in the 1830s and 1840s. Within Ohio, strong regional differences intensified the slavery debate. Historian James H. Rodabaugh captured the tension in his history of the university:

> "The antislavery movement met bitter resistance in southwestern Ohio, especially in the Cincinnati area. The abolitionists in the "Queen City" were few in number, a fact which, however, seemed to increase their determination. The result was that the Garrisonians made a great noise and sometimes resorted to vigorous tactics. This was politically a Democratic Region and one of the last northern sections to break with the old Democratic Party just before the Civil War. Many inhabitants of southern Ohio had ancestral connections with the South. A number of the residents held interests, through inheritance especially, in plantation and slave property south of the Ohio River. The propinquity of southern Ohio to the southern people was a cultural factor that cannot be overlooked. Butler County, in which the village of Oxford is located, was no exception among southern Ohio counties. In 1840 Van Buren carried the county by a large majority, in spite of an intense campaign by the Whigs."[174]

By the mid-1830s, anti-slavery sentiments coalesced into local societies and abolitionist groups. "By 1836, according to the third annual report of the American Anti-Slavery Society, there were 133 antislavery societies in the state of Ohio."[175] Active participation in the antislavery movement by Miami University students predated this general public statement.

Slavery triggered turmoil within the University consumed the Board of Trustees, the administration, the faculty, and the student body. University President Bishop, anti-slavery in sentiments, adopted the "gradualist" philosophy of abandoning slavery. Bishop's position succeeded in drawing the ire of both pro-slavery

[174] Rodabaugh. Chapter 5. Page 8.
[175] Rodabaugh. Chapter 5. Page 8.

advocates and those abolitionists advocating slavery's immediate abolition. The Board of Trustees split over the slavery issue but the pro-slavery faction wielded the greatest power and "was determined to exterminate all abolitionism."[176] Following years of conflict, President Bishop resigned as President of Miami University in August 1840, replaced by Rev. George Junkin.

Rev. George Junkin

George Junkin's tenure as President of Miami University lasted a mere three years. He resigned from the university October 12, 1844. When Junkin resigned he described the inherited situation, as "it was early impressed upon my mind, that his brand (abolitionism) had already kindled up a fire which had well nigh consumed Miami University. To such a ruinous degree did the fire burn within her bosom, that the Trustees took up the subject and passed strong resolutions condemnatory of this wild fire."[177]

A professor under Junkin described him thus, "Two other of his hobbies were extreme Calvinism, as opposed to Arminianism, and anti-abolitionism, to the extent of the justification and defense of American slavery."[178] Junkin became a lightning rod for controversy and after leaving Miami University ended up at Washington University in Lexington, Va. where a daughter married Thomas Jonathan "Stonewall" Jackson.

For Lud, and the entire student body, involvement in the increasingly bellicose debate was unavoidable. Professors injected slavery into their classes. Prof. Bledsoe managed to integrate slavery into his mathematics lectures. Regularly, morning and

[176] *A History of Butler County, Ohio*. Page 69.
[177] *A History of Butler County, Ohio*. Page 24.
[178] *A History of Butler County, Ohio*. Page 69.

evening chapel sessions entertained discussion. Those students who were members and leaders of the campus's anti-slavery organization aggressively drove the topic at every opportunity. The university's literary societies, President Junkin indicated, continually stirred the debate.

Lud faced the slavery debate in chapel, in each class and as a member of the Erodelphian Society. Off campus, in the grog houses, debate often moved from civil discourse to physical aggression. There was no respite at home. The "town and gown" culture seamlessly merged to two endeavors. University guest speakers drew village audiences and the discussion was carried back to the home hearth.

When Lud surfaced in western Missouri politics fifteen years later, the public debates he willingly accepted on states' rights and slavery, were performances first rehearsed in Franklin Hall's third floor Erodelphian room. The argument's finer, emotional points had been loudly and forcibly rehearsed in Oxford's grog shops. Lud honed his thinking and his oratory in these early venues.

On December 4, 1838 the Erodelphian Society debated, "Should slavery be a valid objection for admission of any territory into the Union?" Several months later the society debated the question, "Is the representation of slaves in Congress just?" Both debates provided frightening preludes to Lud's electric and incendiary speeches of a later day.

---------- Graduation ----------

Miami University President, George Junkin, the assembled faculty and staff on July 30, 1841. Following prayer and due deliberation the assemblage approved 24 graduates.[179] Each graduate received a Bachelor of Arts degree. Fourteen of the 24 graduates were Ohio natives. Kentucky provided five graduates, Indiana three, while Missouri and Tennessee provided one each.

[179] **Note**: See the Appendix for a complete listing of the graduates.

Lud and the lone Missouri graduate, Charles H. Hardin of Columbia, left graduation destined to be closely linked for the next 20 years. Both young men eventually settled in Missouri practicing law. Each would be elected to the Missouri Senate in the late 1850s and attend Gov. C.F. Jackson's 1861 Rebel Legislature at Neosho, Mo. Hardin survived the Civil War to become Missouri's Governor in 1874, eleven years after Peyton's death.

Lud was one of six of the Erodelphian Society members graduating in 1841. The six graduating Erodelphians were:

P.B. Calhoun	Wilson County, Tennessee
George W. Gowdy	Xenia, Ohio
James A. Lowes	Oxford, Ohio
Wm. H. Moore	Rising Sun, Indiana
David Mack	Preble County, Ohio
R.L.Y. Peyton	Oxford, Ohio[180]

Thomas Millikin of Hamilton County, Ohio delivered the society's graduation address. Millikin's address, *The Dignity of Labor*, encouraged the graduates to value hard work as the "unwavering force of will," building "independence of character," cultivating integrity, and instilling "moral dignity."[181] The "Valedictory" ended, in retrospect, with a haunting shadow for Peyton's generation: "Let your own deeds, be the attestations of your own worth. Go forth now into the scenes of your future lives. And let it never be said of your times, that the generation has passed away, but the Nation has not advanced. Go Forth!"[182]

--- Alexander McGonigle Peyton's Miami Experience ----

Lud's younger brother, Alexander McGonigle followed Lud in the University Grammar School. Whatever Townshend and Sally's

[180] "An Address Delivered Before the Graduates of the Erodelphian Society of Miami University, August 10, 1841." Millikin, Thomas.
[181] "An Address Delivered Before the Graduates of the Erodelphian Society of Miami University, August 10, 1841." Millikin, Thomas.
[182] "An Address Delivered Before the Graduates of the Erodelphian Society of Miami University, August 10, 1841." Millikin, Thomas.

expectations were for Alexander, he fell far short.

Alexander's Grammar School record was horrific. His poor academic record and unruly behavior diverted his path from any possibility of a professional career. In 1844 Alexander was brought before the faculty and expelled. His expulsion provides a window, not only into his youthful character, but also the school's standards of conduct and disciplinary processes.

On February 4 the entire faculty (excluding Dr. Bishop) convened to review charges of misconduct brought against Alexander. He was charged with:

- The use of profane language
- Lying
- Being an accessory to the theft of the Chapel Key
- Turbulent & unruly behavior, unbecoming a student
- The contemptuous treatment of Professors

Alexander appeared before the Faculty and freely confessed his crimes. Displaying "no evidence of sorrow or shame" for his behavior and actions he was dismissed from the proceedings. The Faculty then suspended McGonigle from all studies at the University. Additionally, and more telling, the faculty banned him from setting foot on University grounds.[183] Considering the Peyton family lived on an "in-lot" virtually on University grounds, the punishment must have carried high public embarrassment as well as proving a challenge for Townshend and Sally.

The faculty's verdict and Alexander's punishment were announced the next morning in the College Prayer Chapel – he was rung out!

---------- University of Virginia ----------

Lud's Bachelor of Arts degree did not prepare him for a specific profession or career path. Just 17 years old at graduation, holding a

[183] "Faculty Minutes - 1844." Special Collections. Miami University Archives.

liberal diploma, he still faced unanswered career questions and decisions. Living in Oxford with two brothers in the mercantile business he could easily have joined them and stayed close to home. There is a good chance he gave business a try because he graduated from Miami University in 1841 but did not go back to school until the fall of 1842. The daily grind of the merchant world under his brothers' supervision may have chafed. As time would show, Lud was not possessed of high ambition and an unrelenting work ethic.

In the months after his graduation he decided to pursue law. The law profession offered a steady income and geographic mobility without the rigorous demands of the mercantile business. Lud's oratorical confidence, debating skills and quick mind fit courtroom demands.

In the mid 19th century, two avenues to the bar were available to aspiring young men. They could either "read law" under an experienced attorney and be admitted to the bar by the local court or study law at a university, graduating fully licensed to practice. Lud opted for the academic route. His fellow Miami graduate, Charles Hardin also chose law but returned to Missouri and "read law." Hardin quickly met the standards and opened a law practice.

Two schools in the early 1840s, Transylvania University in Lexington, Kentucky and the University of Virginia Law School in Charlottesville, boasted strong reputations. Each law school offered a curriculum advocating strict interpretation of the U.S. Constitution. Within the legal profession, both universities became known as "states' rights" schools.

Lud chose the University of Virginia Law School and he was back on the National Road traveling east. He was returning to Virginia just nine years after he had moved west. Henry St. George Tucker was appointed Professor of Law at the University of Virginia in 1841. Judge Tucker came to the university from the Virginia Court of Appeals' bench. John Howe Peyton, Lud's "distant uncle" and the father of cousin, John Lewis Peyton, was a close associate of Tucker's. When Tucker left the bench for the university, John

Howe wrote a letter of appreciation to Tucker from the Court of Appeals attorneys.[184]

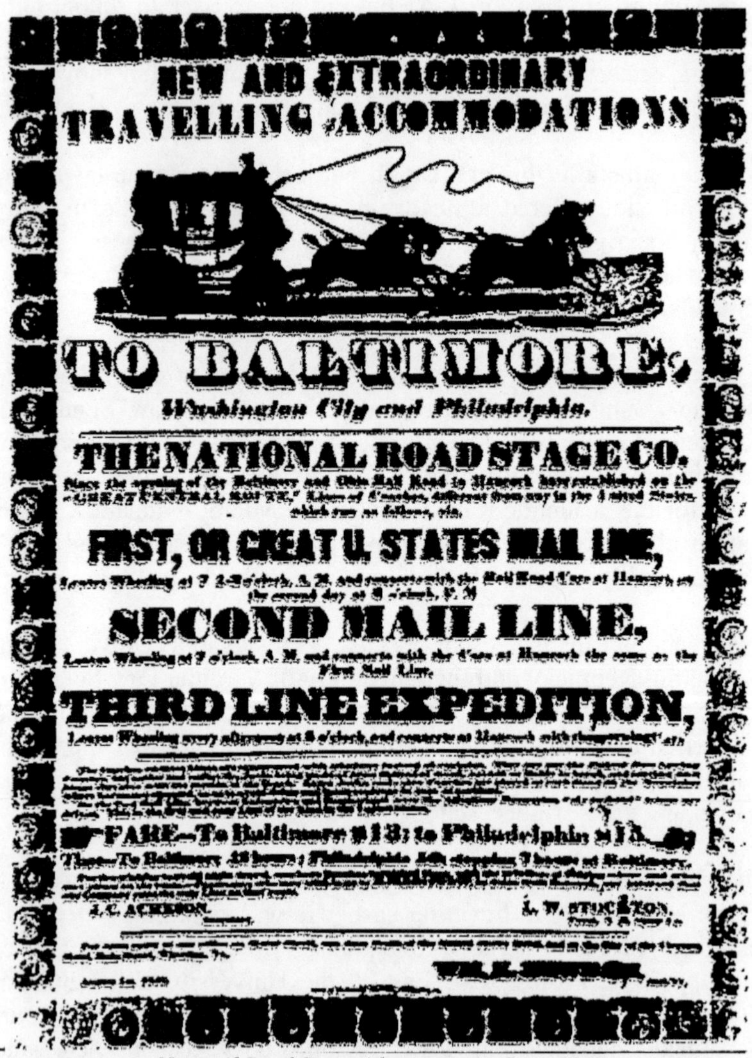

National Road Stage Advertisement Circa 1842

[184] Peyton. *Memoir of John Howe Peyton*. Page 116.

Henry St. George Tucker, Sr.- Author's Collection

Judge Tucker taught law at Charlottesville from 1841 to 1845. Shortly before Tucker's arrival, the law school program had been restructured, allowing students to begin practicing after completing one term. In 1842, the year Lud began his studies at the University Judge Tucker reformatted the law school curriculum. Legal studies now focused on natural law, the law of nations, principles of government, municipal law, and constitutional law. Tucker's strict interpretation of the constitution, the dogma he strongly espoused endorsed states' rights.

In 1843, the same year Lud studied under Tucker, the judge published a treatise, *Lectures on Constitutional Law*. Tucker's treatise introduced, explained and defended the strict, states' rights, interpretation of the U.S. Constitution. Strongly aligned with John C. Calhoun, Judge Tucker's arguments constructed an ironclad defense for Southern rights. Lud and his fellow law students left the university fully indoctrinated in the states' rights interpretation and equally as important, capable of articulating the legal arguments supporting it. In bright minds coupled to brilliant oratorical skills this training was formidable on the political stump – as Lud would demonstrate.

Lud studied law at Charlottesville1842-1843, graduating the summer of 1843. His cousin John Lewis Peyton was also attending the University. An undergraduate, John later enrolled in the Law School graduating two years after Lud, 1845. The cousins became friends and Lud was invited to stay with John Howe Peyton's family at their Staunton estate, Montgomery Hall.

In December 1842, John Howe Peyton, wrote his son:

Staunton, Dec. 29, 1842

My Dear son:

Mr. Kinney has promised to deliver you this letter. Inform me, after Enquiry of the Proctor, what sum I must deposit for the next half term. Write so that I may get your letter a few days before leaving for Richmond.

The young Mr. Peyton, who has just entered the University, is a son of Mr. Townsend Dade Peyton, formerly of Loudoun County, Va., then of Frederick, who emigrated to Ohio, and a son of Col. Francis Peyton, of Revolutionary fame. His grandmother was a Miss Dade and a sister of my grandmother on the mother side. He is, therefore, on both the paternal and maternal sides a blood relative of your. I hope he is a worthy, studious young man and that you may become friends.

Be kind and attentive to him and encourage him I would like to know and to have him at my house. Invite him to spend the entire vacation with you here, and at Jackson river and at William's in Roanoke.

In haste your affectionate father,
John H. Peyton[185]

Lud would have found it impossible to pass up the invitation to visit Montgomery Hall and deepen family ties. John Howe Peyton and his family were a prominent Virginians. The Peyton estate at Staunton contained over 800 acres.[186]

---

[185] Peyton. *Memoir of John Howe Peyton*. Page 148.
[186] "Montgomery Hall: A Plantation and a Park." *Augusta Historical Bulletin*. Vol. 53. 2017. Page 105.

John Howe Peyton
Authors Collection

John Howe was a prominent jurist and Virginia politician. His "social and political circles included U.S. Presidents Thomas Jefferson and James Madison and U.S. statesman, Henry Clay, all of whom stayed at Montgomery Hall and engaged in political discourse".[187]

Montgomery Hall had also hosted Missouri Senator Thomas Hart Benton. Lud's stay at Staunton exposed him to the national stage; a world where thought and deed had formed the nation. Lud's visit reinforced the strong sense of the Peytons' heritage and contribution.

Montgomery Hall

[187] "Montgomery Hall: A Plantation and a Park." *Augusta Historical Bulletin*. Vol. 53. 2017. Page 105.

The year of study at the University of Virginia proved seminal. The time had provided the opportunity to reconnect with his immediate family while opening new relationships. Lud's next visit to Virginia would be occasioned, 18 years later, by the Civil War.

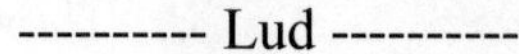

Lud left Virginia, 19 years old, talented, highly educated and confident – he headed west. Just over six feet, a lanky, dark haired and good-looking teenager, still growing into manhood, his youth belied both his formal education and life experience. Lud's basic core remained that of the cavalier Virginians.

A native Virginian, Lud carried a natural comfort with the frontier. The worldly National Road had expanded his character, instilling confidence. Lud was relaxed and at ease with folks from all walks. He instinctively related to the frontier Kentuckian and Virginian. Although accustomed to the world of the landed gentry, Lud easily moved in the hard knuckle frontier. Oxford, initially a frontier village had evolved into a frontier town. During his formative years, Lud lived the hardships imposed by frontier development.

Slavery was a natural element in Lud's world. From infancy until the move to Ohio, slaves had nurtured and surrounded him. The Nat Turner rebellion, a decade past, nonetheless informed Lud's vigilance. Slavery represented the natural order. Lud's participation in the fiery abolitionist debates at Miami University had hardened his attitude. Now battle scarred, future responses proved immediate and aggressive.

Already at 19, Lud understood and owned the states' rights doctrine. As with slavery, states' rights was a given. He had the talent and mental dexterity to defend it in open, public debate. Tutelage from A.T. Bledsoe at Miami and law studies under Judge Tucker at Charlottesville forged and steeled an ironclad conviction in the strict interpretation of the U.S. Constitution. This principle would lie silent within Lud until the mid-1850s when circumstances in western Missouri awakened it.

Lud was gifted. High intelligence had fueled his rapid movement through Miami University's Grammar School and university studies. Miami's reliance on oral recitation and testing produced a quick, "on your feet," wit. Years of debating with the Erodelphian Society honed his natural oratorical skills, building a confidence that proved brilliant in the courtroom and on the stump.

---------- Harrisonville, Missouri ----------

In the months following his graduation Lud returned to Oxford and stayed the winter, leaving for the west in the spring. Western Missouri, on the frontier, offered opportunities for the enterprising. Lud arrived in Harrisonville, Missouri sometime the spring of 1844.

> "Young men moved West because their home communities were already supplied with older men who had made reputations as seasoned practitioners. On the frontier the beginner thought he saw an opportunity to rise to some prominence immediately in the profession and in politics because there were few elderly men."[188]

Harrisonville in 1844, a county seat, had been incorporated for less than 10 years providing ample opportunity for a young, fledgling lawyer. Harrisonville fit the profile, as "many young men who migrated in the early period sought out important county seats on the farthest border of settlement as the place to begin."[189]

> "Western lawyers usually were the sons of poor or middle class farmers. Although some had only a common school background, others had studied Latin, Greek, philosophy and mathematics at an academy, and a number had attended college. Whereas the northern lawyer often had collegiate training the southern lawyer usually had a very limited academic experience."[190]

---

188 English. Page 12.
189 English. Page 13.
190 English. Page 13.

Lud rode into Harrisonville a bit unusual. Young, approaching his 20th birthday, he had no relatives in the area. Fluent in Latin and Greek, University educated, Lud joined a largely uncultivated frontier community. In 1844, he was the most highly educated individual on the lower western Missouri border.

Chapter Five
Missouri's Prairie Frontier

September 20, 1879, sixteen years after Lud's death, Cass County celebrated its first "Old Settlers" meeting. In order to be certified an "old settler" the resident had to have settled in the county before 1846 and had to have been at least 21 years when they first arrived. Had Peyton survived the Civil War, and returned home to Harrisonville, he would not have qualified for this august group. Although he arrived in 1844 he fell just short of being 21 – but for him, perhaps, they might have waved the age requirement.

Lud arrived in Harrisonville and stayed for 17 years, nearly half his life. During these years Peyton, Harrisonville, and Missouri's borderland melded, evolving together from a fresh, vast, prairie frontier to a burgeoning community and finally to the edge of obliteration. Harrisonville's welcoming frontier energy and southern culture proved the perfect safe haven for Lud. His life in Harrisonville unfolded into two distinct chapters.

Chapter one covered ten years, from 1844 until 1854. Lud lived something of a recluse, practicing law, integrating with his community, becoming something of a beloved and respected, although eccentric resident. Western Missouri's early settlement revolved around prairie trade, outfitting westward bound immigrants, the Indian Territory, and agriculture. Missouri was a slave state but the increasingly intense slavery debate was almost half a continent away. Lud's battle with Ohio abolitionists faded further into the past with each passing year. Slavery's constitutional crisis thundered, barely heard, over the horizon.

Chapter One closed with the 1854 Kansas-Nebraska Act. In a heartbeat, the Indians were relocated south, Indian Territory becoming the Kansas Territory. An inrushing population of land hungry settlers replaced the Indian Tribes. Missouri families, some owning slaves, quickly moved into the territory staking land claims. New England settlers, with outside financing, moved to the Kansas Territory dedicated to blocking the expansion of slavery. A clash between abolitionists and slave owners erupted first in the Territory finally bleeding over the border. Discord over slavery, aggravated still deeper by the cultural divide between the New England Puritans and the Missouri frontier's Virginian-Kentucky ethos. The sudden abolitionist reappearance in Lud's world challenged his core beliefs – Harrisonville's quiet reclusive lawyer morphed into an agent of rebellion.

But in 1844 Chapter Two slept in the distant future. In these early days, western Missouri's vast prairie overwhelmed newly arrived settlers. A frontier of few villages, scattered farms and mostly open space, the border offered settlers, traders, and young lawyers an opportunity to prosper in a yet unbroken and often hostile, unforgiving environment. Early settlers, mostly Kentuckian, Tennessean, and Virginian, some with their few slaves, populated several thousand square miles abutting the Indian Territory. When Lud arrived, western Missouri was sparsely populated.

---------- The Frontier Border ----------

Van Buren County's civic leaders had voted to replace the original log courthouse with a solid brick building. Once completed, the brick courthouse would signal the county's first step away from a raucous frontier court to formal a judiciary.

Van Buren County claimed over 1,200 fertile square miles containing two muddy villages, Pleasant Hill and Harrisonville. A deeply rooted, unwelcoming, tall grass prairie greeted farmers. These early farmers, believing the prairie un-tillable, restricted cultivation to cleared land near streams and woodlands. Indian agencies and overland trade fueled local commerce. Lud, almost twenty, university educated, and untested, arrived in Harrisonville.

The Missouri River, frozen shut in winter, began its spring thaw in March and April. The thaw triggered a surge in steamboat travel and in the early 1840s, waves of new settlers. More often than not, the spring river traffic included families destined for western Missouri. Normally the men, husbands and fathers, scouted the area, selected farm sites, and built rough homes. Families and livestock arrived next. Animals, families, and slaves crowded steamboats' lower decks. Some families arrived overland by wagon, but in these early days, the absence of roads and bridges made overland travel slow, arduous, and dangerous.

The steamboats stopped and unloaded at Lexington and Independence. Both towns thrived outfitting the needs of prairie traders, emigrants and the military. Settlers destined for Missouri's western border disembarked at either of the towns. Westport, west of Independence and Lexington, sitting on the Indian Territorial border, served as the gateway to Santa Fe, Oregon, and California. At this early date, Kansas City, or the "City of Kansas," existed only in the dreams of a few local businessmen; not until 1852 would these entrepreneurs begin the town's development.

Western Missouri from the mid 1840s to the mid 1850s pulsed with frontier energy and diversity. Independence, Lexington and Westport gained national reputations as the "jumping off" points for immigrants and adventurers heading still further west. The Missouri River's traffic increased with steamboats moving people and supplies westward. The steamboats and river ports churned diverse folk. Francis Parkman described his fellow passengers in 1846 as being, "Santa Fe traders, gamblers, speculators, and adventurers of various descriptions" mixing with "Oregon emigrants, 'mountain men,' negroes, and a party of Kansas Indians."[191] Parkman's steamboat arrived at Lexington met by "thirty or forty slavish-looking Spaniards, a group of Indians belonging to a remote Mexican tribe, and two French hunters from the mountains."[192]

Independence, the disembarkation and outfitting point for the emigrants hummed and clanked. Lud and Parkman stepped of their boats into a town that, "… was crowded. A multitude of shops had sprung up to furnish the emigrants and Santa Fe traders with necessaries for their journey; and there was an incessant hammering and banging from a dozen blacksmiths' sheds, where the heavy wagons were being repaired, and the horses and oxen shod. The

[191] Parkman. Page 2.
[192] Parkman. Page 3.

streets were thronged with men, horses, and mules."[193] The long distant travelers shuttled out of Independence to Westport.

"Westport was full of Indians, whose little shaggy ponies were tied by dozens along the houses and fences. Sacs and Foxes, with shaved heads and painted faces, Shawanoes and Delawares, fluttering in calico frocks and turbans, Wyandots dressed like white men, and a few wretched Kansas wrapped in old blankets."[194] Merchants, one such A.G. Boone the grandson of Daniel Boone, supplied adventurers, traders, and emigrants alike. Westport exemplified the stereotypical Wild West. Parkman wearily noted, "whiskey, by the way, circulates more freely in Westport than is altogether safe in a place where every man carries a loaded pistol in his pocket."[195]

Families destined for farms in Van Buren and Bates counties usually began their trip at Lexington. Lexington anchored the northeastern tip of the Harmony Mission Trail. The Harmony Mission Trail ran southwest from Lexington to Pleasant Hill and then dropped due south along Van Buren county's eastern border until it reached the Osage River. The Harmony Indian Mission ceased operation several years before Lud arrived. Travelers bound for Harrisonville, pulled off the Harmony Trail east of Harrisonville and veered west into town. Harrisonville, in 1844, "a town" by virtue of its aspirations was but "a village" in size and population.

Lud's disembarkation at Lexington immersed him in the diverse, bustling and loud chaos of a river town in spring. On foot and traveling light, he bought a horse. Heading south to Harrisonville, Lud left the noise for the pervasive hum of the tall grass prairie. He rode south through changing landscape, "sometimes through a narrow prairie, sometimes through a wooded point. A point is a narrow stretch of wood along a stream of water."[196] A bit further south in Van Buren County, "the prairie became wider and the

[193] Parkman. Page 5.
[194] Parkman. Page 3.
[195] Parkman. Page 7.
[196] Tixler. Page 106.

woods became scarcer and thinner. The grass, low and thick, covered a series of small wooded hills and plains crossed by many brooks flowing between two lines of trees, along the edge of which were small farms."[197]

Western Missouri's Prairie Frontier: Circa 1844

The further south Lud moved, the signs of settlement became fewer and fewer. He, and before him Francis Parkman, saw "The woods and the houses gradually became scarcer," and "the prairie seemed to widen constantly."[198] The farms are far apart and the houses

[197] Tixler. Page 106.
[198] Tixler. Page 108.

surrounded by "fences…made of very long pieces of wood piled up and forming projecting and reentering angles." The cultivated areas are also fenced in. The farms are located near streams and woods because "on the prairie one cannot grow anything."[199]

Lud entered a diverse culture. White settlers, most from southern climes, Kentucky, Tennessee, and Virginia greeted him. Farmers with slaves worked side-by-side with their slaves. Missouri traders supplied Indians and the military. Government Indian Agents managed the exchange of goods and services between the Missouri traders and the individual tribes. Although restricted from Missouri, Indians meandered across the border, mingling with settlers and joining in local activities. Prairie freighters depended upon western Missouri for men and oxen. Mexican traders were not infrequent visitors in the villages. Lud blended into this frontier broth of white settlers, slaves, Indians, Indian agents, traders, and teamsters.

A six rail fence- Author's Collection

[199] Tixler. Page 108.

--------- Harrisonville ----------

Lud arrived at Harrisonville the spring of 1844. That spring, the rain never stopped! He may have waded into Harrisonville, muddy if not soaked. Eighteen hundred and forty-four, the year of the great flood, etched into western Missouri memory. For three months, heavy rain deluged the land, filling creeks and rivers and streams. In Indian Territory, on the Kaw River, Grinter's Ferry and the ferry landing disappeared when the Kaw swept its banks clean. At Sibley, in Jackson County, the raging Missouri River easily defeated the town. The "Big Muddy" swept away all of Sibley's hemp warehouses. Further south along Missouri's western border, Sugar Creek devoured a 275-foot bridge. The heavy rains temporarily stopped construction of the Military Post Road from Ft. Leavenworth to Ft. Scott; the road's last mile delayed until November. In future years, when asked about his arrival in Harrisonville, Lud responded, "The year of the great flood!"

Harrisonville, 1844, existed primarily because it was the Van Buren County, county seat. The county, named for Martin Van Buren quite literally defined the American frontier's western border. To the west stretched the tall grass prairie, at the time better known as the Great American Desert. Trees thrived only near streams and rivers. The hills and knolls faced westward over a sea of six-foot tall grass extending deep into the Kansas Indian Territory. The land south of Jackson County, was over 70% prairie.[200] Settlers arriving from Kentucky and Tennessee's tree laden hills lamented western Missouri's dearth of trees; "there was not a stick of timber in sight, and what could a Kentucky mountaineer see in a level country without wood."[201]

Harrisonville's founders platted the village on a hill. Lud, like Charles Tixler four years before, "arrived at the foot of a wooded hill on the top of which is Harrisonville."[202] The town, atop the hill fixed midway between Van Buren County's eastern border and Indian Territory on its west, commanded the surrounding

[200] Schroeder. Page 7.
[201] Dean. Page 1.
[202] Tixler. Page 107.

countryside. The county's western border existed as nothing more than an invisible survey line. Soon after Lud's arrival, completion of the Military Road from Ft. Leavenworth to Ft. Scott created a physical, albeit meandering demarcation between the state of Missouri and Indian Territory. North to south, Harrisonville lay in Van Buren County's northern third, making it an inconvenient destination for those south county citizens living near the Osage River.

Although, the county seat, Harrisonville remained but a village, the settlement "had three dozen inhabitants and twelve or fifteen log houses, one dry goods store, one hotel and a saloon."[203] Young Sam Weddle recalled, "The saloon did the largest business."[204] On the square, the Hansbrough brothers, Enoch and H.M. operated a dry goods store, "which kept anything like a general assortment."[205] Dr. Lynch Brooks maintained a "small stock of drugs" and "he and his son-in-law, Mr. Wilson kept some dry goods but were closing out the stock."[206] This "Wilson and Brooks Dry Goods" served both as mercantile and mingling spot. The courthouse was a log structure. Based on the above, Lud's arrival increased the population from 36 to 37!

Harrisonville's predominate celebrity was Martha "Granny Burnett" - "every child in Harrisonville and Cass County knew" her.[207] She lived alone in Harrisonville. Granny "was slightly humped between the shoulders, wore spectacles that looked like gig-lamps and was a terror to anybody whom she suspected of harboring an intention of meddling with her rights."[208] Granny baked ginger cakes. Children hounded parents for money to buy the ginger cakes. Mrs. Burnett gained local renown as the "old cake woman." Two and perhaps

[203] *The Old Settlers History of Bates County, Missouri*. Page 174.
[204] *The Old Settlers History of Bates County, Missouri*. Page 174.
[205] Smith, A.B. Letter. October 2, 1879. *Cass County Democrat*. May 3, 1917.
[206] Smith, A.B. Letter. October 2, 1879. *Cass County Democrat*. May 3, 1917.
[207] Brooks, Frank H. "Harrisonville Back Numbers – No. 2." October 5, 1916.
[208] Brooks, Frank H. "Harrisonville Back Numbers – No. 2." October 5, 1916.

three generations of children sat on the ground near the Wilson and Brooks dry goods eating Mrs. Burnett's ginger bread cakes.[209]

"The spring of 1846 two more stores, and a carding machine added very much to the business and importance" of the village.[210] As with all other frontier villages, "brick" marked the transition from frontier to civilization, from a village to a town. Harrisonville's first brick home went up in 1848; built by Winchester Payne for John Cummins.[211] Druggists, Abram Cassell and Maxwell built the first brick commercial building and by 1860 brick structures surrounded the Harrisonville Square.

Within weeks of settling in Harrisonville, the myth and legend of Lud Peyton began to crystallize. On Independence Day, 1844, local dignitaries tapped 19-year old Lud to deliver the July 4th keynote address. It was not unusual for an attorney to give the Independence Day speech. "At the public celebrations held on the Fourth of July and on other festive days, lawyers and business men were the leaders, and a lawyer was usually chosen to deliver the principal address. They often wrote their speeches for the occasions and the local newspaper sometime would carry these in full."[212]

Sensing an opportunity to test the newly arrived upstart, the locals may have been looking for some good sport. Given the stage, the tall six foot, gangly youth stood before a crowd of mostly strangers. Lud began and within minutes held the mesmerized frontier audience in the palm of his hand! Lud's listeners expecting an uneasy and awkward performance instead received a hand clapping, flag waving, stand and shout celebration of Independence!

Lud's performance thrust him into the community's spotlight. The young man gained substance. In an age when oratory provided

[209] *The Old Settlers History of Bates County, Missouri*. Page 174.
[210] Smith, A.B. Letter. October 2, 1879. *Cass County Democrat*. May 3, 1917.
[211] Smith, A.B. Letter. October 2, 1879. *Cass County Democrat*. May 3, 1917.
[212] English. Page 122.

primary entertainment and instruction, Lud's natural talents instantly transformed him into a community treasure. This initial foray into the public eye began his reputation as western Missouri's most electric orator.

The small community now knew the tall quiet, reclusive young lawyer harbored both a talent and willingness to entertain. Lud's Fourth of July performance opened hearts, the first step to becoming Harrisonville's loveable eccentric.

---------- "I'll Put You in My Pocket! ----------

Before Harrisonville, as Lud's steamboat approached St. Louis's river quay he could see and hear slaves. Across the water he heard slaves talking among themselves and responding to their white overseer. Slaves lined the dock's edge holding towropes waiting for the chance to throw. Later black backs and black hands pulled the steamboat alongside the dock. They guided the bow and pushed the gangplank onto the deck. All the heavy lifting, all the manual labor was handled by slaves. Lud walked down the gangplank, setting foot in Missouri, setting foot in a slave state.

The journey from the steamboat to his hotel further reinforced the world Lud had entered. A slave loaded his light luggage into the wagon for the trip to the hotel. Once at the hotel, "a negro porter, who belonged to the establishment, stowed" his luggage away.[213]

Lud's first order of business was booking passage to Lexington. Railroads as yet were non-existent and overland travel proved both risky and time consuming. He booked a ticket on the *Lewis F. Linn* named for a recently deceased Democratic U.S. Senator from Missouri, both the name and the steamboat fit. Scheduled for a late Monday afternoon departure, the *Lewis F. Linn* would arrive in Lexington on Thursday. Three days on the river providing ample opportunity to absorb his new state and socialize with other passengers.

213 Peyton. *Over the Alleganies*. Page 267.

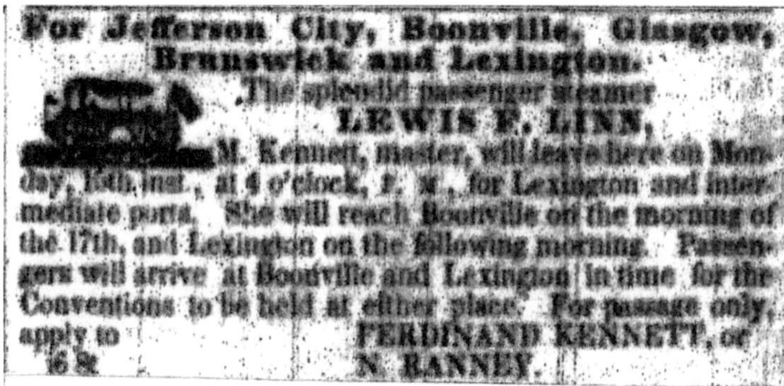

For Jefferson City, Boonville, Glasgow, Brunswick and Lexington.

The splendid passenger steamer

LEWIS F. LINN,

M. Kennett, master, will leave here on Monday, 15th inst., at 4 o'clock, P. M., for Lexington and intermediate ports. She will reach Boonville on the morning of the 17th, and Lexington on the following morning. Passengers will arrive at Boonville and Lexington in time for the Conventions to be held at either place. For passage only, apply to

FERDINAND KENNETT, or
N. RANNEY.

The Lewis F. Linn headed upriver-The Republican July 12, 1844

The next day, time on his hands, Lud tarried in the Missouri Hotel's lobby reading St. Louis's leading newspaper, *The Republican*. The paper provided an introduction to St. Louis and an education on Missouri. Lud patiently absorbed each page. Filled with business advertisements, local news and political articles *The Republican* was a window into the Missouri frontier.

Back in a slave state he noted with interest the number of slaves advertised for purchase or hire. Slave labor obviously fueled the local economy. A Mr. E.B. Cockney had died leaving in his estate five negroes, a woman with two children and "1 boy about 18 years of age and 1 girl about 11 years of age." All five properties, dehumanized, were available for hire. The ad made the offer as a simple matter-of-fact. Lud read the ad with interest, then stoically read on.

PUBLIC HIRING OF SLAVES.

THERE will be hired for the term of one year, on Friday the 19th day of July next, at the Court House door, in St. Louis, between the hours of 11 and 1 o'clock, five negroes belonging to the estate of E. B. Cockey, deceased, as follows: 1 woman with two children; 1 boy about 18 years of age, and 1 girl about 11 years of age. The postponement of the hiring of the above negroes from the 12th to the 19th inst., was in consequence of the sickness of one of the children. [j13 eod td] JABEZ FERRIS, Adm'r.

The Republican- July 13, 1844

Turning to the next page, he perused the "Auction Sales." William Brush announced an offering at auction, listing after a "pair of matched ponies, fast travelers," "a negro woman who is a first rate cook, washer and ironer." Also a special auction, for private sale, "A family of negroes" described as consisting of "a sound healthy woman and two children."[214] Lud, read with interest, untouched, moving to the next offering.

A large auction offered twenty-six slaves, men, women, and children available for a one-year hire. The auction ordered by the Probate Court to be held at the Courthouse Door. Lud pondered the financial opportunity and imagined the scene, pulling in distant Virginia memories. As a young boy, he had attended slave auctions in Leesburg. He remembered slave mothers holding their children.

SLAVES TO HIRE AT AUCTION.

THE undersigned will, by order of the Probate Co[urt] of St. Louis county, hire to the highest bidder, on Mo[n]day the 15th day of July, 1844, at noon, at the co[urt] house door in the city of St. Louis, for one year, twen[ty] six slaves—men, women and children. Persons hiring [must] be prepared to execute notes and bonds, with security [at] the time of hiring: hire payable at the expiration of six [or] twelve months from the day of hiring.

GEO. W. COONS,

j4 eodts Adm'r of estate of Milton Duty, dec'd.

The Republican – July 12, 1844

He remembered looking up into their terrified faces. He read on. The number of runaway slaves caught his attention! Lud was familiar with the runaway problem. St. Louis like Cincinnati occupied the border between bondage and freedom. Lud mused about the temptation to run, Illinois was just across the river and Canada beckoned just a few weeks away. George Clark offered one hundred dollars for ALEXANDER, no last name provided because he was owned by Clark, thus he was known as, Clark's Alexander. Alexander, literate and well spoken, was however noted to be

[214] *The Republican*. July 26, 1844.

"rather impudent," another uppity darkey, Lud judged. Alexander had last been seen heading for Canada on a sorrel horse.

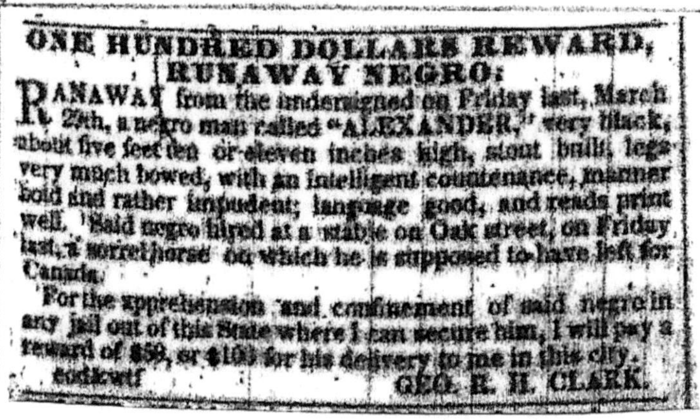

ONE HUNDRED DOLLARS REWARD,
RUNAWAY NEGRO:

RANAWAY from the undersigned on Friday last, March 29th, a negro man called "ALEXANDER," very black, about five feet ten or eleven inches high, stout built, legs very much bowed, with an intelligent countenance, manner bold and rather impudent; language good, and reads print well. Said negro hired at a stable on Oak street, on Friday last, a sorrel horse on which he is supposed to have left for Canada.

For the apprehension and confinement of said negro in any jail out of this State where I can secure him, I will pay a reward of $50, or $100 for his delivery to me in this city.

eodkwtf GEO. R. H. CLARK.

The Republican- July 24, 1844

The next runaway GEORGE, although 30 years of age was however still a "boy." Dorseu's George was "very black" had a scar on his chest and a knot on his jaw. George's beard, ear to ear, ran under his chin and would easily give him away. The reward for George was stair-stepped, $50 if caught in the city of St. Louis, $75 if caught in the county, and $100 if apprehended in the state.

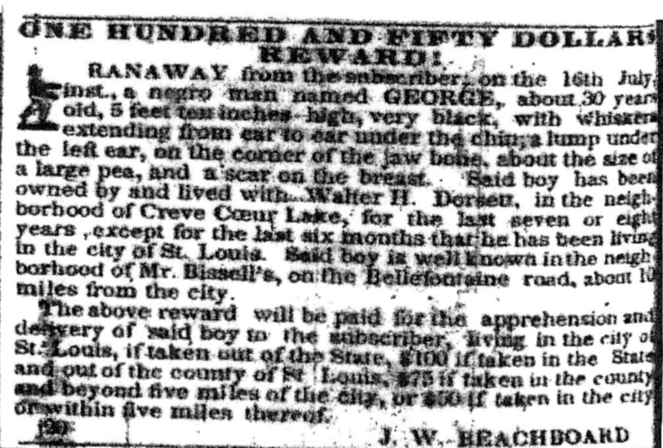

ONE HUNDRED AND FIFTY DOLLARS
REWARD!

RANAWAY from the subscriber, on the 16th July inst., a negro man named GEORGE, about 30 years old, 5 feet ten inches high, very black, with whiskers extending from ear to ear under the chin; a lump under the left ear, on the corner of the jaw bone, about the size of a large pea, and a scar on the breast. Said boy has been owned by and lived with Walter H. Dorseu, in the neighborhood of Creve Cœur Lake, for the last seven or eight years, except for the last six months that he has been living in the city of St. Louis. Said boy is well known in the neighborhood of Mr. Bissell's, on the Bellefontaine road, about 10 miles from the city.

The above reward will be paid for the apprehension and delivery of said boy to the subscriber, living in the city of St. Louis, if taken out of the State, $100 if taken in the State and out of the county of St Louis, $75 if taken in the county and beyond five miles of the city, or $50 if taken in the city or within five miles thereof.

130 J. W. BRACHBOARD

The Republican - July 25, 1844

Lud noticed that even the women were running off. SARAH, Hardage Lanes' Sarah, had disappeared. She was 22 years old, a "slender made woman, of good manners and insinuating address." Lane's ad further described *his Sarah* as dressing "with neatness and taste." Having read the ad, Lud set the paper in his lap wondering why? What sort of man was this Hardage Lane? Had a look from Lane scared Sarah? Had an unwelcome touch turned her cold? Lud recognized an all too common theme.

FIFTY DOLLARS REWARD.

RANAWAY from the subscriber on the 21st ultimo, a negro woman named SARAH. She is a fine looking slender made woman, of good manners and insinuating address, and is supposed to be about 22 years of age; dresses with much neatness and taste: had on, when she left, a striped callicoe dress; usually wears a head dress. I will give the above reward if taken without the county or State, or $20 if apprehended within the city or county and delivered to me, or lodged in jail.

aug6 tf HARDAGE LANE.

The Republican-August 8, 1844

The next day boarding the *Lewis F. Linn* for Lexington Lud again noticed and watched the slaves' efforts. Standing on the upper deck, reserved for the affluent and the white, he took in the dock and the boat's lower, main deck. The lower deck, open to the elements, was crammed with livestock, Indians, poor immigrants and slaves. They floated, cooked and mingled in the open air. On shore the slaves' overseers barked orders, threatening the lash for slow reactions.

Finally the riverboat launched and headed upriver to the confluence of the Missouri and Mississippi Rivers. The *Lewis F. Linn* entered the "big muddy" chugging west toward Lexington and Independence. Past Jefferson City the steamboat continued up river stopping at Boonville, Glasgow, and Brunswick. From here to the western Missouri border Lud noticed a steady increase in the number of slaves. The heavy slave population brought Virginia memories to mind. Later to become known as "Little Dixie," mid-Missouri's agriculture, tobacco and hemp production, both labor intensive crops, relied upon slave labor.

Lexington's river quay bustled constantly from spring to the winter freeze. The largest port in western Missouri, immigrants, freighting, and agriculture fed the town. Lexington was the major river shipping center. Settlers and immigrants disembarked at Lexington. When Lud set foot ashore the number of slaves caught his attention. The town and surrounding area had four times as many slaves as his destination, Van Buren County.[215] Lexington's slaves participated in all commercial and agricultural businesses - blacksmithing, the river trade, hotel and livery services, hemp manufacturing, and farming.

During the upriver voyage to Lexington Lud had listened to excited conversation about Missouri's increasing dominance of the hemp industry. Growing up he had known about Kentucky's influence but Missouri was now overtaking Kentucky. Hemp production flourished along the Missouri River, with Lexington priding itself as Missouri's hemp capital. Lexington's hemp industry already supported three hemp factories and several ropewalks.

Kentucky Hemp Break
Author's Collection

The demand for rope used in ship rigging and cotton baling was steadily increasing. Before the steamboat docked at the Lexington quay, standing on the upper deck, Lud saw line after of line of hemp bales stacked and lined near the river's edge, all destined for east coast manufacturers. Each bale weighed 500 pounds and each had been moved, positioned and stacked by slave labor.

Lud's route to Harrisonville followed the Harmony Mission Trail south out of Lafayette County.[216] He traveled past enclosed fields where slaves, in the spring heat, bent over planting hemp. He

[215] **Lexington Slaves**: The 1840 census counted 943 slaves in Lexington Township of Lafayette County. Van Buren County's slaves numbered 214.
[216] **Harmony Mission Trail**: The trail generally followed the route of present day Highway 7. See the map.

passed hemp breaks that although idle now would, after harvest, be used by the slaves from daylight to twilight "breaking the hemp" so it could be shipped to market.

Hemp seeds planted in rich soil, shot to heights of eight feet. During August's 90 to 100 degree days, the eight-foot stalks were each hand cut. Not an inch to waste, the stalks had to be sheared as near the ground as possible. Slaves, bent over at the waist, faced the ground, swinging sickles. In August, even the mornings are hot, slaves at sunup walked to the edge of standing fields, looked out over the acres to be cut, bent over and began swinging the curved-sickle's. Razor sharp, one misdirected swing, and callused hands, fingers, or legs bled.

Lud often watched as hemp stalks were cut and laid to "dew rot."[217] Slaves, a few weeks later, again labored in the hemp fields, this time shocking the hemp stalks, standing them and bundling them to dry. The final steps, the most dreaded, still waited.

Hemp production was an emerging crop in Cass County. Partners, Tarlton Railey and George E. Moore, specialized in producing Chinese Hemp seed.[218] Visiting Railey's plantation outside Harrisonville, Lud watched as slaves painfully broke the hemp. Acres of shocked hemp had to be broken, as only the plant's pith fiber was needed for rope. The breaking process, twelve daylight hours a day, broke hemp, broke fingers, broke backs and broke slaves. Simple machines, hemp breaks, required two hands, one to hold a bundle of 8-foot stalks the other to grip the break handle, lifting the slats then violently slamming down to pound the hemp stalks on the break frame.

[217] **Note**: The term "dew rot" describes how the cut hemp was laid on the ground, for several weeks, allowing rain and dew to begin the rotting process. This softened the stalk so it could later be broken and the hemp fiber harvested.

[218] Missouri Secretary of State. State Archives. Missouri Supreme Court Records. Box 257, Folder 03.

From daylight to sundown slaves worked their way through acre after acre, shock after shock, and bundle after bundle. Each bundle required the slave to beat the 8-foot stalks, over a 100 times!

Hemp Break Early 20th Century
Author's Collection

As Lud moved south toward Harrisonville, the farms spread out and distances grew. Farms and slaves became scarcer. Lud passed fields being planted, slaves and masters working side-by-side. Very few plantations with large slave populations existed. Most slave owning farmers owned 1 or 2 field slaves.

Cass County's name itself repudiated the non-slavery ideal, openly embracing human bondage. Originally named Van Buren County after Martin Van Buren, county leaders triggered a name change when Van Buren moderated his slavery position. February 19, 1849, Van Buren County became Cass County, now named for Lewis Cass who held firm on slavery.

Cass County whites watched. The whites watched for fugitive blacks. Constant escape attempts demanded constant white vigilance. Fugitive slaves by necessity passed through the county, a border county in a border state. Temptation, possible freedom, beckoned just 15 miles west of Harrisonville. When Lud arrived the county's slaves numbered slightly more than two hundred, congregated around Pleasant Hill, Harrisonville and Papinville. Thirty-one free blacks lived in the county in the mid-1840s.

Cass County whites watched. Lud settled into the community and became a watcher. He soon recognized local community slaves on sight. Suspicious whites stopped unrecognized blacks demanding to see their passes.[219] Darkies without passes were thrown in jail

[219] Missouri Supreme Court Records. Box 232. Folder 6.

and the Sheriff announced the capture by placing runaway slave ads in area newspapers. If unclaimed, the Sheriff auctioned the slaves on the courthouse steps.

Border whites watched whites! Any white encouraging and/or assisting runaway slaves faced severe punishment. Lud's friends and neighbors arrested, tried and banished a Methodist Minister for encouraging slaves to escape. Labeled "Black Abolitionists," whites aiding runaways faced imprisonment and worse – one captured abolitionist was caught within a few miles of the border, tied on a horse facing backward, ridden 90 miles back and given to the vigilantes. A nearby community sentenced a white neighbor, found guilty of hiding a runaway, to "40 lashes, less one,"[220] – strapped to a wagon wheel, the guilty white received the first lash standing and the 39th on his knees.

Many summer afternoons and evenings Lud lounged, visiting the Brown, the Price and the Tarkington plantations. At the Brown plantation, Wayside Rest, the "house slaves'" quarters, behind the plantation house, regularly hosted neighborhood slave gatherings. Lud listened as they had darkey "music, dancing, barbecued rabbits, quails."[221] The Browns' Maria, well known to Lud and the entire community, seemed to manage the Brown household. Brown's Maria, nanny to the Brown children, periodically allowed the children to visit the darkey festivities, "playing fiddles, banjos – guitars – accordions & jew harps."[222] Such happy times, were long remembered, through the eyes of a child. Lud watched, listened, and laughed contentedly - and vigilantly.

It often seemed the slaves and their masters were one big happy family. Too often female slaves found themselves in a "family way," taken advantage of by owners. The community noticed. Wives noticed! Lud wondered what Cassandra Simpson thought when their house slave gave birth to a mulatto child. How did Eliza Crawford, Sarah Strong, or Mary Sanders react when mulatto

[220] *History of Lafayette County, Missouri*. Page 404.
[221] Tennessee Historical Society. Lizzie Brown's Material. "Autobiographical Sketches – Elizabeth Daniel Brown." Page 57.
[222] Ibid. Page 57.

babies appeared in their Van Buren County households? For Lud, the mulattoes triggered uncomfortable memories of his father and his mulatto half-brother Beverly Tyler.

Slavery's ugly, barbaric side was never discussed in open public forum. But the whites knew. The darkeys knew. Both knew the reality. The white's comforted their consciences believing Missouri's slavery to be milder, and gentler. Newspapers, in small notices, merely noted the villainies. The details, the circumstances and horror, arrived by mail and word of mouth.

Lud knew of, had seen instances where slaves, generally good slaves, became saucy. Forgetting their place, these slaves required the whip. This happened even on small farms. One owner wrote,

"This is the first time that I whipped any of them, and they began to think that I dare not do it, and were very saucy."[223]

Celia's owner, George Newsom, repeatedly raped her. A woman of color, a mother and a victim, Celia begged, pleading for him to stop. Newsom continued to rape, and Celia retaliated! She stabbed him and then burned his body. Found guilty of murder, Celia was hung.[224] Lud heard the details from other lawyers. Judge John Ryland had upheld the death sentence.

Elsewhere, white crowds gathered cheering as vigilantes tied a slave to a stake and burned him alive.[225] In yet another episode, visions of Nat Turner, visceral fear and anger surfaced in Lud as he listened to accounts of slave violence. Again white crowds gathered, cheering as mobs lynched two slaves and burned a third alive. Slaves from miles around were gathered and forced to

---

[223] Overdyke, W. Darrell. *"A Southern Family on the Missouri Frontier: Letters from Independence, 1843 – 1855.*

[224] McLaurin, Melton A. *Celia, A Slave: A True Story*. University of Georgia Press. 1991.

[225] *"How George Vest Came to Missouri."* Kuhr, Manuel Irwin. *Missouri Historical Review.* Vol. LIX, No. 4. July 1965. Page 427.

witness the horrific murders.[226] These villainies juxtaposed and subjugated against images of happy slaves dancing to banjos and fiddles on the Brown's plantation.

"I said, 'I'll put you in my pocket,'" Jabez Smith chuckled as he shared the story with Lud. One of Smith's slaves, a bit saucy, had been told if he didn't straighten up, the slave would end up in Smith's pocket. The threat, short, soft and indirect curdled the blood of any slave. In translation, "You are my property, if you anger me again, I'll put you at auction and sell you and put the money in my pocket!" Lud, often on Saturday visits to the Independence Square, had casually passed as "auctioneers sold 'niggers' to the highest bidder."[227] The crying and sobbing slaves fearing their children would be ripped away from them and also fearing being sold to a slave dealer and shipped south to the plantations of Mississippi or Louisiana. Knowing the fears, Lud thought of his sister Fanny living on the Davis's Canton, Mississippi plantation with its 100 slaves, maybe a future destination for some of these western Missouri slaves.

As a lawyer, Lud witnessed firsthand how human property and greed tore at the family and community fabric. Often a deceased's most valuable assets were slaves. Easily valued in the hundreds of dollars the value of two field slaves could exceed a small farm's value. John Gallimore's death triggered a fight between in-laws when Wesley Gallimore sued Joseph Tarkington for Gallimore's Jane.[228] Jane had been a wedding gift from Hannah Tarkington to her daughter and new husband. After the young couple's untimely deaths the Tarkington's reclaimed Jane. Just eleven years old, Gallimore's Jane became the tug-of-war treasure between two feuding families. The dispute ended up in the circuit court and then moved into Harrisonville square conversation and then into parlor gossip.

---

[226] "*Judge Lynch in Saline County.*" *Missouri Historical Review*. Volume 89, Nos. 3 & 4.

[227] *Cass County Democrat*. "Missouri Bygones: No. 1." April 12, 1917.

[228] Cass County Circuit Court Records. *Court Minutes*. Book 275-9.

John Seagraves' death put "one negro woman slave named Elya about 18 years old and her female slave child about one year old" in harm's way.[229] Seagram's death placed Elya and her baby girl at risk of separation. Elya's daughter has reached an age where she could survive without her mother. Elya and her baby girl entered Harrisonville's square conversation and parlor gossip, but more threatening, into the slave market conversation. Elya waited, worrying how Lud and the court would decide their fate. Elya, knowing the character of all the local white masters, feared the wrong decision. Elya, holding tight to her baby.

And then "Emeline a woman of color" absolutely unnerved every Harrisonville heart and mother, white or black. "Emeline a woman of color" gave birth. Rather than allow the child to be a "slave for life," Emeline killed her newborn baby! Arrested for infanticide, "Emeline a woman of color," a Mother and murderer, fell to the supervision of the court.[230]

Simultaneous with Emeline, Cass County's white populace recoiled from the jolt delivered by Harriet Beecher Stowe's *Uncle Tom's Cabin*. Stowe's novel and the "Beecher" name triggered Lud's memories, harsh memories of the Beecher family in Oxford and the Miami abolitionist movement. Emeline suddenly became Stowe's anonymous slave mother who committed suicide rather than deal with the horror of losing her baby, a baby destined to be a slave for life. Lud's father stared up from the novel's pages as Stowe's Mr. Shelby, a caring man, but in the end willing to sell slaves for the money. Harrisonville's white population unsettled by visits to Independence's slave auctions, touched but not changed as slave families were ripped apart. Tarlton Railey, and other western Missouri, hemp farmers taunted by Stowe's hero and runaway, George Harris. Stowe's Simon Legree, reflected in Samuel Ralston's disciplinary whipping of his saucy slaves, Sam and Riley. Did Stowe's slave dealer, Mr. Skeggs, unnerve and come a bit too close to Cass County's Skaggs family? Stowe's Cassie brought to mind Hardage Lane's runaway SARAH.

---

[229] Cass County Circuit Court Records. *Minute Book*. Book 275-14.

[230] Cass County Court Records. *Book 80-8. November 1849 – September 1858.*

Stowe's novel, accurately or inaccurately, put a permanent stain within every white Cass County neighbor. Some may have, like Shakespeare's Lady Macbeth, privately prayed, "Out damned spot! Out, I say!"[231] As one Missouri Southerner wrote, "The story of *Uncle Tom's Cabin* was indignantly repudiated by every Southerner, even those who deplored slavery but it served the purpose of arousing almost fanatical sentiment in the North."[232]

---------- Charles Sims ----------

Lud Peyton began his law practice as a member of the Missouri Circuit Court's Sixth Judicial District. Twice a year, the Circuit Court convened in Harrisonville; court sessions, one in the spring and one in the autumn, lasted several days. When the court adjourned, the judge, circuit attorney, and several lawyers moved on to the circuit's next county seat. Peyton traveled the circuit, moving from county seat to county seat, all within the Sixth Judicial District. Harrisonville however remained Lud's permanent home and the community became his family.

From the beginning, Charles Sims and Lud Peyton formed a loose professional bond. Lud and Sims became Harrisonville's most prominent attorneys during these early years. Although the two lawyers worked the same courtrooms, lived in the same town, and partnered on the same cases, their lives, personal and professional, unfolded in stark contrast. Sims was more the prototypical frontier lawyer. Energetic and ambitious Sims had a singular focus on success in the judiciary and politics.

> "When the lawyer arrived in a western community he was usually without funds or property, and anxious to make money. Fees were usually moderate in the West and even though a lawyer practiced over a wide territory and handled all kinds of cases, he could not hope to become wealthy through practice alone. Therefore he often engaged in other sidelines. A

[231] Shakespeare, William. *Macbeth*. Act V, Scene 1.
[232] *Glimpses of the Past. Vol. I – III.* "Aunt Lizzie's Story." St. Louis Historical Society. 1933-1936. Page 72.

> lawyer might be a real estate agent, farmer, surveyor, teacher, merchant, horse trader, speculator, preacher, or editor."[233]

When Lud arrived in 1844, Sims already occupied a public position in Van Buren County. He had helped design and construct the county's first log courthouse. Sims, a bit older than Lud, had been in practice two years.

In 1843 Sims joined one of Van Buren County's most prominent families. Charles married Polly Briscoe. Polly's father, John Briscoe, pioneered Van Buren County. Briscoe, having previously served as a judge on the Saline County, County Court, later became a judge on the Van Buren County Court. Polly's brother, William M. Briscoe, was active in the county's political community. William through the years served as a Justice of the Peace, County Court Judge, Sheriff of Van Buren County, and county representative in the State Assembly. The Briscoe family's political savvy and established connections helped Sims ascend regional and statewide politics.

Sims's ambitions for professional status, wealth, and political clout typified the aspirations of his contemporaries; Peyton's ambitions, initially, led to different, intangible ends. Where Sims sought wealth, Lud sought friends. Where Sims typified frontier energy, Lud was lethargic. Where Sims's legal process was documented, Lud argued from the top of his head. Where Sims willingly stepped into the political arena, Lud, in the beginning, wandered in or was pushed. Where Sims's oratorical skills were ordinary, Lud's were electric. Through almost two decades, the lives of these two young Harrisonville attorneys intertwined and influenced, each other, their lives and fates taking different trajectories.

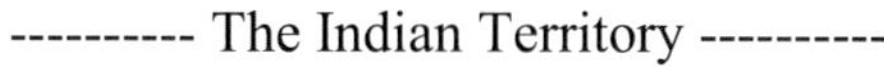

---------- The Indian Territory ----------

Indian Territory abutted Missouri's western border and "by 1840, the boundary of the permanent Indian Country was complete."[234]

[233] English. Page 13.
[234] Andrist. Page 10.

The southern boundary began at Texas's northern edge and zigzagged all the way to Canada. Over 300,000 Native Americans now lived west of the boundary. From Westport south along the boundary several tribes lived on reservations administered by government agents. The Shawnee and Osage Tribes represented the largest populations. By 1846 the Miami Tribe had arrived and was settled on land just west of Van Buren County. Distributing food, supplies, and shelter to the tribes fed much of western Missouri's commerce. The Indian presence fueled Lud's early law practice as well as drawing him into the frontier's social and business networks.

Indian Territory and Missouri's Prairie Frontier: Circa 1844

A soft boundary separated Missouri and Indian Territory. Indians, traders, and settlers moved through and across the border without inhibition. In 1840, when Charles Tixier crossed the boundary heading to the Osage's village, he commented, "we passed a line traced with a plough – it was the border."[235] After 1844, the Missouri – Indian Territory boundary, generally was defined by the meandering route of the Military Road from Ft. Leavenworth to Ft. Scott.

The "soft border" made it easy for Indian traders to outfit in Missouri then cross into Indian Territory. Traders, usually seeking animal skins and pelts, offered an array of goods in return. St. Louis suppliers advertised directly "To Indian Traders" and "Indian Outfitters," guaranteeing "a general assortment of goods adopted to the trade, to which they would invite the attention of purchasers."[236] The Indians' attention generally grabbed by clothe, beads, pipes, blankets, and knives (even "scalping" knives).[237] Other vendors offered the traders wrist bands, ear drops, and kettles. Harrisonville and West Point were common assembly points for the traders.

INDIAN OUTFIT,

SUCH as iron and tin camp kettles, medals, breast plates, wrist bands, broaches and ear drops, &c.

The above articles can be furnished by S. V. FARNSWORTH & CO., No. [illegible] North Main street, St. Louis, Mo., at as low rates as they can be purchased at the east. Persons wishing to purchase any of the above articles, are invited to call and examine them. [illegible]

The Republican- July 12, 1844

Missouri's border population from Westport to Arkansas contained a dynamic mix of Indians, white settlers, slaves, and prairie traders. This chemistry did not change until 1854 when the Indians were relocated to present day Oklahoma. "The Indians of various tribes were numerous. The different tribes I remember were the Sacs, Foxes, the Delawares, Pattowotomies and Osages."[238] The government settled the Miami Tribe, from Ohio, west of Van Buren County in the late 1840s. The Miami's arrival reunited Lud with the tribe that had populated his Oxford, Ohio boyhood neighborhood.

---

[235] Tixier. Page 114.
[236] *The Republican*. July 12, 1844.
[237] *The Republican*. July 12, 1844.
[238] *History of Cass and Bates Counties, Missouri*. Page 801.

TO INDIAN TRADERS.

POWELL & WILSON, No. 82 Main street, are this day in receipt, per Manhattan, of the following goods, adapted to the Indian trade:

CLOTHS—Sav'd list scarlet, blue and grey;

BLANKETS—Mackinaw, ass'd, from 1 to 3 points; scarlet, blue and green do;

RIBBONS—Scarlet, green, yellow, light and dark blue, and ass'd colors and widths, (bright colors;)

SHAWLS - 8-4 and 10-4 chintz shawls, assorted colors and styles;

GARTERING—Scarlet, green, red, and assorted colors and widths;

KNIVES—Butcher, cartouche, scalping, and inlaid handle;

AWLS - Assorted;

PIPES—D pipes, a superior article;

BEADS—Assorted;

Together with a general assortment of goods adapted to the trade, to which they would invite the attention of purchasers.
m29

The Republican- July12, 1844

For the first ten years of Lud's Harrisonville life, Indians were a daily presence. Indians ignored the invisible border, moving into Missouri communities, mingling with people in the villages, on the roadways, and on the scattered farms. By and large, the relationship was peaceful although the culture clash created some abrasions.

Indians could, and did, suddenly appear on farms and the children were warned to be weary. The Indians, men, squaws, and children, viewed pioneer property as "available" and the settlers viewed them as being "great beggars and thieves."[239] Indians were known to stroll into farm homes and "would walk through our kitchen eating everything they could find."[240] Although the settlers' children found the Indians "a thrilling sight," the adults found them an annoyance.

Borderland farmers were not above flogging Indians when pushed to a limit. In Lud's early day's one farmer violently flogged Indians who had appeared on his land and stolen his dog. The flogging came very near erupting into a more violent

[239] Daniels, Elizabeth Brown. "Autobiographical Sketches." Folder 1. Page 9.
[240] Daniels, Elizabeth Brown. "Autobiographical Sketches." Folder 1. Page 9.

confrontation.[241] On another farm, flogging was triggered when a group of Indians set fire to the prairie; the prairie fire quickly spread and incinerated crops.[242]

Winter's hardships increased the Indians' eastward flow from their reservation homes into Missouri's borderland. Hunger and near starvation drove them to desperation. Even with their increased presence in the winter, "they did little harm except a little stealing."[243]

Missionaries had accompanied the eastern Indians when they were relocated to the Indian Territory. White religious determination to convert the Indians never abated. When camp meetings were held near Harrisonville in the late 1840s and early 1850s Indians were always welcome attendees. The camp meetings held southwest of Harrisonville at times attracted as many as 500 Shawnee and Delaware. The Indians "seemed to enjoy religious services as much as the whites."[244]

Although Indians and religion seemed to mix well, Indians and alcohol proved a continual problem. "The Indian Intercourse Act strictly forbade the sale of alcohol to tribesmen, but it took a strong-principled trader to resist the lure of the tremendous profits which a brisk trade in firewater brought in."[245] Missouri had stringent laws prohibiting the sale of liquor to the Indians but nonetheless the sale of whiskey continued. Being found guilty of supplying alcohol to Indians carried an automatic $100.00 fine – for that time, an extremely large and severe financial penalty.

Lud's cousin, John Lewis, observed, "The Indians who remained near these spots presented a sad picture of filth and wretchedness. When observing them loitering around the grog-shops of the West, spending in spirits every cent they could earn by hunting and

[241] *History of Cass and Bates Counties, Missouri*. Page 825.
[242] *History of Cass and Bates Counties, Missouri*. Page 818.
[243] *History of Cass and Bates Counties, Missouri*. Page 812.
[244] *History of Cass and Bates Counties, Missouri*. Page 812.
[245] Andrist. Page 13.

fishing, it was easy to understand the rapid process of extinction which is going on among them."[246]

Between Lud's arrival in Van Buren County and the beginning of the Civil War, indictments for selling liquor to Indians regularly appeared on the circuit court docket. These Indictments continued even after the majority of the tribes had been moved south after 1854. For Lud and other border lawyers, an unfortunate source of regular income flowed from representing clients accused to selling whiskey to Indians.

Lud's first large case involved a dispute between locals who had contracted with the Osage Indian Agent to build houses for the Osage Tribe on the Verdigris River. Thomas B. Arnett and William C. Brown signed a contract, February 1, 1845, to build 21 houses. Later, Arnett and Brown sub-contracted part of the work to two local carpenters, James Cook and Tim Whitehead. Cook and Whitehead, soon over extended, borrowed money from Eli Dodson. Construction delays and arguments resulted in Dodson never being repaid. Subsequently, Dodson filed suit against Arnett and Brown. Lud handled Dodson's initial complaint.[247] Charles Sims represented Arnett and Brown.

The dispute eventually reached Missouri's Supreme Court where a judgment was handed down in July 1847. For Lud the lawsuit's significance was twofold. The dispute immediately immersed him in the complexities of dealing with federal Indian Agents and local merchants' commercial interests. This experience in Indian issues would later be called into action when Lud as a Confederate Senator was appointed a member of the Committee on Indian Affairs. Secondly, handling Dodson's lawsuit immersed Lud in the network of traders tied to the Indians and prairie commerce.

These frontiersmen, Lud's senior in age and experience, heavily influenced the young lawyer. Nathan McKinney, a hardened veteran freighter, lived in Van Buren County. One of the border's

---

[246] Peyton. *Over.* Page 264.
[247] Missouri Secretary of State. Supreme Court Records. Box 59. Folder 12.

best wagon masters, McKinney's shared knowledge of Santa Fe, the Indians, and the northern trails deepened Lud's understanding of the west. Lud's time with veteran Indian agents, Richard Cummins and John Peck, provided insights into the Indian culture and the issues associated with the territory. Joseph Clymer's broad business interests straddled all aspects of the frontier.

Joseph Clymer became Lud's friend and eventually, a political ally. Clymer had arrived in western Missouri in the 1830s settling on a large farm southwest of Harrisonville, in an area that later became a part of Bates County. The Clymer farm lay within a stone's throw of Indian Territory. In 1840 Clymer also had an outfitting store in Westport. By 1844, Clymer operated "Clymer's Trading Post" at the Osage Agency station. When the Pottawatomie Tribe signed its treaty in 1846, Clymer witnessed the event in support of Indian Agent Richard Cummins. Granted a license to trade with the Miami Tribe, Clymer contracted to build houses at Miami Village. In addition to working with the Indian Tribes, Clymer contracted with the army to transport supplies across the prairie.

Although there is no evidence Lud himself invested in prairie freighting or got involved in supplying the Indians, his association with McKinney, Cummins, Peck and Clymer became an education. During conversation, over a whiskey, while smoking a cigar, a deep working knowledge of frontier business passed. More importantly, Lud's personal network grew and solidified.

---------- Frontier Men ----------

Following Lud's arrival and highly successful speech at the July 4th picnic in 1844, he settled into Van Buren County's frontier community. Lud assumed a very private persona, generally avoiding the community's social scene. Friends remembered that although Lud was "well fitted both by nature and education to shine and adorn society, soon after his settlement here he became a sort of recluse, and for years rarely entered society at all."[248] Because Peyton never purchased a house or owned property, his contact with

[248] *The History of Cass and Bates Counties, Missouri*. Page 377.

the larger community unfolded when, for extended periods, he lived-in with local families and boarded in Harrisonville's hotels. Although generally avoiding the social scene, Lud, from his arrival, blended comfortably with the frontier male community.

Van Buren County's early settlers imported a strongly southern, Kentucky and Virginia culture. This male dominated, hierarchical world enjoyed and highly prized sport and gaming. Card games and horse racing occupied special places when attention turned to entertainment. Billiards also gained a place in the gaming hearts of frontier males. Participation seemed open to everyone regardless of social status – it seems many men were periodically able to set aside religious scruples for a bit of fun.

Horse racing in particular captured male hearts. Kentucky and Virginia hosted formal races, and had done so for decades. Racing and wagering went awkwardly hand-in-hand because although the state assembly legalized racing as gaming, placing wagers on a game was illegal. That said, what was a race without a small bet. Betting could get out of hand. There are documented instances where slaves became the currency used to settle bets.[249]

Lud took full advantage of the races. The interest in horse blood and debates over the fastest horse feed daily conversation. Russell Hicks, a Jackson county lawyer whose estate was five miles north of Lone Jack, maintained his own horse track. George Douglass, one of the borderland's richest men, prided himself on owning "a magnificent stallion, an offspring of the famous, 'Sir Archer.'"[250] Charles Younger, Cole Younger's grandfather, owned one of the largest stables of racers in western Missouri.

Frequently, community transgressors were indicted and hauled before the circuit court. As a matter of judicial process, the county court convened a grand jury in advance of circuit court sessions. It was the duty of the grand jury to provide indictments against neighbors who had strayed from the law. These local citizen grand

[249] "The Story of a Kansas Freedman." *Kansas Historical Quarterly*, Vol. XI, No. 4. November 1942.
[250] Tixler. Page 111.

juries, closeted and secreted, arraigned friends and neighbors regardless of wealth or social position. Lud fell victim to one of these grand juries not long after he settled in Van Buren County.

The spring of 1848 a Van Buren County grand jury convened in advance of Judge John Ryland's Sixth District circuit court arrival. The grand jury provided Judge Ryland with a list of over 30 indictments for "gaming." Among those indicted, with Lud, were John Briscoe, Henry Hawkins, and John Callaway. Prominent county leaders, John Briscoe and Henry Hawkins, both served as judges on the county court at one point. Equally prominent and influential, John Callaway would later be elected to the Missouri House of Representatives.[251]

Lud, a relatively new practicing attorney, appeared before Judge Ryland. Placed in the awkward and unusual position of being a defendant, Lud pled "guilty" as charged. Judge Ryland slapped a hefty $10.00 fine on him.[252] The fine, accompanied by a lecture from Ryland, evidently had an impact on Young Lud because he never again stood before the bench for gaming – at least he wasn't caught.

In 1847, Peyton and several Van Buren County men, organized a new Mason's lodge at Harrisonville. For the next 14 years this organization and its members played a central role in Lud's life. Lud's Mason membership and leadership reflected the prevailing culture – lawyers "were especially active in the Masonic Grand Lodge. Furthermore, lodges were for the select within the community, and such connections advanced their professional and political careers."[253] Harrisonville's "Old Prairie Lodge, No. 90" had humble beginnings.

The Harrisonville Masons first met, on the old square, above Joseph January's dry goods store. The chapter's charter was dated October

[251] Cass County Circuit Court Minutes. September 1846 to September 1856.. Book 275-9.
[252] Cass County Circuit Court Minutes. September 1846 to September 1856. Book 275-9.
[253] English. Page 121.

12, 1847. Charles Hamilton, Hugh Glenn, and Joseph January were elected the lodge's first officers. Hamilton Finney, the Van Buren county clerk, also a charter member, crafted the lodge's first jewels, "'out of the bottom of tin coffee pots, they were daisies and lovely to behold.'"[254]

These Mason friendships remained constant through Lud's Harrisonville life. In 1860 Lud boarded at one of the Harrisonville hotels, sharing it with January's widow and children. Hamilton Finney and Hugh Glenn remained close friends up to the Civil War.

Harrisonville's Mason membership included a broad, diverse political and social spectrum. Hiram B. Standiford, Cass County Sheriff and later State Representative, was a member. In the mid-1850s Standiford's personal stand on slavery eventually took him to the Kansas Territory and into the Free State movement. James Christian, a legal apprentice under Peyton, moved to Lawrence, Kansas Territory and became James H. Lane's law partner. Within the same Masons lodge, Hamilton Finney officiated. Finney, County Clerk and an ardent Southerner, would later smuggle gunpowder stolen from the Liberty Arsenal. Dr. Joseph F. Brookhart, son of David Brookhart, carried equally strong beliefs and would participate in the Battle of Osawatomie.

Elias P. West, Harrisonville attorney, also served as an officer of the "Old Prairie Lodge." During the Civil War, West commanded Harrisonville's Union Enrolled Militia Company stationed at Harrisonville. Despite the diverse opinions and allegiances held by its membership, the Masonic link superseded all differences. Once fighting began, flashing the Masonic sign saved numerous lives.

---------- Mexican War & the Gold Rush ----------

History and circumstance provided Lud and other young men, two opportunities for military glory and potential wealth. The first door opened when the United States declared war on Mexico in May 1846. The allure of war and fame awaited those who enlisted. The

[254] *The History of Cass and Bates Counties, Missouri*. Page 181.

second door, this one for riches, opened in 1849 when gold was discovered in California. Both national events, offered opportunities and each required a personal decision by men throughout the country. In both instances, Lud opted to remain in Harrisonville.

The Mexican War did not receive universal national or local support. The diary of one Westport merchant, June 6, 1846, lamented, "The Mexican quasi war – our frontier is all in commotion. Volunteers preparing and organizing, drilling and equipping themselves 'to march over the hills and far way' to the Mexican frontier to reap laurels of renown. The worst of all is our government is in fault. We are actually the aggressors."[255] Lud concurred.

Several Missourians enlisted returning home with well-publicized reputations. Their Mexican War exploits aided public careers in the 1850s. The men, ambitious and civic minded, benefited from their service. Lud's decision not to enlist placed him at a decided disadvantage politically, but then, at this early point in his life he suffered no ambitions. He was however destined to work closely with several of the veterans.

Waldo P. Johnson, a young Osceola lawyer, enlisted. During the 1850s and later during the Civil War, Johnson and Lud became political allies. Johnson became a political force in southwest Missouri. At Lud's death in 1863 Johnson replaced him in the Confederate Senate.

John W. Reid, also an attorney, enlisted. Reid moved to Jackson County after the Mexican War. Reid leveraged his war reputation into a seat in the Missouri legislature. He emerged as a military leader during the border conflict and led Missouri forces at the Battle of Osawatomie. Lud and Reid, both Democrats, later vied for party leadership in western Missouri.

[255] State Historical Society of Missouri. Manuscript Collection. Walker Diary.

Sterling Price, upon his return from the Mexican War, was elected Missouri Governor. Price's war experience leveraged him into the Governor's chair. Lud and Gov. Price enjoyed a long and often unsteady relationship. Price's personal commitment to Southern issues came into question. However, when the Civil War began Price commanded the Missouri State Guard and Lud led a cavalry regiment under Price.

Gold! Missouri's frontier was just as electrified by the discovery of gold in California as the rest of the county and "the gold fever reached Harrisonville like an epidemic. It seemed for a while that no one would be left. For days, the Courthouse Square was parked with covered wagons, in which many citizens were assembled, their objective point being the land beyond the wide wastes then known as the desert."[256] Aaron Smith, Harrisonville's wool carder and a close friend of Lud's wrote his father the spring of 1849 he didn't "believe there is one man in every three from this vicinity that talks of going will do it."[257] Already, the "exciting topic – Gold – has greatly abated" and "a large number of our citizens here who intended going have declined going."[258] Although Smith and Peyton avoided temptation, a great many did not.

Lud and the entire Harrisonville community were devastated by the death of Dr. John McReynolds. Dr. McReynolds, accompanied by his slave Asa, left wife and family in 1850 for the California gold fields.

Whereas Lud avoided the magnetic draw of California's gold fields, his brother Alexander succumbed. Alexander still living in Oxford, Ohio, caught the fever. The *Indiana American* announced on March 9, 1850, "gold fever was now raging in Oxford" due to one Mr. Wadley having returned from California with $14,000.[259]

---

[256] Brooks, Frank. "Harrisonville Back Numbers – No. 4"
[257] Missouri History Museum and Archives. Manuscripts. A.B. Smith Letters. April 18, 1849.
[258] Missouri History Museum and Archives. Manuscripts. A.B. Smith Letters. April 18, 1849.
[259] Smith. Page 1.

Alexander joined a group of sixteen Oxford adventurers bound for California. The party took with them "a very special wagon in which to haul their tents and supplies, its bed 'waterproof and water-tight.'"[260]

The adventurers, under the leadership of Hiram Ogle left Oxford on March 26, 1850. By way of Cincinnati they boarded a steamboat headed west on the Ohio River and then north to St. Louis on the Mississippi. Initially they landed at St. Joseph but finding "much sickness" they fled back to Independence, Jackson County, Missouri. They arrived at Independence on April 21, 1850. Seventeen days later, outfitted for the trip west, they left for California. One of the party, Samuel Boke, became ill and the group stopped for his recovery. Finally, May 15, 1850 the party traveled 25 miles west into the Kansas Indian Territory and camped for the night above the Wakarusa River.

This would be a night long remembered. Ezra Bourne's diary recorded: "Before setting up our tents we killed three rattlesnakes. After looking around we found that we were on a den of the reptiles, as the ground was absolutely perforated. It was dark and we were surrounded by swamps or water, so it was impossible to change our residence that night. We made the best of it by plugging up the holes with dirt, mud, and grass. Then after spreading our blankets we tried to sleep, but sleep was a stranger to us that night. This made us very cautious, thereafter, in selecting our camp grounds." The next morning Dr. John Barber and Alexander Peyton, "concluded that the experiences, encountered so far did not tally with their expectations or suit their tastes, so they faced about leaving for the more peaceful haunts of Oxford."[261]

---------- What's Going On? ----------

For many years Lud announced "the news" to Harrisonville residents. On mail stage days Harrisonville residents listened, quiet

[260] Smith. Page 2.
[261] Ezra Bourne Diary. Page 2.

and mesmerized, as he dramatically shared statewide and national news. On these days Lud stepped into the public eye.

The frontier borderland craved news! Unfortunately, by the time national or statewide news reached western Missouri, the events were old "news" and in most cases the world had moved on. The news appetite was no different than today but newspaper delivery was unpredictable and slow, in winter it was glacial. Aaron Smith, Lud's close friend and Harrisonville's sole wool carder, lamented in February 1849, "we have had no mail for at least 2 weeks & I have had no paper for the last 3 or 4 weeks. Consequently I know but little of what is going on below."[262] People relied heavily on newspapers and letters for world, national and state news. Travelers and occasional visitors supplemented, sometimes replaced, the newspapers.

Often, by the time news arrived, it was already history as evidenced by the death of President William Henry Harrison. President Harrison died April 4, 1841. The *Jefferson City Inquirer* did not publish the death until April 15, 1841, eleven days after the event. Copies of the *Inquirer* did not arrive in Harrisonville for several days.[263] President Harrison had been dead nearly a month when Harrisonville first heard.

News rippled across the country, east to west, at a slow pace. In 1847 the first telegraph began operation in St. Louis reducing the *Inquirer's* delay to press from 11 to two days. Even so, western Missouri readers were still days behind. The mail delivery from Jefferson City, or St. Louis, to Van Buren and Bates counties was slow and fraught with obstacles.

Missouri's borderland relied heavily upon St. Louis's *Missouri Republican* and the Jefferson City *Inquirer* for the news. The *Inquirer* had subscription agents in Van Buren and Polk counties as early as 1840.[264] Newspapers headed west from both cities by

[262] Missouri Museum and Archives. Manuscripts. Aaron Smith Letters. February 1, 1849.
[263] Sparlin. Page 162.
[264] Sparlin. Page 161.

steamboat. At Lexington and Independence the newspapers were delivered to the nearest post office. Combined with mail, the newspapers were loaded on stages. In the 1840s the stages to Pleasant Hill and Harrisonville only ran twice a week.

If the newspaper pipeline operated without error the papers would arrive within five days. Steamboats hit snags and/or grounded themselves on sand bars delaying their schedule. Heavy rains often turned country roads into mud pits and flooded streams, delaying stages until the roads dried and the streams lowered. The Big Blue and Little Blue rivers in Jackson County often overflowed delaying the mail as evidenced by this 1849 complaint: "No mail came to Kansas, because as usual 'Blue is up.' The contractor ought to be drowned in the Blue!"[265] During the winter, when the Missouri River froze solid, newspaper delivery from down river ceased. Subscribers regularly deluged newspaper editors under piles of complaints.

The stagecoach's arrival, and the news it delivered, newspapers, letters, and travelers, was a major event in all frontier villages. In 1849 the *Jefferson City Inquirer* had subscriptions from 153 Missouri Post Offices.[266] Few individual citizens subscribed to the newspapers and others, illiterate, relied on a public reading to stay afoot of the news.

Once the mail was delivered to the postmaster, the newspaper would be read out loud to any and all who cared to listen. Designated readers, selected by the postmaster, read the newspapers. Harrisonville was no different.

John C. Christian, Harrisonville's postmaster, crotchety, critical and demanding, controlled mail sorting, mail delivery, and newspaper distribution with an iron hand. When the mail stage neared Harrisonville the driver blew his horn announcing the stage's approach. The horn alerted local residents to gather outside the post office praying Christian would allow an early reading of St. Louis's

---

[265] State Historical Society of Missouri. Kansas City Manuscripts. Native Sons. Walker Diary. January 25, 1849.
[266] Sparlin. Page 161

Missouri Republican.[267] Young and old alike gathered, eager for the latest news.

Hamilton Finney reading latest newspaper at Harrisonville
Brian Hawkins, Artist

Christian's flinty disposition approved precious few public readers. Only Hamilton Finney, Richard O. Boggess, and Lud Peyton were permitted the privilege of entering the post office, grabbing the latest newspaper and reading to the crowd.[268] Lud's lyrical, clear voice interpreted the "*Republican*" to attentive adults and enraptured children. His dramatic talents, supported by musical voice inflection and flowing gestures made the news jump alive out of the paper. The scene, oft repeated, week-to-week, and month-to-month imbued Lud with a special community presence and persona. The news and Peyton's oral rendering became synonymous.

---------- "Living Around" ----------

The 17 years Lud Peyton lived in Harrisonville he never owned his own a home. Fifty-five years after Peyton's death, Frank Brooks

[267] *Cass County Democrat.* March 31, 1938.
[268] *Cass County Democrat.* March 31, 1938.

fondly described Peyton's life style by remembering "He just 'lived around.'"[269] When Lud landed in Harrisonville, 20 years old, he had no relatives and no known sponsors. Without funds, without associations, but with a quiet and refined way about him, Lud was "taken in" by families. Through the years he moved, rotating between families and local boarding hotels, seemingly, due to his charm and unassuming ways, never lacking for a place to hang his hat.

Lud's "living around," resulted in him occupying an unusual standing in the community. In many of the prominent local families he was not a stranger or an occasional visitor but a member of the family. He had been, and remained, a member of the family household. Lud's long term stays with families created relaxed, informal and personally intimate relationships. Overtime Lud endeared himself to the community.

Lud lived light. He lived an unencumbered life style. Like most frontier residents, he lived on credit. Frontier lawyers' incomes were largely driven by circuit court case volume. When the number of cases dropped, Lud's income dropped. Joseph January, a local dry goods merchant, died in the mid-1850s. When January's estate was settled Lud's unpaid tab totaled $33.52![270] The unpaid balance was one of the largest owed January's estate. Similarly, Lud's unpaid bills at Hugh Welden's ale house reflected his penchant for canned oysters, crackers, and whiskey – all on credit![271]

Although Lud lacked possessions and property, what he lacked in tangibles he made up in relationships. Lud collected friends. He was never alone, albeit often out of public sight. Through the years, it became apparent to the community that although Peyton, by nature, shunned public attention, he willingly stepped on stage when circumstances dictated.

The Harrisonville families who welcomed Peyton into their homes followed the southern tradition of "open hospitality." Under the

[269] *Cass County Democrat*. November 30, 1916.
[270] Cass County Probate Records. January, Joseph.
[271] Cass County Probate Records. Welden Hugh. Till Box 93.

custom, "the doors of these homes were rarely closed to strangers," and long-term "visitors" (such as Lud) were not unusual or unwelcome.[272] Within the homes' confines the term "family" expanded to "include all the people who slept under" the roof.[273] Robert A. Brown's home and plantation, "Wayside Rest," just outside Harrisonville developed a reputation for epitomizing this welcoming southern hospitality.

Nineteenth century homemakers, regardless of social station, valued their parlors as the centers of family gatherings and socializing. "Even in log houses of the frontier, which consisted of two square cabins joined by a breezeway, or dog trot, the room in which the family entertained guests (as opposed to the 'family room' where the family cooked and ate and some of it slept), was called the parlor."[274] Those with means built parlors with enough space to accommodate pianos, furniture, and bookcases.

The family gathered in the parlor each evening and, when entertaining, the parlor welcomed all guests. Following dinner, as darkness neared, families congregated in the parlor. The parlor was a "common room in which all ages and sexes met for family entertainments."[275] "Reading was a popular activity, but instead of reading silently and individually, the family was more likely to listen to someone reading aloud. Typically the man of the house would read aloud while women engaged in some form of sewing or handiwork."[276]

Reading aloud in both family and social settings was the norm. All manner of printed material was read aloud from books to letters. "Letters were often read aloud, in the parlor, to an audience that might consist of family, friends, boarders, and servants."[277] Newspapers were read aloud. Novels and stories were read aloud. "Shakespeare and Milton were familiar to the younger generations

---

[272] Fischer. *Albion*. Page 278.
[273] Fischer. *Albion*. Page 279.
[274] "The Parlor." *American Heritage*. Vol. 14, Issue 6. October 1963.
[275] Hedrick. Page 291.
[276] Horton, Laurel. "History: The Parlor." *Southern Spaces*.
[277] Hedrick. Page 77.

because they were accustomed to hearing them read aloud."[278] Harrisonville's parlors provided the intimate and unintimidating environment where Lud's talents and quiet presence flourished.

Educated and talented, Lud livened the family's parlor hours reading and conversing. Peyton's musical talents with the fiddle entertained the young and old alike. His love of Shakespeare surfaced during evening recitations and in a culture that thrived on all things "out loud" Lud excelled. Sitting in the parlor lit by gas lamps and candles, Lud, book in hand, stretched his lanky frame and brought *Richard III* to life! When cramped by the chair, he rose and paced, book in hand, his small audience mesmerized.

Shakespeare held a special place in Lud's heart, his appreciation for the English playwright was well known.[279] Lud in the courtroom and on "the stump" infused Shakespearean quotes in his oratory. Allusions to the classics lifted his speech. Miami University's curriculum included Shakespeare's complete works, both the plays and sonnets. At an early age Lud's exposure to Shakespeare in reading and recitations shaped his approach to oratory and expanded his literary vocabulary. Miami University's proximity to Cincinnati provided ample opportunity to witness Shakespeare's plays on stage.

Cincinnati, along with St. Louis, and Lexington, Kentucky, formed an early frontier stage circuit. Five years before the Peyton family settled in Oxford, Junius Booth performed in Cincinnati.[280] Booth played Richard III in Shakespeare's play of the same name. On July 3, 1837 the New National Theatre opened in Cincinnati; this theatre the most recent in a line of theatres stretching back to 1811. During the period of Lud's early education, 140 Shakespearean productions filled Cincinnati stages.[281] Frontier audiences favored *Richard III* above all of Shakespeare's plays.[282]

[278] *The Nineteenth Century*. Page 974.
[279] Sloan, Charles W. "Robert Ludwell Yates Peyton." *The Green Bag*. Vol. X, No. 10. Page 414.
[280] Rusk. Page 399.
[281] Rusk. Page 413.
[282] Rusk. Page 414.

Lud brought his love of Shakespeare to Harrisonville in 1844. Western Missouri's frontier did not provide opportunities to enjoy Shakespeare's plays on stage. Harrisonville's nearest theatres, and this not until the late 1850s, were in Lexington and Boonville. "Lexington's Arcana Hall was probably as adequate a theatre as any in rural Missouri, with the exception of Boonville's Thespia Hall, completed in 1857."[283] As a result, Shakespeare's plays and sonnets were shared and enjoyed by oral reading.

It is natural to envision a youthful Peyton reading aloud, his expressive and explosive oratorical style, capturing his listeners' imaginations – sometimes the young boys in Cole Younger's circle. They sought him out! Missouri's educational guidelines suggested each township library contain copies of Shakespeare's plays and sonnets.[284] By 1858 Cass County's 55 local teachers and almost 1,400 students carried a basic knowledge and appreciation for Shakespeare.

During Lud's later political campaigning and stump speaking, his electrifying oratory, invoking Shakespeare's work, rang true to audiences familiar with the Bard.

Evening parlor gatherings began first with news. Sharing news kept everyone informed about the family, school activities, and the community. As a lawyer, Lud interacted with a broad range of individuals and families throughout western Missouri. He was a constant source of news. Returning from the court circuit Lud brought the distant news from Independence, Lexington, Warrensburg and other stops along the way.

At heart a quiet, solitary soul, Lud was an easy houseguest, seemingly not wearing out his welcome. Lud's character and personal warmth endeared him to the entire Van Buren County community. He was honest and exhibited obvious affection for the people around him. His intimate friends described him as "kind,"

---

[283] Bowen. Page 70.

[284] *Journal of the State of Missouri*. 20th General Assembly (Adjourned Session). Page 300.

"gentle," "affectionate," and "genial."[285] Years after Lud's death, Cole Younger, just a lad in the 1850s, fondly missed his gentle friend. Another youngster, Frank Brooks, could not but remember how Lud cared about Harrisonville's children. Throughout his life, Lud exercised an admired character trait lauded in Lewis M. Ayer's eulogy. Ayer praised Peyton's "consideration," as the one word best describing the man.[286]

---------- Families and Friends ----------

A solitary man, naturally reserved, Lud strolled a quiet social path avoiding the common matchmaking gatherings. Through time his personal warmth and magnetism opened doors and hearts; Harrisonville's families, large and small, invited him into their homes. Although not shy when put on stage, Lud's life, public and private, remained very low key and reclusive. Lud's polite, quiet and unassuming presence, melded into the Harrisonville community.

Soon after his arrival Lud formed a lasting bond with the Brooks clan. Dr. Lynch Brooks had played an active community role from Van Buren County's initial organization. Dr. Brooks, a Kentucky native, settled in Johnson County, in 1835 but soon moved to Van Buren County. Between 1838 and the mid-1840s, Dr. Brooks served as the Harrisonville postmaster on three different occasions. In 1842 he served as the county Treasurer. Three of Dr. Brooks' sons, Newton, John, and Philip accompanied him to Van Buren County.

Lud became closely associated with all three brothers. Newton went into the dry goods business in Harrisonville. John farmed while Philip, like his father became actively involved in county government. Prior to Lud's arrival, Philip served the county as Treasurer, Deputy Clerk, and in 1847 was the Harrisonville Postmaster. Lud and Philip formed a tight friendship and Lud became a "live-in" member of the Brooks family.

285 *The Green Book*. Volume X, No. 10. October 1898. Page 416.
286 *Proceedings and Speeches on the Announcement of the Death of Hon. R.L.Y. Peyton of Missouri*. Sentinel Job Office, Print. Lewis M. Ayer. 1864.

Philip Brooks met and married his wife Chelnissa Anderson in Johnson County. Chelnissa's sister, Harriet, had earlier married James Dolan and moved to western Van Buren County. Soon after Philip and Chelnissa married they moved to Harrisonville. Philip, following in his father's civic footsteps, served as Deputy Clerk of the Circuit Court and later Treasurer of Van Buren County. Shortly after Lud settled in Harrisonville the Brooks had their second son, Frank. Lud became a member of the Brooks household.

The two young men, within two years of each other, enjoyed each other's company and shared interests. Lud's extensive travel and knowledge of the East excited Philip who developed a severe case of wanderlust. During the 1850s Phillip "lived around" inside Missouri along the Missouri River – he moved the family to Independence, St. Louis, Glasgow, back to Harrisonville and then to St. Joseph. Lud and Philip each held deep allegiance to the South. Philips's strong pro-South beliefs led to his banishment from St. Joseph during the Civil War.

Lud fit comfortably into Chelnissa's parlor, noisy with two young boys running about. She welcomed the education and entertainment Lud provided. Lud's fiddle found its way to the parlor as well as outside where the boys danced to Lud's playing. Lud became a favorite of the two Brooks boys, Beverly and Frank. Frank, years later, memorialized Lud in a series of vignettes about frontier Harrisonville and its people.

Lud also "lived-in" with the McReynolds family. Although a bit older than Lud, John and Polly, offered a welcoming southern hospitality. Dr. John and Polly McReynolds arrived in Van Buren County shortly after Lud. In a remarkably short period of time Dr. McReynolds endeared himself to the entire community and welcomed Lud into the family. Polly's family, the Callaway's settled in Van Buren County from Tennessee. Dr. McReynold's cousin, also a physician, Dr. Logan McReynolds lived in Pleasant Hill and also married into the Callaway family.

In Harrisonville and the surrounding community, "Doctor (John) McReynolds was the fine old family physician, who ministered to the physical ailments of the citizenry, town and county."[287]

Dr. John and Polly's home, like the Brooks' home, resonated with children's noise. The McReynolds' had five young children, including a set of twins. The McReynolds's young boys, John and David, played constantly with the Brooks brothers. Lud brought the same easy connection into the McReynolds's home he enjoyed with Philip and Chelnissa Brooks.

When gold was discovered in California, Dr. John got the fever. In 1850 he made the tragic decision to leave Polly and the children in Harrisonville while he made his fortune in the gold fields. Dr. McReynolds and a slave, Asa, packed and joined the caravan of gold hunters on the Harrisonville square. "For days the Courthouse Square was parked with white-covered wagons. The square became a 'wailing spot.' More farewells were spoken then, and more tears shed than have been said or shed since on the old square."[288] Having promised to help Polly in Dr. John's absence, Lud stood among those remaining, waving as the wagons disappeared to the west, heading to Council Grove in Indian Territory, before moving to California.

Dr. McReynolds died in Asa's arms in California shortly. Like so many of the 49ers, Dr. McReynolds died in the quest. Asa however made the return trip to Harrisonville. He carried a bit of gold and the doctor's belongings.

Lud, along with the community, gathered in support of Polly. Silas Price and James M. Simpson stepped in to help settle Dr. McReynold's estate. Polly and the family made it through the tragedy of his death only to be devastated by cholera. Polly, Asa, and Asa's wife, Jennie, were all victims of the horrific cholera epidemic that swept through Harrisonville in 1854. Lud, a family

287 Brooks. "Harrisonville Back Numbers. No. 1.

288 Brooks. "Harrisonville Back Numbers. No. 4."

member, helped carry Polly to her grave.[289] The McReynolds's Asa was buried next to her.

After Dr. McReynolds's departure for California, Lud moved into the Harrisonville boarding house operated by Squire G. Allen and his wife Susan. Allen's 70-year old mother, Anna, lived with them. In 1850, Lud celebrated Thanksgiving and Christmas with the Allen's and the only other guest was influential Jackson County attorney, Henry Bouton.[290]

Allen expanded the boarding house and after 1850 it became known as the "Allen House," the first hotel/boarding house in Harrisonville. Allen's hotel occupied the southeast corner of the block north of the courthouse. Mrs. Allen, with slave assistance, provided the meals. In 1855 Allen sold the hotel to William "Bill" Taylor who renamed it the "Arizona House" in 1856. The Taylors, strong southerners, managed the hotel giving their children free rein.[291]

The Arizona House buzzed with the constant flow of travelers and local boarders. Dining room conversation as well as front porch talk hit all current rumors and topics. Travelers, hailing from Lexington, Independence, Westport, and Kansas City, shared the latest news.

Taylor's Arizona House faced competition from the Southern Hotel owned by Silas Price and Charles Keller. When Lud first arrived in Harrisonville he roomed at what became the Southern Hotel. At that time Sam Wilson was the proprietor. Billed as a "hotel" Wilson's place "was a log house with two rooms, one above and

289 Brooks. "Harrisonville Back Numbers. No. 4."

290 **Henry B. Bouton**: Bouton married Mary Jane Peery, a daughter of Edward T. Peery, a prominent early pioneer in Jackson County. During the 1850s Bouton became one of Kansas City's founding fathers. He was influential in railroad development and Kansas City's growth. A residential sub-division in Kansas City bore his name.

291 **William Taylor Family**: The Taylors continued as proprietors of the hotel until the Civil War. Bill and Margaret fled to Louisiana and never returned to Missouri. One of their daughters, Louisa, eloped with a Union officer she met at the hotel.

one below."[292] Wilson left Harrisonville during the California gold rush and the hotel eventually fell to Price and Keller

.

Lud became a Harrisonville fixture. Although he "lived-in" with families he boarded for more than a decade at the Allen/Arizona House and the Southern Hotel. Lud, if not on the court circuit could be found on or near the square. He read newspapers out loud to the locals when the mail stage arrived. He was always available for conversation. All travelers and news funneled through the square and the hotels – he was there.

Southern Hotel-Courtesy Cass Co Historical Society

Lud's relationship with Squire Allen ensured Lud knew the county and town's pulse. During the late 1840s and early 1850s, Allen orchestrated Harrisonville's early development. Allen, a "jack of all trades," plied his skills in many avocations, as a hotel proprietor, a Baptist minister, a merchant, a politician and civic leader. In 1855, he served as Harrisonville's first Mayor. Allen seemed at the center of most events, Lud on the periphery kept pace.[293]

---

[292] State Historical Society of Missouri. Manuscripts Collection. James, David. C4126. Folder 22.

[293] **Squire Allen**: Allen was born April 17, 1806 in Campbell County, Kentucky. He married Susan McCollom in Kentucky and the couple moved to Van Buren County in the late 1840s. Early in the Civil War they left Missouri and never returned. After leaving Missouri they lived in Arkansas and Tennessee finally settling in Kenton County, Kentucky.

The hotel's location, across the street from the courthouse, meant fast and easy access to the county business. Hamilton Finney, as the County Clerk, quite literally knew everything happening in the county. Lud and Finney were tight friends. From land deals or County Court activity Lud knew the skinny. When the Circuit Court was in session, Lud was front and center because his profession, his community, and local disagreements swirled in and through the square.

Lud's best friend, certainly one of his closest friends, Silas Price co-owned the Southern Hotel. Price, ten years Lud's senior, had followed his brother Edmund to Westport in 1841 or 1842. In 1843 Price bought land in Van Buren County and the next year brought his bride, Mary, to the log home he built. The Price place was 2 ½ miles northwest of Harrisonville very near the Robert Brown plantation. Charles Keller, Silas's brother-in-law soon joined him in Harrisonville. As partners, Silas and Charles managed one of Harrisonville's largest mercantile businesses.

Silas Price
Circa 1858- Courtesy Cass County Historical Society

Silas and Mary, in 1846 or 1847, began construction of a classic two-story colonial style house. The home contained five brick fireplaces. Walnut and oak woodwork highlighted an interior mirroring the Virginia homes they were accustomed to.[294] Mary's new home boasted "eight large rooms, a parlor, a sitting room and keeping rooms, with a bedroom above the keeping room."[295] When completed the Price home was the first magnificent place on the Van Buren County frontier.

The Price Mansion- Courtesy Cass County Historical Society

The Price plantation in all respects was a Virginia transplant. Mary Price managed a growing household supported by a number of house slaves. Hospitality, the open door to guests, was a central element Mary's welcoming atmosphere. The home's parlor and sitting room provided the venue for evening socializing and entertainment.

Lud accepted the invitation to visit, becoming a frequent member of the Price household. Lud's Virginia manners, his parlor presence and his love for the children all served to endear him to Mary and Silas.

[294] Price. Page 72.
[295] *Crossroads*. "Price Farm Home Burns." Winter 2004. Page 7.

This was a comfortable friendship. Silas's beliefs, personal and political, mirrored Lud's. Silas was an entrepreneur whose business contacts into the Kansas Territory and Jackson County afforded Lud the opportunity to establish a relationship network beyond Cass County.

When Mary gave birth to twin boys, February 12, 1855, Silas named one of his new sons, Peyton. Nothing could have reflected the Prices' deep attachment more than making Lud a namesake.

Silas died suddenly in 1858, just a month after Lud was elected to the Missouri Senate. His sudden death deprived Lud of his closest friend and trusted advisor at the very time he needed him most. Silas's early death preceded that of David Brookhart by a year. The Brookhart's, David and Theresa, also hosted Lud as "live-in" guest. They settled in Harrisonville in 1852. Off the southeast corner of Harrisonville the Brookhart's built an estate, naming it "Brookhart Hill." Their son, Dr. Jacob F. Brookhart, also settled in Harrisonville and opened a practice.

David and Theresa Brookhart
Author's Collection

David arrived in Cass County a seasoned politician and wealthy landowner. He had served several terms in the Maryland House of Delegates. Lud and David shared strongly held Democratic beliefs. Prior to his death in 1859, Brookhart and Lud represented Cass County at statewide Democratic conventions. The older, more experienced politician mentored Lud's early political and government career.

---------- Harrisonville's Boys ----------

Lud's memory and legacy survived in no small part because of the relationship he enjoyed with Harrisonville's youngsters, particularly the town's boys. Lud's age was not far removed from the boys he mentored. His bachelorhood allowed them constant, open access. Lud's presence, a fixture in town around the square, brought them into regular contact. Although an adult, Lud lived in many of their homes as often happens the boys were drawn to him. Lud and Aaron Smith, the town carder, attracted the boys.

One of the boys, Frank Brooks wrote on several occasions about Peyton.[296] Lud lived with the Brooks family in the late 1840s and 1850s. Frank's Peyton stories, especially Lud's epic battle at the ladies' picnic, memorialized Lud's life and legend.

Cole Younger remembered Lud and wrote fondly of him after the Civil War. One of the Harrisonville youths during the 1850s, Cole remembered Lud reading aloud the newspapers when the stage arrived.

Two other youngsters, John and David McReynolds also had similar personal relationships. Not only had Lud lived with the family, but also in 1854 Peyton, a pallbearer, helped carry the boys' mother, Polly, to her grave after cholera took her.[297]

---------- A Lud Legend ----------

Despite ironclad bachelorhood and reclusive way, Lud retained a place in the hearts of Harrisonville's ladies. A shade over six feet tall, handsome with coal black hair, by nature a Virginia gentleman, and a notable public figure, Lud seemed to be a target for the fair sex. About Lud, John Lewis Peyton wrote, Lud "never knew any of

[296] **Frank Brooks**: Brooks published a series of articles, "Harrisonville Back Numbers" in the *Cass County Democrat* in 1916.

[297] Brooks. "Harrisonville Back Numbers. No. 4."

the delights of coquetry and stolen kisses, and never knew any of their pains and penalties."[298] Lud's reclusive nature coupled to his minimalist lifestyle discouraged the more serious ladies, yet there remained, mystery and magnetism.

For decades after the following event, the Lud's legend remained, retold on numerous occasions. With each retelling, the epic proportions of his superhuman, effort, near tragic ending, and heroic rescue grew ever larger. Witnesses to the adventure never tired of proclaiming, "I was there!"

With most of the men off to a Camp Meeting, Harrisonville's ladies scheduled a large picnic, women and children only. Blankets were tossed near the banks of the slow flowing "Scaly Bark" providing the outing's perfect venue. Lud, the town's preeminent orator and storyteller, was called upon to deliver the day's entertainment. Dr. Ben Hocker accompanied Lud, as male companion and chaperone.

The weather and picnic conditions were perfect! However, early in the proceedings, as the women and children assembled, a sudden medical emergency summoned Dr. Hocker. Lud, now the sole male presence, charmed the ladies, playing intermittently with the children.

Plum trees encircled the picnic grounds. Owing to the season, plum tree limbs bent over, heavy with ripened fruit. The plums glistening in the sunlight became too great a temptation. The ladies, genteel members of the fair sex, encumbered with dresses, unable to climb the trees, pleaded with Lud to scale the heights – to harvest the perfect plums.

Lud, ever the gallant, dressed in his suit, agreed to ascend the tree, harvest the ripe plums, and satisfy the appetites of the women and children. As Lud prepared to climb the tree an admiring crowd of women and children gathered. The plum tree thus challenged didn't move, mocking Lud's six-foot frame and gangly manner.

[298] Peyton, John L. "Sketch of Hon. Robert L.Y. Peyton of Missouri." *The Magazine of American History*. Volume XVI. July-Dec. 1886. Page 397.

Then, to ahs and oos, up he went, easily conquering the low branches.

Lud failed to notice, beginning his heroic climb, that six feet off the ground, multiple vines gripped and strangled the plum tree. These same vines hungrily awaited our approaching hero. Undaunted, Lud climbed on. Little tendrils parted as Lud entered the vine's web, suddenly trapped, unable to free his hands. The more he struggled, the tighter the vines clasped! Up high in the tree, Lud disappeared into the vine's cocoon. The end seemed near. Far below, Harrisonville's fairest, wringing hands, lost breath and hope.

Panic swept through the onlookers fearing Lud's public demise. The vine's tightening iron grip trapped Lud's arms - he was unable to weld his knife and cut himself free. So cruel a fate to be eaten alive, by a serpentine vine with all of Harrisonville's fair sex watching. Fearful squeals flew from the helpless damsels, Lud in distress.

Then, just at the apex of crisis, a posse of local knights rode by the fair grounds. Alerted by squeals of panic and appeals for help, the rescuers halted, racing to the plum tree. Among the rescuers, John Cummins, one of Lud's best friends arrived first. Looking up, Cummins immediately ascertained the gravity of the situation – Quickly drawing his knife, Cummins scaled the tree, hacked through the vines and freed Lud Peyton.

Back on "terra firma" Lud regained composure. Sweat dabbed, he straightened his suit – arranged his hair. The Harrisonville ladies, giggles subsiding, entreated Lud to resume his oration. Lud obliged.

Harrisonville history records that Lud's picnic oratory stirred imaginations, carrying his listeners to far off lands and heroic deeds. That said, the content of his remarks have lost but Lud's harrowing near death experience and his dramatic rescue lived for decades. The legend and the spirit in which Lud accepted the numerous comic retellings merely tightened his bond with the Harrisonville community.

---------- Lud's Family ----------

Townshend Peyton died September 30, 1852. He had lived 78 long and productive years. Although Sally and Alexander were with him in Oxford, his other children were scattered across the country. Three lived in Missouri. Lud was in Cass County. Alfred and Maria, with her husband Henry Luckett, lived in St. Charles County. Fanny and husband Joe lived on their Canton, Mississippi plantation. Townshend's other daughters lived in Maryland and Virginia.

Frank Peyton handled Townshend's estate. Once the estate was settled Frank moved his family to Springfield, Illinois. Harriet, Frank's wife, bore three children in Illinois, but died after the third birth. Frank, now a widower with six children returned to Oxford. Never remarrying, Frank operated a mercantile store for the remainder of his life.

Alexander returned to Oxford from his failed attempt to get rich in the California Gold Rush. In April 1853 he sold the farm his father left him to Sally for $2,000. Now fully funded Alexander left Oxford for parts unknown.

Beverly Tyler, Townshend's mulatto grandson, lived in Oxford. Beverly had married several years before, the ceremony performed by the Rev. Hiram R. Revels. Rev. Revels was destined to be the first African-American U.S. Senator. After Townshend's death, Beverly and his family moved in with Sally becoming her caregivers.

By 1852, when Townshend died, the Luckett's had settled into life at St. Charles. They had arrived in St. Charles, Mo., from Springfield, Illinois around 1850. In St. Charles, Rev. Luckett continued his religious calling. Strong southerners, the family owned 15 slaves. When the Civil War erupted they fled to Memphis.

Alfred, estranged from his father, had followed the Luckett's to St. Charles. Alfred arrived in St. Charles a bachelor but soon met and proposed to Laura Baswise, a Cincinnati native. Alfred was 37, twenty years Laura's senior when he proposed. The couple was married October 20, 1853. They settled on a St. Charles farm and soon had three small children.

Laura's father Thomas Baswise had moved to St. Charles County from Cincinnati in 1846. "A year later, Baswise, became one of the largest landowners in the county when he purchased 1,700 acres near Portage des Sioux."[299] Baswise, initially a Whig, became active in local politics and took the Oath when the Civil War began in 1861. He was a Conservative Unionist during the war, becoming a staunch Democrat following the cessation of hostilities.[300]

Lud's cousins, Balie and John Lewis lived at distant points. Balie Peyton, the U.S. Consul to Chile, left Chile September 23, 1853, heading for San Francisco. He arrived at San Francisco on November 9. San Francisco's population had exploded from 2,000 to 40,000 in just six years. From 1853 until 1859 Balie carved a niche for himself in politics, a law practice, and San Francisco history.

John Lewis Peyton lived in Staunton, Virginia. During his odyssey to the west in 1848 - 1849 he had formed a tight friendship with Stephen Douglas. John Lewis was back in Chicago in the early 1850s where he worked as a newspaper correspondent and Douglas political advisor.

---

[299] Ehlmann, Page 80.
[300] Ehlmann. Page 190.

Chapter Six
Frontier Lawyer

Attorney Lud Peyton rode into Harrisonville, young, well educated, and green. Six months shy of his 20th birthday, Lud hardly seemed seasoned enough to handle the variety of cases arriving at the circuit court. Lud did arrive in Harrisonville well educated by the standards of the time, because many beginning lawyers were admitted to the bar having "read law" rather than studying law and carrying a law degree. Although a novice before the bar, Lud was hardly inexperienced in the ways of the frontier having been raised in Oxford, Ohio.

As the frontier had pressed west from Ohio to Missouri, Harrisonville found itself the frontier's new edge. The youthful lawyer and the seven-year old town were a good match. Lud felt comfortable and at home, with the people and the culture. Van Buren County was part of Missouri's Sixth Judicial District, operating within the jurisdiction of Judge John F. Ryland.

Judge John F. Ryland, a Lexington resident, assumed the Sixth Judicial District's bench in 1830 by appointment and held the seat until 1848. At this early period, Missouri's governor appointed circuit court judges. Frontier justice was administered wherever the court met; it was common for early circuit courts to hold sessions in open fields, beneath shade trees, in the homes of local landowners, in school houses, and when lucky, in crudely constructed log cabin courthouses. County grand juries, summoned in advance of the circuit court session, met in similar rustic settings to discuss and present indictments. Lud's cousin, John Peyton attended a Cole County circuit court session in the late 1840s:

> "The session of Court attracted a considerable number of country people to the town, and these were principally collected about a miserable, naked-looking edifice made of mud in the form of brick, called the Court House, where a set of half educated muddy-headed lawyers, made a muddle in attempting

> to make the 'wrong side appear the better cause.' A rougher set of citizens, whether regarded with reference to dress, manners or physical appearance, separately or combined, could not be imagined. Bear-skin caps, Mackinaw blankets, leather leggings, old Bess rifles and hunting knives, entered into their dress and equipments. Tall, square-shouldered, broad-chested, stout men made up of bone and gristle, they drank whiskey, chewed tobacco, and while waiting for the opening of Court, engaged in athletic sports …"[301]

In a like manner, circuit court judges hewed from the same frontier timber, administered justice forcibly, without appeal. Most were well armed and aggressive. "Turbulent conditions … subjected the judges to unusual dangers. They had to go armed even while on the bench, and several times they were threatened by litigants because of adverse decisions.[302] John Peyton described the story of a judge, who was left unprotected when the sheriff left the court. In the sheriff's absence an unhappy plaintiff confronted the judge. "His honour rose from the judgment seat, drawing a revolver from the table drawer, and whipping a bowie knife from a scabbard worn down his back, was about to execute judgment, when the sheriff appeared."[303] These early frontier jurists, in partnership with equally rough-hewn lawyers laid Missouri's judicial foundation.

Lud seems to have easily joined Missouri's unpolished legal fraternity. The state's, largely southern population, and culture, while an inducement for Lud made it uncomfortable for some northern lawyers.[304] That said, many northern lawyers integrated enjoying successful careers. Missouri's lawyers rode a judicial circuit, moving from county seat to county seat. They lived in difficult conditions, most followed secondary occupations. Collectively the legal fraternity loved gaming, horse racing, and storytelling. As a rule, these lawyers were better educated than the general population, providing prominence and station. Most

---

[301] Peyton. *Over.* Page 269.
[302] English. Page 60.
[303] Peyton. *Over.* Page 271.
[304] English. Page 99.

enjoyed membership in the Masons, a strong elite frontier fraternity.

Missouri lawyers, when Lud arrived, still operated within the lingering, but still present, "honor culture." Most lawyers were armed even in court, "their pistols and ataghans on their persons or by their side at all times and that dirks could be seen peeping from the bosoms of all members of the bar."[305] Flamboyant courtroom oratory easily led to slighted honor. Missouri's fledgling legal system encouraged entertaining courtroom oratory as much as nuanced legal argument. Lud's Virginian heritage, college education, and oratorical gifts naturally fit. Harrisonville also proved a natural fit. Lud, like other beginning lawyers, settled in a young town where "starting a practice he could develop with the community."[306]

---------- Routes to the Missouri Bar ----------

Aspiring young men seeking admittance to Missouri's bar generally followed three avenues. The most common path to the frontier bar required reading, and studying the basic law books while working as a clerk under an experienced, successful, and practicing attorney. Normally, frontier bar admittance required knowledge of Blackstone's *Commentaries*, Chitty's *Pleadings*, and Missouri's *Revised Code of 1835*. This route, although common, was not particularly easy. Law clerk wages were low. The required reading and study were accomplished on the clerk's time, not that of the mentor.

Judge John F. Ryland, the presiding judge during Peyton's first four years in Harrisonville, followed this arduous route to the bar. Before settling in Lexington, Mo., Judge Ryland studied law in Kentucky under Judge Hardin. Admitted to the Missouri bar in 1819 Ryland became Judge of the Sixth Judicial District in 1830. He administered early frontier justice in court settings often as rustic as the people. Soon after being appointed judge of the Sixth

305 English. Page 80.
306 English. Page 95.

Judicial District, Ryland was holding court in the loft of a Saline County stable. "Below the loft a mule was making a considerable noise. Ryland told the Sheriff, 'Mr. Sheriff, go down there and make that fellow keep still, so as to give these other jackasses a chance to be heard.'"[307] Ryland's common sense and compassionate adjudication deeply influenced western Missouri communities. Lud personally benefited from Ryland's tutelage .

Charles Henry Hardin
Courtesy Cass Co Historical Society

The second route to Missouri's bar combined Judge Ryland's early education with a formal education. Charles Hardin, Lud's fellow Miami University classmate and future Missouri governor followed this path. Hardin attended Miami University with Lud, the pair graduating in 1841. Neither however left the university with a law degree. Hardin returned home to Columbia, Mo. where he immediately began reading law in the offices of Judge James M. Gordon. Bright and driven, Hardin was quickly accepted to the bar beginning his practice in 1843 at Fulton in Callaway County.

Lud's path to Missouri's bar followed the third route, obtaining a law degree after graduating from a university. Following his from Miami University, Lud set off to study law at the University of Virginia under the tutelage of Henry St. George Tucker. Peyton graduated from the Virginia Law School with a Bachelor of Laws degree in July 1843, following just a year of study. Lud's graduating class contained 25 members. When Lud arrived in Harrisonville the following spring, 1844, his law degree fulfilled the basic requirement for admission to the bar and all he needed to begin practice was admittance by the local circuit judge.

Lud's law degree from the University of Virginia did not endear him to everyone in the Missouri bar. The University of Virginia, as

307 *History of Saline County, Missouri.* Page 210.

well as Kentucky's Transylvania University was known as the bastions of states' rights.

St. Louis lawyer James O. Broadhead praised his son William for deciding to opt out of the University of Virginia's law school. In 1858 Broadhead wrote William, then a student at the University of Virginia:

> "I think it a wise conclusion you have come to, not to remain at the University longer than the present session, unless you should conclude to study something else than law. I think it is one of the best schools in the country for the study of languages and the sciences, but your opinion about the law is just the same that I at first expressed to you. After all a man must depend mostly upon himself in the study of law, and where he has access to a good library, and opportunities and incentives to habits of steady application, he will learn most readily the elementary principles …
>
> The South, however, on this subject of slavery is perfectly mad – and there is no telling to what excesses of folly, the Southern people will permit themselves to be led."[308]

Broadhead's misgivings about the University of Virginia law school reflected the collective opinion of other anti-slavery lawyers in Missouri.

Lud's ironclad commitment to Southern states' rights had been forged at Miami University and further "iron tempered" at the University of Virginia. While at Miami University, Lud had been schooled by Albert T. Bledsoe who would later author, at Jefferson Davis's request, a scholarly defense Southern secession. Judge Tucker at the University of Virginia later reinforced Bledsoe's strict constitutional interpretation.

---

[308] *Glimpses of the Past, Volume I – III*. "Fragments of the Broadhead Collection." St. Louis Historical Society. Page 47.

Lud's judicial contemporaries fully appreciated the import of his education.

---------- Lud's Contemporary, Samuel Sawyer ----------

Lud's decision to settle in Harrisonville to begin his law practice aligned with the country's westward expansion and the steady emergence of opportunities as frontier populations grew. Van Buren County had existed for a mere seven years when Lud arrived in 1844. Harrisonville was barely more than a village. The town's newness, and the population's paucity meant little judicial competition; a good growth opportunity for an energetic, patient, and determined young lawyer. Lud's law degree allowed him to settle in a county seat and begin practice immediately, avoiding the necessity of reading and studying under an already practicing attorney.

Lawyers' appearance in frontier county seats, like Harrisonville, coincided with the establishment of local government institutions.[309] Generally, lawyers in these emerging communities were young. "Young men moved west because their home communities were already supplied with older men who had made reputations as seasoned practitioners. On the frontier the beginner thought he saw an opportunity to rise to some prominence immediately in the profession and in politics because there were few elderly men. Rarely did a lawyer of experience and reputation go to a new county unless he had suffered reverses in his home community."[310]

For most ambitious and aspiring young men, hoping to enter the bar, the selection of a specific county seat was more difficult and the journey to practice law more arduous than the course Lud followed. Samuel L. Sawyer, Lud's legal contemporary, friend, and eventual political adversary, settled in Lexington, beginning his study, apprenticeship, and practice there. Sawyer, alone, arrived at Lexington from New Hampshire, by way of Cleveland, Ohio, in the

[309] English. Page 9.
[310] English. Page 12.

late 1830s. Sawyer walked off the steamboat without friends, without means, without legal knowledge, and without a sponsor. He did however arrive with energy, determination, and ambition. Sam Sawyer's situation was typical of many who disembarked at Lexington and Independence in the 1830s.

Lud, upon arrival in Harrisonville, enjoyed one benefit Sam Sawyer faced as a challenge, the Missouri frontier's social context. Most early western Missouri settlers arrived from Virginia, Kentucky, and Tennessee, Southern slave holding states. Quite naturally these immigrants lived in a social milieu much different from their northern neighbors. Where Lud found a natural comfort, Sam Sawyer sensed the difference. Soon after his arrival at Lexington, Sawyer wrote his father, Aaron, encouraging him to consider moving to Missouri – but with a caveat. Sam cautioned his father, "perhaps you would not enjoy the society. The country is principally settled by Virginians, Kentuckians, and others still further south."[311] Sam further wrote, however, "the people here are not picayune by any means but intelligent, high minded and friendly. They certainly are here."[312] Sawyer seemed to smoothly assimilate with his Southern neighbors while struggling to start his law career.

Lexington's Judge Ryland took Sawyer under his wing. Ryland advised Sawyer "to procure a supply of books and go to reading and he would ensure success."[313] Sawyer's basic challenge was to find the books. He lamented to his father, "There are no good libraries that I have seen" and he would be unable to "commence practice unless I have a tolerable supply of books."[314] Sawyer eventually persuaded his father to send him basic law books. After the books arrived Sam began his study in earnest and Judge Ryland assisted him in gaining admittance to the bar.

311 State Historical Society of Missouri. Manuscripts, C1833. Samuel Sawyer Letters, 1836 – 1849. Letter July 7, 1838.
312 State Historical Society of Missouri. Manuscripts, C1833. Samuel Sawyer Letters, 1836 – 1849. Letter July 7, 1838.
313 State Historical Society of Missouri. Manuscripts, C1833. Samuel Sawyer Letters, 1836 – 1849. Letter September 4, 1838.
314 State Historical Society of Missouri. Manuscripts, C1833. Samuel Sawyer Letters, 1836 – 1849. Letter July 7, 1838.

Sam Sawyer's struggles to acquire the legal texts and build a library for his practice were seemingly foreign and unnecessary for Lud. In marked contrast to most of his contemporaries, Peyton viewed law books and a law library as generally unnecessary. "He had not in his library a dozen law books, and he had little or no use for more."[315] Lud "tried cases without books."[316]

Sam Sawyer landed in Lexington and practiced in a number of nearby county seats, assessing them as permanent homes. Soon after beginning to practice he considered Ray County, the county north just across the Missouri river from Lexington. Ray County has "about five thousand inhabitants and contains two lawyers. There is but little business and few lawyers."[317] Later in the autumn, 1838, Sawyer wrote his father, "I think of settling there (Jackson County) or in Johnson County or here (Lexington). The prospect is less inviting here than either of the adjoining counties. There is no lawyer in Johnson County, two here and four in Jackson."[318] At this early date, Harrisonville and Van Buren County, new and rough fell from consideration.

---------- Survival ----------

By 1844, the number of lawyers in the surrounding county seats had grown. Sam Sawyer stayed in Lexington with its full stable of lawyers. Independence, Warrensburg, Marshall, and Georgetown were taken. Van Buren County, and Harrisonville, distant from the Missouri River, and abutting the Indian Territory remained largely unrepresented. When Lud appeared in Harrisonville, Charles Sims had already become the most active local attorney. For the next 13 years, Sims and Peyton, living in Harrisonville built law practices. Each man approached the challenge of making a living in dramatically different fashion.

[315] *History of Cass and Bates Counties, Missouri*. Page 378.
[316] *History of Cass and Bates Counties, Missouri*. Page 378.
[317] State Historical Society of Missouri. Manuscripts, C1833. Samuel Sawyer Letters, 1836 – 1849. Letter July 7, 1838.
[318] State Historical Society of Missouri. Manuscripts, C1833. Samuel Sawyer Letters, 1836 – 1849. Letter September 8, 1838.

Practicing law on Missouri's early western frontier did not in itself provide sufficient income to survive and prosper. Survival required that young lawyers "engage in other sidelines. A lawyer might be a real estate agent, farmer, surveyor, teacher, merchant, horse trader, speculator, preacher or editor."[319] The low volume of business in the individual county seats required the lawyers to ride the local circuit and pickup business in the other counties. Additionally, the nature of legal income on the frontier was not tied to criminal cases or litigation but rather to civil cases regarding debt collection.

Frontier lawyers were largely debt collectors, "the collection of debts proved a very lucrative practice."[320] Until communities grew to the point where settlers and merchants accumulated debt, lawyers struggled financially. Samuel Sawyer, early on, worried about his income potential, lamenting, "the business is principally litigation, no collections of consequence."[321] Pioneer merchants sold goods to locals on credit. The merchants also bought on credit. Customarily, goods were sold to the merchants on six month credit, and the merchants sold goods to "the people" on 12 month credit. "The people" were not good when it came to repaying the local merchants. As customer debts accumulated and went unpaid "the notes given to merchants were collected by lawyers by suit."[322]

At Harrisonville in 1851 Aaron Smith complained to his father, "money is harder to collect now than I have known it to be here for the last 4 years. It is a general complaint with merchants, lawyers, doctors, mechanics and farmers that there is no money in the country."[323] Merchants, pushed near bankruptcy by debtors, pleaded for reimbursement in local newspapers. Some ads pleaded for payment while others took a more threatening tone. Desperate for money, the merchants declared in print, I "will have the

[319] English. Page13.
[320] State Historical Society of Missouri. Manuscripts, C0678, File 1. Autobiography of Thomas L. Anderson.
[321] State Historical Society of Missouri. Manuscripts, C1833. Samuel Sawyer Letters, 1836 – 1849. Letter September 8, 1838.
[322] State Historical Society of Missouri. Manuscripts, C0678, File 1. Autobiography of Thomas L. Anderson.
[323] Missouri Historical Society. Museum and Archives. Manuscripts. Aaron Smith Letters. March 23, 1851.

MONEY!"[324] The following declaration by William J. Taylor ran for weeks in Harrisonville's *Western Democrat.*

TO MY DEBTORS.

ALL those who are indebted to me are hereby respectfully informed, that I want them to come forward *immediately*, and *pay* the MONEY. My creditors are pressing me to pay my debts and so I *must* and *will* have the MONEY *from* my debtors. Mark what I say, I need money and must and will *positively*, have it from *those* who owe me. WM. J. TAYLOR.

February 27, 1858.—tf

Wm. J. Taylor's public announcement-
Western Democrat May 1, 1858

As frustrating as the debt situation was for Missouri's merchants, the issue was the lifeblood of the frontier lawyer's business. Multitudes of individual debts ended up in the circuit court where lawyers presented the case, later becoming the debt collectors.

In new and growing frontier communities, like Harrisonville, until the general population and the number of merchants grew to a sufficient size, lawyers struggled to survive solely on their law practices. As the population increased, debt increased, litigation increased, civil suits increased and criminal cases increased. Charles Sims supplemented his legal income actively speculating in land. Sam Sawyer, elected as the Sixth Judicial District's Circuit Attorney, received regular compensation because the state's attorney position carried guaranteed annual income. In contrast to Sims and Sawyer, Lud survived following an alternative course.

Lud lived on credit and what little income he could generate from his law practice. A close friend described Peyton as rarely exhibiting "any energy in business. He might with great propriety have been called physically lazy."[325] Wealth accumulation fell

[324] *Western Democrat.* February 27, 1858.
[325] *History of Cass and Bates Counties, Missouri.* Page 377.

outside Lud's basic ambitions. Whereas Sims, developed a reputation for diligent legal work and accumulated considerable wealth through land speculation, Lud strove to maintain himself solely on what litigation and friendship would provide.

---------- The Sixth Judicial District ----------

Lud practiced law in Missouri's Sixth Judicial District from 1844 until the Civil War erupted. Throughout this 17-year period, the Sixth District Circuit Court contained the same seven counties, and roughly, the same 5,000 square miles. Although the geographic jurisdiction remained constant, the judicial district's population exploded from 35,000 to almost 100,000 in 1860; slaves represented over 20% of the district's population. New villages sprouted throughout the district. The burgeoning population brought expanding commerce. The area thrived as river commerce increased, feeding not only the local area but also fueling growing traffic as settlers headed west. Expanding commerce fueled litigation increasing opportunities for attorneys. Missouri's western border, until 1854 abutting Indian Territory, dealt with legal cases surfacing from the friction between the Indian population and the settled white communities.

The Sixth Judicial District's judges and attorneys personified Missouri's frontier energy and character. Traveling on horseback and often working in primitive conditions the jurists became a close fraternity. Bonded by shared adventures, in the courtroom and on the road, their stories gave rise to legend and myth. As a group, they loved horse racing.[326] During slack time "they entertained themselves by playing cards, gambling and telling stories."[327] On the road, in rustic accommodations, they shared hotel beds.

The judicial profession became a cultural focal point for western Missouri society. These frontier lawyers, often larger than life, set the tone and direction for much of western Missouri's history. During his 17-year practice, Lud plied his legal skills before five

[326] English. Page 124.

[327] English. Page 101.

different circuit court judges. Each judge, expressing different character and personality, influenced local communities and shaped the jurists practicing before them. Twice each year the judges' arrival, anticipated and celebrated, enervated district's seven counties.

Missouri's Sixth Judicial District

In 1845, responding to Missouri's growth, the state assembly expanded the number of judicial districts, from seven to 14. The general assembly also mandated each circuit court's route and travel schedule. The Sixth Judicial District convened two terms per year in each county, a spring term and an autumn term. The Governor appointed all 14 circuit court judges until 1850 when a law change required that the judges be elected by popular vote. Jacksonian Democracy's steadily growing influence eventually resulted in the election of all judges, circuit and Supreme Court.

---------- The Circuit ----------

The judge and the state's attorney of the Sixth District Circuit Court routinely traveled a circuit of 365 miles. The journey began in Independence, Jackson Co., then moved to Harrisonville, Van Buren County's county seat.[328] After Harrisonville the court traveled south to Papinville, Bates County. In 1855 Butler replaced Papinville as the county seat. The Bates County term completed, the circuit entourage turned back north to Warrensburg, Johnson Co., and then moved to Georgetown, in Pettis Co. Marshall, the Saline County seat, next welcomed the travelers. Lexington, Lafayette Co. hosted the final term of the circuit. The full circuit required six weeks of horseback travel and differing accommodations, regardless of the weather.

Lawyers could accompany the judge and state's attorney on the entire circuit, but it is doubtful many regularly rode the entire circuit. The volume of legal business varied greatly by county and a county's local attorneys exercised an advantage over "foreign" lawyers. The more distant courts in Papinville, and later Butler, offered primitive accommodations and few lawsuits, and that discouraged attendance. Most frontier attorneys necessarily supplemented their unreliable legal fees with income from other pursuits and often these other avocations took precedence. Sometimes family responsibilities pulled them off the circuit. Lud's practice generally encompassed those counties within a day's ride of Harrisonville; initially his low ambition and energy kept him close to home.

The Sixth Judicial District's tour began and ended in the circuit's two largest, and rival towns, Independence and Lexington. Missouri River commerce and outfitting the overland trail industry fueled both towns. Local outfitters supplied wagons, animals and supplies to the hundreds of prairie freighters and thousands of westward bound emigrants. Each town also supported a stable of experienced lawyers. In Independence, spring's approach heralded an upsurge

328 **Note**: Van Buren County was renamed Cass County in 1848.

in river traffic, a reenergized overland trail outfitting business, and the opening session of the Sixth District Circuit Court.

The anticipated convening of the circuit court swelled Independence's population. The public square surrounding the Jackson County courthouse often took on a carnival atmosphere. Locals looked forward to the entertaining oratory of the attorneys and the public disclosure of individual problems. In the days before court opened, the judge, the state attorney, and local lawyers began to arrive and settle into the surrounding hotels.

Independence's Smallwood Noland Hotel hosted most of the district's attorneys when court was in session. The hotel dominated the northeast corner of the town square directly across from the courthouse. Lavish, two stories tall, with a broad porch along the east side, the hotel could accommodate 400 guests.[329] That said, single rooms were not often available, so most often, guests slept two to a bed with an additional sleeper on the floor.

The Smallwood Noland Hotel's cuisine greatly exceeded normal frontier fare. The menu offered a wide variety of entrees, desserts, and libations. Main course possibilities included Macedonia of Wild Fowl, Buffalo Tongue, Braised Duck, and Omelet with fine herbs. Fourteen different "Cake and Confectionary" offerings lined the menu. For those wanting something beyond cake, 11 different "Ice Creams and Jellies" were available.[330]

Smallwood Noland, the hotel's owner, catered to the circuit court's community. A Noland nephew described the importance ascribed to the opening of the circuit court. "The regular meetings of the Circuit Court were great occasions in Uncle Wood's estimation. Much preparation for the reception of guests was necessary. The house went through a thorough cleaning from top to bottom – the rooms were newly furnished and everything in readiness when the courts opened. The lawyers throughout the district (which was a

[329] Wilcox. Page 282.
[330] State Historical Society of Missouri. Manuscripts, C4121, Folders 56 & 143. David A. James Papers.

large one) arrived on horseback, were shown to their rooms and a jolly good time they had of it."[331]

Lud's early stays at the Smallwood Noland Hotel introduced him to men with whom he would associate until the Civil War. Judge John F. Ryland, a Lexington resident, occupied the bench. The judge, "was excessively fond of the law, but his kind heart and pacific disposition often led him to discourage suits which in his opinion were calculated to engender strife and bad feeling among neighbors and families."[332] Ryland shared with Peyton a love of books and Latin. Ryland loved history. On the bench, and off it, Ryland, always, "a gentleman, easy, natural and commanding" with a "high sense of honor."[333] The attorneys facing Ryland, with whom Peyton worked, formed a varied and competitive legal brotherhood.

Lud often partnered with, and opposed, a very competent group of Jackson County attorneys. Samuel H. Woodson, William Chrisman, and Abram Comingo eventually formed a partnership in 1854 known as "Woodson, Chrisman and Comingo."[334] All three lawyers actively supported the American Party in the mid 1850s. Peyton and Woodson, in particular, shared a strong belief in Calhoun's strict, interpretation of the U.S. Constitution. Woodson's legal career transitioned to politics and he represented western Missouri in the U.S. House of Representatives prior to the Civil War.

At Independence Lud first encountered Russell Hicks. These two men, friends and legal associates, formed a bond based on respect, politics, and shared interests. Russell Hicks, in the mid 1850s, succeeded William T. Wood as Judge of the Sixth Judicial District. Hicks was an unusual, forceful presence. A contemporary described Hicks as "…one of the roughest diamonds I ever saw in a court house."[335] Hicks was "certainly unpopular with the lawyers in

[331] Webb. Page 141.
[332] Bay. Page 273.
[333] Bay. PP. 271 & 275.
[334] Monaco. Page 74.
[335] Crittenden. *MHR*, Vol. 26, No. 1. Page 6.

his circuit," according to another.[336] Russell Hicks, in person and memory, acquired mythical proportions. He, "had red hair which he colored black, a large head, and usually shaved his temples and forehead, and when the red bristles stood out when the shaving process had been neglected for a few weeks, he presented a savage appearance."[337] Hicks never married, "in fact, he never spoke to a woman if he could avoid it,"[338] and he "was never known to laugh and seldom smile."[339] On the bench, as the circuit court judge, Hicks was however regarded as "one of the ablest and most honest judges I ever saw on that or any bench."[340]

Russell Hicks established a village in southeast Jackson County, two miles northeast of Lone Jack, and named it Hicks City. Hicks' slaves built the estate including his racetrack. "He was passionately fond of fine horses, especially racers, and maintained on his farm a racetrack, more for amusement than profit."[341] Hicks and Peyton shared a love of horse racing as well as a love for politics.

Russell Hicks
Author's Collection

The circuit court's opening session occasioned a flurry of activity in Independence – especially on the square surrounding the courthouse. For the week, the square became a daily farmer's market, good of all types available for purchase. William Walker, Nebraska's first territorial governor, in 1851, described the square resounding with "noise and confusion." The noise emanating from auctions "selling negroes, horses, mules, etc."[342] "Court days were holidays."[343] In all of the county seats, taverns were a short walk from the courthouse and they were "invariably

[336] Bay. Page 44.
[337] *History of the Bench and Bar of Missouri.* Page 402.
[338] Wilcox. Page 139.
[339] *History of Jackson County.* Page 238.
[340] Crittenden. *MHR.* Vol. 26, No. 1. Page 6.
[341] Wilcox. Page 139.
[342] O'Brien. Page 133.
[343] English. Page 19.

crowded at court times, and many excellent yarns of frontier wit and humor have come down from the pranks played when the lawyers and judges were on circuit."[344]

Jackson County Courthouse-
Courtesy of State Historical Society of Missouri

Jackson County's two-story brick courthouse dominated central Independence. Through two decades, the courthouse had evolved from a two room, hewn log cabin to a brick courthouse. In 1848 the courthouse was remodeled and given a spire. The Jackson County courtroom accommodated a raised judge's bench and enough room for spectators behind tables for the plaintiffs and defendants – and the circuit proceedings did draw spectators. "Pioneer Missourians traveled miles over rough roads to attend the court sessions to see the judges and hear the lawyers plead."[345] Court proceedings provided entertainment, and those lawyers with high oratorical skills drew audiences. "In the French and Spanish era, orator had been the word used to designate a petitioner in a suit, and as late as 1819, attorneys in Missouri called themselves orators."[346]

Leaving Independence the circuit court entourage moved south to Harrisonville, Cass County's county seat. The 40-mile trek

[344] English. Page 101.
[345] McCurdy. Page 1.
[346] McCurdy. Page 2.

required two travel days. The traveling jurists were welcomed at homes and villages along the way as their hosts saw an opportunity to get the news from known dignitaries. "Many people considered it an honor to have the judge and bar stop with them and looked forward to their arrival."[347] Dirt roads, dusty in dry weather and knee deep in mud in wet weather, connected Independence and Harrisonville. On horseback, judges and lawyers, were mindful of both the weather and the depth of streams and rivers they had to ford.

Arriving at Harrisonville, the traveling jurists registered at either of two hotels, neither of which met the splendor of Independence's Smallwood Noland Hotel. Both hotels offered livery services, either themselves or via nearby stables. The Arizona Hotel occupied the northeast corner of Cass County's square. Lud often lived, for long stretches, at the Arizona Hotel. The hotel served as a center for the mercantile and county political interests and its convenient location drew the jurists. The Southern Hotel, owned by Lud's close friend Silas Price and his brother-in-law Charles Keller, also welcomed the travelers. The Southern Hotel was located two blocks south of the courthouse.

Harrisonville's hotels offered guests services and accommodations more typical of the period – basic creature comforts. "Every accommodation and convenience," as an early tavern advertised, probably meant sleeping in a common room, perhaps sharing a bed with a stranger. If you arrived late and the bed space was taken, you could sleep on the floor, feet facing the fireplace, side by side with other tavern patrons."[348]

Sanitation in the 1840s and 1850s met minimum standards. "Patrons 'washed up' on the front or back porch from a pail or basin and toweled off with a communal towel. A traveler in need of 'relief' would take a walk in the woods. An accommodating tavern keeper would provide a shovel for those wishing to cover their tracks. The later taverns and inns were equipped with outdoor

[347] English. Page 101.
[348] State Historical Society of Missouri. Manuscripts, C4121, Folder 143, Page 11. David A. James Papers.

privies or 'outhouses.' An inn would provide guests with a washbasin and a pitcher of warm water in the morning, with a towel. Later, a chamber pot was added by the smaller hotels."[349]

The circuit's judges and lawyers were welcome guests to locals with the space to provide accommodations. The opportunity to acquire the latest news could not easily have been passed up. As Harrisonville grew its mercantile network and social network stretched to welcome the judicial travelers. For the jurists, staying with a family easily surpassed communal hotel living.

The same county courthouse welcomed the circuit court during Lud's 17-year legal practice. Charles Sims, Harrisonville's other prominent attorney, designed and supervised the construction of the courthouse in 1844. Made of brick, the two-story courthouse's first floor housed the county clerk and the county recorder. The first floor also provided a room for the use of the circuit court. The courtroom occupied the entire second floor and like the Jackson County courthouse had space for the bench and bar as well as seating for spectators.[350] Within this courtroom Lud Peyton's oratorical magnetism drew crowds of local citizens.

Harrisonville's courthouse grounds were superb. The courthouse was "inclosed by a handsome iron fence" and "the ground surrounding the courthouse is planted in shade trees and blue grass, and is one of the most attractive features of the town."[351] During the earlier period in the courthouse's history, high traffic on and through the courthouse grounds wore the grass down, although the surrounding iron fence always ensured a signature view.

[349] State Historical Society of Missouri. Manuscripts, C4121, Folder 143, Page 34. David A. James Papers.
[350] *History of Cass and Bates Counties, Missouri*. Page 291.
[351] *History of Cass and Bates Counties, Missouri*. Page 291.

Cass County Courthouse-Courtesy Cass County Historical Society

When Cass County's term adjourned the Sixth Circuit Court traveled south into Bates County. Harmony Mission hosted the circuit court from 1841 until proceedings were moved to Papinville in 1847.[352] Papinville served as the county seat from 1847 until October 1856 when the county seat was relocated to Butler. Both Papinville and Butler offered the traveling jurists more primitive destinations.

The route from Harrisonville to Papinville was well traveled and well known. As early as 1824 the Old Mission Road from Lexington to Harmony Mission had been documented.[353] Originally an Indian Trail, the Old Mission Road passed through Van Buren County's (Cass County's) eastern edge before entering Bates County. The Sixth Circuit Court used this route before the county seat was relocated to Butler.

However, potential water hazards faced the jurists as they moved south. The Grand River traversed all north-south roads and during times of heavy rain high water and floods challenged the jurists. It was not uncommon for the travelers to disrobe, tie their clothes to

[352] *History of Cass and Bates Counties, Missouri*. Page 963.
[353] *Jackson County Democrat*. October 26, 1961. Page 7D.

their saddles, wade across the stream and dress again on the other side. Once the court moved to Butler in the mid 1850s the jurists, although not free of the water threat, could ferry across the Grand River rather than fording it at Settle's Ford.

Papinville anchored the northern most steamboat landing on the Osage River. The county did not have a courthouse during the early circuit court visits and as a result the court met in schoolhouses or the residences of local citizens. When the court convened a Grand Jury, the jury received its orders inside and then "repaired out of doors (there being no jury room)."[354] Finally in 1852, the Bates county court directed that a courthouse be constructed at Papinville and dedicated $2,500 to the effort. The county court hoped the construction of a new brick courthouse would certify Papinville as the permanent county seat but that hope soon faded.[355] The new Papinville courthouse was completed in 1855 just before the county seat was moved to centrally located Butler. A local merchant purchased Papinville's new courthouse.

By virtue of the reorganization of Bates County, Butler simultaneously became a town and the county seat. It was located in the county's geographic center. In 1855 Butler was a mere village, not surveyed and laid-out as a town until October 1856 - coincidentally, the date of the circuit court's inaugural session at Butler.

The presiding Circuit Court Judge was the Honorable Russell Hicks who convened the county court in "an old school house."[356] Lud attended this first session. It is of interest that of the four lawyers present at Butler, all lived in different counties. Thomas H. Starns lived and practiced in Butler. Waldo P. Johnson, already a Missouri political presence, lived and practiced at Osceola, in neighboring St. Clair County. The fourth attorney, Thomas Freeman, lived in Polk Co. at Bolivar.[357] A Grand Jury was called and "they held their

---

[354] *Old Settlers History of Bates County, Mo.* Page 17.

[355] *Old Settlers History of Bates County, Mo.* Page 16.
[356] *Old Settlers History of Bates County, Mo.* Page 17.
[357] *Old Settlers History of Bates County, Mo.* Page 17.

sessions on a dry knoll in the high prairie grass, but as no complaints were laid before them they were soon discharged."[358]

Ten years before Butler's initial Grand Jury, 1846, Lud's first significant civil case surfaced in what was to become Bates County at West Point. Thomas B. Arnett and William C. Brown signed a contract to build 21 houses on the Osage Reservation near the Verdigris River in southeast Indian Territory. Joel Cruttenden, the Osage tribe's subagent, negotiated the contract with Arnett and Brown. Eli Dodson, a Van Buren County resident, funded two subcontractors but was not paid for the work. Angered, as well as being out several hundred dollars, Dodson retained Lud Peyton to sue for his funds.

February 19, 1846 Lud filed a suit against Arnett and Brown in the Sixth Judicial Court, Judge John F. Ryland presiding. Dodson alleged he was owed $600.00, quite a substantial sum for the day.[359] Judge Ryland found for Dodson but Arnett and Brown appealed to the Missouri Supreme Court. In its July 1847 term the Supreme Court reversed the decision, finding for Arnett and Brown. Lud found himself opposing Charles Sims in the courtroom.

After Bates County, the circuit court's journey turned north from Papinville and Butler to Warrensburg, Johnson County's county seat. The trip, the longest segment on the circuit, covered 75-miles requiring three days. The most efficient route from Bates County to Warrensburg took the men out of the Sixth Judicial District to Clinton in Henry County. A night's stay in Clinton provided the chance to renew friendships and strengthen professional ties.
Once at Warrensburg, the weary travelers checked into one of two hotels. The Bolton House, located on the southwest corner of the square, began hosting travelers in the mid 1840s. The Mansion House rivaled the Bolton House. The Mansion House had originally been built in 1837 as a log building. During the years it was modified and enlarged.

---

358 *Old Settlers History of Bates County, Mo.* Page 17.

359 Missouri Secretary of State. Supreme Court Records. Box 59. Folder 12.

The Johnson County Courthouse had already been in use for six years when Lud first visited it. Functional but dated, the courthouse remained in use until 1870. A one-story brick structure, the courthouse had space for spectators separated from the bench and bar by a wooden fence.

Lud first became associated with attorney Michael C. Goodlett in Warrensburg. Goodlett became a prominent civic and political figure in Johnson County. During the border troubles, 1858 and 1859, Goodlett commanded Johnson County's militia.[360] He also served with Lud in the Missouri General Assembly.

Johnson County Court House-
Courtesy State Historical Society of Missouri

Departing Warrensburg the circuit court headed 30 miles east to Georgetown in Pettis County. Pettis County, Saline County, and Lafayette County, the last three stops in the circuit identified strongly with Missouri's slaveholding interests. Abutting the area that later known as "Little Dixie," these three counties hosted horrific slave episodes during the 1850s. Tension between civil law and vigilantism shaped and changed the judiciary in the area. These

[360] Missouri Secretary of State. Special Collections. Missouri-Kansas Border War, 1858-1860. Goodlett Letter. January 5, 1859.

three counties contained 64% of the slaves in the Sixth Judicial District while similarly home to around 40% of the free white population. This unbalanced population coupled to abolitionist attacks sparked fear and paranoia in the white community.

George R. Smith founded Georgetown in the early 1830s and the town served as the Pettis County seat until after the Civil War. Smith occupied the largest home in Georgetown, a three-story brick house built in 1849.

The Pettis County courthouse had been commissioned by the county court in 1835. By the time Lud practiced in western Missouri the courthouse had been in use for almost 10 years. Facing south, the courthouse was striking.

> "It was square, with a large door in the center of each of three sides, and a large window on each side of the doors. The north side had two windows but no door, the space between being occupied by the judge's bench. This was a platform about four feet high with chairs on it, and terminated at the two windows with four or five steps. A balustrade followed the whole length of steps and platform, and continued at right angles, inclosing a square in the center of the building which had benches just inside the railing. This space was floored, and served some grand purpose for the primitive courts … The rest of the floor was brick, with some benches. A stairway, which I suppose now was a common one, led magnificently with its balus-trade to the second story … The roof was beautiful, not simply a board covered comb, like our common cabin homes, but square and shingled, and terminated at its top with a lovely octagonal observatory, with green shutters hung to white posts; and this also had a beautiful shingled roof. The cupola in turn was surmounted by a tapering spire that held a gilded globe with an arrow above, on which was pivoted a fish of gold that turned in the wind."[361]

[361] *Life of George R. Smith.* PP. 29 – 30.

George G. Vest was the most notable attorney practicing in early Georgetown. Vest arrived in 1852 and practiced there until 1856 when he moved to Boonville. A graduate of Transylvania University, Vest served in the Confederate Congress throughout the war. History holds the story that Vest decided to stay and practice in Georgetown after a defendant, a slave, for whom Vest successfully gained an acquittal, was burned alive in front of 2,500 locals.[362] Although mob leaders threatened Vest's life, he decided to stay in Georgetown. Lud and Vest served together in the Missouri Assembly, both earning reputations as formidable orators.

The route north from Georgetown to Marshall, Saline County's county seat covered a mere 30 miles. The trip to Marshall, generally devoid of large rivers and streams, ensured a smooth and uneventful journey. In 1839 the county seat had been relocated from Arrow Rock to Marshall. The Saline County courthouse was built in the early 1840s and remained in use until burnt by Confederate Partisan Rangers in 1864.

Similar to other courthouses in the Sixth Judicial District, the Saline County courthouse stood two stories. Forty feet by forty-five feet, the building was constructed of brick. Inside, two staircases led to the second floor. Thirty-one windows flooded the interior with light.

Marshall was the smallest of the towns visited by the Sixth Judicial Court. The town's population on the verge of the Civil War was advertised as being 250. Sandwiched on the circuit schedule between Georgetown and Lexington, Marshall undoubtedly was not the high point of the circuit. In addition to its small size, Marshall also lacked outside entertainments and its hotel accommodation provided only basic creature comforts.

Edward Dance operated Marshall's "Dance Hotel" in the 1850s. Previously the hotel had been known as the "Old Ming Hotel."

---

362 Kuhr, Manuel Irwin. "How George Vest Came to Missouri." *MHR*. Vol. LIX, No. 4. Page 427.

James Gibbs operated a competitor hotel, advertising his livery stable. Neither hotel offered marquee accommodations.

G. Douglas Brewerton, a New York newspaper correspondent, stayed in Marshall in the mid-1850s and vividly described the rustic nature of his hotel. Brewerton shared his hotel room with his "*almost* sober stage-driver."[363] The hotel was a "two-story 'hotel,' log cabin."[364] His shared bed was "a large double-bed, of the old-fashioned, short-legged, four-poster breed." [365] The candle provided was crammed into an empty whiskey bottle. The room itself, …the dingy walls are literally papered with "circus bills," unreadable business cards, notices of sheriffs' sales, stray cattle, and patent medicines "good for the chills;" nor are these all; cloaks, hats, riding-whips are suspended from every available peg, and a rifle, flanked by its bullet-pouch and horn, rests above the door, while the tobacco-stained floor under our feet is littered with a mingling of buffalo over-shoes, robes, Mackinaws, and such like traveling gear.[366]

Marshall's Dance Hotel, and its proprietor, played major roles in 1859's tumultuous events, tragedies that overturned the Sixth Judicial District. Missouri, and particularly the Little Dixie environs, were nervous and on-edge in 1859. John Brown's slave raid into western Missouri, coupled to another slave abduction raid in Ray County, Mo. sounded alarms. The raids, in the minds of the whites, encouraged what seemed to be an increasing number of slave runaways. A perfect storm of fear and violence came to a horrific culmination in Saline County the summer of 1859.

July 19, 1859 three slaves, abducted from legal authorities by a mob of white vigilantes were murdered at Marshall. Russell Hicks, the Sixth District Circuit Judge, had convened a special session of the court to hear the cases. As court proceedings moved slowly and seemingly against the wishes of the mob, the slaves were abducted. One of the accused slaves, John, was tied to a walnut tree and

[363] Brewerton. Page 70.
[364] Brewerton. Page 70.
[365] Brewerton. Page 70.
[366] Brewerton. Page 71.

burned alive.[367] The other two slaves, Jim and Holman, were hung from the same limb of a nearby by tree. These three murders followed by one day the lynching of another slave, witnessed by an estimated 1,000 people, at Arrow Rock in eastern Saline County.[368] These events ignited abolitionist ire and drew national attention not just to Missouri but more specifically to central Missouri and Saline County.

Within days of the murders, Russell Hicks resigned as judge of the Sixth Judicial District appalled by the violence and blatant disregard for civil law.[369] Judge Hicks was replaced on the bench by Jackson County's Robert G. Smart. Smart remained on the bench until the start of the Civil War; Union Home Guards murdered Smart shortly after the war began. The Sixth District's Circuit Attorney, John W. Bryant, a Saline citizen, remained in his position following Hicks' resignation.

However, in the years before 1859, Russell Hicks and the circuit court adjudicated Saline County's more routine cases before departing for Lexington, the last stop on the circuit.

Just 40 miles west of Marshall, Lexington, the last stop, welcomed the Sixth District judiciary to a different universe. The traveling jurists left the smallest county seat in the circuit for the largest; Lexington's reported population of 5,200 exceeded Marshall's by almost 5,000. Whereas Marshall lay embedded in central Saline County, miles from the Missouri River, Lexington sat on the river's south bank, the largest western port.

For many jurists, including Judge Ryland and Circuit Attorney, Samuel Sawyer, Lexington was home. These men leaving Marshall, headed west anticipating family and the comforts Lexington offered.

Multiple Lexington hotels provided accommodation options well beyond the other county seats, excepting Jackson County. By 1860

---

[367] Dyer, Thomas G. *Missouri Historical Review.* Vol. 89, No. 3. Page 288.
[368] Dyer, Thomas G. *Missouri Historical Review.* Vol. 89, No. 4. Page 380.
[369] *Missouri Historical Review.* Vol. 89, No. 4. Page 372.

visitors could find rooms at the Virginia Hotel, the Union Hotel and the Washington House.[370] Earlier in the period travelers with a more rustic taste, stayed at Jenkin's Tavern, "near the steamboat landing."[371] The Walton Hotel welcomed guests in the 1850s. G. Douglas Brewerton's room at the Walton Hotel contained "a bed-chamber, two tallow candles, a shaky table, and pen, ink and paper for company."[372] Brewerton also appreciated the convenience of the nearby saloon and "a 'drink of old Rye (which is at times regarded in Missouri as the pledge of peace, though it is oftener the cause of a feud), costs just one dime per glass."[373]

Lafayette County Courthouse-
Courtesy State Historical Society of Missouri

Three months before Lud initially disembarked at Lexington, the citizens of Lafayette County commissioned the design of a new courthouse. February 3, 1844, "John F. Ryland, Street Hale,

[370] State Historical Society of Missouri. Manuscripts, C4121, Folder 68. David A. James Papers.
[371] State Historical Society of Missouri. Manuscripts, C4121, Folder 68. David A. James Papers.
[372] Brewerton. Page 76.
[373] Brewerton. Page 76.

William T. Wood, Henderson Young, William Early, and James Crump were appointed commissioners to prepare a plan for a new courthouse to be erected in the city of Lexington."[374] Three members of the commission, Ryland, Young, and Wood, at different times, served as judges of the Sixth Judicial District. Construction began on the new courthouse in 1847 and it was completed in 1849.[375] The third courthouse in Lexington, and designed by local architect William Dougherty, this courthouse was "a two-story brick structure of handsome colonial design with a tall clock tower and massive stone columns."[376]

---------- The Murder of Billy Smith ----------

When requesting a change in venue, attorneys in the Sixth Judicial District often requested Lexington. The town's size ensured necessary accommodations. Also, the town was home, over the years, to several judges, the attorneys hoped the town's convenience would smooth the way for an approval of a change of venue.

In 1851 a horrendous murder rocked Cass County, and the defendants immediately retained Lud. The brutal nature of the killing and the community's universal outrage deemed the probability of selecting an impartial jury almost impossible. The circuit court granted a change of venue and the murder trial was moved to Lexington.

The murder occurred July 30, 1851 just outside Harrisonville. Five Harrisonville men, Joel Elliott, James Gillespie, Hiram Chapman, Michael Ellison, and Billy Smith headed northwest from Harrisonville to Brown's Mill; Robert A. Brown owned and operated the mill. Smith, Elliott and his son-in-law, Gillespie, had signed on as wagon train teamsters and were headed to Ft. Laramie. Chapman and Ellison had agreed to accompany the three to their

---

[374] *History of Lafayette County, Missouri.* Page 284.

[375] *Lexington, Missouri: 1822 to 1972. Official Commemorative Book.* Page 25.

[376] *Lexington, Missouri: 1822 to 1972. Official Commemorative Book.* Page 25.

rendezvous point and then return with the horses to Harrisonville. The seemingly routine trip soon took a turn to disaster.

All members of the party were neighbors. They had known one another for a while. Billy Smith, a slight, undersized 18 year-old, lived near the Elliott and Gillespie families. When Joel was off working as a teamster, his wife, Lydia, managed the household and the couple's six children. James Gillespie lived next to the Elliott's. Gillespie had married Joel and Lydia's daughter, Reedy. The couple had two children, Joel and Martha.

Both families, well established in Harrisonville, were solid members of the community although Joel and James had a history of crossing the line. Two years earlier the pair had been indicted for "disturbing the peace."[377] Three months before the trio set off for Laramie, Elliott had been indicted for "disturbing a religious service." Violence, or even threatened violence, had never been an issue. There were no warning signs that July 30, 1851 would turn bloody.

Joel Elliott began the trip in an ugly mood. He carried a grudge against Bill Taylor, the eventual owner of the Arizona House. As the group began their trip to Brown's Mill, Elliott began to interrogate Hiram Chapman about Chapman's friendship with Taylor. At one point in the argument Chapman intoned, "he (Chapman) was a friend to every man that was a friend to him and as good a friend to Elliott as he was to Taylor."[378] Chapman then "proposed that they drop the subject and be friends which was agreed upon."[379]

Elliott however was not fully prepared to let it go and by the time the travelers arrived near Brown's Mill, he had worked himself into frenzy. Arriving near the mill and stopping, Elliott, now in a full

[377] Cass County, Missouri. Trial Docket. Sept. 1849 to Sept. 1856. Book 275-10.
[378] Lafayette County Circuit Court Records. Box 27. Hiram Chapman Affidavit.
[379] Lafayette County Circuit Court Records. Box 27. Hiram Chapman Affidavit.

rage pulled Chapman from his horse, threw him to the ground and began to beat him.

Chapman ended up on top of Elliott pleading for the others to separate them; Chapman did not want to hurt Elliott. Hearing Chapman's plea, Gillespie, supporting Elliott, drew his knife threatening to stab anyone who interfered. Chapman freed himself and raced into the brush with Elliott pursuing. When Elliott neared, Chapman grabbed a piece of wood clubbing Elliott into a retreat.

Elliott's escape brought him back to where Gillespie, Smith, and Ellison stood. Gillespie told Elliott, now thoroughly enraged, that both Billy Smith and Mike Ellison were against him. Now out of control, Elliott grabbed Billy, who had earlier attempted to separate him and Chapman, and "drew his knife across Smith's throat."[380] Ellison had seen "the point of the knife near Smith's throat and then looked away, but instantly looking back again saw the blood running from Smith's throat."[381] As Ellison jumped on his horse, to run for help, he saw Elliott and Gillespie throw Billy Smith to the ground.

Upon his return to the scene, Ellison found Billy Smith lying 40 or 50 feet from the point of the original attack. Elliott and Gillespie, had now fled the scene. As Ellison approached, Smith cried out, "I am a dead man!" In addition to the wound on his neck, "he was also wounded by a cut on his left side some four inches in length and so deep that his bowels and stomach were protruding at the wound."[382] Bill was moved to the nearby home of William Gillenwater's.

Billy died the next day about 2:00 in the afternoon. Before dying Billy told Gillenwater's, Joel Elliott had stabbed him; but before

[380] Lafayette County Circuit Court Records. Box 27. Michael Ellison Affidavit.
[381] Lafayette County Circuit Court Records. Box 27. Michael Ellison Affidavit.
[382] Lafayette County Circuit Court Records. Box 27. Michael Ellison Affidavit.

slicing him open had proclaimed, "You are the man that moved my house and now I will kill you."[383]

All of the witnesses gave depositions to the two local Justices of the Peace, Thomas M.T. Jackson and Samuel Saunders. Dr. Benjamin D. Hocker verified Smith's wounds. Dr. Hocker added that prior to his death, Billy shared Elliott's threat, "Damn you, you are the man that pulled my house down and now I will kill you."[384]

Joel Elliott and James Gillespie, having fled the scene of the fight, immediately retained Lud as their defense attorney. When the two men were deposed, August 1, they pled "innocent" and refused to discuss the charges further on advice of their attorney. Both were taken into custody and jailed pending legal proceedings.

Lud's fee, for representing the two was $200.00. In as much as Elliott lacked $200.00 in cash, he and Lydia, August 1, 1851, signed a Deed of Mortgage. The provisions of the deed stipulated Peyton would be paid in land in the event the Elliott's were unable to pay in cash by December 1851.

Harrisonville's mounting anger and growing appetite for revenge swirled around Elliott and Gillespie. A September Grand Jury, with Robert A. Brown as foreman, indicted the two for first-degree murder. Lud filed for a change of venue, moving the upcoming trial to Lexington, Lafayette County. The change in venue was approved and Lud transferred the pair's defense to Lexington attorney, William T. Wood.

The following summer, in the courtroom of Judge Henderson Young, a Lafayette County jury found Joel Elliott guilty of first-degree murder and he was hung at Lexington. Those present when the jury's verdict was read, reported Elliott "never minded it when the jury brought in their verdict.[385] James Gillespie, six months

[383] Lafayette County Circuit Court Records. Box 27. William T. Gillenwater's Affidavit.
[384] Lafayette County Circuit Court Records. Box 27. Dr. Benjamin D. Hocker Affidavit.
[385] Aaron B. Smith Letters. July 23, 1852.

later, was found guilty of second-degree murder and sentenced to 40 years in the Missouri penitentiary.

James Gillespie had been in custody since the murder and following his trial was transferred to the state penitentiary where he began serving his 40-year sentence. While in the Jefferson City penitentiary, he developed health problems. His parents, John and Mary, lobbied the Governor for a parole. John Gillespie, wrote a letter to Gov. R.M. Stewart in January 1858, pleading for his son's release. He wrote, "…but I consoled my poor blind wife by calling you to think of your official business. I pray that it is consistent with your views to remember James E. Gillespie in his weak affirmaties and if possible let him come to the bosom of a broken hearted Father and Mother before they are confined to the chambers of the tomb."[386] Gov. Stewart relented and granted James Gillespie a full pardon effective February 22, 1858.

Although Elliott's trial was conducted in Lexington, the Harrisonville community remained intensely focused on the outcome. Many local men had been called as witnesses. Several witnesses returned home bringing severe diarrhea and the threat of deadly cholera.[387] Aaron Smith, the Harrisonville carder, surmised Gillespie's trial was delayed due to the outbreak of disease in Lexington but, in fact, a missing witness caused the postponement.

Elliott's conviction enraged Lud. At the time of Elliott's trial, he had been ill, bedridden and unable to make the journey to Lexington. Lud felt the defense a sham.

Another of Elliott's attorneys, John W. Reid, did not make an appearance until the trial was already in session. Judge Young appointed William T. Wood to represent Elliott and was reported to have "made a very able defense."[388] Despite Wood's defense, Elliott was found guilty. Lud was "perfectly enraged at the trial, he says Elliott did not have a fair trial or they never would have done more than send him to the penitentiary – Peyton told me (Aaron

[386] Missouri State Archives. Record Group 5. Pardons. Box 10, Folder 3.
[387] Aaron B. Smith Letters. July 23, 1852.
[388] Aaron B. Smith Letters. July 23, 1852.

Smith) he would never have been better prepared to defend him than he was at the present moment – but I know he only intended to go to the trial as the last resort – for he intended to have it put off again if possible & I have no doubt would have done so if he had been there, for he told me since the trial, that if Elliott's counsel had been there he could have had his trial postponed."[389]

Shortly before 2:00 p.m., September 12, 1852, Joel Elliott rode to the gallows through a crowd some believed "the largest ever assembled in Lexington."[390] *The Lexington Express's* editor observed that most of the multitude was not from Lexington or Lafayette County. "Of his guilt, no one entertains a doubt; yet a considerable number of persons, sympathizing with his family, and pitying the prisoner on account of his age, signed a petition for commutation of his punishment."[391] Governor Austin A. King denied the petition and Elliot died on the gallows. To the people of Lexington, Elliott was a "stranger to us. We never saw him, except while on trial. He was brought to this county by a change of venue from Cass County, granted on his own affidavit, that he could not get justice done in his own county."[392]

Following Joel Elliott's trial and execution, Lydia and the children remained in Cass County. The Harrisonville community enfolded Lydia and the children, supporting them through the tragedy. Joel Snyder represented the estate and in January 1853, Snyder along with prominent citizens, Hiram B. Standiford (the County Sheriff), William J. Taylor, Abram Cassell, T.D. Pearson, and Robert A. Brown provided a $2,000 bond. Legal debts mounted and the Elliott farm (360 acres) was ordered sold. April 3, 1854 Lydia Elliott made the highest bid when the farm was auctioned. Her bid, $5.00, allowed her to retain the farm and family home. The Harrisonville community and its leaders provided Joel Elliott's widow and children with security.

[389] Aaron B. Smith Letters. July 23, 1852.
[390] *Lexington Express*. September 14, 1852.
[391] *Lexington Express*. September 14, 1852.
[392] *Lexington Express*. September 14, 1852.

---------- Peyton's Practice ----------

Lud's frontier legal practice survived handling routine cases. Civil suits, rather than criminal cases generally populated the local dockets and these cases ran the full gambit of complaints. That said, Lud's courtroom reputation attracted criminal defendants and he seemed "always employed in every important criminal case which arose in" the county.[393]

The vast majority of the legal suits handled by the circuit court involved debt. That said, not far behind debt, and handled on a regular basis were cases involving alcohol. Alcohol's availability and consumption was prolific. State law dictated very specific rules regarding alcohol's distribution and use within the community including the prohibition of sales to Indians. Indictments for selling to Indians were common in each court session.

Lud's practice also was built on representing locals who violated the law enjoying entertainment and social pursuits. State law and local authorities strictly enforced "Gaming." Card playing, billiards, and horseracing fell beneath gaming's rather large umbrella. Those indicted by local Grand Juries for gaming were pulled into the circuit court and fined. During Peyton's 17-year practice, the community's most notable citizens ended up in front of the judge.

Lud developed a solid and regular clientele handling divorce and other social issues. Divorce filings came before the circuit court in almost every session during the 1840s and 1850s.

---------- Divorce Cases ----------

Domestic unhappiness was as much a part of the frontier social fabric as it is now. The triggers of divorce filings were diverse. The personal trauma and public drama inflicted on the parties magnified because of the open nature of the divorce process administered in small communities. Circuit court sessions,

[393] *History of Cass and Bates Counties, Mo.* Page 377.

considered holidays, became spectator sport. Once filed, divorce petitions plodded through the circuit court process often taking years to resolve, holding participants in the public conversation. Lud's reputation in the community seemed to draw an unusually high number of clients. Two divorce cases were particularly noteworthy.

The two divorce filings, that of the Parsons, Samuel and Jane, and the Gillenwater's, William T. and Mariah, both handled by Lud Peyton provide a window into the time. Both cases center on widowers, abandoned by a second wife, following a long and successful first marriage. Samuel Parsons filed for divorce under an unusual circumstance. In most abandonment situations, it was the wife who had been abandoned by the husband, but in Samuel's case Jane had disappeared. The Gillenwater's' divorce is unique because the process, and public interest, began in 1854, reached the Missouri Supreme Court in 1859, and survived the Civil War. The Gillenwater's' suit was one of two Cass County divorce cases to reach the Missouri Supreme Court in the 1850s.

Samuel Parsons, 44, and Jane Allen, 41, were both widowers when they married December 22, 1853 in Jackson County. Sam's first wife of over 20 years, Barbary, had recently died. Jane's husband William had died September 10, 1852. Sam and Jane had been near neighbors and each owned considerable land. Jane's estate contained not only her deceased husband's land but also that of her brother, George Carriger, who had died in 1850 leaving his entire estate to his sister. Following their marriage, Sam and Jane lived in Jackson County until one day in 1855 Jane disappeared – she left seemingly without advance warning.

For two years Samuel languished with children and searched for Jane. By Missouri law, following an abandonment, the spouse had to wait two years before filing for a divorce. In the interim Sam moved to Cass County, five miles west of Harrisonville. Finally, frustrated and angry, he contacted Lud. When the next term of the circuit court convened in Harrisonville, October 1857, Lud filed a divorce petition for abandonment.

The search for Jane continued as Samuel's petition remained on the court docket in the spring of 1858. The court ordered Lud and Parsons to publish in the *Western Democrat*, for four weeks running, notification of the divorce filing and ordering Jane to appear in Harrisonville at the October term.[394] The "Order of Publication" both common and routine, placed the divorce in the public eye and put a spotlight on it. Sam faced the same ongoing question from friends and neighbors, "Have you found Jane yet?" He had not.

Lud continued the proceedings on Parsons's behalf. When the circuit court reconvened in April 1859, Lud noted Jane's continuing absence and Sam's inability to locate her. April 5, 1859, Judge Russell Hicks granted Samuel Parsons a divorce.[395] Four years after Jane's disappearance and 18 months after Sam's initial petition, Lud procured the divorce. Although Sam endured four years of anguish, his process compared lightly to that of the Gillenwater's divorce saga.

Lud represented William T. Gillenwater from 1854 until the Civil War. The Gillenwater's divorce proceedings began in Harrisonville eventually reaching Missouri's Supreme Court in January 1859. Lasting years, highly public, and intensely confrontational, the divorce riveted the community. The public prominence of both parties elevated Lud into a larger public profile. It is not difficult to imagine Cass County's interest in the never-ending drama surrounding one of the county's most prominent families.

William T. Gillenwater and Mariah Thomas were married in Jackson County, November 16, 1852. William's first wife, Elizabeth, had died in January 1851. Following the marriage ceremony the newlyweds returned to Cass County where William had lived since arriving in the late 1840s. William was the father-in-law of Robert A. Brown. Brown, by 1852, was one of the county's wealthiest citizens and one of its largest slave owners.

---

[394] Missouri Secretary of State. Archives. Cass County Case Files. Case 1134. Box 11. Folder 48.
[395] Cass County. Circuit Court Records. Book C. Page 21.

Although Robert Brown never held public office, his prominence and positive reputation ran wide and deep in western Missouri.

The couple's marital bliss lasted but a short period, 16 months, ending for good on April 8, 1854. Following a heated argument, Mariah fled the Gillenwater's home on horseback, taking $300.00 and accompanied by one of the house slaves. She raced toward Pleasant Hill hotly pursued by an angry, screaming William.

Mariah pulled off the road at the home of a neighbor, Charles Mills. She collapsed once inside the Mills' home and was carried to a lounge. William soon followed her into the house and their argument continued. Surrounded by a host of friends and neighbors, they fought about the $300.00 and Mariah's motives. Finally, William left, but not before publically declaring she was not now, nor would ever be welcome in his home. He left with the horse and house slave. [396]Three days following their split, William deeded all of his land and personal property to his son-in-law, Robert A. Brown.[397]

Mariah fled to the home of William Bronaugh. Following an extended illness she retained the legal counsel of William Chrisman and Abram Comingo. Chrisman and Comingo were two of Jackson County's most prominent attorneys; the attorneys filed a petition for alimony on Mariah's behalf in Cass County. Mariah then fled western Missouri, returning to Danville in Boyle County, Kentucky. William meanwhile engaged Lud as his legal counsel and filed for divorce.

Thus began a six year, highly public, divorce contest featuring a decision from the Missouri Supreme Court, a recess for the Civil War, and a conclusion only coming with William's June 1865 death in Texas. Regularly, as the circuit court convened in Harrisonville every six months the Gillenwater's divorce surfaced for public

[396] Missouri Secretary of State. Supreme Court Records. Box 231. Folder 5.

[397] Missouri Secretary of State. Supreme Court Records. Box 231. Folder 5.

consumption and discussion. No fewer than 12 depositions were taken from prominent local citizens who had participated in the couples' dramatic 1854 split. As the community took sides in the contest, Mariah filed for a change of venue fearing a fair hearing in Cass County could not be had – her request was denied. With Mariah living in Kentucky, William was left alone to tell the tale.
At the fall term of the circuit court in 1857, Judge Russell Hicks ordered William to pay Mariah $65.00 alimony until the next term of the court. Over the holidays in 1857, the Harrisonville newspaper printed an "Order of Publication" regarding the Gillenwater's divorce proceedings. Finally, at the court's spring session in 1858 Judge Hicks dismissed William's divorce petition and ruled Mariah should "recover against said plaintiff her costs and charges."[398] Lud filed for a re-trial on April 1, 1858 but Judge Hicks "refused and overruled" the motion for a new trial.[399]

Lud and William refused to accept Judge Hicks' decision. June 13, 1858 Peyton filed a "writ of error" with Missouri Supreme Court clerk William E. Dunscomb.[400] This was the second Cass County divorce petition accepted by the Missouri Supreme Court within a six-year period. The Supreme Court issued its ruling in January 1859: "It is clear that the plaintiff (William) was as anxious for a separation as the defendant, and the little arts he practiced in hope of keeping the law on his side serve only to evince his real desire. The record does not show that he is an innocent and injured party, and therefore he cannot be divorced." [401] Judge Scott delivered the opinion and Judge Richardson concurred.

The Supreme Court decision did not end the fight. The drama continued through 1859 and up to the beginning of the Civil War, Lud in the thick of it.

[398] Missouri Secretary of State. Supreme Court Records. Box 231. Folder 5.
[399] Missouri Secretary of State. Supreme Court Records. Box 231. Folder 5.
[400] Missouri Secretary of State. Supreme Court Records. Box 231. Folder 5.
[401] Missouri Secretary of State. Supreme Court Records. Box 231. Folder 5.

---------- The Missouri Supreme Court ----------

Lud carried three other civil cases to Missouri's Supreme Court in the 1850s. The three cases, all involving plaintiffs and defendants from Jackson, Cass and Bates counties, open a window into the period's culture and business activities. One of the cases provides considerable insight into the constant debt problem. Debt plagued merchants and citizens to equal degrees, as credit purchases and personal loans operated as normal tools in the frontier's economic process. The second case Peyton carried to the Supreme Court involved slander. Maintaining honor, having a "good name" was a cornerstone of frontier culture. Affronts to reputation triggered the threats of a duel or a civil lawsuit. Lud's third Supreme Court case involved shipping liability for hemp seed consigned by steamboat to buyers downstream.

October 6, 1849, Daniel Mead obtained a $50.00 personal loan from Abram Fonda.[402] The debt's repayment eventually required eight years and a verdict by the Missouri Supreme Court. The lawsuit became convoluted as a Justice of the Peace judgment, land transfers, a divorce, a disappearance, and an auction on the Cass County courthouse steps created a long and confusing road.

Abram Fonda, frustrated by Daniel Mead's apparent refusal to repay the loan, brought suit against Mead. August 6, 1853, almost four years from the date of the original loan, Justice of the Peace Hiram Stephens found in Fonda's behalf and ordered Mead to repay. Mead's only asset was his 40-acre farm, but when Stephen's judgment was given, Mead admitted to the debt but said he didn't own the farm. In February 1853 Mead had transferred ownership of the farm to Elias Owens for nothing. Owens later transferred the 40-acre farm to Hamilton Foster for nothing.

April 4, 1854 the Sheriff, Hiram B. Standiford auctioned the farm to cover the debt. At the auction, Henry L. Franse bought the 40-acre farm but when he moved to occupy, Hamilton Foster contested

[402] Missouri Secretary of State. Archives. Supreme Court Records. Box 218. Folder 14.

Franse's ownership. The argument over ownership continued until September 1856 when Franse retained Lud and filed suit.

The lawsuit and court proceedings became even more muddled for three reasons. Daniel Mead, although accessible early in the process, had in the interim, fled Cass County and disappeared. Additionally, he and wife, Jane, had divorced. There were procedural problems with Hiram Stephen's verdict as the Justice of the Peace. Also, Sheriff Hiram B. Standiford left Cass County and moved to the Kansas Territory before filing the record of sale with the county clerk. As a result, Judge Russell Hicks disallowed Stephen's verdict, and found for the defendants, Elias Owens and Hamilton Foster.

Incensed by the circumstances and the verdict, Lud advanced Franse's case to the Missouri Supreme Court. In July 1857 the Supreme Court reversed Hick's decision and reinstated Franse as the farm's owner.

Two months after the Supreme Court's ruling for Henry Franse, Jeremiah Jackson of Bates County retained Lud to defend him in a slander suit. September 17, 1857, Lawrence T. McManus, represented by attorneys Thomas W. Freeman and Thomas H. Starnes, filed suit against Jackson for slandering McManus.[403]

The Bates County, County Court had contracted Lawrence McManus as a road overseer. McManus's responsibilities required that he supervise the road's construction while local citizens supplied the labor. County residents were required by statute to assist in roads' construction. McManus accused Jackson of refusing to supply the workers as required by law. McManus then reported Jackson's failure to the local Justice of the Peace, Lewis Speece.

Little seems to have come of McManus's accusation until a public confrontation occurred on September 17. During their verbal

[403] Missouri Secretary of State. Archives. Supreme Court Records. Box 232. Folder 06.

sparring McManus mentioned Jackson's refusal to participate in the road building. Jackson rebutted McManus's accusation and in doing so, in McManus's opinion, severely impugned his reputation and slandered him.

McManus alleged Jackson's comments were so severe that he (McManus) was "brought into public scandal and lost the company and society of many of his good neighbors and acquaintances."[404]

McManus also alleged Jackson to have said, in front of the gathering, "I wonder if McManus is not the same man who gave a Negro a free pass?"[405] This accusation, if true, implied McManus had given a pass to a slave allowing free movement by saying the slave had been emancipated. Such an act was clearly against the law, endangering the safety of local white citizens.

Both statements, McManus stated, had slandered his reputation and destroyed personal relationships to the extent of $10,000 – a truly excessive amount in 1857. Jackson denied the charges and retained Lud to represent him. The feud continued for a full year until October 10, 1858 when Judge Russell Hicks found for the defendant, Jackson, and further ordered McManus pay the full court costs.

McManus refused to accept Hicks' decision and through his attorneys appealed to Missouri's Supreme Court. The court ultimately again found for Jeremiah Jackson, and McManus lost his case.

While the feud between McManus and Jackson festered in Bates County, another Supreme Court case unfolded in Independence involving two Cass County farmer-merchants and two Jackson County shipping agents. Lud, a personal friend of the plaintiffs, Tarlton Railey and George E. Moore, became involved in the case

[404] Missouri Secretary of State. Archives. Supreme Court Records. Box 232. Folder 06.
[405] Missouri Secretary of State. Archives. Supreme Court Records. Box 232. Folder 06.

after the initial filing. Events triggering the lawsuit began March 15, 1857.[406]

Tarlton Railey and George E. Moore shipped 18 sacks (containing 18 bushels in total) of Chinese hemp from Cass County to Lexington, Missouri. The hemp seed was shipped to Independence on March 15 and by April 4 was stored in the warehouse of Robert G. Smart and James Porter at Maxwell's Landing in Jackson County. The seed was transferred to the steamboat "A.C. Goddin" and moved to Lexington. At his point tragedy occurred because the seed was never delivered to Curtis O. Wallace for sale. Instead it was delivered to one T.B. Wallace, who surprised by the delivery, accepted the seed and then just let it sit until selling it at clearance rates to just get rid of it.

When Railey and Moore approached Robert Smart and James Porter for reimbursement the request was denied. Smart and Porter pushed all of the liability off on the steamboat. Railey and Moore retained the services of William Chrisman and Abram Comingo, two Jackson County attorneys and sued Smart and Porter for damages. During the course of the legal proceedings, Judge Russell Hicks resigned, replaced on the bench by Judge Robert G. Smart, one of the defendants. When the case returned to court, Judge Smart excused himself, and the Fifth District Judicial Court judge, George W. Dunn presided. Judge Dunn's ruled in favor of the defendants and he further ruled the plaintiffs should pay the court costs.

The plaintiffs reached out to Lud who joined Chrisman and Comingo. Judge Dunn's ruling was appealed to the Missouri Supreme Court. In January 1861 the Supreme Court reversed the circuit court's ruling and found in favor of the plaintiffs.

406 Missouri Secretary of State. Archives. Supreme Court Records. Box 257. Folder 03.

---------- Lud's Legend ----------

George Beck and James Preston hated each other. The two traded threats, passing a point of no return. One day in 1854 the antagonists, both unaccompanied, unexpectedly met on the Morristown – Harrisonville Road. Suddenly alone and face-to-face, angry words led to violence leaving one of the men bleeding to death in the road. The bloodshed provided the platform that catapulted Lud in the pantheon of local lore and opened the door for his political rise. Lud's closing defense at the ensuing trial so amplified his oratorical brilliance, he was elevated from man to myth. Forty years after the trial and 550 miles from the old courthouse, Peyton's now mythical oratory, hit the pages of the *Chicago Chronicle*.[407]
Twenty-nine year old James Preston, his wife, Martha and their children farmed in western Cass County. Their farm adjoined that of James's father, George Preston. James "was respectably connected, and ordinarily was a peaceable and quiet citizen, except when under the influence of intoxicating liquor."

The Beck families lived several miles south of the Preston's. John Beck and his son George also farmed. George, 36, and his wife Sarah Ann had two children. George Beck took a strong dislike to James Preston. Overtime, the animosity became a shared dislike intensifying to the point George and James became enemies; their hate was common knowledge throughout the community. George Beck's threat to kill Preston was also common knowledge.

The two enemies, both farmers and fathers, unexpectedly, met on the Harrisonville road west of town. An argument erupted between the two. Beck "according to the fashion of the times, wore a heavy blanket around him with his head through the center."[408] During the face-off, Beck appeared to Preston, to be reaching for a weapon beneath his blanket. Preston, operating under the knowledge Beck had publically threatened to kill him, pulled his pistol and fired. Preston's bullet caught Beck squarely and he later died.

[407] *Sunday Chicago Chronicle*. Vol. I, No. 209. December 22, 1895. Page 15.
[408] *History of Cass and Bates Counties, Missouri*. Page 364.

Following the killing, James did not flee but remained in the county. He was taken into custody and jailed in Harrisonville. On April 5, 1854 James was indicted for murder. Tensions within the community did not subside, as Beck's family threatened quick justice. Fearing vigilante justice, the Sheriff transferred Preston to the Jackson County jail in Independence, "for safe keeping."[409]

For the two years following his indictment, James's upcoming trial polarized Cass County. Local neighbors sided with one of the two families, and became witnesses for either the prosecution or the defense. Neighbors, and several prominent county leaders, posted for James's $7,000 bond.[410] Tensions mounted.

Finally, March 31, 1856 Preston's murder trial began in the courthouse at Harrisonville, Judge William T. Wood presiding. A 12-man jury climbed the steps to the second floor courtroom and took their seats. Spectators filled all the available seats and many stood lining the outside walls.

Saline County's John W. Bryant, circuit attorney for the Sixth Judicial District began the proceedings and presented the prosecution's case.[411] For two days, under Bryant's skillful prosecution the state's case gradually moved opinion against Preston. When prosecuting attorney Bryant finished building his case, court proceedings shifted to the defense, and anticipation soared when word spread that Lud would be the last to speak presenting the defense's closing arguments.

Outside the courthouse the surrounding square filled with locals. When a murder trial occurred "it always drew. Farmers came in with their families and camped out in order to hear the trial. It was the only diversion they had."[412] The Preston trial was high drama.

---

[409] Cass County Circuit Court Records. Special Session. May 25, 1854.
[410] Cass County Circuit Court Records. 1855. Page 135.
[411] **John W. Bryant**: Bryant, later in 1859, would be deeply involved in Saline County's slave lynching; murders that led to the resignation of Judge Russell Hicks.
[412] *Sunday Chicago Chronicle*. Vol. I, No. 209. December 22, 1895. Page 15.

This was murder. This was life or death! This was the Beck family against the Preston's. For three days, the square surrounding the courthouse buzzed with the trial's ebb and flow.

Lud and Charles Sims working together constructed Preston's defense. The "theory of the defense by which it sought to acquit Preston was that he had killed Beck in self-defense."[413] The two lawyers brought different skills that blended into a double-barreled shot.

Sims rose first and addressed the jury. Sims "was ready, cool, and logical and very ingenious in argument, well calculated, by reason of his plausible manner, to make 'the worse- appear the better reason,' although he did not appeal to the sympathetic nature."[414] The defense's closing arguments were left to Lud.

The day Lud presented the final arguments the courtroom swelled beyond capacity. Many ladies filled seats, pulled into the drama by Lud's reputation.

Lud rose to address the jury. In appearance he "was long and gangling in his gait; his hair was like a brush heap; his arms were always in the way, and his nose was like that which sculptors and artists give Julius Caesar."[415] In a day when oratorical skills were appreciated and treasured, Lud's magnetic oratory drew crowds. A listener wrote, "…his great forte was in swaying juries by his persuasive eloquence. His voice was exceedingly musical, enunciation and articulation perfect, his command of language wonderful."[416] As Lud began speaking the Sheriff "removed the sash and doors from the courtroom so that the people without could hear Peyton."[417]

---

413 *History of Cass and Bates Counties, Missouri*. Page 363.
414 *History of Cass and Bates Counties, Missouri*. Page 364.
415 *Sunday Chicago Chronicle*. Vol. I, No. 209. December 22, 1895. Page 15.
416 *History of Cass and Bates Counties, Missouri*. Page 364.
417 *Sunday Chicago Chronicle*. Vol. I, No. 209. December 22, 1895. Page 15.

The courtroom scene set, Peyton did not disappoint. For three hours Lud led the packed courtroom and jury through the events. His closing arguments and the jury's verdict became legend.

> "Mr. Peyton, in a masterly speech of three or four hours, concluded the case for the defense. When he began to speak the court house was packed. From the start he held perfectly the attention of both jury and audience. In his usual fascinating and forcible style he dwelt on the salient points of the defense; showed how Beck had 'hounded' Preston at every step; compared Beck to the 'hyena' and Preston to the lamb, being pursued, etc. His peroration was delivered with truly dramatic effect. The orator seemed at his best, carried both audience and jury by storm.
>
> The effect was electrical. The jury was in tears.
>
> One of the ladies in the audience was so affected by the pathos of the speaker that she was completely overcome, and fainted. The argument being concluded, the jury went out and returned in a few minutes with a verdict of "Not Guilty."[418]

When the jury had returned to the courtroom the written verdict was handed to the judge who read it "first in silence,' and "before it was read aloud the court said, 'I don't want any levity or demonstration in this courtroom when the verdict is read. If you people who are here want to cut up any capers about it you must go out of doors and do it."[419]

News of Preston's release and Peyton's brilliant defense spread. There could have been no venue better suited for establishing a lawyer's reputation than a winning verdict for first-degree murder in a packed courtroom. Peyton's brilliant oratory in Preston's defense "must have been an argument of force, and convincing, for, twenty-five years ago when the writer (Frank Brooks) was a visitor in Harrisonville, he heard people who had come upon earth long

[418] *History of Cass and Bates Counties, Missouri*. Page 364.
[419] *Sunday Chicago Chronicle*. Vol. I, No. 209. December 22, 1895. Page 15.

after the effort in question talking about the great speech of Lud Peyton, which their grandfathers had heard."[420]

Over time, with each retelling, the trial's drama and Lud's electric performance rose to ever-greater heights. Forty years after the trial, and over 30 years from Lud's death, the *Chicago Chronicle* revisited his magnificent moment with a bit of embellishment.

The newspaper asserted Peyton not only enraptured the jury with oratory but also swayed their verdict with his fiddle playing. The story described Lud as being a "natural musician."[421] Rather than returning a verdict in minutes, this later version described an overnight deliberation, and as "the night wore on" suddenly "the sound of a fiddle was heard. It was soothing and restful as all music is when it comes in the night."[422] The jury gathered at the courtroom window and listened as Lud played. Soon a verdict was reached, the jury denying Lud's soothing fiddling swayed the decision.

Lud fiddling to jury-
Chicago Chronicle December 22, 1895

[420] *Sunday Chicago Chronicle*. Vol. I, No. 209. December 22, 1895. Page 15.
[421] *Sunday Chicago Chronicle*. Vol. I, No. 209. December 22, 1895. Page 15.
[422] *Sunday Chicago Chronicle*. Vol. I, No. 209. December 22, 1895. Page 15.

In 1856 Lud's dramatic, successful defense, elevated him onto a higher Missouri stage, and four decades later it crystallized the man to myth.

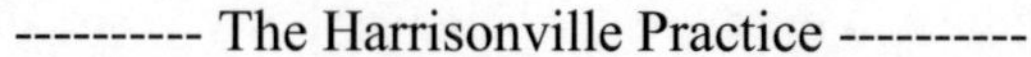

---------- The Harrisonville Practice ----------

Lud, although practicing throughout the Sixth Judicial District, largely confined his scope to Cass County and the adjacent counties. Western Missouri's expanding population created more legal business and as a result attracted more attorneys. For many years Lud preferred to practice law alone on his own while his contemporaries joined in partnerships. Lud's lack of ambition and drive during his early years at Harrisonville precluded any desire to join forces with another attorney.

During the 1840s and early 1850s Cass County's (previously Van Buren County) legal environment generated such a low volume of business forming partnerships made little sense. For much of the period Lud and Charles Sims handled the bulk of Harrisonville's legal needs although other lawyers settled and practiced in town. Although sharing the same courtroom and often working on the same cases they never established a formal partnership. Sims's interests in land speculation and Missouri politics carried him in a different direction.

Lud's office, and scant legal library, traveled with him. His office seemed, most often, to be where he was living at the moment. When he resided with friends his office was at the residence. When he lived at the Arizona House his office was his room, the hotel's lobby or the front porch. Sometimes "Peyton's office – for it seemed he had a place where he could be found, occasionally – was a room in the courthouse."[423]

Regardless of Lud's meandering office location and the ongoing reluctance to push himself for a higher station in life, his local practice provided ongoing income. His business increased as a natural result of the increase in population and business. Within the

[423] *St. Louis Post-Dispatch*. January 5, 1896.

legal community he mentored and encouraged fledgling attorneys. One of the more intriguing relationships Lud developed involved James Christian.

James Christian emigrated from Ireland to the United States in 1834. Twelve years later Christian was living in Kentucky where he married Malinda Ross. While in Kentucky he began reading and studying law. By the early 1850s James and Malinda had settled in Harrisonville. James joined the Harrisonville Masons where he fell under the tutelage of Lud and Elias West. Lud took Christian under his wing, helping him enter the bar. Christian, having lived in Kentucky then settling in Missouri, had acclimated to the Southern culture. Harrisonville provided a comfortable home for the Christians but the legal field was already crowded. The creation of the Kansas Territory in 1854 opened new career and business opportunities. The Christians packed and moved to Lawrence. At Lawrence, Christian quickly involved himself in the local government. While retaining his pro-slavery views, he became the Douglas County clerk. As Lawrence filled with abolitionists, Christian held fast to his beliefs and assimilated.

While serving the county he began advertising for legal clients. A Lawrence abolitionist newspaper, the *Herald of Freedom* published Christian's business solicitation in September 1855. The advertisement recommended R.L.Y. Peyton, John Cummins, and Hamilton Finney as Christian's references. Although prominent men, Cummins was on the Cass County Court and Finney was the County Clerk, Christian's references seem a bit surprising. They were all strong pro-slavers and Missourians.

During the Wakarusa War New York reporter, G. Douglas Brewerton, interviewed Christian.[424] Christian explained he was a "member of the pro-slavery party," and although he has "never had the good fortune to 'own a darkey' but would like a couple if he could afford that luxury, as he thinks they might be made useful."[425]

[424] **Wakarusa War**: The term "war" is a bit harsh. The confrontations and events occurred in late 1855 and bled into 1856. Brewerton arrived at Lawrence in 1856.

[425] Brewerton. Page 283.

Christian's declaration of his pro-slavery beliefs, endorsed by Lud, in the abolitionist stronghold signals the fluidity of the time. Christian's law career took another surprising turn.

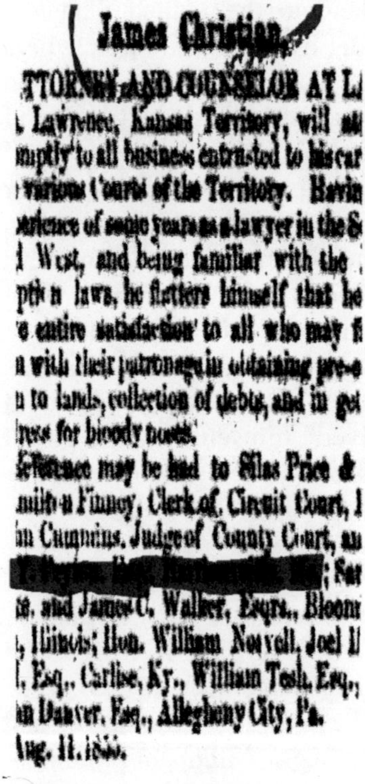
James Christian.
TTORNEY AND COUNSELOR AT L
Lawrence, Kansas Territory, will at
mptly to all business entrusted to his car
various Courts of the Territory. Havin
perience of some years as a lawyer in the S
d West, and being familiar with the
ption laws, he flatters himself that he
e entire satisfaction to all who may f
n with their patronage in obtaining pre-e
n to lands, collection of debts, and in get
ress for bloody noses.
Reference may be had to Silas Price &
milton Finney, Clerk of Circuit Court,
hn Cummins, Judge of County Court, an
[redacted]; Sar
e, and James C. Walker, Esqrs., Bloom
, Illinois; Hon. William Norvell, Joel
, Esq., Carlise, Ky., William Tosh, Esq.,
an Danver, Esq., Allegheny City, Pa.
Aug. 11, 1855.

James Christian Card-
Herald of Freedom

In May 1858 Christian entered a law partnership with James H. Lane, the territory's most radical and violent abolitionist, who just three years later because the scourge of western Missouri. This seemingly unlikely partnership however, fit the "practical workings of law firms that specialize in political law business. Lane was the outstanding Free-State lawyer- Christian was the prominent Democrat, or so-called Pro-Slavery lawyer in the territory. The firm was ambidextrous, therefore, and could meet any legal emergency where a judicious use of political influence might be of advantage to the success of clients."[426] Just a month after the two formed their partnership Christian defended Lane when Lane faced murder charges in the killing of Gaius Jenkins.

Thus, James Christian, during a short eight-year period found himself the close friend and business associate of two quite different men - a fire-eater, Lud Peyton and a radical abolitionist, James H. Lane. The two adversaries represented the most radical extremes in the slavery debate and would shortly become sworn, to the death, enemies.

[426] Malin, James. "Identification of the Stranger at the Pottawatomie Massacre. *Kansas Historical Review*. Vol. 9, No. 1. Page 3.

R.O. Boggess
Kansas City Daily Journal, August 4, 1896

In 1857 Lud finally entered a law partnership with Richard O. Boggess. Their association wedded individual strengths creating Harrisonville's dominant legal team. Lud's long tenure in Cass County and deep ties to the community brought credibility and trust. Richard Boggess brought energy, ambition and drive. In the years leading to the Civil War, the "Peyton & Boggess" law firm expanded and flourished.[427]

Richard O. Boggess, known in public circles as R.O. Boggess settled in Harrisonville early in 1856. He was an ambitious 23-year old bachelor and he arrived with legal credentials. Lud mentored Boggess and sponsored him April 4, 1856 before Russell Hicks at the spring term of the Sixth District Circuit Court.[428] Lud also sponsored Boggess with the Harrisonville Masons.

Filled with energy and drive, Boggess purchased the *Cass County Gazette* late in 1856. His interest in the newspaper was not unusual, often "lawyers were leaders in establishing and editing newspapers."[429] Editing the newspaper provided Boggess local exposure and supplemented his legal income. He renamed the newspaper the *Western Democrat*, changing its politics to the Democratic Party.[430] On May 15, 1858 Boggess announced to *Western Democrat* readers that he had sold the newspaper to Thomas Fogle. Fogle, Boggess assured his readers, would remain true to the politics and direction the newspaper had taken under his leadership – a very strong States' rights position on the political spectrum's far right.

[427] **R.O. Boggess**: Richard O. Boggess resumed his law practice after the Civil War. He was deeply involved in the railroad bond scandal. In 1873 he moved to Kansas City. He died August 3, 1896.
[428] Cass County Record Book. 1855 – 1858.
[429] English. Page 121.
[430] "History of the County Press." Organ, Minnie. *Missouri Historical Review.* Vol. 4, No. 4. July 1910.

Shortly after selling the *Western Democrat* Boggess advertised as a Harrisonville "Attorney at Law."[431] By July 1858 he had expanded his business beyond legal representation and began advertising himself as "Attorney at Law, Notary Public, and General Collecting Agent." Debt collections plagued those with the capital to loan money, merchants and the more affluent citizens. Boggess stepped openly and aggressively into debt collecting. The profession carried two elements, danger and profit. By the end of the year, Peyton and Boggess joined as partners, their professions and politics the same.

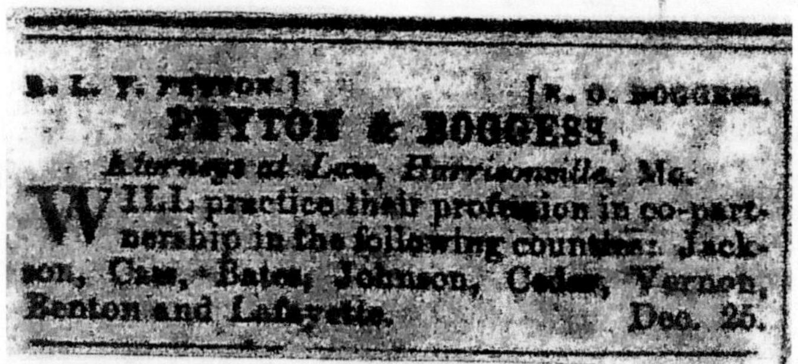

R. L. Y. PEYTON.] [R. O. BOGGESS.
PEYTON & BOGGESS,
Attorneys at Law, Harrisonville, Mo.
WILL practice their profession in co-partnership in the following counties: Jackson, Cass, Bates, Johnson, Cedar, Vernon, Benton and Lafayette. Dec. 25.

Peyton-Boggess business announcement Western Democrat July 21, 1860

The partners expanded their business beyond the Sixth Judicial District. By 1860 their advertisements targeted the Sixth Judicial District counties of Jackson, Lafayette, Johnson, Bates, and Cass as well as Cedar, Benton, and Vernon counties.[432] Richard married Sally Railey, the daughter of Lud's close friend, Tarlton Railey. On the eve of the rebellion Lud and the newlyweds were living in the Arizona House.

431 *Western Democrat*. May 1, 1858.
432 *Western Democrat*. July 28, 1860.

Chapter Seven
Awakening & Rise to Prominence

In 1854 Lud Peyton lived and practiced law, an obscure lawyer, on Missouri's western border. In September 1860, headlined as one of Missouri's most electric orators, he shared a St. Louis podium with two U.S. Senators and Missouri's Governor elect. He was lauded, a young, political rising star. Lud's awakening and rise to prominence narrates a story as engaging and compelling as it was unimaginable!

Lud arrived in Harrisonville, despite his youth, a committed and uncompromising ultra-Southern individual. By birth and cultivation Lud was a native Virginian and he identified as such. Reared in southwest Ohio, an area developed by transplanted Virginians that retained Virginia's southern culture.While at Miami University, Lud's pro-slavery stance had hardened in the ongoing abolitionist conflicts mentored by the family of Harriet and Henry Ward Beecher. The University of Virginia Law School curriculum reinforced Peyton's pro-Southern proclivities anchoring them in constitutional law.

For ten years Peyton's core values and beliefs, were not challenged. Although Lud shared his feelings with friends and acquaintances there was little occasion to publically voice them, and besides, such was not his nature. Western Missouri's communities accepted slavery as a normal part of life. Abolitionist agitation was distant, far off in the east. Politically the people were moderate and status quo. Although slavery entered discussion, Indian issues, railroads, and prairie freighting dominated dialogue. Lud's easy way endeared him to the Harrisonville community and bespoke little of the fire-eater.

Peyton's life, on a variety of levels, hardly hinted at a rapid political ascent. Barely into his 30s, Lud's youth imposed limitations in a political structure where age and hardened political experience were valued. In a frontier society anchored by family and networked by marriage, Peyton's bachelorhood and lack of any immediate family seemingly set him a bit outside. The frontier prairie culture thrived on energy. Although driven by ambition Lud's reputation for procrastination and laziness belied political success. Lud owned no land, no slaves, followed no secondary occupation, and seemingly avoided wealth accumulation like the plague. In a world valuing wealth and status, Lud lived by subsistence. Lud Peyton stood as the antithesis of the American frontiersman! Yet in a matter of years he emerged from comfortable obscurity to statewide notoriety, advocating war.

---------- The Kansas Territory ----------

The Kansas-Nebraska Act, passed by Congress in May 1854, triggered a sequence of events turning the world upside-down. Missouri communities, business, religious, family and individuals, heretofore-distant observers in the national slavery struggle took "front and center." Lud awakened!

In the months immediately preceding the passage of the Kansas – Nebraska Act, Missouri's western border counties positioned themselves to engineer the Kansas Territory's statehood as a slave state. Well before the Kansas–Nebraska Act became law, David R. Atchison and Benjamin F. Stringfellow began organizing the "Platte County Self Defensive Association."[433] Atchison and Stringfellow lived north of the Missouri River. Their organization, initially, begun in April 1854, transitioned into what became known as the Blue Lodges. By the autumn of 1854 Blue Lodge chapters

[433] Ralston. *The Journal of Southern History*. Page 233.

met in most of Missouri's western border counties. Jackson County's lodge membership exceeded "600" men.[434] Cass County's Blue Lodge chapters met in Harrisonville and Pleasant Hill. A Blue Lodge convention in November 1854 directed Jackson and Cass Counties to send representatives to Mississippi, Alabama, and Louisiana soliciting support and financial donations.[435]

Blue Lodge chapters organized Missourians to vote in the Kansas Territorial elections of October 1854 and March 1855. The first election, for a territorial Congressional representative, generated intense interest in Missouri. Missouri voters flowed to Kansas territorial polls. Territorial elections in March 1855 attracted thousands of Missouri voters and Missouri leaders stood as candidates for the territorial legislature.

The first territorial election, scheduled for November 29, 1854, chose a territorial "Delegate to Congress." Three candidates stood for the position, and one Pro-Slavery candidate, J.W. Whitfield ran against two Free-State candidates. Ft. Scott was one of 17 designated polling stations.

Cass and Bates county leaders, Lud among them, rapidly organized a group of Harrisonville men to vote. As the November election day approached, the men loaded wagons with provisions for the three-day trip to Ft. Scott. Their route carried them through West Point and then south to Ft. Scott on the Military Road. Witnesses later reported "a party of about one hundred men from Cass County, and the counties south of it, went into the Territory."[436] When the Missourians arrived at Ft. Scott they set up camps and raised their tents.

---

[434] Ralston. *The Journal of Southern History*. Page 234.
[435] Ralston. *The Journal of Southern History*. Page 234.
[436] *Report of the Special Committee to Investigate the Troubles in Kansas: 1856*. Page 5.

Cass County's contingent contained a host of the community's most influential citizens. Lud represented the legal community. Robert A. Brown, the county's largest slave owner and most respected landowner journeyed with Peyton. Physicians, G.D. Hansbrough, Jacob F. Brookhart and A.B. Sloan, joined the contingent. At this early stage in the opening of the Kansas Territory, there was high interest along the border in Kansas entering the Union as a slave state. Although an influx of New England emigrants had begun, expectations, local and national, were that Nebraska would enter the Union a Free State and Kansas a Slave State. The high number of Cass County voters underscored the importance of the issue in Missouri.

Ft. Scott's voting proceeded peacefully and uneventfully. When voters appeared, "some attempts were made to swear them, but two of the judges were prevailed upon not to do so, and none were sworn."[437] Voting commenced; Lud was voter 101 of the total 105. J.W. Whitfield, the Pro-Slavery candidate, received all 105 votes. When voting concluded, "the Missourians went to their wagons and commenced leaving for home."[438] There were no reported incidents of confrontation or violence.

As new settlers established residence and began interaction, the Kansas Territory began to assume an early identity. Lawrence, named for New England abolitionist Amos Lawrence, became known to Missourians as "the abolitionist capital" because of the flood of eastern settlers funded by the New England Emigrant Society. Missourians also moved into the territory staking land claims and establishing farms. Many arrived in the territory with their slaves.

---

[437] *Report of the Special Committee to Investigate the Troubles in Kansas: 1856*. Page 5.

[438] *Report of the Special Committee to Investigate the Troubles in Kansas: 1856*. Page 5.

In addition to differences over slavery, a natural culture clash ensued. The Missouri settlers, products of the traditions of Virginia and Kentucky, rose from frontier stock. Hard work, heavy drinking and entertainments were cultural foundations. The New England emigrants, of traditional English puritan stock, chaffed against the rough hewn humanity of the Missourians. Each group took exception with the other.

It did not take long for serious tensions to surface. Lawrence's abolitionists requested arms from their eastern benefactors. The first Sharp's Rifles arrived at Lawrence by mid-summer 1855 and soon terrified settlers along the border.[439] At the time, Sharp's rifle reinvented rifle accuracy, distance and payload. These weapons, universally known as "Beecher's Bibles" because of Henry Ward Beecher's efforts to supply them to the abolitionist settlers, immediately swayed the balance of power along the border.

The Beecher name, linked to rifles aimed at western Missouri, by abolitionist agitators set Lud aflame. Both the Beecher's and abolitionist assaults held fast in his early Oxford memories. The unfolding events in Kansas represented physical aggression against all he believed. For Lud, it was a call to action.

---------- Cass County's Political Reach ----------

Cass County politicians exercised statewide influence throughout the decade of the 1850s. This was particularly true from 1854 to 1861. Like most of Missouri, Cass County had historically voted with Senator Thomas Hart Benton's Democracy party. The Whig Party had a presence in western Missouri but never enjoyed a political base as strong as the Benton Democracy. However, after

439 Reese. 484-V1.

1848, Benton's political foundation eroded, then quickly evaporated.

Sen. Thomas Hart Benton
Author's Collection

Benton's fading power surfaced in local elections, as did the demise of Missouri's Whig party. Politicians waded in a divisive, turbulent river where slavery, railroads, land, and immigration defined debate. Throughout the 1850s Missouri's chaotic political world dissolved from a two party (Democracy and Whig) contest to a four party free-for-all during the 1860 Presidential election. Cass County politicians played significant roles, regionally and statewide, in the events that opened the doors for Lud's political emergence.

Charles Sims, one of Harrisonville's earliest lawyers, accepted the Anti-Benton Democrats' nomination for Missouri Lt. Governor in 1856. Although initially a Benton Democrat, Sims split with Benton, as did many fellow Democrats. Sims had represented Cass County in the Missouri House of Representatives from 1848 to 1854.

He set his political sights next on a seat in the Missouri Senate. In 1854, in a closely contested senatorial election against Harrisonville Whig, Hugh Glenn, Sims won by less than a hundred votes. Sims's statewide political base grew. In 1856, when the anti-Benton Democrats nominated Trusten Polk for Governor, Sims had positioned himself to accept the party's nomination for Lt. Governor.

When Sims moved into the Senate, in 1854, Hiram B. Standiford replaced him in the Missouri House of Representatives. Standiford was elected as a Benton Democrat and he remained steadfast to the Benton cause. A long time Cass County resident, Standiford had served as County Sheriff. His election to the House was a testament to his character because the county electorate was moving away from Benton.

Richard W. Cummins moved near Westport in Jackson County, Missouri in 1831. For almost twenty years Cummins worked as an Indian Agent, earning respect for his fairness and honesty. Cummins became a personal friend of Senator Thomas Hart Benton and as such, stood a stalwart Benton Democrat. After leaving the Indian Agency in 1849, Cummins moved to Cass County. He had, through two decades, accumulated significant land holdings and wealth; when he relocated to Cass County he was one of its largest slave owners. By virtue of reputation and status, Cummins exercised considerable personal influence throughout western Missouri.

William H. Russell settled in Cass County for a few years in the 1850s. Russell had represented Callaway County in the Missouri House of Representatives (1838 – 1840) prior to moving to California. By 1850 Russell was back in Missouri, settling in Jackson County, before moving to Cass County. He led Cass County's delegation to the 1855 Lexington Pro-Slavers Convention. A former Whig, Russell became a key statewide leader of Missouri's American Party (Know-Nothing Party). Russell's statewide influence and leadership resulted in his being named President of the American Party's state convention at St. Louis in April 1856.

The American Party, largely due to Russell's presence, exercised considerable political clout in Cass County during the 1850s.

Politicians, William M. Briscoe and John F. Callaway, both vocal and respected, carried the American banner. By the mid-1850s, both men were well established, long time residents of Cass County.

David Brookhart, sixty-two years old, moved to Cass County from Maryland in 1852. Brookhart built an estate, "Brookhart Hill," southwest of Harrisonville. His son, Jacob F. Brookhart, opened a medical practice in Harrisonville. Both father and son stepped energetically into local and state politics. David arrived in Harrisonville a seasoned politician and public servant. An attorney, he had served in the Maryland House of Delegates eight terms, 16 years.[440]

Immediately upon arrival in Cass County Brookhart stepped into local politics as an Anti-Benton Democrat and later was elected a Judge of the Cass County Court. The 1856 Missouri Democratic State Convention selected Brookhart as an alternate delegate to the Democratic National Convention.

Dr. W.H.H. Cundiff- Author's Collection

Dr. W.H.H. Cundiff settled in Pleasant Hill in 1855 opening a medical practice. A Benton Democrat, Cundiff ran for the Missouri House of Representatives in 1856 as a member of the Union Democratic Party. A slavery opponent, Cundiff lost the election in a closely contested race, only to challenge the result and have the initial tally overturned. Cundiff's political

[440] *Cass County, Missouri, Families*. PP. 36-37.

position aligned with that of his neighbor, Joseph Christopher. Christopher had served in the Kentucky legislature and had also settled near Pleasant Hill.

These Cass County politicians flexed political muscle locally, regionally, and statewide. Their divergent positions covered a broad political spectrum. In 1854 and 1855 the presence and power of these men left little room for Lud Peyton's radicalism. That said, circumstances and events quickly changed the political landscape.

---------- Political Winds Shift: 1848 to 1854 ----------

Lud won a seat in the Missouri Senate the first week in August 1858. He defeated his opponent, James Hudson, by a total vote of 3,389 to 309. The vote belies Lud's journey to victory as well as the overall circumstances of his win. Up to this point, Lud's 10-year political odyssey followed failure, rejection, and fortuitous circumstance.

Six years before the Kansas – Nebraska Act, Lud, then just 24 years old, had thrown his hat into judicial politics. In 1848, four years after arriving at Harrisonville, Lud ran for Circuit Attorney of the Sixth Judicial District. At the time, the Sixth District contained seven counties: Jackson, Cass, Bates, Lafayette, Johnson, Saline, and Pettis. Lud's opponent, Samuel L. Sawyer of Lexington, was already an experienced Circuit Attorney and seasoned politician. Politically a Whig, Sawyer's sterling reputation served him well in heavily Democratic western Missouri.[441]

[441] **Note**: Samuel L. Sawyer's political career was long and productive. Sawyer was elected to the Missouri Constitutional Convention in 1861, the Convention voting to remain in the Union. Sawyer eventually moved to Independence, Mo. Sawyer served in the U.S. House of Representatives from 1879 to 1881.

Lud entered the election late, either on a personal whim or pushed by local Democrats needing a candidate against the Whigs. Lud prevailed in Cass and Bates counties, but was soundly defeated in the other five counties. Defeated and humbled, he disappeared from the political spotlight, not to reappear for six years.

The same year of Lud's defeat, slavery's explosive, divisive presence surfaced in Missouri politics and put its stamp on Van Buren County. Charles Sims, Van Buren County's newly elected state representative, introduced a bill to change the county's name. Martin Van Buren, the county's namesake, had "softened" his position on slavery during the presidential campaign. Van Buren's presidential opponent, Lewis Cass, held firm to the U.S. Constitution's codification of slavery. In response, Sims championed a name change and in 1848 Van Buren County became Cass County. The county's name change reaffirmed its place in Missouri's slave culture.

Five months after Samuel Sawyer's victory over Lud, Claiborne F. Jackson introduced the "Jackson Resolutions" to the Missouri assembly. Jackson's resolutions declared,

> "…that Congress had no constitutional power to legislate on the subject of slavery in the territories except on the question of fugitive slaves, that any right to prohibit slavery in any territory belongs exclusively to the people there and could only be exercised by them at the time of the framing of a constitution for statehood, and that the conduct of the northern states on the subject of slavery had released the slaveholding states from adherence to the Missouri Compromise line, even if such act ever did impose any obligation upon the slaveholding states. The resolutions sanctioned by the application of the principle of the Missouri Compromise to the newly

> acquired territory for the sake of harmony and the preservation of the Union, but in the event of the passage of any act in conflict with the above principles they declared that Missouri would cooperate with the slaveholding states in such measures as might be necessary for their mutual protection against northern fanaticism. The resolutions further instructed Missouri's United States senators to act in conformity with their terms."[442]

Jackson's resolutions passed both Missouri houses with large majorities. Senator Benton, upon learning of the resolutions, declared them "fundamentally wrong."[443] He returned to Missouri from Washington, D.C. traversing the state opposing the resolutions. The rift between the Missouri General Assembly and Senator Benton eventually resulted in the split of Missouri's Democratic Party into Benton and Anti-Benton factions. This division had an impact in Cass County, eventually aiding Lud's political ascent.

Elections during the summer of 1850 put Benton's 30-year grip on Missouri to the test. In western Missouri, Richard W. Cummins, a 62-year old Cass County slave owner and Benton Democrat ran for the state senate. Cummins entered the race late, drafted by 45 local Benton Democrats just five weeks before Election Day.

Cummins accepted the nomination and in early July stated, "I am his (Benton's) personal as well as political friend; and you cannot find any man who will sustain him, that I will not support. I have been personally acquainted with Col. Benton for at least forty years, and I always regarded him as a high-minded, independent and honorable gentleman. I think his enemies have done him great

[442] McCandless. Page 247.
[443] Phillips. Page 172.

injustice."[444] Cummins's political opponents were Alvan Brooking, a Whig, and Duke W. Simpson, both Jackson County residents.

The first week in August 1850 the votes were counted and the election was a clear defeat for the Benton Democrats. . Alvan Brooking carried Jackson County by a significant majority and overall, defeated Cummins by 154 votes.[445] Duke W. Simpson came in a distant third. After the election, Cummins permanently retired from politics, and moved to Bates County. The statewide vote went against Benton and he lost his seat in the U.S. Senate ending his 30-year tenure. Benton continued fighting to regain control of Missouri's Democratic Party but never succeeded.

Although Cummins's defeat put a crack in the Benton Democrats' hold on western Missouri, the defeat did not completely eliminate Benton's power and presence. The same day Richard Cummins lost to Brooking, Charles Sims, then a stalwart Benton Democrat, won Cass County's seat in the House of Representatives. Sims handily defeated his Whig opponent, Martin Rice, by a vote of 455 to 278.[446] Two years later, 1852, Sims ran unopposed retaining his seat in the House.

In 1854 Sims decided to take a step up to the state Senate and he ran against a Harrisonville Whig, Hugh Glenn. The 25th Senate District included Jackson, Cass, Lafayette, and Johnson counties. Although losing to Glenn in Jackson County, Sims carried Cass and Bates counties by huge majorities securing a victory.[447]

Cass County's electorate supported individual character and reputation, over political party affiliation. In August 1854, when Charles Sims, a long time Benton Democrat switched sides and ran

[444] *Jefferson Inquirer*. July 20, 1850. Page 3.
[445] Missouri Secretary of State. Election Returns. Box 4. File 38.
[446] Missouri Secretary of State. Election Returns. Box 4. File 38.
[447] Missouri Secretary of State. Election Returns. Box 5. File 32.

successfully on the Anti-Benton ticket, his vacated seat in the House was filled by Hiram B. Standiford. Standiford ran as a Benton Democrat and slavery opponent. Standiford's success stands out because Bates and Jackson counties elected anti-Benton, strong pro-slavery proponents, John E. Morgan and John W. Reid respectively.

Cass County's mid-1850s voters, although pro-slavery, supported moderate, mainstream political positions. There is no evidence the community, in total, subscribed to the ironclad, ultra-Southern doctrine Lud advocated. This chemistry makes Lud's successful move into political office the more intriguing. Other issues and events were afoot; fear factors increased local anxiety and opened opportunities.

---------- Slavery, Religion and Abolition ----------

Missouri's border counties were acutely sensitive to fugitive slaves and abolitionist efforts encouraging runaway slaves. This sensitivity prevailed in all of Missouri's border counties, those abutting Illinois, Iowa, and the Kansas Territory. Border counties, susceptible to slave stealing and slave runaways, responded by vigilance and regular patrols sealing the border.

The Methodist Church, having split into "North" and "South" denominations in 1844, became a magnet for slave driven confrontations. The Methodist presence in Missouri was significant and the friction between Methodist South congregations and Methodist North ministers intensified over time. Furthermore, along Missouri's western border Kansan abolitionist activity ratcheted the tension. In 1855 these three volatile elements, fugitive slaves, Methodist North abolitionists, and the border intersected in Lud's community and indirectly began to open doors.

Friction between Missouri and newly arrived abolitionists in Kansas, prompted Missouri's slave interests to convene a Pro-Slavery Convention at Lexington in Lafayette County. Twenty-four Missouri counties sent delegates. The convention met for three days and issued an "Address: To the People of the United States;" the address discussed slavery defining Missouri's position. Wm. B. Napton, Sterling Price, Mordecai Oliver, and Samuel H.Woodson[448] signed the 15-page document. At the time, all four men were leading governmental and judicial leaders.

Cass County's delegates to the convention were:

Squire G. Allen	Tarlton Railey
John F. Callaway	H.D. Russell
T.R. Crockett	William H. Russell
T.F. Freeman	J.T. Thornton
Dr. G.D. Hansbrough	Clayton Van Hoy
F.R. Martin	Caleb T. Worley
William Palmer	

The convention adjourned in mid-July and the delegates, acutely sensitive to abolitionist attacks, returned home, ever more vigilant. Several of Cass County's delegates became immediately involved in the capture, trial, and expulsion of a Methodist North minister, the Rev. W.H. Wiley.

The Rev. Wiley had been temporarily assigned to Cass County as a replacement for Wiley Jones, a Methodist North circuit minister and abolitionist, who had thoughtfully relocated to Prairie City in the Kansas Territory.

Rev. Wiley's expulsion elevated Cass County into Missouri's limelight, also attracting attention in the Kansas Territory. The

[448] **Note**: Samuel H. Woodson served two terms in the U.S. Congress representing western Missouri. Woodson was elected as an American Party candidate.

Daily Missouri Democrat, at St. Louis, published a letter from Rev. Wiley on August 11, 1855.[449] Rev. Wiley wrote that on July 26 two men, one of whom was Col. (Caleb) Worley stopped him on a Cass County country lane. Shortly thereafter 16 additional riders joined Col. Worley. The posse accused Rev. Wiley of "inciting slaves to escape, and of preaching abolitionist doctrine."[450]

Wiley was escorted to Harrisonville to "have charges investigated."[451] Suspicion against him had surfaced three weeks prior to his capture when John A. Tuggle, a Methodist South congregant, wrote an accusatory article published in the *Cass County Gazette*. Two weeks later, "two negroes attempted to escape from Harrisonville" and Wiley was charged with inciting the attempted escape to Kansas.[452]

Rev. Wiley was escorted to Harrisonville and placed under guard at the Harrisonville Hotel. The next morning William J. Taylor, the Rev. S.G. Allen, and one Mr. Bailey examined all of the minister's papers searching for incriminating evidence. Conducted to the courthouse Rev. Wiley was examined by a local tribunal. Dr. Joseph L. Maxwell chaired the proceedings. Dr. Guilford D. Hansbrough, Col. Caleb Worley and the Rev. Squire G. Allen seconded Maxwell. Dr. Hansbrough had just returned from Lexington where he had been a delegate to the Pro-Slavery Convention. Once proceedings began at the courthouse, Dr. Hansbrough informed Wiley the investigation had found Wiley guilty of "aiding some negroes in running off."[453] Additionally, Hansbrough continued, Wiley had been "preaching abolitionist doctrines and circulating abolitionist documents."[454] The Rev.

[449] *Daily Missouri Democrat*. August 11, 1855. Page 2.
[450] *Daily Missouri Democrat*. August 11, 1855. Page 2.
[451] *Daily Missouri Democrat*. August 11, 1855. Page 2.
[452] *Daily Missouri Democrat*. August 11, 1855. Page 2.
[453] *Daily Missouri Democrat*. August 11, 1855. Page 2.
[454] *Daily Missouri Democrat*. August 11, 1855. Page 2.

Wiley was given seven days to leave Missouri and forbidden from going to the Kansas Territory.

Rev. Wiley fled to St. Louis. His letter to the *Daily Missouri Democrat* stated that the assembly at the Cass County courthouse contained 200 citizens. Two weeks later, Lawrence's abolitionist newspaper the *Herald of Freedom* published excerpts from Wiley's letter. Border divisions widened and the intensity of the angst rose.[455]

Cass County citizens had also recently discussed and endorsed the Fabius Township Resolutions.[456] The Fabius Township Resolutions, had been issued by residents of Marion County, Mo., February 18, 1854 in response to the disappearance of 15 slaves.[457] Methodist North ministers had encouraged the slaves to flee Missouri. The Fabius Township Resolutions contained five points. Collectively the five resolutions banned abolitionists from "'visiting and preaching'" and empowered the residents "'to resort to the use of such means as will afford us protection.'"[458] The resolutions strongly affirmed slavery. Similar meetings and resolutions followed in Jackson and Cass counties.[459]

These events, the summer of 1855, amplified the anxiety level of Cass County citizens and voters. The community understandably viewed itself as being under attack from without and within. The public dialogue assumed a higher pitched, more aggressive tone. Lud entered the public forum with a ferocious message.

---

455 **Note**: See the Appendix for a complete transcription of the newspaper articles.
456 Leftwich. Page 104.
457 Leftwich. Page 100.
458 Leftwich. Page 101.
459 Leftwich. Page 104.

---------- Doors Open & Peyton's Fire ----------

Angered and awakened Lud stepped on the public stage. When Cass County's Democratic Party met, in Harrisonville, July 1855, Peyton spoke explosively from the steps of the courthouse. Lud unleashed his extreme ultra-Southern opinions, till now privately shared, into public consciousness.

J.T. Leonard, a Peyton friend and proprietor of the Harrisonville Hotel, remembered the speech. According to Leonard, Peyton's oration contained the following:

> "My countrymen, the immortal patriots of the Revolution are looking down from their abodes above upon you. The eyes of the world are upon you. Yet you do not comprehend the gravity of the situation. You have eyes and see not, ears and hear not. Men cry peace, peace, and you believe in peace because no sound of war is yet heard – no plundering army tramples these fields, no ruthless soldiery yet disturbs the fond mother or the tender infant, no hireling robbers have yet violated your homes or applied incendiary torch at midnight to your dwellings. False or delusive belief! Mark my words!
>
> Unless we take in the situation at once and become united – unless the South presents a solid front to her enemies – it united, knit together in a solid phalanx, we are lost. The invader will come like the barbarians of old from the North, and before another harvest sweep over these peaceful fields, tramping you down with the iron heel of war, and finally delivering you and your posterity over to the soul-piercing agonies of tyranny and oppression."[460]

Lud's spewed vehemence, deeply sincere, differed significantly from the attitudes of his listeners. Although the audience shared concerns about slavery and changes in the Kansas Territory, they remained moderate, not yet accepting the apocalyptic threat Lud

[460] Peyton, John Lewis. Page 396.

forewarned. Lud's message and the community's listening remained divergent.

Shortly after Lud's fiery appeal to Harrisonville's citizens, the first of several fateful events, occurred that would open the door for Lud's ascent. Hiram B. Standiford, Cass County's representative in the state assembly, and devoted Benton Democrat, announced his resignation. His resignation was reported in Columbia's *Weekly Missouri Statesman*, "Capt. H.B. Standiford, Representative from Cass County has resigned his position in the Legislature. Col. Wm. Russell and Joel Snyder, Esq., are proposed in the *Gazette* as candidates for the vacancy."[461] Simultaneous with his resignation, Standiford announced his intention to move to the Kansas Territory.[462]

Standiford's departure opened Cass County's House seat. William Russell stepped out as a potential replacement candidate and Lud announced for the open seat. He evidently, "became a candidate a few days before the election, and was defeated by a small minority."[463] This report of Snyder's margin of victory may have been misleading.

The local powers and the electorate were not quite ready to endorse Lud's extreme political doctrine. Joel Snyder the local Democratic moderate carried the election over Lud on October 29, 1855. The election results were reported in the *Weekly Missouri Statesman*: "The election to fill the vacancy in the Mo. legislature, caused by the resignation of H.B. Standiford of Cass County, came off on

[461] *Weekly Missouri Statesman*. November 2, 1855.
[462] **Note**: Hiram B. Standiford did move to the Kansas Territory. He founded the town of Stanton. Standiford died January 2, 1858 of natural causes at the age of 58.
[463] *History of Cass and Bates Counties, Mo.* Page 378.

Monday week, and Joel Snyder (Whig) was elected over R.L.Y. Peyton, by near, one hundred majority."[464]

Three months after winning the seat, Snyder died of natural causes, February 4, 1856. The county's seat in the Missouri House remained vacant until filled in the elections of August 1858.

Undeterred, Lud returned to his law practice while remaining deeply involved in the Anti-Benton Democratic Party. The month following Joel Snyder's untimely death, Lud entered the Cass County courthouse to partner with Charles Sims in defending murder suspect, James Preston. Preston was acquitted largely due to Lud's closing arguments. This magnificent oratorical performance resonated throughout western Missouri's political and legal communities.

In 1856, politics dominated Missouri's spring and summer. The upcoming August elections would select a Governor, Lt. Gov., and other state officials as well as Congressmen. The statewide political structure had evolved into three parties: (1) Benton Democrats (2) Anti-Benton Democrats and (3) the American or "Know-Nothing Party." Cass County politicians played significant roles in the Anti-Benton Democrats and the American Party – both parties held state conventions in April 1856. The American Party held its state convention in St. Louis. The convention began "…April 17, 1856. George R. Smith of Pettis County called it to order. William H. Russell of Cass County was elected permanent chairman and Thomas A. Harris of Marion County, Secretary."[465] William Russell's statewide leadership in the American Party tied him closely to three prominent western Missouri politicians, Lafayette County's Robert C. Ewing, Pettis County's George R.

---

464 *Weekly Missouri Statesman*. November 9, 1855.
465 Ryle, Walter H. "Slavery and Party Realignment in Missouri in the State Election of 1856." Page 327.

Smith, and Jackson County's Samuel H. Woodson. Robert Ewing won the American Party's gubernatorial nomination while Woodson ran for the U.S. Congress as an American Party candidate. Woodson, the previous July, had been President Pro-Temp of the Lexington Pro-Slavery Convention.

Russell's American Party exerted considerable clout in Cass County. John F. Callaway and William M. Briscoe were strong American Party members. Over the next few years both ran for public office on the American Party ticket.

Several Cass County leaders played key roles in the 1856 Anti-Benton Democratic convention at Jefferson City. Charles Sims, the State Senator representing the 24th Senatorial District, led the county's delegation. Joining Sims at the convention were Lud Peyton and David Brookhardt.

Wednesday, April 23, the convention nominated Trusten Polk for Governor. Shortly thereafter the convention nominated Charles Sims for Lt. Governor. Sims's nomination was unanimously adopted.[466] The *St. Joseph Gazette* praised the Sim's selection:

> "Charles Sims, the second name on our ticket, is a high-minded gentleman, and has long been the gallant leader of the Democracy of his county. First a member of the House, and then of the Senate, in both an active and influential representative. So go on through the whole ticket. Each gentleman is eminently qualified for the station for which his name is offered, and if elected, will, do honor to themselves and reflect credit upon the sagacity of the people."[467]

During the convention David Brookhardt was chosen an alternate to the National Convention from the Fifth District.[468] In an ironic

466 *Jefferson Examiner*. May 2, 1856.
467 *Jefferson Examiner*. June 21, 1856.
468 *Jefferson Examiner*. April 26, 1856.

twist, Robert T. Van Horn from Kansas City was chosen as the other alternate; just five years later, Van Horn, having switched allegiances, would lead Union troops into Cass County in the first major battle of western Missouri's Civil War.

Lud was chosen to be the Cass County Elector during the upcoming campaign. J.W. Torbert of Cooper County was designated as the overall Fifth District coordinator. Other Fifth District county electors were Capt. John W. Reid of Jackson Co., George W. Seibert of Cooper Co., William Anderson of Lafayette Co., John W. Bryant of Saline Co., Major Martin of Benton Co., and A. Glasscock of Pettis County.[469] Bryant had been the Prosecuting Attorney in the James Preston murder trial just three weeks before the convention. John W. Reid was among the most prominent Missouri pro-slavery leaders and within a matter of months would lead Missouri troops into the Kansas Territory to fight John Brown at Osawatomie.

Lud's participation in the Anti-Benton Convention played a critical first step in his political ascent. Under Charles Sims's tutelage, Lud gained experience and knowledge in political organization. During the convention Lud was able to expand and deepen his network of political contacts.

The months following the convention, May through September, were among the most violent along the Missouri – Kansas Territory border. The crisis drew national attention to Missouri's western border. The disorder and escalating violence created opportunities for political radicals on both sides of the confrontation – Lud's position remained constant while escalating tensions opened the community's thinking about the threat.

[469] *Jefferson Examiner.* May 2, 1856.

The period between the spring political conventions and the August elections, captured the nation's attention. Border violence escalated. A.G. Boone, a Westport leader, issued a call for assistance to all western Missouri counties. Boone's appeal was published in the *Cass County Gazette*.[470] The day following Boone's plea for help Missouri "Border Ruffians" torched downtown Lawrence. In response, John Brown planned and led the bloody Pottawatomie Massacre. Charles Sumner was beaten senseless and nearly killed on the floor of the United States Senate.

Violence crisscrossed the border and common criminals joined the chaos taking full advantage of the situation. Horse thieves from Kansas were captured and jailed in Harrisonville.[471] David Atchison's "Army of Law and Order" invaded the Kansas Territory. Throughout the summer of 1856, as Missouri's political campaigns rolled toward August elections, events inside the Kansas Territory and along Missouri's western border shaped the mood of the local electorate.

Then, just days before the August election, Charles Sims made an announcement that would have a profound impact on Lud's political aspirations. Sims withdrew from the Lt. Governor race and removed his name from the Anti-Benton Ticket. The *Jefferson Examiner* reported that Sims's decision was driven by "his proposed removal to Kansas. He heartily approves the Democratic Platform, and supports Polk for Governor."[472] Sims was replaced on the ticket by Randolph County's Hancock L. Jackson.

As later events foretold, Charles Sims would have been Missouri's Governor had he remained on the Anti-Benton Democratic ticket. Trusten Polk won the gubernatorial election and then almost

[470] *Cass County Democrat*. August 20, 1963.
[471] Conrad. Page 213.
[472] *Jefferson Examiner*. July 19, 1856.

immediately decided to vacate the Governor's chair for the open seat in the U.S. Senate. Hancock Jackson, Sims's last minute replacement on the ticket, then became Governor. Thus, had Sims not removed himself from the ticket, he, rather than Hancock Jackson would had become Missouri's Governor.

Throughout the tumultuous summer of '56, Lud campaigned vigorously for the Anti-Benton Democratic Ticket. There is no evidence he participated in the Kansas Territorial violence. Charles Sims's announcement created a political, leadership vacuum in western Missouri, and Lud unexpectedly found himself positioned to fill the vacuum.

The 1856 election results reflected both the times and the populace's mood. Strong pro-slavers John W. Reid and James Chiles were chosen to represent Jackson County in the Missouri House. Bates County placed John Clymer, a slave owner and long time border resident, in the Missouri House.

Cass County's contest for the Missouri House between John F. Callaway and W.H.H. Cundiff was surprisingly very, very tight. Callaway ran on the American Party ticket. Cundiff, a Pleasant Hill resident, ran on the Union Democratic Party Ticket (Benton Democratic Party).[473] When the votes were counted Callaway had bested Cundiff by a mere two votes, 501 to 499.[474] When the House convened Callaway's credentials were accepted and he took Cass County's seat. Cundiff contested the vote and won; two votes on each side were reversed giving Cundiff a two-vote victory. Cundiff took Callaway's now empty seat in the House.[475] Samuel H. Woodson won the Congressional race. Woodson represented the

[473] *History of Cass and Bates Counties, Mo*. Page 487.
[474] Missouri Secretary of State. Archives. Elections. Box 6. File 13.
[475] *Journal of the House of Representatives of the State of Missouri*. Nineteenth General Assembly. Page 217.

strongest pro-slavery positions and espoused the American Party's nativist doctrine.

Following the 1856 elections Lud continued his law practice and watched as the political landscape moved in his favor. The 1857 August elections produced results conducive to Lud's political beliefs. David Brookhardt won a chair on the County Court. Brookhardt, a slave owner and Anti-Benton Democrat, remained Lud's close ally.

Russell Hicks' successful election as circuit judge of the Sixth Judicial District was equally promising to Lud's political aspirations. Hicks represented a long-standing and traditional affinity for the South. He had been one of the original trustees in Kansas City. Within the judicial community Hicks was both respected and feared. Hicks had become, through their long association, Lud's friend and mentor.

A final 1857 political result foretold Lud's future. Robert M. Stewart became Governor, defeating James S. Rollins by "slightly more than 300 votes in a total over 95,000" cast.[476] Stewart carried Jackson and Bates counties by significant majorities but lost in Cass County 494 to 592 receiving 45.5% of the total vote. Rollins's victory in Cass County can be attributed to his American Party affiliation; the American Party continued to hold sway in Cass County. The county's electorate demonstrated a willingness to move away from its moderate position.

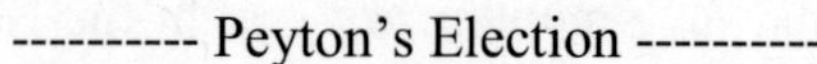

---------- Peyton's Election ----------

Lud's political ambitions brightened in 1858 but his success was uncertain until the August elections. Two major developments fueled Lud's rise to the Missouri Senate.

[476] McCandless. Page 283.

The first major factor was the deteriorating situation along the Missouri – Kansas Territory border in 1857 and 1858. James Montgomery's presence at Ft. Scott and his aggressive behavior toward pro-slavery families in both the Kansas Territory and western Missouri escalated tensions. Vernon, Bates and Cass counties were flooded with refugees driven out of the Kansas Territory by Montgomery's men. In April, Montgomery issued a threatening proclamation to pro-slavers to leave the territory. Tensions between Montgomery and the town of West Point in Bates County reached a climax in late May 1858.

Charles Hamelton, a disgruntled pro-slaver, led a party of 25 to 30 men into the territory, May 19, where they murdered five men and wounded five others.[477] Hamelton's attack became known as the Marais des Cygne Massacre. The massacre ignited the entire western border. Missouri Gov. Stewart sent Adjutant-General G.B. Parsons to Cass and Bates counties to assess the trouble.

Throughout the summer, jayhawking raids into Missouri increased tensions. Missouri's electorate, unsettled, anxious and fearful, began listening to voices, like Lud's, championing aggressive responses and warning of the imminent danger.

The second salient factor assisting Lud's political ascent was the unusual political landscape in western Missouri. Charles Sims, the sitting State Senator, left an open seat when he moved to the Kansas Territory. Hiram B. Standiford, Cass County's Representative had also moved across the border. John F. Callaway had lost his seat in the Missouri House to W.H.H. Cundiff. Cundiff, although House incumbent, championed a political position being daily undercut by border violence. David Brookhardt although recently elected to Cass County's County Court battled failing health. Joel Snyder, the

[477] Welch. Page 103.

moderate Democrat, who had defeated Lud for Standiford's vacant House seat, had suddenly died. In total, all created a huge political vacuum, and significant opportunity.

William M. Briscoe announced his 1858 candidacy for Cass County's seat in the Missouri House. Briscoe's opponent was A.S. O'Bannon. Briscoe ran on the nativist American Party (Know-Nothing) platform while O'Bannon's position closely aligned with Cundiff's Unionist position.

----- Two Open Seats: U.S. House & State Senate -----

Charles Sims's announced move to Kansas vacated his seat in the Missouri Senate. In addition to Sims's Missouri Senate seat, western Missouri's Congressional seat, hotly contested, seemed up for grabs.

Congressional House incumbent, Samuel H. Woodson, of the American Party, faced growing opposition from splinters of the Democratic Party as well as from ultra-Southern voices demanding an aggressive response to the Kansan abolitionist threats. Until the final Congressional candidates surfaced, potential candidates for Sims's vacant Missouri Senate seat waited. Further complicating the murky political waters, squabbles between competing Democratic county organizations, split Jackson, Cass and Bates counties.

The 5th District Congressional seat remained up for grabs. Lud was in the running for Congress. The Democrats met at Georgetown, April 26, and were unable to agree on a candidate. In mid-May the Cass County National Democrats announced they favored Lud as their first choice and the incumbent Woodson as their second choice. Over the next eight weeks Jackson County's John W. Reid and Samuel Woodson surfaced as the final candidates. On July 5,

Pettis County's George R. Smith threw his hat into the ring. The strength and public recognition of these three candidates terminated Lud's Congressional ambitions.

Missouri's Fifth Congressional District

The state's 14th District open senatorial seat, initially attracted the interest from a host of willing candidates. Traditionally the nomination process dictated that local conventions select candidates and make the announcements in April – four months ahead of the August elections. The 14th district's Democratic convention convened at Butler, Bates County, the spring of 1858. When the district convention adjourned no state senatorial candidate had been named.[478] The race remained open.

Two men seemed reasonable choices to "step-up" to the state Senate. John W. Reid and James Chiles were Jackson County's incumbents in the Missouri House. Both were politically seasoned, well known, and a comfortable political fit for the electorate. Reid took himself out of a possible Missouri Senate candidacy when he announced for Congress, opposing Woodson.[479]

Missouri's 14th Senatorial District

478 *The Liberty Tribune*. June 18, 1858.
479 *The Liberty Tribune*. July 2, 1858.

The *Liberty Tribune* announced, "Col. (James) Chiles of Jackson County, has announced himself as a candidate for Senator, from the Counties of Jackson, Cass and Bates."[480] The same article announcing Col. Chiles as a candidate also mentioned the possibility of James M. Cogswell, of Butler, running as Chiles's opponent. Cogswell, advanced in years, never formally announced as a candidate.[481] Others however did throw their hats into the ring. Harrisonville's Squire Allen and Jackson County's Dr. Caleb Winfrey announced their intentions to stand for election.[482]

Bates County Democrats backed Squire Allen at a convention in early July. Squire Allen's ambitions sprang from his long tenure and leadership at Harrisonville. Allen operated one of the town's hotels and had long participated in local government. He was well respected in both Cass and Bates Counties. James Chiles and Dr. Caleb Winfrey labored under the weight of being from Jackson County. The recent border confrontations were centered in Cass and Bates Counties and these two counties strongly opposed further political power being anchored in Jackson County. In mid-July when the Democrats met at Harrisonville the candidacies of Chiles, Allen, and Winfrey evaporated when Lud, no longer a favorite for Congress, announced his availability for the Missouri Senate and grabbed the nomination.

At this juncture in his political career, Lud had never won an election, having lost to Samuel Sawyer in 1848 and Joel Snyder in October 1855. Lud had never held public office. However, when the votes were tallied Lud received 91.6% of the 3,694 votes cast.[483]

---

[480] *The Liberty Tribune*. June 18, 1858.

[481] **Note:** James M. Cogswell, prior to moving to Butler, had resided in the northeast corner of Jackson County. The Cogswell family had lived in Jackson County for over a decade before their move to Bates County. Undoubtedly, James M. Cogswell and James Chiles, a neighbor, had a longstanding relationship.

[482] *Harrisonville Western Democrat*. July 10, 1858.

[483] Missouri Secretary of State. Elections. Box 7. File 10.

His lone opponent, James Hudson, was less known; Hudson had never run for office, or held an office and following the election sank again into political obscurity. Essentially Lud had run unopposed, the electorate not given the choice of a moderate candidate. With his victory, Lud, like his grandfather and father before him, stepped into significant public service.

---------- The Missouri Senate ----------

Prior to taking his seat in the Missouri Senate, Lud formed a partnership with Harrisonville attorney Richard O. Boggess. Boggess also edited and published the Harrisonville Democratic newspaper. When Lud departed for Jefferson City, Boggess assumed responsibility for their law practice.

In late December 1858, Lud journeyed to Jefferson City to take his seat in the Missouri Senate. Four western Missourians accompanied him, traveling to take their seats in Missouri's House of Representatives. Cass County's American Party candidate, William M. Briscoe, had also triumphed in August 1858, ousting incumbent W.H.H. Cundiff. Briscoe had defeated A.S. O'Bannon, receiving 57.3% of the vote.[484] Briscoe, in the House, and Lud, in the Senate, would serve and partner together, in Jefferson City and along the western border into the Civil War. When the Civil War erupted they served together in the Missouri State Guard.

Jackson County's two state representatives were George W. Tate and James B. Yeager. Tate, 68 years old, had long been a fixture in Jackson County initially at Westport but in 1858 he lived in Lone Jack. Yeager, a 48-year old Kentuckian, had a long established record in Jackson County and best known for his prairie freighting business.

[484] Missouri Secretary of State. Elections. Box 7. File 10.

James Edgar represented Bates County. Edgar, 40 years old and new to politics, had soundly defeated incumbent Joseph Clymer in the August election.

Monday, December 27, 1858 the Missouri Senate accepted Peyton's credentials and he took his seat representing the 14th Senatorial District. Lud arrived on Missouri's largest political stage at a deciding moment in the state's history. Twenty-four newly elected Senators presented their credentials and took their seats along with Peyton. The twenty-four included James S. Rains and Mosby Monroe Parsons. Parsons's fiery ultra-Southern beliefs coincided with Lud's. James S. Rains rapidly became Lud's close friend as well as a political and military mentor. Hancock L. Jackson, President of the Senate, another staunch Southern politician had replaced Cass County's Charles Sims in 1858 on the Anti-Benton ticket and figured prominently in Lud's future.

Missouri State Capitol – 1858
Courtesy of Missouri State Archives

Events that fateful week unfolded in a manner scripted by the fates. Lud's strong ultra-Southern beliefs, his "fire-eater" ferocity, and his electric oratorical skills required only an opportunity to catapult his career. Two days after Peyton took his seat, John Brown invaded Missouri's western border counties, providing Lud the public platform and audience that would launch his career.

Wednesday, December 29, 1858, John Brown, assisted by abolitionists and horse thieves, invaded Missouri, abducted 11 slaves, plundered settlers' homes, and murdered Missouri citizens. Brown's invasion marked the first step toward his eventual attack, less than a year later, on Harper's Ferry, ending with his execution and martyrdom. Men who accompanied Brown in December 1858 remained in the Kansas Territory to orchestrate and execute, during the Civil War, the total destruction of Lud's 14th Senatorial District.

Brown's Missouri invasion traumatized the entire border a precursor to countless future intrusions. The abolitionists attacked at night. They invaded homes. They held families at gunpoint and often kidnapped the men. They stole personal property. They abducted slaves. They murdered.

On this first foray into western Missouri they descended upon three different families. H.G. Hicklin and John Larue suffered from Brown's plundering and theft. Five slaves were abducted from each farm. Aaron D. Stephens led another of Brown's bands. Stephens invaded David Cruise's farm. Cruise fought back and was killed in the fight. The murderers robbed the Cruise farm liberating one slave.[485]

Several of Brown's gang associated with this raid became well known to Missourians the next few years. John E. Stewart, already

[485] Welch. Page 191.

notorious as a border horse thief, plundered Jeremiah Jackson's home and burned his store to the ground.[486] Charles R. Jennison, and James Montgomery, participants in this early raid, later led Kansans in the destruction of western Missouri.[487]

---------- 1859 ----------

Lud, new to Missouri's Senate and representing three of the western border counties, rose in the Capitol's Senate Chambers, to address the rising threat. A member of the Senate's "Committee on Federal Relations," Lud addressed the Senate recommending the passage of a bill calling on Gov. R.M. Stewart to protect the border counties against Kansas marauders and appropriating $30,000 for the purpose; accompanying the bill was a "Special Message" from Governor Stewart. Stewart's message provided a succinct history of the violence along the western border and his futile communications with the Kansas Territorial Governor as well as the President – all to no avail.

Lud slowly rose from his Senate seat and strode to the chamber's podium. He was little known to his fellow senators both a newcomer and a stranger. Lud's six-foot, lanky frame and flowing black hair garnered attention. Lud's youth, he was but 35, one of the youngest members of Missouri's highest assembly, would have normally compelled his silence but circumstances along the border hastened his public christening. With a volatile mixture of adrenaline, youth, and fire-eating passion Lud launched into his speech – the cameo oration propelled him into the political limelight.

[486] Mildfelt. Page 75.

[487] **Note**: Todd Mildfelt's *The Secret Danites: Kansas' First Jayhawkers* and G. Murlin Welch's *Border Warfare in Southeastern Kansas: 1856 – 1859* provide in-depth accounts of the men and events.

Lud's fiery call to arms fit the crimes but not, as yet, the times. He warned, "We can submit no longer," against a "band of thieves, midnight assassins and robbers."[488] Lud's language, classic and powerful, described Missouri's western border as being destroyed by "fire and sword" while "murder and rapine" operated along Missouri's "hearthstones and firesides."

Lud further traced the history of the "Abolitionist fanatics" along Missouri's western border, from his personal experience, while expanding to record the country's struggle the past 30 years. Lud points to the "Black Republicans" march under "the banner of a higher law" while insulting the civil rule of law. He related to the Senate how (William Lloyd) Garrison, (William H.) Seward and (Henry Ward) Beecher have created the situation "under the garb of religion, preaching murder and war."[489]

In closing, Lud implored the Senate not to submit to abolitionist aggression. "We shall never obtain peace by submission. We scorn, spit upon and reject so disgraceful a proposition: our own strong arms will protect us." Finally Lud called for support of the bill being proposed that Missouri's soil might be "avenged."[490] On this larger stage, Lud's oratory, for the first time, encompassed the entire state of Missouri, not just his 14th Senatorial District. His language and the scope of his rhetoric expanded beyond a small Missouri border community, beyond the state of Missouri, to include the entire country and the conflict being waged.

The initial reaction to Lud's oratory and the call for state militia assistance fell short of his hopes. A number of elected officials, in both the Senate and the House, objected to the bill's placing money

[488] **Note**: All quotations from Peyton's speech survive in a transcript published in *The Liberty Tribune*, January 21, 1859.

[489] *Liberty Tribune*. January 21, 1859.

[490] **Note**: The full text of Senator Peyton's speech is provided in the Appendix.

and power in the hands of Governor Stewart. The issue of protecting Missouri's western border became entangled in political feuding. As debate over the bill continued, the depth of the political fissure surfaced. February 5, the *Weekly Jefferson Inquirer* pleaded, "Protect the border by all means, but do so by placing the money in the hands of a sober and competent man."[491]

Gov. R.M. Stewart
Author's Collection

In addition to the political issues of giving Gov. Stewart too much authority, members of both houses of the Assembly, disputed the seriousness of the threat from James Montgomery, John Brown and the Kansas abolitionists. Boone County's Representative Odon Guitar, cautioned, "...this War Bill is a measure dangerous in the extreme, lest the flame, once kindled, shall sweep beyond the power of control."[492] Other representatives shared the same opinion triggering William Briscoe to rise and respond in the House "...do you mean to force the people on the border to organize into mobs to protect themselves: Or will you give them aid? He knew the reports from Bates and Vernon counties were true, and that the half had not been told."[493]

The ferocity and violent theme of Peyton's speech, probably among the first southern fire-eater orations in the Assembly, surprised many. Waldo Johnson, Osceola's established representative, backed off the legislation while he condescended in describing Lud as "a noble and intellectual young man."[494] The reporter for St.

[491] *Weekly Jefferson Inquirer*. February 5, 1859.
[492] *Weekly Missouri Statesman*. January 21, 1859.
[493] *Weekly Jefferson Inquirer*. January 29, 1859.
[494] *Weekly Jefferson Inquirer*. January 15, 1859.

Louis's *Daily Democrat* was not as diplomatic. The newspaper's correspondent described Lud's speech as "an inflammatory and silly speech," while suggesting that Lud "…is a young man, and will grow more discreet as he grows older, and be wiser when he knows more than he knows now."[495] In a later newspaper issue the same correspondent wrote, "It is painful to see him squirm and twist while other Senators are excusing his indiscretion on the ground of his *youth* and *inexperience*."[496]

Lud's fire resonated with others with whom he would form close ties. M.M. Parsons of Cole County and Clay County's J.T.V. Thompson joined arms with Lud as "the principal advocates for war."[497] They, along with Lud, advocated "'war to the knife and knife to the hilt.'"[498]

The border defense bill passed into law February 24. Border tensions and pressure continued to build throughout the following months. As acute as the situation was along the border itself, away from the flashpoint, Missouri's newspapers, although continuing to report events, minimalized the Kansas threat and headlines moved to other issues.

During debate on the border defense bill, William Briscoe pronounced "The people of Cass County were able to protect themselves."[499] The attitude also reflected the citizens of Bates and Vernon counties, even though they had petitioned Gov. Stewart for military protection. Militia companies formed throughout the spring. At Butler, Bates County, a militia company of 100 men was

[495] *Daily Democrat*. January 8, 1859.
[496] *Daily Democrat*. January 12, 1859.
[497] *Daily Democrat*. January 12, 1859.
[498] *Daily Democrat*. January 12, 1859.
[499] *Weekly Jefferson Inquirer*. January 29, 1859.

organized under the leadership of Capt. William Doak.[500] Sen. Peyton participated in the militia's organization assuming the rank of "General" while Rep. Briscoe became a militia "Major."[501] Both men's prominence grew along the border as they added military responsibilities to their political duties.

In the Kansas Territory, Lawrence's, *Herald of Freedom*, continued to fan hostility along the border. On March 26 the newspaper published the first installment of Philip Fowler's *The Jayhawker*, a serialized, unflattering account of the territory's abolitionists. Advertised to be an "inside" account of the abolitionist movement's discord and intentions. Readers on both sides of the border followed the story for three months the spring of 1859. Fowler's story exposed the shady and illegal activities of the abolitionist movement while unveiling the true character of its leaders, James Lane, James Montgomery, John Brown, and Charles Jennison. The final installment was mailed from Harrisonville on May 1, and fearing a return to Kansas, Fowler found refuge in Cass County as a schoolteacher.

By summer Lud's prestige had reached new heights. When initial discussions about Missouri's next Governor began, Lud's name was thrown into the conversation. As early as June the *Bolivar Pilot* published an article on possible gubernatorial candidates. The paper rejected other candidates "while such men as James S. Rollins and Peyton of Cass County, live."[502] Three months later the *Liberty Tribune* reported "not only has Col. Peyton been named for this office, but there are troops of men who are anxious for it."[503]

500 "The Democratic State Convention of Missouri in 1860." Snyder, John F. *Missouri Historical Review*. Vol. 2, No. 2. Page 297.
501 "The Democratic State Convention of Missouri in 1860." Snyder, John F. *Missouri Historical Review*. Vol. 2, No. 2. Page 297.
502 *Bolivar Pilot*. June 5, 1859.
503 *Liberty Tribune*. September 16, 1859.

In less than a year, Lud had risen from political obscurity to be mentioned as potential candidate for Missouri's highest office.

Lud's first Senate session, the first session of the 20th General Assembly convened on December 27, 1858 and adjourned 63 days later, March 14, 1859. Although Lud's impassioned speech in early January elevated him to a larger stage, his legislative duties quickly became a day-in and day-out grind. Three days after the session's opening, Senate members received their committee assignments. Lud became a member of five Senate committees: Federal Relations, Internal Improvements, Education, Lunatic Asylum, and Swamp Lands.[504]

The Senate committee on Federal Relations handled the legislative bills and issues tied to Missouri's western border. Lud served on this committee along with Samuel B. Churchill, James S. Rains, J.T.V. Thompson, and William McFarland. Federal authorities arrested Churchill and Thompson, Southern sympathizers, early in the Civil War while Rains fought with the Confederacy.

---------- Missouri's 1860 Democratic Meltdown ----------

In 1860, events outside the western border, and indeed outside Missouri, propelled Lud's continued political ascent. Just as his 1858 election to Missouri's Senate was occasioned, by a sudden, unexpected political vacuum in the 14th District at the precise moment K.T. (Kansas Territory) abolitionist aggression alarmed the electorate, Missouri's 1860 political meltdown opened a new pathway.

When the year opened, the anticipated national party conventions, in advance of the November Presidential election, strongly

[504] *Senate Journal. First Session of the 20th General Assembly.* Pages 40 – 41.

influenced Missouri's political landscape. The state's Democratic Party began the year a single entity but by the November Presidential Election had splintered into three independent movements. This disintegration of the Democratic Party opened the door for Lud.

In January Missouri's Democrats enjoyed the temporary confidence of a unified party. Politicians outside the Democrats swam in less certain waters. The Whig party had effectively died five years earlier, the American Party's divisive beliefs doomed the party to a short life, and the Republican Party was just emerging from an embryonic stage. Like sailors thrown overboard, abandoned and swimming for lifeboats, these unaffiliated politicians formed a loosely grouped "Opposition" to the Democrats.

The "Opposition," seeking conciliation and common ground, convened a convention in Jefferson City in February. The opening gavel fell on February 29 and adjourning gavel dropped on March 1. The men gathered represented such a wide divergence of political opinion, their failure hardly surprises. James O. Broadhead and Arnold Krekel, who both eventually, led Missouri's Republican Party attended. James S. Rains, later a pro-Southern Breckinridge Democrat and General in the Missouri State Guard, was in attendance. Also present was George R. Smith from Pettis County, a former American Party candidate whose political wanderings covered the spectrum.

This Opposition Convention adjourned leaving a committee to (1) Appoint delegates to the National Constitutional Convention (2) Support the nomination of Edward Bates for President and (3) Convene a state convention in Jefferson City in April. Slavery was the convention's "elephant in the room." The convention did not address slavery; "there was no controversy on the slavery question; but at the same time, no principle was enumerated in the platform from which the most scrupulous Free Democrat or Republican can dissent."[505] Short lived, this "Opposition" quickly splintered and dissolved.

The Republicans met in St. Louis just nine days after the Opposition Convention adjourned. One hundred and thirty-four delegates met and nominated Edward Bates for President. Delegates were selected for the Republican National Convention scheduled for mid-May, in Chicago.[506]

Lud's Democratic Party convened at Jefferson City April 10. Three days before the opening gavel, the capitol began filling with delegates. Correspondents reported "the city is rapidly filling up with members and strangers who intend to be present at the Convention. The hotels are jammed and every boat that arrives is crowded with passengers. The delegates from the river counties are here, and also a large number from the Southwest."[507]

Throughout the convention, enthusiasm, partisan opinions, and alcohol melded to create an undisciplined environment - "the Delegates seemed bent on having a glorious drunk before proceeding to the transaction of business for which they were assembled, and the bawling drunkards, the yelling and swearing of rowdies and the scrambling of bullies has engrossed the whole time."[508] Inside the Convention proceedings, especially the night sessions, "John Barleycorn controlled the whole arrangements," with sober delegates allowing the drunks to prevail because "an attempt to enforce good behavior might result in a fight, in which sobriety would be severely punished."[509]

[505] *Weekly Missouri Statesman*. March 16, 1860.
[506] *Daily Missouri Republican*. March 12, 1860.
[507] *The Bulletin*. April 7, 1860.
[508] *Weekly Missouri Statesman*. April 13, 1860.
[509] *Weekly Missouri Statesman*. April 13, 1860.

The state convention's business and the delegate assembly's chemistry warred over the same policy conflicts and disagreements that were soon to split the National Democratic Party. A small cadre of young, radical, pro-South delegates attempted to move the deliberations and decisions of the convention to the far right. The *Jefferson Examiner* noted that when "youthful enthusiasm or over-heated zeal led the younger and more fiery portion of the convention beyond the bounds of prudence, the sage counsels of the veteran (Sterling) Price, aided by (James) Young, (F.) Roland, and others at once restored order and quiet."[510] Despite this observation, the ultra-Southern advocates, led by James N. Burnes, succeeded in having "unrelenting opponents of Douglas and his doctrines" appointed to all the key convention seats.[511]

C.F. Jackson
Courtesy State Historical Society of Missouri

Over three days, the convention passed resolutions, nominated a candidate for Governor, and selected delegates to the upcoming national convention at Charleston, South Carolina. Following hours of debate the convention adopted resolutions aligned with the "Jackson Resolutions," supporting the "principles proclaimed by the Democratic National Convention at Cincinnati in 1856," and fully supporting slavery in the territories.[512] Bolivar's John F. Snyder, a delegate and convention leader, wrote later, "the Democracy of Missouri, by their platform of principles adopted at the State convention held in April, was committed to the

[510] *Jefferson Examiner.* April 14, 1860.
[511] Snyder, John F. "The Democratic State Convention of Missouri in 1860." *Missouri Historical Review.* Vol. II, No. 1. Page 114.
[512] Snyder, John F. "The Democratic State Convention of Missouri in 1860." *Missouri Historical Review.* Vol. II, No. 1. Page 118.

policy advocated by the Breckinridge, or Southern, wing of the now dissevered party."[513] C.F. Jackson defeated Waldo P. Johnson for the gubernatorial nomination.

During the Democratic National Convention, held at Charleston, Missouri's delegation made an "on site" decision that drove a wedge between the state's Democratic southern wing and the moderate democrats. At Charleston, Missouri's delegates departed from the State Convention's instructions supporting Stephen Douglas, rather than solidly adhering to the convention's resolutions, and thereby letting the eventual Presidential candidate surface secondarily. Nathaniel C. Claiborne, of Jackson County, led Missouri's delegation in making Douglas their primary commitment; upon his return to Missouri the southern wing labeled Claiborne as a "traitor."

The Charleston Convention adjourned without settling upon a Presidential nominee. The delegates agreed to reconvene in Baltimore late in June. Sandwiched between these two Democratic conventions, the Republicans and Constitutional Unionists each held conventions. In May, the Constitutional-Union Party met in Baltimore nominating John Bell for President while the Republican Party nominated Abraham Lincoln at Chicago.

In late June, when the Democrat's National Convention reconvened in Baltimore, a final, fatal split occurred. Stephen Douglas was nominated for President, without a strong pro-south platform. Angry, the ultra-Southern Democrats stormed out of the convention, reconvened several blocks away, and nominated John C. Breckinridge for President.

---

513 Snyder, John F. "The Democratic State Convention of Missouri in 1860." *Missouri Historical Review*. Vol. II, No. 1. Page 124.

This national Democratic party split put Claiborne F. Jackson, Missouri's gubernatorial nominee in the uncomfortable position of choosing between Douglas and Breckinridge – regardless of Jackson's choice, he would anger and alienate a significant segment of Missouri's Democrats. With the campaign clock ticking, Jackson announced his choice less than a week after Douglas and Breckinridge were nominated.

-- Lud Peyton and Missouri's Breckinridge Democrats --

Straddling a fault line, gubernatorial candidate Claiborne Jackson announced at Fayette, Mo., June 30, he would support Stephen Douglas for President. Immediately Missouri's Democratic southern wing split. Led by both U.S. Senators, James S. Green and Trusten Polk, the bolters announced they would stand for Breckinridge and nominate candidates for the state offices.

These now, "Breckinridge Democrats," had but five weeks until the August gubernatorial and congressional elections. With no time to waste, and no time for a state convention, the Breckinridge supporters assembled in St. Louis July 3 and drafted candidates for Governor and Lt. Governor. Hancock L. Jackson, Missouri's incumbent Lt. Governor, received the gubernatorial nomination while Jefferson City's Mosby M. Parsons garnered the Lt. Governor nomination. By July 7 both men had accepted their nominations with just a month remaining until the August election.

Across Missouri ultra-Southerners scrambled to organize and support the Breckinridge ticket. The week after Hancock Jackson and Mosby Parsons accepted their nominations, candidates for the Congressional seats were lacking. July 13, the *Liberty Tribune* announced R.H. Musser as a Congressional candidate from the 3rd District.

Lud surfaced and announced as a Congressional candidate for the 5th District's seat. A Kansas City newspaper denied Lud's candidacy as a rumor on July 14.[514] By July 19 his candidacy was an established fact. The next week the newspapers in Liberty and Glasgow carried stories announcing his place on the ballot; the "Hon. R.L.Y. Peyton, State Senator from Cass County has announced himself a candidate for Congress."[515] The *Liberty Tribune* carried an abbreviated Breckinridge ticket that included Lud.

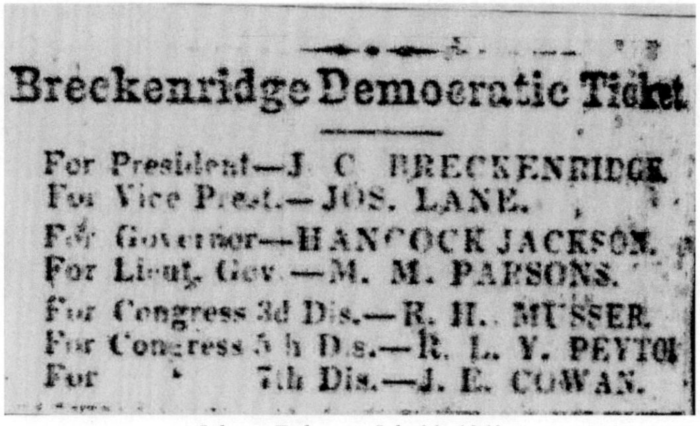

Breckenridge Democratic Ticket

For President—J. C. BRECKENRIDGE
For Vice Prest.—JOS. LANE.
For Governor—HANCOCK JACKSON.
For Lieut. Gov.—M. M. PARSONS.
For Congress 3d Dis.—R. H. MUSSER.
For Congress 5th Dis.—R. L. Y. PEYTON
For 7th Dis.—J. E. COWAN.

Liberty Tribune - July 20, 1860

Missouri's Fifth Congressional District already sported two candidacies. John W. Reid, of Jackson Co. and Lafayette County's Frank T. Mitchell were debating across the Fifth District when Lud announced. Reid ran on the Douglas ticket while Mitchell ran as a Constitutional Unionist. Reid's reputation was well established in western Missouri. He had served in the State Assembly and led the Missouri forces at the Battle of Osawatomie. Frank T. Mitchell was a Methodist Minister.

514 *Lexington Express*. July 21, 1860.
515 *Glasgow Times*. July 19, 1860.

When Lud entered the race, the canvassing debates between Reid and Mitchell had been low key. Lud's entry meant the debate's tenor would change. One observer wrote, "Mr. Mitchell will have to do his work over again and will probably have a warmer time with Mr. Peyton, who is an eloquent debater, and occupies ground more in harmony with the people of the District, than Douglas-Reid Squatter Sovereignty."[516]

When Lud entered the race, Reid and Mitchell had completed 16 of their scheduled 28 debates. There is no evidence Lud ever shared the podium with the two candidates. Overall the Breckinridge candidates lacked a cohesive organization and time was against them. The short schedule denied the opportunity to build an organization and populate all the ballots. Although Hancock Jackson and Mosby Parsons appeared on ballots statewide, the Congressional candidates did not. When the election was held early in August, Lud's name did not appear on the ballot in the Fifth District.[517] Reid defeated Mitchell for the Congressional seat.[518]

Both Hancock L. Jackson and Mosby M. Parsons were defeated in the August elections. Claiborne F. Jackson and Thomas Reynolds became the Governor elect, and Lt. Gov. elect, respectively. The Presidential election still remained three months off in the future. The Breckinridge Democrats regrouped after their August defeat and announced a state convention that would convene in Jefferson City, September 20.

---

[516] *Glasgow Times*. July 19, 1860.

[517] **Note**: Candidates' names were submitted for inclusion on the ballot by officials of the political party. Evidently, due to the limited amount of time before the election and the disorganization of the Breckinridge Democrats, Congressional candidates were not submitted. Per archivists at the Missouri State Archives.

[518] **Note**: Both John W. Reid and Frank T. Mitchell joined the Missouri State Guard when the Civil War began in 1861. Mitchell served as an aide to Claiborne F. Jackson and settled in Texas after the war.

Hancock L. Jackson and Mosby M. Parsons
Courtesy of State Historical Society of Missouri

Lud had made good use of the opportunity to stand for Congress. The Breckinridge Democrats welcomed his ultra-Southern stance. Lud was no longer overshadowed and muted by the larger, more politically diverse Democratic Party. During the summer of 1860 his reputation soared given the opportunity to stand apart and speak to the multitudes.

September 1, 1860, the Cass County Democratic Club met to select delegates to the upcoming Breckinridge state convention. "Resolutions were adopted approving the call of the State Convention – endorsing Breckinridge and Lane – Senators Green and Polk."[519] The *Jefferson Examiner* wrote, "We notice the name of R.L.Y. Peyton, among the list of delegates," solid recognition of Lud's rising celebrity.[520]

Lud had become a sought after public speaker. His oratory, powerful and emotive, swayed audiences. Invitations exceeded his

---

519 *Jefferson Examiner*. September 15, 1860.
520 *Jefferson Examiner*. September 15, 1860.

availability and he was unable to honor all the speaking opportunities he received.

The following letter from Lud to protégés in Johnson County, Mo. was published in St. Louis's *Daily Bulletin*. This correspondence, the only known existing Peyton letter, clearly expounds his political views. It also serves as evidence a broader general public was now keenly interested in his thoughts and opinions.

Letter from R.L.Y. Peyton:

> "Harrisonville, Mo., Sept. 6, 1860
>
> Messrs. Gibson, McCowan, and others:
>
> Your letter of the 1st inst., inviting me to address the Democratic party of Johnson, at Warrensburg, on the 8th of this month has been received. I have purposefully delayed any answer to this kind invitation of my friends in hope that I might be able to comply with their wishes, but I regret to find that it will be utterly out of my power to present on that occasion.
>
> Sincerely regretting any division at this time in the ranks of the Democracy of Missouri, yet regarding Mr. Breckinridge and General Lane as the true exponents of Democratic principles, as men whom the who South may take with honor, safety, and ,confidence, and ought to unite upon with perfect unanimity, and the only ones by whom Democrats can rally or stand by – so believing as a Democrat, a nation, and a southern man, I shall support them as the only true Representatives of old Democratic doctrines and those great, national ideas of justice

and protection to all the people, all the interests and all the property – slaves as well as others – of the whole country, wherever the national flag floats and the arm, power and jurisdiction of the National Government shall reach.

In this contest it does indeed seem to me that even the instincts of a southern man would counsel him to the side of Mr. Breckinridge, not because he comes from the South, or, as Chief Magistrate of these States, would lend himself to a partial administration of the government to the favor the peculiar views of that section, but for the reason that he holds to doctrines and follows a line of policy that will secure the interests and guards the rights of the southerner equally with all others. This is no time for the South to halt, divide or quarrel – it is no time now to concede or recede, even one solitary inch from the high ground of constitutional principle.

There was never a period the whole history of the Republic when the southern people were more persistently and bitterly assaulted, more definitely, wantonly and fiercely pressed both in State and territory. The contest of 1860, on our side, is emphatically one of defense against war and aggression, worthlessly waged upon us in both State and territory, and thus to expel from the joint domain, and then cleave down in one-half the Union the slave institutions of fifteen southern commonwealths. Our peace, honor, safety, equality and whole existence is staked upon the struggle, and our manifest duty is to stand united and fight it out up to the full measure and strength of our whole constitutional privileges.

I will not doubt the loyalty, courage and discern-ment of the southern people. The path of safety and of victory lies straight ahead of them, and even though

as wayfaring and foolish as their enemies would have them, they could not err therein. This path found in a calm, stern, steadfast and united support of Breckinridge by the whole southern people, with destruction of party, and upon the majority of platform adopted at Charleston. Would we do so, a peace would be conquered, durable and lasting, the Union and the Constitution saved and vindicated, and a new lease of life given to the government, to last forever, and spreading tranquility over the whole country. In this great contest, Missouri will be found true to her ancient principles, true to the great doctrines of constitutional equality, and when the ides of November come, will tell the whole world, in an unmistaken language, that she loves as little the unfriendless action of Mr. Douglas as she does the Black Republican restrictions of Mr. Lincoln. She submits to neither, and will spurn both as she would dishonor and degradation. She demands peace and safety here at home, peace and
protection for slave property in their territories.

Again regretting my inability to be present with you,
I remain, very respectfully, your obedient servant,
R.L.Y. Peyton"[521]

------- The Breckinridge Democratic Push ------

In September 1860, at Jefferson City, Peyton shone brightly in the Democratic gathering that became known as the Breckinridge Convention. "The Democrats opposed Douglas in all but seven counties of the state sent delegates to the September convention. It was well understood the purpose of this convention was to effect a radical realignment of the Democratic party of Missouri, and to place it in thorough accord with that of the southern states. The

[521] *St. Louis Daily Bulletin.* September 14, 1860.

program laid down for its guidance was to ratify the nomination of Breckenridge and Lane;"[522]

Delegates began arriving in Jefferson City September 19. Cass County's Democrats sent two delegates to the convention, Guilford D. Hansbrough and R.L.Y. Peyton.[523] Hansbrough and Peyton arrived with smiles and a high step because all delegates to this convention were Breckinridge men, wholly against Stephen Douglas, violently against Lincoln. The *St. Louis Daily Bulletin* wrote that a festive mood prevailed as delegates arrived in Jefferson City to parades and music in the streets.[524] It further described, "Several hundred delegates are now marching in procession with music, banners, and transparencies. The old leaders of the party are here. Among them are Polk, Green, Hunter, Halliburton, Burlin, Wilkes, Snyder, Hoy, Burnes, *Peyton*, Davis, Knott, and others."[525]

James Green
Courtesy Library of Congress

Trusten Polk
Courtesy Library of Congress

The Democratic Convention began September 20 and lasted but two days. Dr. John F. Snyder later described the atmosphere as having "intense enthusiasm" and "strict order and decorum were

[522] Snyder, J.F. "The Democratic State Convention of Missouri in 1860." *Missouri Historical Review*. Vol. II, No. 1. October 1907. Page 125.
[523] *Jefferson Examiner*. September 22, 1860.
[524] *St. Louis Daily Bulletin*. September 20, 1860.
[525] St. Louis *Daily Bulletin*. September 20, 1860.

maintained."[526] The raucous and contentious atmosphere that had dominated the April convention was absent. Speeches on the second day of the convention focused solely upon the defeat of Abraham Lincoln and the rejection of the Douglas Democrats. The agenda driven business of the convention was handled efficiently and on the second day resolutions were easily passed solidifying the party's Breckinridge position.

At this point the convention evolved into what Dr. Snyder described as a "political love feast."[527] Lud then ascended the stage and unleashed his oratorical magic.

DEMOCRATIC STATE CONVENTION.

INCREASING ENTHUSIASM.

THE MEETING ON THURSDAY NIGHT.

SPEECHES BY
POLK, GREEN and PEYTON.

Democracy of Missouri sound to the core

Gov. Claiborne F. Jackson addresses the Convention and endorses the Breckinridge Platform.

THE BALL CONTINUES TO MOVE.

[Special Report for the St. Louis Daily Bulletin.]

JEFFERSON CITY, Sept. 21.

EVENING SESSION.

On the re-assembling of the Convention at half-past seven o'clock. Mr. Jas. M. Hughes moved that the President appoint a committee of five to prepare an address to the Democracy of Missouri. The following gentlemen were appointed on said committee: James M. Hughes, Thomas L. Snead, Gen. E. L. Edwards, J. T. Hughes, and Col. J. F. Snyder.

Mr. Halliburton desired to offer the following resolution, by instruction of the people of Linn county. He did it because he considered the defeat of Lincoln paramount to everything else:

St. Louis Daily Bulletin
September 22, 1860

526 Snyder, J.F. "The Democratic State Convention of Missouri in 1860." *Missouri Historical Review*. Vol. II, No. 1. October 1907. Page 127.
527 Snyder, J.F. "The Democratic State Convention of Missouri in 1860." *Missouri Historical Review*. Vol. II, No. 1. October 1907. Page 129.

> "Having then no other special question before the convention resolved itself tacitly into a "committee of the whole on the state of the Union." Hon. R.L.Y. Peyton, State Senator from Cass County, an eloquent and very able statesman, opened the symposium with a speech of matchless force fiercely arraigning the Abolitionists of the North for their aggressive encroachments upon the rights of the patient, long suffering South; and demonstrating, to the satisfaction of all present, that Douglas though masquerading as a Democrat, was in reality a more dangerous enemy of the South than Lincoln. The sentiments and facts, he so impressively presented were then echoed, reiterated, and elaborated, with theatrical and oratorical embellishments, in addresses by D.H. Donovan, Col. Churchill, and General Ranney, of St. Louis, Peter S. Wilkes, of Green County, Parson, Buffington, and others."[528]

Certainly within the ranks of the Breckinridge Democrats, Lud's star was rising. His reputation preceded him to the convention. The crowd had loudly called for him and he did not disappoint. Again, the *St. Louis Daily Bulletin* vividly described the setting and Lud's impact:

> "After Gov. Jackson had concluded his remarks, loud cries made for Peyton. Hon. R.L.Y. Peyton, of Cass County, then came forward, and for more than an hour held the audience spell-bound by his eloquent words. He exposed the fallacies of the Douglasites, showed the ridiculousness of the Bellites,and pointed out the alarming consequences of the Black Republicanism. Then, in words of burning eloquence, he appealed to his Democratic friends to stand firm to

[528] Snyder, J.F. "The Democratic State Convention of Missouri in 1860." *Missouri Historical Review*. Vol. II, No. 1. October 1907. Page 128.

> principle and never yield to the seductive wiles of the enemy. Mr. Peyton was frequently interrupted by the most enthusiastic applause, and at the close of his speech the audience rose to their feet and gave three cheers for the young and rising Senator from the southwest. The Convention then adjourned, It being 11 o'clock."[529]

Lud's late night speech to the Breckinridge Convention did not meet with universal acclaim. In St. Louis, the *Republican* was not completely supportive, in its evaluation of Lud, criticizing his content and delivery. The *Jefferson Examiner* came to Lud's defense on October 20, 1860: "The Squatter *Republican* attempts to belittle Hon. R.L.Y. Peyton's abilities as an orator, by characterizing his eloquent efforts in the late Democratic State Convention, as a 'spread eagle speech,' &c. It is remarkable perhaps, how the *Republican* changes. Speaking in reference to a speech delivered by this same Peyton not a great while ago, in the Senate, it declared that it was the most eloquent effort ever delivered in that hall. But Peyton don't like Squatterism. That is where the shoe pinches."[530]

Immediately following the convention's adjournment Lud was off to St. Louis. A "Grand Democratic Rally" was held Tuesday, September 25 in front of the courthouse. Peyton was featured in the announcements as a key speaker.[531] He shared the podium with Senators James S. Green and Trusten Polk. Others speaking that night were Wesley Halliburton, James N. Burnes, James B. Bowlin, and Samuel B. Churchill.

The St. Louis rally placed Lud among Missouri's highest elected officials. In Jefferson City he had shared the podium with the

[529] *St. Louis Daily Bulletin*. September 24, 1860.
[530] *Jefferson Examiner*. September 29, 1860.
[531] *St. Louis Daily Bulletin*. September 25, 1860.

Governor elect. In St. Louis he spoke on the same agenda as both United States Senators. Churchill and Halliburton were both established, notable political leaders. Lud and Burnes represented the party's young rising stars.

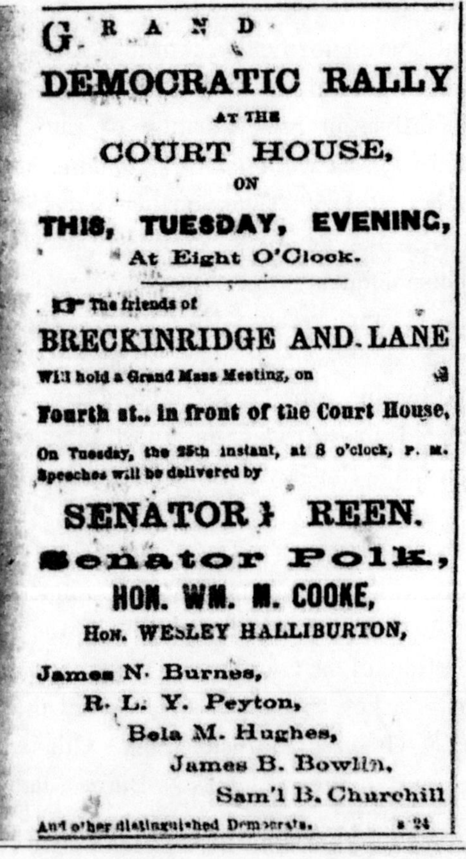

GRAND

DEMOCRATIC RALLY

AT THE

COURT HOUSE,

ON

THIS, TUESDAY, EVENING,

At Eight O'Clock.

The friends of

BRECKINRIDGE AND LANE

Will hold a Grand Mass Meeting, on

Fourth st., in front of the Court House,

On Tuesday, the 25th instant, at 8 o'clock, P. M.
Speeches will be delivered by

SENATOR GREEN.

Senator Polk,

HON. WM. M. COOKE,

HON. WESLEY HALLIBURTON,

James N. Burnes,

R. L. Y. Peyton,

Bela M. Hughes,

James B. Bowlin,

Sam'l B. Churchill

And other distinguished Democrats. s 24

St. Louis Daily Bulletin
September 24, 1860

---------- 45 Days to the Election ----------

When the Jefferson City convention adjourned, only 45 days remained until the Presidential election. Lud left the convention having been selected one of nine Breckinridge/Lane Electors.

DEMOCRATIC ELECTORAL TICKET.

1st District....E C MURRAY............Pike county.
2d District....WESLEY HALLIBURTON Linn;
3d District....WILLIAM Y SLACK......Livingston.
4th District....JAMES N BURNES.......Platte;
5th District....R L Y PEYTON..........Cass;
6th District....THOS. W FREEMAN.....Polk;
7th District....MONROE M PARSONS....Cole;
8th District....CORBIN ALEXANDER....St Francois;
9th District....JAMES B BOWLIN......St. Louis.

FOR CIRCUIT ATTORNEY,
ROBERT S. VOORHIS.
FOR ASSISTANT CIRCUIT ATTORNEY,
WARREN MONTFORT.

St. Louis Daily Bulletin, September 26, 1860

Lud's selection as one of the key nine campaign managers may have been a last minute decision. On September 15, the Jefferson City *Examiner* had reported George G. Vest, of Cooper Co., to be the Fifth District Breckinridge elector.[532] The *Examiner* also indicated John B. Hale, of Carroll Co., would be the Third District's elector.

In reality, both Vest and Hale ended up standing for Stephen Douglas.

The nine men charged with campaigning on Breckinridge's behalf and bringing home an election victory were:

District	Elector	County
1	E.C. Murray	Pike
2	Wesley Halliburton	Linn
3	Wm. Y. Slack	Livingston
4	Jas. N. Burnes	Platte
5	R.L.Y. Peyton	Cass
6	Thos. W. Freeman	Polk
7	Monroe M. Parsons	Cole
8	Corbin Alexander	St. Francois
9	Jas. B. Bowlin	St. Louis

532 *Jefferson Examiner*. September 15, 1860.

Lud's Fifth District included the counties of Jackson, Cass, Lafayette, Johnson, Henry, Saline, Pettis, Benton, Cooper, Morgan, Moniteau, Miller, and Cole.

Lud chaired the Executive Committee for the Fifth District; the Executive Committee included a member from 11 of the 13 counties. The organization included "Sub-Electors" and "Assistant Electors" from each county. Lud's Harrisonville law partner, R.O. Boggess, was an Assistant Elector for Cass County. The Fifth District "Executive Committee" members were:[533]

County	Committee Member
Jackson	D.E.W. Robinson
Cass	Dr. G.D. Hansbrough
Lafayette	Col. Lewis Green
Johnson	P.B. Walker
Henry	R.K. Murrell
Pettis	Dr. Watson
Saline	E.S. Clarkson
Cooper	Dr. Phil Dimitt
Morgan	W.C. Hedrick
Benton	Wm. D. Barkley
Moniteau	R.Q. Roach

Campaigning began full speed following the September convention and the St. Louis rally. Lud's responsibilities as a Breckinridge Elector were twofold. Primarily he orchestrated the development of the Fifth District's Breckinridge campaign organization. All 13 counties of the district needed local leadership to maintain an active campaign.

As an elector, Lud was responsible for "canvassing" the district on Breckinridge's behalf. Electors for each of the Presidential candidates spoke and debated on their candidate's behalf. Often the

[533] *Jefferson Examiner.* September 29, 1860.

electors traveled together, visiting county seats and other large towns. The debates drew large crowds supplying audiences with entertainment as well as the opportunity to hear firsthand the candidate's virtues. It was common for the orators to talk for one or two hours, sometimes longer.

Lud's rising notoriety generated numerous speaking invitations from Breckinridge political clubs throughout western Missouri. Even though Ray County fell outside the Fifth Congressional District, his reputation garnered an invitation to speak in Richmond October 15.[534] He had however already accepted an invitation from the Jackson County Breckinridge Democrats to speak at a large rally on the 15th.

Jackson County's Breckinridge clubs planned a huge Monday rally. Well in advance of the event newspaper announcements advertised the rally and encouraged citizens to attend the full day celebration. The organizers promised "There will be no fireworks nor tomfoolery to attract the thoughtless and excite the wonder of the simple, but there will be solid arguments, eloquent exhortations, and patriotic appeals –'thoughts that breathe and words that burn.'"[535]

Westport's *Border Star* announced on October 6, that Lud, along with other notable leaders would speak at the rally. He again shared the podium with U.S. Senator Trusten Polk, State Senator Samuel B. Churchill and Platte County's James N. Burnes.

534 *Jefferson Examiner.* October 6, 1860.
535 *Border Star.* October 6, 1860.

Breckinridge Rally in Independence
Westport's *Border Star*
October 20, 1860

The October 15 rally began with an 11:00 a.m. parade. A brass band led the parade through Independence ending at the Jones Hotel where Senator Polk was staying. Jackson County township clubs composed the parade groups, all on horseback; the townships, Kaw, Blue, Sni-a-bar, Ft. Osage, Van Buren, and Washington all participated. All of the clubs carried hickory poles with banners reading, "The Old Constitution, the Old Bible, and the Old God." The Sni-a-bar contingent was the largest with over 200 riders.[536] After speaking at the Jackson County rally Lud was back on the canvas circuit traveling to speak at Boonville.

Lud's Boonville speech, both for content and delivery, stunned his listeners. Lud held the audience's rapt attention "for three long hours."[537] A St. Louis correspondent present in the Boonville audience, hearing Lud for the first time wrote: "From the little we have heard of Mr. Peyton, we had been led to anticipate a fair Democratic address from a tolerably fair Missouri orator. But shades of Webster! Never before, have I listened to anything in the way of a political address even approaching to it, in this State; and this was in substance the language of nearly everyone who heard it."[538]

[536] *Border Star*. October 20, 1860.
[537] *Western Democrat*. October 27, 1860.
[538] *Western Democrat*. October 27, 1860.

Following the speech Lud returned to his hotel where, for the remainder of the day, "proud and admiring friends (even politically differing from him)" filled his room. In the evening he was serenaded by a band. The crowd demanded another speech. Lud "responded in a short speech, enthusiastically received."[539] The next day he was off to Jefferson City and then back to Clinton for his final canvassing speech.

---------- Elsewhere ----------

During October 1860, as Lud campaigned for Breckinridge in western Missouri, his cousin, Balie Peyton, campaigned in Tennessee for the Constitutional Unionist's candidate John Bell. Peyton had been instrumental in the founding of the Constitutional Unionist Party. A St. Louis newspaper reported, Balie Peyton had commented about Lincoln: "He did not believe if Lincoln was elected he could find a man in the South who would accept any important office under him. If such a man could be found, he was a traitor and deserved to be tortured to a terrible death."[540]

John Lewis Peyton had maintained close contact with Stephen Douglas. John lived in Chicago for several years in the early 1850s. September 1, 1854, in Chicago, John accompanied Douglas on stage when Douglas defended his role in the Kansas-Nebraska Act. Although Peyton had returned to Stanton, Va. and married, he continued regular correspondence with Douglas. April 14, 1860, just days before the Charleston Convention, Peyton assured Douglas his nomination was "fait accompli."[541]

[539] *Western Democrat*. October 27, 1860.

[540] *St. Louis Daily Bulletin*. October 6, 1860.

[541] University of Chicago. Special Collections. Stephen Douglas Papers. Box 32. Folder 17.

Three cousins, all active politicians canvassing different geographic locations, supporting opposing candidates in the same Presidential election: John L. Peyton for Douglas, Balie Peyton for Bell, and Lud Peyton for Breckinridge.

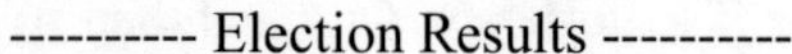

---------- Election Results ----------

The Presidential election results in the Fifth District did not reflect positive returns for Lud's efforts. Bell's Constitutional Unionist Party won the popular vote in eight of the Fifth District's 11 counties. Stephen Douglas and the Northern Democrats won the other three. Breckinridge ran a distant third in 10 of the 11 counties. Only in Cass County, Lud's home county, did Breckinridge come in second, receiving 607 votes. It would seem Lud's influence moved many local voters into the Breckinridge column but not enough to provide a victory.

Chapter Eight
Rebellion and Civil War

Abraham Lincoln became President Elect November 6, 1860. Exactly one year later, November 6, 1861, Lud Peyton was selected to represent Missouri in the Confederate Senate. Between Lincoln's election and Lud's journey to the C.S.A. Senate in Richmond, Va. events within Missouri accelerated at breakneck speed. Missouri struggled, from a state in search of an identity to a state at war with itself, as two governments faced off. Simultaneously Kansas's Jayhawkers assailed the state from the west.

Although Lud's constituents sent him to Missouri's Senate in 1858, these same voters remained moderate, maintaining a steadfast Union loyalty. Lud's ultra-Southern doctrine attracted only the radical minority. His fiery message never wavered from 1854 to Lincoln's election. His continued willingness to advocate violence under the States' Rights umbrella placed him well outside the norms of his community.

Western Missourians, like the state itself, remained "tolerant toward slavery," while continuing to be "averse to secession."[542] The secession cause would not gain heavy momentum until, during the Civil War, atrocities by Kansan abolitionists (in federal uniform) pushed moderate Missourians into the Southern camp.

A year after Lincoln's election, Lud Peyton, no longer merely an angry young fire-eater from Harrisonville, became a primary architect of rebellion and secession. By November 1861 Lud held an influential seat within Gov. Jackson's inner circle. Long the voice of Missouri's border conflict, others now listened to him as one of the original voices for Missouri's Southern identity. Also, Lud now spoke with the authority accorded a veteran regimental cavalry commander.

[542] Peckham. Page vii.

---------- Lincoln's Election ----------

Stephen A. Douglas won Missouri's Presidential election, the only state Douglas carried. His margin of victory was a miniscule 429 votes over Constitutional Unionist John Bell. Missouri's electorate had little appetite for secession, voting for the Union. The three Union candidates, Lincoln, Bell and Douglas, combined received slightly more than 81% of the vote.

Lud's 14th Senatorial District, Jackson, Cass, and Bates counties also exhibited little inclination for secession. The three Union parties, although below statewide levels, still tallied 71.1% of the Presidential vote. Despite six continuous years of confrontation and violence, these border counties held firm to the Union. Even in Cass County, Lud's political base, the ultra-Southern candidate, Breckinridge, received less than 40% of the vote.

Hidden beneath the overwhelming local Union vote, stirred a violent rejection of Lincoln's "Black Republican" doctrine. Lincoln received a mere 244 votes in Lud's district, less than .5% of the total vote. Presidential choices were cast "viva voca," each voter required to publically, orally, cast his vote. The 244 courageous men who voted for Lincoln became targets of ostracism and threat.

In Bates County, Lincoln voters' names were published in the local newspapers. Posters nailed on buildings and trees identified the "Black Republicans." The same held true in Cass County. The threats were quite clear – "Black Republicans" should be publically identified and driven out. In the days and weeks following Lincoln's election many who had voted for him fled western Missouri. Threats of violence as well as attempted assassinations became a part of daily life. One Lincoln voter recalled, "we never slept in the house until Sumter was fired upon."[543]

---

[543] "Memorial Monuments and Tablets in Kansas." *Kansas Historical Collection*. Volume XI. Fn. Page 276-277.

Lincoln's victory further widened the seismic divide between Missouri and the Kansas Territory. Kansas's radical abolitionists interpreted Lincoln's election as sanctioning violence, and the immediate abandonment of the rule of law. Terrorist intentions stepped out of the shadows and into the open light of day. Lud's long-standing warnings about approaching violence and invasion were about to come true, personified in Charles R. Jennison.

-----Russell Hinds's Murder and the Southwest Expedition -----

Within a week of Lincoln's victory, emboldened by the election results, jayhawker Charles R. Jennison and a few followers kidnapped and hung Bates County resident Russell Hinds. Accusing Hinds of pursuing runaway slaves, Jennison pinned a note on his victim's swinging corpse:

> "This man was executed by the (citizens erased) of Kansas for being engaged in hunting (in erased) kidnapping negroes in 1859.
> November 11, 1860
>
> P.S. As all others will be that is found in the same occupation"

Russell Hinds' death was but the first of others along the border. For the second time in Lud's senatorial term, border violence in his constituency moved him into the public spotlight. Lud's district, long threatened with invasion by James Montgomery and other Danite abolitionists, recoiled under the blatant crime. The cold, ferocious nature of Hinds's murder, Jennison's conscious rejection of civil law in favor of terrorism shifted the border conflict outside civilized norms.

The alarm sounded, Missouri Gov. Robert M. Stewart ordered the State Militia from St. Louis to Missouri's western border. Led by General David Frost, the State Militia embarked upon what became known as the "Southwest Expedition." In late November, Gen. Frost led 600 men from St. Louis to Missouri's western border.[544] A strong opinion existed among some Missouri politicians that the Southwest Expedition was an overreaction; they believed the threat of an abolitionist invasion was overblown. This view held despite John Brown's raid of December 1858 and James Montgomery's repeated threats.

The border communities requested arms, not a St. Louis militia. Companies of poorly armed neighborhood home guards had existed for several years; given weapons they felt capable of self-defense. These local militia companies had organized and trained, they patrolled their border neighborhoods but needed the firepower. They resented St. Louis help.

Despite the debate over necessity, the expedition arrived at the border in Bates and Vernon counties in late November. The encampment lay squarely within Lud's constituency. Lud's elected position as the area's state senator required his continued leadership of the border militia. Thereafter, when Lud took the public platform, he did so as a leader and veteran of the border troubles – speaking from personal experience.

John S. Bowen
Author's Collection

The Southwest Expedition brought Lud together with John S. Bowen. These two men, of identical political persuasion, met and formed an association that continued through the Battle of Vicksburg. The upward trajectory of both careers began along Missouri's western border. Bowen's concrete Southern foundation mirrored Lud's. Both harbored a deep hatred for abolitionists and shared a tight allegiance to Missouri Governor Elect, C.F. Jackson.[545] Bowen later became a Confederate Major

[544] **Note**: For a detailed discussion of the Southwest Expedition see *Cinders and Silence*.

General heralded as the "Stonewall of the West." The summer of 1863, the two men died within miles and days of each other following the Confederate defeat at Vicksburg.

John Bowen, a native Georgian and West Point graduate, had just turned thirty-one when he arrived in Bates County. In 1854 Bowen had been appointed Adjutant of St. Louis's Jefferson Barracks.[546] This promotion followed by just two months his marriage to Mary Kennerly. Mary had been born on the Jefferson Barracks' grounds and came from an established military family.

Col. John F. Snyder, commander of Missouri's Sixth Military District, joined the Southwest Expedition at the border. Snyder was Lud's military superior and a friend through politics. In early December Snyder reported to Gov. Stewart, "the State has not been invaded, nor is there any possibility at present of its invasion."[547] That said, Snyder requested "the Governor to establish an arsenal here for greater emergencies."[548] An arsenal was never established.

December 10, Gen. Frost and the main body of the expedition returned to St. Louis. Bowen however remained at the border commanding a four-company battalion. Three of the companies were created from expedition volunteers and the Polk County Rangers formed the fourth. The battalion spent the next five months patrolling Missouri's western border. Bowen's influence and character had a lasting impact. He assisted local militia companies in Cass, Bates, and Vernon counties. In late April 1861, after four months patrolling the border, Bowen's battalion, returned to Jefferson Barracks.

-------Quantrill's December Morgan Walker Raid ----------

By late 1860, cross border raids, by Kansans and Missourians, had become all too common. Kansan raids into Missouri became

---

545 **Note**: Although Claiborne F. Jackson was elected Missouri's Governor in August 1860 he did not take the Oath of Office until January 3, 1861.

546 Tucker. Page 32.

547 *Daily Missouri Democrat*. December 4, 1860.

548 *Daily Missouri Democrat*. December 4, 1860.

increasingly frequent between 1858 and 1860. Abolitionist raids to liberate slaves, and then move them into the Underground Railroad, increased dramatically. Common criminals joined abolitionists, both eagerly stealing livestock, horses, and property as well as slaves. The practice of "running slaves" thrived. Abducted slaves, shepherded to Kansas were sold back to their owners. In response to the raids, Missouri communities established border patrols.

Already on alert and itchy due to the Russell Hinds's murder, followed by the arrival of the Southwest Expedition, border communities were pushed to the edge with the night raid on Morgan Walker's Jackson County farm, December 10. Four armed Kansas raiders, including a then unknown William C. Quantrill, appeared on the Morgan Walker farm, outside Blue Springs, intending to liberate 30 slaves, while stealing livestock and horses. Quantrill betrayed his three cohorts, and they were all killed during the foray.

The attack's brazen nature rocked western Missouri slave owners and non-slave owners alike. It provided proof of the looming threat Lud had warned against. The day following the attempted theft nineteen Jackson County leaders, including Congressman John W. Reid, met in the Independence Court House to "organize local protection against such future acts."[549]

Within a week Jackson County's County Court appointed armed patrols. Eighteen Patrol Captains were appointed for one-year terms. The Captains represented individual districts within county townships and notable among the Captains were Upton Hays, Samuel Ralston, John McCoy, Minor T. Smith and the McGee's, F.M. and James. The patrol rosters contained 95 residents.[550]

The charged atmosphere "added more fuel to the fire" for Lud and others in Missouri advocating an armed, aggressive response to the increasing Kansan threat.

---

[549] *Border Star*. December 15, 1860.
[550] Jackson County Court Records. Book 11. Entries 99,728 – 99,745.

---------- Missouri: Union or Secession ----------

Lud Peyton arrived in Jefferson City in late December 1860 for the 21st Session of the Missouri General Assembly. South Carolina, on December 24, had voted to secede from the Union. Missouri's Assembly began its session December 31 amid apprehension and swirling speculation about the state's direction. As the uncertainty continued a dedicated group of ultra-Southerners, Lud paramount among them, began the push for secession.

January 3, 1861 Missouri's outgoing governor, R.M. Stewart, and incoming governor, C.F. Jackson held center stage. South Carolina's recent secession underscored the occasion.

John T. Tracy, Stewart's secretary, delivered the outgoing Governor's message. Stewart raged against the abolitionists, "the leaders and movers of this faction are infidels or fanatics in religion," and invoked the presence of *Uncle Tom's Cabin* attacking "novel writers" and "play actors" for feeding the abolitionist frenzy.[551] Stewart captured the moment's mood noting "a great crisis is not merely to be feared as approaching – it is already upon us. We see it in every man's face; we hear it in every man's voice."[552] Despite the threat and South Carolina's decision Stewart warned against "…the mad chimera of secession," and the "violence and blood" it would unleash in Missouri.[553] In conclusion, the Governor cautioned against "...unwise and hasty action," standing by his "unalterable devotion to the Union."[554]

The State Assembly reconvened in joint session during the afternoon to hear incoming Governor Claiborne F. Jackson's inaugural address. Jackson's address acknowledged South Carolina's secession decision and tied Missouri, unalterably to the

---

551 *Journal of the Senate of Missouri, First Session, Twenty-First General Assembly*. Page 21.

552 *Journal of the Senate of Missouri, First Session, Twenty-First General Assembly*. Page 23.

553 *Journal of the Senate of Missouri, First Session, Twenty-First General Assembly*. Page 25-26.

554 *Journal of the Senate of Missouri, First Session, Twenty-First General Assembly*. Page 27.

Southern cause: "So long as a State continues to maintain slavery within her limits, it is impossible to separate her fate from that of her sister States who have the same social organization."[555] Gov. Jackson requested the assembly to support two requests. Anticipating a convention of southern states, he requested a Missouri State Convention to define and act on the state's support the southern cause. Secondly, he asked for "a thorough organization of our military" in order to defend the state.[556]

Lud and the other ultra-Southern senators listened to Jackson's inaugural address fully prepped for his message and also poised for steps to secession. The morning following the inaugural, Lt. Gov. Thomas Reynolds chaired a meeting of the secessionists in the capitol's basement.[557] Unionists believed Reynolds, "a short chubby fellow of forty, with black hair and beard and eyes, and black moustache and dark skin," to be "the leading spirit of the secession cause in Missouri."[558] Plans in place, the legislative secessionists set about delivering Jackson's requests.

January 18 a Senate committee composed of Lud, Samuel Churchill, and Robert Wilson invited Daniel R. Russell to address a joint assembly session. Russell had arrived in Jefferson City as "Commissioner from Mississippi," ten days after Mississippi had seceded. In his evening speech, Russell "expressed the hope that Missouri would cooperate with her (Mississippi) in the adoption of efficient measures for the common defense and safety of the slave-holding states."[559]

On January 21 Gov. Jackson signed into law a bill convening a state convention. Convention delegates were to be elected February 18 and the convention called to order February 28. Each state senatorial district sent three times its number of senators; Lud's 14th

---

[555] *Journal of the Senate of Missouri, First Session, Twenty-First General Assembly*. Page 49.
[556] *Journal of the Senate of Missouri, First Session, Twenty-First General Assembly*. Page 53.
[557] Parrish. Page 5.
[558] Peckham. Page 27.
[559] Barnes. Page 323.

District was allowed three delegates to the convention. Lud, and his fellow secessionists, had misread the mood of the state's electorate. Expecting voters to be swept up in the pro-south, secession current, sending secessionist delegates to the convention, they were caught off guard by the election results.

Lud's 14th District, despite scars inflicted by the Fugitive Slave Act, despite the accelerating violence along the border, despite Peyton's fiery oratory to the contrary, elected three moderate Unionist delegates. Robert A. Brown, although one of Cass County's largest slave owners, supported the Constitutional Unionists and opposed secession. Jackson County supplied the other two convention delegates, Abram Comingo and Judge J.K. Sheley. Both men "were opposed to secession."[560] Statewide, voters sent Unionist delegates to the Convention.

The Missouri State Convention met for 19 days, February 28 through March 22, ultimately rejecting secession. The Convention's decision refuted Gov. Jackson's inaugural commitment to the South, and forever after, discounted Missouri's commitment to the Southern cause in the eyes of other Southern states. Secondarily undermining Confederate confidence, Sterling Price, later Major General of the Missouri State Guard, chaired the State Convention. Price "took strong ground in the canvass preceding the election of its members and in the convention itself, in advocacy of the Union and opposition to secession."[561]

The State Convention's decision to remain in the Union triggered "Southern Rights" rallies throughout Missouri. The rallies, in addition to condemning the Convention, passed resolutions "favoring immediate secession" and "recommending the Legislature to pass a secession ordinance."[562] Lud and other advocates attended the rallies fanning flames on behalf of the South.[563] The overall weight of public sentiment however continued with the Convention's judgment.

---

[560] *History of Jackson County*. Page 467.
[561] Duke. Location 738.
[562] *Missouri Statesman*. May 3, 1861.
[563] *Glasgow Weekly Times*. May 9, 1861.

---------- May Madness ----------

In May 1861, Lud's life and Missouri's history slid into the dark depths of Civil War. Although the State Convention had reaffirmed Missouri's commitment to the Union, Lud and his fellow ultra-Southern brethren worked feverishly to push the state into the Confederacy. Uncertainty predominated. Throughout April, tensions between unionists and dis-unionists escalated within a heartbeat of violence. Following the Confederate attack on Ft. Sumter, Lincoln requested Missouri troops as a part of his overall call for 75,000 troops. Gov. C.F. Jackson refused Lincoln, instead calling for a Special Session of the State Assembly to convene May 2 in Jefferson City.

On Thursday May 2, Lt. Gov. Thomas C. Reynolds called the Senate to order. Friday morning Gov. Jackson was notified both houses were present and prepared to begin deliberations. St. Louis's Senator Sam Churchill read Jackson's message to the Senate. The Governor reminded the assembly he had received a request from President Lincoln, on April 15, to supply four regiments "to aid in the prosecution of the civil war about to be inaugurated," and that he had responded to the federal government "Missouri would not furnish one man to assist in such a war."[564]

The Governor's statement, "Our interests and our sympathies are identical with those of the slaveholding States, and necessarily unite our destiny with theirs," blindly ignored the sentiments of the State Convention, moving the state into the southern camp.[565] Jackson requested that the assembly revise the Militia Law to prepare the state for defense. Additionally, he asked for the funding needed to enable the military buildup.

For the next 12 days the Missouri Assembly met in deliberation, many sessions were "secret" with the public galleries and chamber doors closed. Secrecy fueled rumors! The capitol building and Jefferson City became the center of a swirling vortex, amplified by

[564] *Journal of the Senate of the State of Missouri, Called Session*. Page 9.
[565] *Journal of the Senate of the State of Missouri, Called Session*. Page 10.

telegraph wires humming with events unfolding in St. Louis. General David Frost's state militia encamped at Jefferson Barracks near the federal arsenal. Frost's Camp Jackson drew the concerned attention of Federal authorities, fearing Frost intended to seize the arsenal for secessionists.

Jefferson City's explosive atmosphere expanded with uncertainty and the moment's significance. A St. Louis correspondent reported, "Let me assure you that this locality is overwhelmingly for the Union and the American flag," but "they have no arms and are forced to suppress their sentiments."[566] Streets and sidewalks also contained vocal secessionists, with more arriving from surrounding communities. Secessionist flags sprouted up in the city, one "from a pole within a few yards of the Governor's residence."[567] Rumors flew through hotels and bars fueled by the assembly's "behind closed doors" machinations. The secessionists especially seemed "constantly involved in exciting conversation."[568]

Jefferson City, Missouri
Harper's Weekly

Lud and fellow secessionists worked feverishly inside the capitol building to deliver Missouri to the South. Led by Lt. Gov. Tom Reynolds, the cabal included Jackson County's Nathan Claiborne, Johnson County's Mike Goodlett, Cooper County's George Vest, Polk County's Thomas Freeman, Ray County's Thomas Conrow, Cole County's Mosby M. Parsons and St. Louis's Sam Churchill. The entire club was deemed those "hot headed boys."

566 Peckham. Page 170.
567 Peckham. Page 170.
568 Peckham. Page 171.

In capitol chambers the dis-unionists walked into a strong headwind. Although holding a decided majority over dedicated Unionists, the fight over Gov. Jackson's two requests intensified. Generally the Senate met twice daily, conducting morning and afternoon sessions. Of the 12 sessions between May 3 and May 10, ten went into "secret session," with no tangible legislative result – outside chambers it was known every issue was "fiercely debated."[569]

Secret sessions fueled fear. Generally it was believed "a secession ordinance will be prepared as soon as thought practicable."[570] The general public objected to the Assembly's secrecy and newspapers riled against it. Editorials called the secrecy "tyrannical, uncalled for, and an usurpation of the rights of the people."[571] As tensions rose, some members of the Assembly began entering the chambers "with loaded guns."[572]

Despite the lack of a southern breakthrough, Lud and the secessionists scheduled a Confederate flag raising ceremony for Thursday night, May 9. Placards began appearing around Jefferson City a couple of days before announcing the event.

In the late afternoon, early evening, legislative dignitaries and the general public gathered "on the bluff immediately east of the Governor's mansion" overlooking the Missouri River.[573]

Come One, Come All!

The Flag of the Confederate States
Will be Flung to the breeze on
Thursday afternoon at 4 o'clock
At the foot of Madison Street

Ladies are all Invited to Attend

Speeches will be made by
Lt. Gov. Reynolds
Peyton
Vest
And Others

Event flier Prototype

569 *Daily Missouri Democrat.* May 7, 1861.
570 *Daily Missouri Democrat.* May 7, 1861.
571 *Daily Missouri Democrat.* May 9, 1861.
572 Peckham. Page 172.
573 *Missouri Daily Republican.* May 11, 1861.

As the proceedings began "several ladies, as per programme, hoisted the secession eight star flag to the top of the pole amid cheers."[574] As a spring thunderstorm rolled in, five men addressed the crowd, Lud being the third.[575]

Ladies Raising Confederate Flag,
May 9, 1861
Brian Hawkins, Artist

[574] *Daily Missouri Democrat*, May 11, 1861.
[575] **Note**: The five speakers were Michael C. Goodlett, George G. Vest, R.L.Y. Peyton, Thomas W. Freeman, and Nathan C. Claiborne.

Lud Peyton Demands Secession
May 9, 1861
Brian Hawkins, Artist

Not surprising, Lud's incendiary oratory sparked the most fire. The *Daily Missouri Democrat's* correspondent reported:

> "Peyton made an out and out secession speech. He alluded to the cause of the present troubles as viewed by him. The Union was dead never to rise again. The separation was final and Missouri must go with her Southern sisters. Every interest, State, and National ties, commanded her. He denounced the war policy of Lincoln as tending to make slaves of the Southern states. For the last 10 years the sardonic grin of death has been on the face of the Union. The man who in any public position armed neutrality, or that the Union could be again co-joined, was a *(illegible)* heart and would cut the throats or set fire to the buildings of the citizens of the State. True enemies, not treacherous friends, for him. His speech in fine, was one of the most ultra and called for immediate secession."[576]

When the speeches finished, "the crowd then separated, and a thunder storm shortly came up, and the flag was taken in out of the wet."[577] The approaching prairie storm, blotting out the sun, dispersing its lightning and thunder, strangely foreshadowed the following day's explosive events.

Friday, May 10, Missouri's heretofore, contentious debate between Unionists and dis-unionists jumped to armed confrontation, riot, and Civil War. At St. Louis, General Nathaniel Lyon overthrew Gen. David Frost's command, conquering Camp Jackson. Lyon marched Frost's command into St. Louis. Along the route riots erupted, Lyon's troops fired into the raucous crowd killing civilians, including children. Mayhem ruled! Telegrams ricocheted between St. Louis and Jefferson City. Friday afternoon the Senate, informed of the Camp Jackson episode passed a bill giving Gov. Jackson the authority and power to do what was necessary to "protect the people."[578]

---

576 *Daily Missouri Democrat*. May 11, 1861.
577 *Daily Missouri Republican*. May 11, 1861.
578 *Journal of the Senate of the State of Missouri, Called Session*. Page 76.

Later that night, both Houses met in extraordinary session. Each received communication from the Governor that "two regiments of Blair's are now on the way to the capital."[579] Although this later proved to be fictitious rumor, late in the night, Jackson County's Nathaniel Claiborne, following Gov. Jackson's instructions, boarded a train destined for the Osage River bridge. Basil Duke and "other legislators," including Samuel Hyer, assisted Claiborne in burning the bridge.[580] Duke had just arrived from New Orleans via St. Louis having successfully transported armaments, on the steamboat *Swan*, delivering them to Camp Jackson."[581] The first violent steps to war had been taken, and as the days ahead proved, there would be no coming back!

Gen.Sterling Price
Harpers Weekly Etching

Lud remained in Jefferson City until the legislature's "Special Session" adjourned on Wednesday, May 15. The panic triggered by the Camp Jackson affair incented the assembly to rapidly pass the legislation necessary to fund and staff what became the Missouri State Guard. Gov. Jackson's call for the men needed to defend Jefferson City resonated throughout the state. May 16, a company of about 100 men left Harrisonville, bound for Jefferson City.[582] Gov. Jackson appointed Sterling Price Major General of the State Guard May 15 and Price assumed his commission May 18.

Price's appointment carried uncertainty that would haunt him throughout the Civil War. Ultra-secessionists, Lud included, questioned Price's commitment to the South. Just days before Jackson granted Price's commission, the Governor had voiced

[579] *Journal of the Senate of the State of Missouri, Called Session*. Page 77.
[580] Duke. *Reminiscences*. Location 1,100.
[581] Duke. *Reminiscences*. Location 1,046.
[582] *Western Democrat*. May 18, 1861.

doubts "of General Price's being heartily with the South."[583] Lud Peyton's hesitancy in supporting Price, "unless he should come out plainly and unequivocally as a southern rights man," was well known.[584] The recent State Convention's Union endorsement, with Price as the Convention's President, tainted him forever in the eyes of the fire-eaters. Moderates however welcomed Price's appointment as taking some of the power away from the dedicated secessionists. After the war, Lt. Gov. Reynolds recounted a conversation with Andrew County's state senator, Robert Wilson. Upon hearing of Price's selection Wilson commented, "'I am glad Price is to take command. If these hot-headed boys who are now commanding are left to themselves, they will carry us to the devil.' Wilson alluded to Parsons, Peyton, Calton Green, and others who were taking charge of the volunteers arriving."[585]

James S.Rains
Courtesy State Historical Society of Missouri

Price appointed James S. Rains Brig. Gen. of the Guards Eighth Division on May 18. Immediately, Lud and Rains left Jefferson City initiating a recruiting trip. The two men hit all the southwest Missouri counties before moving north up the border to Harrisonville. Lud and Rains had become friends while serving in the Missouri Senate. Rains hailed from Sarcoxie in southwest Missouri. He had gained military experience in California and after settling in Missouri worked as an Indian Agent.

One of the towns the pair visited that spring was Carthage, Jasper County. Each of the men addressed the crowd in the Jasper County courthouse. Among the listeners stood a young John Maloy; Maloy would later become Lud's personal and business secretary in Richmond, VA. Years later, Maloy reminisced:

583 Reynolds. Page 31.
584 Reynolds. Page 23.
585 Reynolds. Page 26.

"'Colonel Peyton addressed an immense crowd in the courthouse. His speech was a flame of fiery eloquence; sometimes persuasive and soothing, and at times vehemently denunciatory. It was at times picturesque with metaphor and classical illustration. I remember at the conclusion of one of his periods, abounding with climax, I looked suddenly out of the court house window expecting to see the public square filled with blood-thirsty Jay-Hawkers. He assailed the constitutional union man as paltering in a double sense, waiting to see, like the York or Lancaster, whether the red or the white rose predominated. It had a powerful effect on the audience. It greatly impressed me and I shall never wholly forget it, although I was in my teens."[586]

Lud's rhetoric throughout the recruiting tour, continued to call for armed rebellion. Lud spoke in southeast Cass County in late May alarming friends and leaders alike. Harrisonville's Provost Marshal, John Christian, hurriedly wrote Col. F.P. Blake, "I have been told by several that Senator Peyton, in one of his speeches at Austin or Dayton, said that what they could not get at the ballot box, they would take with the bayonet and bullet…"[587]

Lud and Rains separated after Harrisonville. Rains continued recruiting, traveling north to Jackson and Lafayette counties. Lud returned to Jefferson City and Gov. Jackson. When Gov. Jackson and Maj. Gen. Price went to St. Louis to meet personally with Gen. Nathaniel Lyon, Lud remained in Jefferson City. What became known as the Planter's House Conference ended disastrously with Lyon storming out of the meeting, after declaring war. Jackson and Price retreated back to Jefferson City. June 12 Jackson issued a proclamation calling out the Missouri State Guard entreating Missourians to "Rise, then, and drive out ignominiously the invaders."[588]

---

586 Sloan, Charles W. "Robert Ludwell Yates Peyton." *The Green Bag.* Volume X, No. 10. October 1898. Page 415.
587 Missouri Secretary of State. Provost Marshal Records.
588 Peckham. Page 252.

Immediately, the situation became critical for Jackson and his staff, as "Lyon embarked with two thousand men on a military expedition toward Jefferson City, traveling up the Missouri River by boat rather than by rail as Jackson had expected."[589]

Gov. Jackson hastily "wired supporters and troops commanders around the state of the latest events, ordering them to move with all haste to Boonville."[590] He and his staff gathered documents, currency, and other state records. Lud assured Jackson of his allegiance, affirming he would "remain loyal to the bitter end."[591] June 13, as Lyon sped toward Jefferson City, Jackson and members of his government boarded the steamboat *White Cloud* and fled to Boonville. Jackson's political entourage numbered about 10 – Lud among them. Other legislative members were Warwick Hough, Thomas J. Churchill, James H. McBride, Aaron H. Conrow, Thomas W. Freeman, and Thomas A. Harris.[592]

At Boonville, Lyon's Federal forces routed Jackson's militia June 17. Jackson ordered his command to southwest Missouri while he fled to his Howard County home, collecting his family before following the troops. Lud left Boonville quickly moving to join Price and Rains at Lexington.

---------- Rains's Eighth Division ----------

Since the state legislature's adjournment Rains had spent his time recruiting for the Missouri State Guard's Eighth Division. His geographic territory contained two tiers of the western border counties from the Missouri River to the Arkansas line. Cass, Bates, Vernon, and Jackson counties, along with 15 other western Missouri counties fell into the Eighth Division. By a sad twist of fate, the division's portion of Missouri was destined to experience the most horrific, sustained devastation of any area within Missouri during the Civil War. What became known as Missouri's Burnt

589 Phillips. Page 260.
590 Phillips. Page 260.
591 Peckham. Page 169.
592 Phillips. Page 260. Note 25.

District, Lud's 14th Senatorial District, fell squarely in Rains's department.

Missouri's Military Districts 1861

The word spread that Brig. Gen. Rains and Sterling Price were recruiting for the Missouri State Guard in Lafayette and Jackson counties. Ragtag companies made their way to the recruiting assembly points. These "companies" arrived for service in low military standards for readiness. The men, mostly from farms, wore what they had on their backs. As yet, uniforms did not exist. Those who arrived mounted, on their own horses, became the cavalry. Those on foot became the infantry. About a third arrived unarmed and those with arms carried shotguns, squirrel rifles, and old muskets. A few officers had military training and experience but most were elected officers on the basis of local notoriety and status.

Brig. Gen. Rains faced the daunting task of recruiting and training a legitimate fighting brigade. He needed trained infantry. He needed an effective cavalry. He needed seasoned artillery.

Rains placed Col. Richard H. Weightman, in charge of the infantry. "With his infantry in Weightman's capable hands and his artillery under Bledsoe's tutelage, Rains invested his energy into organizing his cavalry. The division's largest and best equipped arm consisted of ten companies spread among three commands, each led by an experienced officer."[593]

Lud Peyton (3rd Mo. Cavalry), Lt. Col. James B. McCowan (2nd Battalion), and Lt. Col. Richard A. Boughman (7th Mo. Cavalry) commanded Rains' three cavalry regiments. Peyton's regiment was the smallest of the three with slightly more than a hundred men. The other two cavalry commands each contained 250 horsemen.

The Eighth's Division's artillery was placed in Hiram Bledsoe's capable hands. Bledsoe assumed command as a veteran of both the Mexican campaign and the border war. Each of the artillery pieces had a name. The more famous was "Old Sacramento," a veteran of the Mexican War. Another piece, a six pounder, was affectionately named "The Black Bitch."[594] Bledsoe, a Lafayette County farmer, survived the war, settling in Pleasant Hill.

Rains's Eighth Division failed to meet the minimum standards of an army command. Many of the recruits arrived without weapons. Because of the lack of weapons, a large segment of the Eighth Division merely watched during the battles of the next few months. Even those arriving with weapons, carried shotguns and squirrel rifles; in battle, these proved of little use because of their short ranges and the painfully slow reloading process.

The new recruits arrived with high energy and enthusiasm but no military training. Largely unarmed and totally untrained, these newly formed companies were unprepared for upcoming fights. The entire army appeared rag tag. Although a few of the officers had uniforms none of the rank and file did. Shoes quickly became a problem. The hours of drilling coupled to long marches destroyed boots and shoes. Many men marched barefoot.

---

[593] Hinze and Farnham. Page 83.

[594] *Confederate Veteran*. Volume XI, 1903. Page 424.

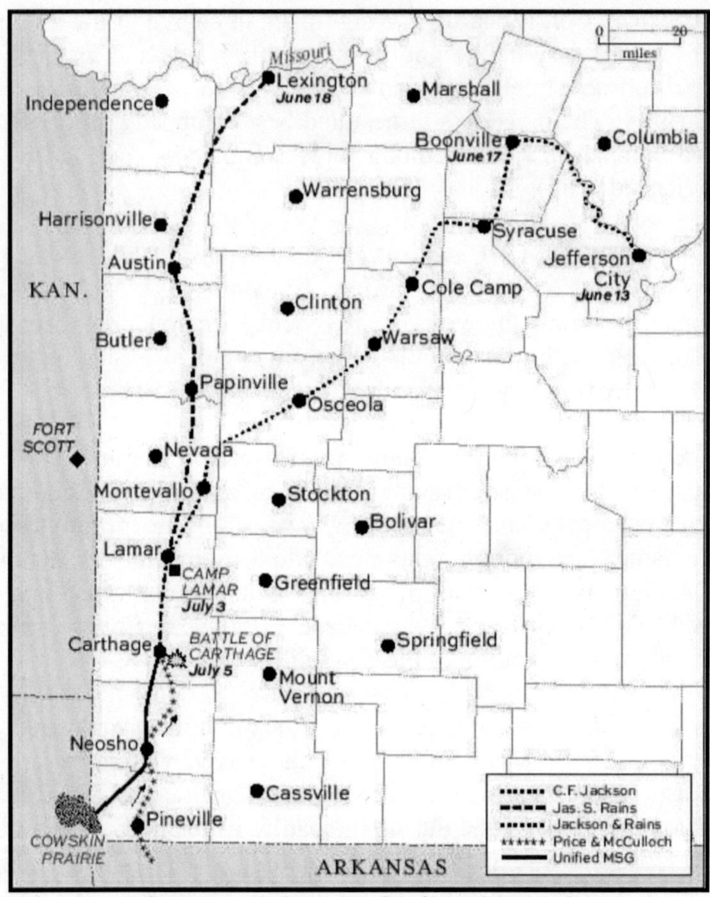

*Secessionist's Retreat to Southwest Missouri**
June-July 1861

June 19, under orders to merge his command with that of Gov. C.F. Jackson, Brig. Gen. Rains left Jackson County marching toward southwest Missouri. The first day, the command covered 20 miles reaching Austin. The next day, June 20, Rains camped at Papinville.

---

*Note: Rains' day-to-day movements in Jackson and Lafayette Counties remain clouded. He gathered recruits in both.

The weather became an obstacle. Heavy unrelenting rains engorged all of the local rivers, slowing progress, making river crossings dangerous. Between Lexington and Warrensburg the Black River overflowed its banks. The raging Grand River at Osceola presented a greater challenge. Rains' new recruits marching in torrential downpours and deep mud, camped without shelter. Tents, along with other basic supplies, were not supplied.

Delayed by the poor weather and heavy rains, the Rain's Eighth Division finally crossed the Grand River followed by the Little Osage River on June 28. By July 2 the command had arrived at Lamar in Barton County, and established "Camp Lamar."

Gov. Jackson's command arrived from Boonville, July 3. "The long awaited unification despite the miserable weather, improved the morale of the army."[595] When Gov. Jackson's contingent arrived Rains'men fired off a cannon. Brig. Gen. Rains and Gov. Jackson inspected the men and "in actuality the army that coalesced on the third day of July was little more than two mobs of men with only a semblance of order and discipline."[596]

---------- Peyton's Third Cavalry ----------

Lud had reunited with Brig. Gen. Rains at Lexington. There a flood of local militia companies, small groups and individual recruits created organizational chaos. Companies and regiments gradually coalesced largely based on geographic identity. Those from Lud's border constituency, already familiar, grouped naturally. These border companies, not yet a recognized regiment, headed south under Peyton's yet unofficial leadership.

When Rains left Jackson County for southwest Missouri (Maj. Gen. Price had departed for Arkansas earlier to solicit help from Confederate forces) to unite with Gov. Jackson's command, not all of the companies from the surrounding counties had arrived. William Marchbank's Bates and Vernon counties cavalry got a late start arriving at Lexington after Rains had marched. Marchbank's doubled back, finally uniting with Rains at Camp Lamar.

[595] Hinze and Farnham. Page 87.
[596] Hinze and Farnham. Page 87.

Marchbank's company, a border unit, was integrated with Lud's cavalry as Company "B."

Brig. Gen. Rains's march to southwest Missouri stopped outside Lamar in Barton County. Camp Lamar swelled when Gov. Jackson's command arrived July 3. Rains took advantage of the brief pause to formalize the organization of many of the regiments and companies. On July 3 Lud was officially elected Colonel of the 3rd Cavalry, MSG. The same day Martin White was elected Lt. Col., Nathan Tyler was elected Major, and David Warren was elected Captain of Company "G."

Lud's military qualifications were thin. He was hardly qualified to train then lead a cavalry regiment in battle. During the Mexican War, rather than enlist and fight, Peyton had elected to remain in Harrisonville. His slim military experience had been gained during the 1856 to 1860 border conflict when he and William Briscoe had led the neighborhood home guard units. Lud's military qualifications were greatly exceeded by another Cass Countian, Edgar V. Hurst. Hurst had been educated at the Kentucky Military Institute and was a veteran border militia commander.[597]

Lud's election as colonel, following the time's custom, resulted from his political station, his passion for the cause, and the recommendation of men like Rains. Known and liked by the men, Lud received their support. Regardless of his qualifications, Lud performed well in the heat of battle.

Lud's Third Cavalry roster was uniquely a hardened border regiment. The Company "A" roster contained Bates County men who had organized in mid-May. Vernon County men largely composed Company "B." Companies "C" through "H" and also included men from those western border counties. The officers and

[597] **Edgar V. Hurst**: Hurst commanded the Missouri State Guard's Third Infantry Regiment. He achieved high recognition for his leadership at the Battle of Wilson's Creek. Slightly wounded, he returned to Cass County to recuperate. In January 1862 he was cornered, near his home, and killed by Federal troops.

men of Lud's regiment were all veterans of the border conflict, acutely and personally aware of the Kansas threat.

None of the officers on Peyton's staff exceeded the reputation and respect of his 58 year-old Lt. Col., Martin White. When Gov. Jackson's plea for men went out, White was living in Bates County near Papinsville. Before moving to Bates County, Martin and his family had settled in the Kansas Territory from Christian County, Illinois. White had served in the Illinois House of Representatives with Abraham Lincoln; Lincoln had represented White in a legal dispute.

In 1855 Martin settled on a tract of land "twelve miles southwest of Paola, Kansas and seven miles from Osawatomie."[598] Shortly thereafter John Brown's family settled in the same neighborhood. Martin and John Brown clashed early on becoming known enemies.

August 11, 1856 John Brown, Sr. accompanied by other abolitionists attacked the White farm.[599] The attack thwarted, Brown fled, in the process stealing all of White's livestock. Three weeks later, August 30, acting to recover his livestock, Martin joined Missourians heading to Osawatomie and John Brown. Jackson County's John Reid led the regiment. As Reid's command neared Osawatomie, an advance scout, of which White was a member, encountered Frederick Brown II, one of John Brown's sons. During the confrontation, White shot and killed Frederick.

Frederick's death moved Martin White squarely into the abolitionist crosshairs. James Montgomery swore to kill White and avenge Frederick's murder.[600] In consequence, White left Kansas resettling in Bates County.

Martin White required no introduction. The fact he was elected Lt. Colonel of the regiment attested to his status. His presence provided identity to the 3rd Cavalry Regiment. Lud and Martin

598 Donovan, Ethel. Page 1.
599 Donovan, Ethel. Page 2.
600 *Daily Missouri Democrat*. January 8, 1859.

shared elevated reputations along the border. Both were veterans of the six-year border conflict. Each brought credibility.

Lud's Regimental Surgeon, Dr. Jacob F. Brookhart had fought with Martin White at the Battle of Osawatomie. Brookhart, a Harrisonville resident, had been a member of Reid's regiment of the "Army of Law and Order." A veteran of the border war and Harrisonville civic leader Jacob's enlistment attracted other local recruits. Lud and Jacob had been friends and political allies for years.

William Doak's reputation preceded him, leading to his election as the Captain of Company "A." A frontiersman and adventurer, in 1857, Doak had led gold hunters to the Colorado gold fields. By 1860, Doak was the Bates County Sheriff, managing state provided muskets and ammunition for the Butler militia. A border veteran, Doak had led local home guard units facing off against James Montgomery. When Civil War flared William was well known, respected and feared along Missouri's western border.

Lud and William were not strangers. They first met during Butler circuit court sessions where, as lawyer and sheriff respectively, they administered the law. When local militia units were organized in the late 1850s they coordinated training and arming. They again crossed paths during the Southwest Expedition.

William Marchbank's, 27, recruited a Vernon County volunteer company in May. Marchbank's, along with the other Vernon County recruits, had lived under the threats and attacks of Kansas's abolitionists. A long time resident, Marchbank's had crossed the border and voted in the Kansas Territorial elections of 1854 and 1855. Ferocious, Marchbank's later in the war surfaced as one of western Missouri's most feared guerilla leaders.

These men, White, Doak, Brookhart, and Marchbank's, along with Lud and William Briscoe, personified the Third Cavalry. Border veterans, devoted to Missouri, they led a regiment already seasoned by years of border conflict. Outside Lamar they were finally, formally merged into a single fighting unit.

Camp Lamar, renamed Camp Jackson upon the Governor's arrival, now contained about 6,000 men, of whom 2,000 were unarmed. The camp, situated on the North Fork of the Spring River, swelled as new recruits arrived. Lud and his contemporaries struggled to integrate the new men into a semblance of military organization. Attempts to integrate the new recruits and initiate some form of military order and training occurred under the increasing stress of the Federal pursuit under Gen. Nathaniel Lyon and Gen. Franz Sigel. Also, rumors circulated, accurately, that Major Samuel Sturgis' federal command had entered western Missouri joining the pursuit.

---------- Battle of Carthage ----------

July 5, around 4:00 a.m., word reached Gov. Jackson, at the MSG camp, of approaching federal troops. Jackson ordered Rains south to Carthage to meet the approaching threat. Brig. Gen. Rains placed Col. Peyton in charge of the division's cavalry. Although, by this time, most of the cavalry had weapons, the lack of ammunition, caused a critical problem. Of the nine companies under Peyton's command, only two companies and a portion of a third had sufficient ammunition to fight. The units without ammunition were held out of the approaching fight.

Rain's division continued its march south and by 9:00 a.m. faced off against Gen. Franz Sigel's federal troops. The cavalry anchored the Missouri State Guard's right flank. "Its commander was Col. R.L.Y. Peyton. Peyton was ordered by Rains just moments before the battle to take command of his own Third Cavalry, together with the battalions of Col. James McCowan and Lt. Col. Richard Boughan, plus two small mounted companies. McCowan's Battalion took up an advanced position 300 yards in front and to the right of Peyton's main body. Peyton's men remained mounted."[601]

Fighting erupted between 9:30 and 10:00 a.m. with artillery exchanges between the two armies. Hiram Bledsoe and Henry Guibor directed the MSG's guns and inflicted heavy damage. The

[601] Hinze and Farnham. Page 118.

federal artillery returned fire as the two armies faced each other. In the midst of the cannonade, Brig. Gen. Rains made the fateful decision to take personal command of the cavalry regiments on his right and lead an attempt to turn the federal left flank. As gallant as Rains's decision may have seemed it left the MSG command leaderless during the height of the fight. Gov. Jackson meanwhile remained in the rear of the MSG's army with 2,000 unarmed men.

The cavalry continued its rushed attempt to turn the federal left. Lud's men followed Rains and Col. James McCowan's men. In his battle report Lud indicated, "This was done under a severe and heavy fire from the cannon of the enemy, both officers and privates bore themselves with calmness and gallantry. Every officer and private in the whole column, as you yourself (Rains) can testify were ready to obey any call you might give them."[602] The 3rd Cavalry's rush through the cannonade was made without suffering the loss of any men but such was not the case for McCown and Boughan's regiments.

With Rains absent from the MSG's main body, commanders were left to fight on their own initiative. Parsons, simultaneous with Rains's decision to turn the federal's left flank, decided to rush around the federal's right flank with his cavalry. Weightman's infantry pushed forward toward the federal center. Sigel, in addition to flanking actions on each of his wings and approaching infantry, had to deal with the fact his artillery was nearly out of ammunition. Given these circumstances, as well as the need to protect his 32-wagon supply train, Sigel retreated back toward Carthage, reforming on the other side of Dry Fork Creek.

With Weightman's infantry leading the way, the MSG hotly pursued Sigel's retreating Federals. As Sigel's troops neared Buck's Branch Creek they saw MSG cavalry had reached the creek crossing ahead of them. Only the cool headed leadership of Lt. Col. Francis Hassendeubel kept the federal troops and the wagon train moving toward the MSG cavalry supported by limited artillery fire.

---

602 Hinze and Farnham. Page 135.

The outmanned and outgunned cavalry had to yield to the approaching federal soldiers.

While fighting raged along the Carthage – Lamar Road, Rains's cavalry was far away on the federal's left. Rains had led the cavalry a mile west of the fighting in hopes of finding a suitable ford. Finally, finding a ford, with the federal retreating back toward Carthage, Rains ordered a halt. He left the cavalry with orders to remain while he returned to the main body. Rains then abandoned Col. Peyton and the other cavalry commanders without orders.

Soon after Rains's departure Lud made the decision to rejoin the fighting. Lud realized that with the Federals in retreat, the opportunity for a complete victory still remained if they could take advantage of the circumstances. Lud's battle report indicated, "Before your return to my command the column was marched forward in order to intercept the enemy at or before he should march to Carthage which movement afterwards met with your approbation."[603]

Rains's inept leadership had taken the Southern cavalry so far from the fighting, Sigel was able to retreat back into and through Carthage, escaping complete calamity. The "Southern cavalry never seriously challenged the Federal column during this segment of the withdrawal."[604] The significance of the lost opportunity was not lost on the remainder of Rains's command. A rumor began to circulate that the cavalry had halted and rested to eat blackberries. "Unable to shake the gossip, Rains' horsemen were thereafter derisively labeled the 'Blackberry Cavalry.'"[605]

Lud performed well at the Battle of Carthage. He entered the fray an untested regimental commander but as nightfall began he had earned the respect of his superiors and his men. In the chaos of battle he demonstrated courage and initiative validating both his rank and leadership. July 5, 1861 marked his military rite-of-passage.

603 Hinze and Farnham. Page 173.
604 Hinze and Farnham. Page 174.
605 Hinze and Farnham. Page 176.

---------- Cowskin Prairie ----------

July 6 Rains's victorious Eighth Division combined forces with Brig. Gen. Ben McCulloch and Major Gen. Sterling Price. Generals McCulloch and Price had been rushing toward Carthage from north Arkansas to join Rains when word reached them of the Guard's Carthage success. When McCulloch's Confederate forces first appeared the Missouri State Guard cheered. A bystander wrote, "No wonder that we burst into loud huzzas when the redoubtable McCulloch came into sight, surrounded by his gaily-dressed staff, and when accompanied by Governor Jackson, General Price, and General Pearce, he rode down our dust-stained ranks to greet the men that fought with Sigel and put him to flight."[606]

The troops Brig. Gen. McCulloch observed appeared far from the normal military standard. "In all their motley array there was hardly a uniform to be seen, and then, and throughout all the brilliant campaign on which they were about to enter there was nothing to distinguish their officers, even a general, from the men in the ranks, save a bit of red flannel, or a piece of cotton cloth fastened to the shoulder, or to the arm, of the former."[607] Considerable effort was needed to transform the rag-tag Missouri State Guard into a disciplined and effective fighting force. Shortly after uniting the units of Gov. Jackson, Price and Rains, the entire command turned to the southwest and Cowskin Prairie.

Cowskin Prairie lies in what today is McDonald County; the county occupies Missouri's very southwest corner. The prairie lies less than five miles north of the Arkansas border and spills west into, what was in 1861, Indian Territory, and what today is Oklahoma. It would not be possible to find a prairie further to the southwest in Missouri.[608] "An open area formerly used as a place for

---

[606] Snead. Page 238.
[607] Snead. Page 238.
[608] **Note**: Cowskin Prairie rests "In the southwest part of the county (McDonald), the Cowskin Prairie extends some five miles square," and is in Prairie Township, "named from Cowskin Prairie which extends over the great portion of its surface." Reference – *Illustrated History of McDonald Co., Missouri.*

slaughtering cattle, it (Cowskin Prairie) was well positioned as a training camp."[609] For the next 16 days, from July 6 to July 25, the MSG forces encamped at Cowskin Prairie drilling to transform the collection of farmers and tradesmen into a disciplined and dangerous army.

Cowskin Prairie Circa 1861

Lud's 3rd Cavalry, although bloodied at Carthage, took full advantage of the time and space at Cowskin Prairie to drill, for the first time since organization. The prairie's size allowed the cavalry to exercise and drill. Diaries recorded that "the daily drill sessions lasted from four to six hours."[610] Throughout the two weeks of intense training, the bonds between man and horse as well as between the officers and cavalrymen tightened.

---

[609] Piston and Hatcher III. Page 114.
[610] Piston and Hatcher III. Page 115.

Col. Peyton in top hat- Courtesy State Historical Society of Missouri

In appearance, Lud's cavalry remained ragtag. Uniforms were a non-existent dream. Men wore the same clothes they had worn at enlistment or makeshift uniforms creatively sown. A sketch of Lud drawn during the summer of 1861 shows him in civilian clothes with a top hat.

The men's energy and enthusiasm overshadowed the non-military appearance but could not offset the lack of proper weapons. Most of the men still carried shotguns and squirrel guns. The weapons, from all vintages and designs, were not suitable for battle and a far cry from the long range rifles carried by the Federals. In total, 2,000 members of the Missouri State Guard at Cowskin Prairie still had no weapons!

July 25, when the Southern command moved out of Cowskin Prairie, Peyton's 3rd Cavalry had been assimilated into a reorganized cavalry brigade led by Col. James Cawthorn. Col. Peyton's 3rd Cavalry represented one of three regiments under Cawthorn. Colonels James McCowan and DeWitt C. Hunter lead the other two cavalry units. A majority of Hunter's regimental roster came from Vernon County. Hunter himself was a veteran of the California gold fields.[611]

Lt. Col. McCowan's 2nd Cavalry roster largely came from Johnson and St. Clair counties, Mo.[612] McCowan himself, like Lud a native Virginian, had lived in Warrensburg before the hostilities. Lt. Col. McCowan survived the war and surrendered at Jackson, Mississippi in 1865.[613] Cawthorn's three regiments sprang from border counties south of the Missouri River and all were staffed by veterans of the

[611] **Note**: DeWitt C. Hunter subsequently joined Jo Shelby's Iron Brigade and achieved considerable military fame.
[612] *Sterling Price's Lieutenants*. Page 367.
[613] *Sterling Price's Lieutenants*. Page 361.

Kansas Territory border troubles. He now commanded 1,200 horsemen.

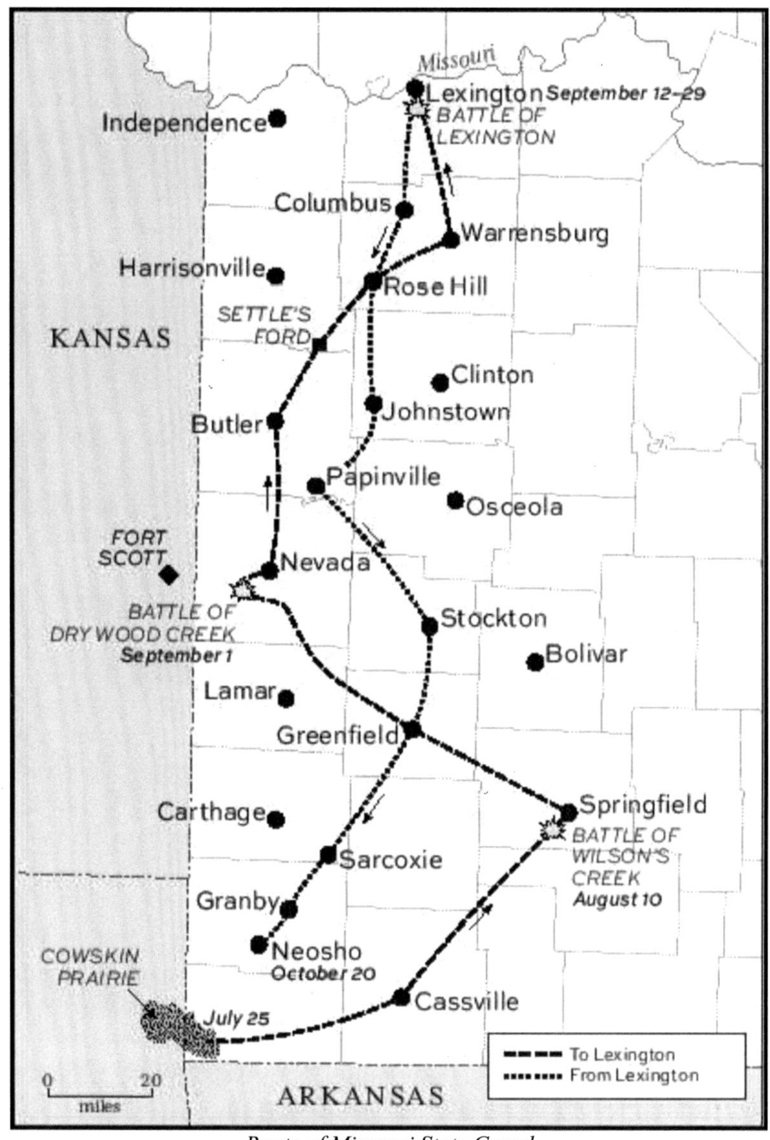

Route of Missouri State Guard
July-October 1861

---------- Dug Springs ----------

Away from Cowskin Prairie, Lyon's Federals pursued Price's army. Gen. Lyon's command had arrived in Springfield, July 13. Price and McCulloch jointly decided to move north and attack the Federals at Springfield. July 25 the Southern army began leaving Cowskin Prairie moving to Cassville just 50 miles southwest of Springfield.

Unfortunately, more than armed soldiers left Cowskin Prairie, "contrary to an understanding he had reached with McCulloch, Price allowed some two thousand unarmed men and a significant number of women to follow along."[614] By July 28, Price had 7,000 men in position at Cassville.[615]

By an ironic twist of fate, the night of August 1, Gen. Nathaniel Lyon and his command, having moved out of Springfield, camped at Wilson's Creek within sight of the scrub covered hill that would soon and forever be known as "Bloody Hill" – the hill would host Gen. Lyon's death. That same evening the main body of the Southern forces camped at Crane Creek miles to the southwest.

Lyon sent an advance battalion under Capt. Frederick Steele ahead of his main force hoping to locate McCulloch's main command. August 2, Steele's battalion, under sweltering 110-degree heat, moved seven miles and camped at Dug Springs. Evening approaching, "around 5:00 p.m. a great cloud of dust became visible in the distance."[616] Rains was on the move, he personally led the fast approaching MSG advance scout.

Steele positioned his men on the high ground surrounding Dug Springs. Neither Steele nor Rains knew the size of their enemy opposition but each feared the worst, an enemy beyond their own size. Rains launched a full-scale attack with his six companies of mounted cavalry. The Southern soldiers were met with withering small arms fire and canister. Rains's men turned tail and raced

614 Piston and Hatcher III. Page 137.
615 Piston and Hatcher III. Page 136.
616 Piston and Hatcher III. Page 140.

back in the direction from which they had come. In their haste to escape the Federals, the scared cavalrymen rushed right through McIntosh's advancing support of 150 cavalrymen.

Although the skirmish at Dug Spring held little military significance, it labeled Rains and his cavalrymen as weak kneed and cowardly. The entire episode became known as "Rains's Scare." Henceforth McCulloch's confidence in Rains and his command disappeared. All of the other fighting units in McCulloch's command had witnessed, and never forgot, Rains's panic filled retreat.

The position of Lud's 3rd Cavalry during the Dug Springs skirmish is not known. When the Guard command left Cassville, Rains's Eighth Division cavalry were the last units to leave. Lud's regiment probably remained with the main army due to unfamiliarity with the local terrain. Rains preferred having his knowledgeable local companies with him on August 2. Regardless, the outcome of the Dug Spring skirmish put a permanent stain on Rains's military reputation.

---------- Battle of Wilson's Creek ----------

General Lyon, fearing the approaching Southern force, retreated back to Springfield following the Dug Spring skirmish. The Southern forces continued their march toward Springfield. By evening, August 6, McCulloch's command had settled in at Wilson's Creek, on Springfield's outskirts. Cawthorn's three cavalry regiments were camped between the huge brush covered hill that rose to the west and Wilson's Creek. From north to south the three regiments encamped with Hunter on the far north, McCowan's Cavalry in the middle and Peyton's 3rd Cavalry on the south.

Between August 6 and August 9 the commanders of both armies debated next steps. Lyon, fearing a considerably larger foe and struggling with supply issues, initially decided to leave Springfield, retreating to Rolla. However, on August 8, he reversed course making the decision to attack the Southerners with all he had the next day.

Price and his subordinates pressured, a tentative Gen. McCulloch into attacking. August 9, McCulloch finally agreed to attack Lyon at Springfield, ordering a 9:00 p.m. night march, but rain forced a delay. Meanwhile, earlier, Lyon's attacking federal troops had launched from Springfield at 5:00 p.m.

Lyon split his force into two separate commands. Lyon, leading the first, would attack McCulloch from the west while Sigel, leading the second, would attack from the east. Lyon would strike the first blow then Sigel, hearing the firing, would initiate his attack. Lyon's troops reached the western edge of the Southerner's camp around 5:00 a.m., August 10.

A small group of Southern foragers skirmished with Lyon's advance guard and the alert was sounded. Southern commanders, heretofore focused on attacking Springfield were instantly forced into defensive measures. Cawthorn ordered Hunter to reconnaissance the approaching Federals. Hunter took 300 cavalrymen and moved up the hill toward Lyon. The Federals were forming a battle line, moving artillery into place. Hunter moved his men in line, causing the Federals to hesitate. "This gave Cawthorn time to sound the alarm and organize the rest of the division's mounted troops, which were camped both in the Gibson's Mill area and on the main portion of Bloody Hill itself."[617]

Lyon's troops charged. Their attack pushed Hunter's Cavalry back down the hill. "Had Rains' troops been camped on a color line, like good troops are supposed to be, instead of promiscuously wherever they chose, our lines (MSG's lines) would have been forced before we were fairly awake."[618]

Cawthorn reacted. "He formed the rest of his mounted brigade, at least six hundred strong, into position on the crest of the main

[617] Piston and Hatcher III. Page 197.
[618] "The War in Missouri." *Southern Bivouac*. April 1886. Page 679.

portion of Bloody Hill to create a second line of defense. He apparently did this on his own initiative, without waiting for orders from Rains. Colonel Robert L.Y. Peyton placed his regiment on the left, while Lieutenant Colonel James McCowan aligned his troops on the right." [619] The cavalrymen dismounted and the horses were moved behind the line. Hunter's retreating men fortified this line.

The federal advance, the First Kansas and the First Missouri, drove the Southerners off the crest of Bloody Hill. "Perhaps because they could see that they would soon be outflanked, the Missouri State Guardsmen raced for their horses, and in the ensuing confusion men became separated. As a result, Hunter's and Peyton's units did not rejoin Cawthorn until much later that morning."[620]

The battle raged throughout the morning, largely focused on Bloody Hill. Sigel's attack from the east failed and he retreated. Between 11:00 and 11:30 General Lyon was killed on Bloody Hill. His next in command, Gen. Sam Sturgis called retreat and by 5:00 p.m. the Federals were back in Springfield. Fearing rapid pursuit from Price, the Federal troops fled Springfield rushing northeast to Rolla in a huge body consisting of over 370 wagons and hundreds of Union civilians.[621]

Lud's regiment, in the immediate aftermath of battle, experienced war's unromantic reality. The intense August sun and heat beat down upon the dead of both sides. Within hours corpses rapidly began decomposition. The stench wafted through the entire battlefield and into Springfield. One member of a Missouri State Guard burial detail remembered, "'the stench was awful then, and what it must have been two days later would baffle imagination.'"[622] Two days after the battle, physician John Wyatt moved through the battlefield and wrote, "Many of the wounded are lying where they fell in the blazing sun, unable to get water and aid

[619] Piston and Hatcher III. Page 198.
[620] Piston and Hatcher III. Page 201.
[621] Piston and Hatcher III. Page 305.
[622] Piston and Hatcher III. Page 301.

of any kind. Blow flies swarm over the living and dead alike. I saw men not yet dead, their eyes, nose & mouth full of maggots."[623]

Price and McCulloch's Southern forces occupied Springfield and its environs. They established a string of camps stretching from Springfield westward to Mt. Vernon, a distance of 25 miles. The encampments, strung out, allowed the thousands of men and horses access to forage and water. Weather conditions remained excessively hot as the soldiers recouped following the battle.

Generals Price and McCulloch debated next steps. Price argued strongly for a push north to the Missouri River. McCulloch, whose responsibilities tied him to Indian Territory, wavered over a push further north into Missouri. Following a series of fruitless discussions, Price made the decision to reassume command of the Missouri State Guard and push north without McCulloch. August 14 Price formally took command of the Missouri troops.

The Missouri State Guard remained camped in and around Springfield for 10 days. Lud's regiment, like others, took advantage of the time to heal and reorganize. Lud's men had been right at the apex of the Battle of Wilson's Creek when the fighting began on August 10. They fought both on horseback and on foot. The entire morning of August 10 Lud's separated regiment had been in the thick of the heat and the fight, on and around "Bloody Hill."

The regiment went into encampment as blooded veterans. Within the space of five weeks they had fought Federal troops at Carthage and Wilson's Creek. Both engagements were victorious. Although ragged in appearance and partially armed, Lud's command eagerly looked forward to a march north to Lexington.

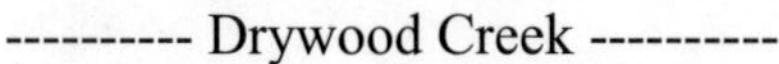

---------- Drywood Creek ----------

When hostilities began the summer of 1861, Kansas's Jayhawkers increased raids into western Missouri. The Jayhawkers entered

[623] Eakins. *Diary of a Doctor, Missouri State Guards*. 1861. Page 10.

Missouri looting, burning and killing before retreating back into Kansas with their booty. By the end of August 1861, these attacks had devastated Vernon and Bates counties. The number of able-bodied men absent in the Missouri State Guard left the border communities defenseless.

Nearby, Ft. Scott became the recruiting depot for abolitionist, James H. Lane who was organizing three regiments of what was to become known as Lane's Kansas Brigade. These regiments, led by James Montgomery, William Weer, and H.P. Johnson soon became the scourge of western Missouri. Simultaneously, Charles "Doc" Jennison was operating well outside both the law and the accepted rules of war with a guerrilla gang of about 50 men.

By the end of August 1861, Nevada, Vernon County's county seat had been virtually destroyed, the population displaced. MSG Surgeon John Wiatt wrote in his diary after passing through Nevada August 31, the town "was a short time ago completely sacked by Jim Lane's Jayhawkers. Vernon joins the Kansas line and has suffered much from them. Only one family now lives in Nevada."[624] Many soldiers in Price's command called Vernon, Bates, and Cass counties home. During the men's absence their families had suffered greatly. Because of the jayhawking raids, and although Lexington was the ultimate destination, the decision was made to amend the route north. The first stage of the march would track along the Kansas border and eliminate the Jayhawkers terrorizing western Missouri.

August 25 Price's command left Springfield and headed north toward Ft. Scott. The army marched through largely undisturbed prairie. One soldier described the prairie landscape, "…the grass, which grows heavier on the prairies here than on any others I have ever seen – sometimes rising above the heads of the cavalry as they marched through it, and presenting under the motion of the breeze a waving view like the gentle roll of the sea."[625] Another described the prairie grass as being "six feet high."[626] On horseback Lud's

[624] Eakins. *Diary of a Doctor, Missouri State Guards*. 1861. Pages 16-17.
[625] Anderson and Bearss. Page 50.
[626] Eakins. *Diary of a Doctor, Missouri State Guards*. 1861. Page 19.

men moved through the tall grass and the heat. August's weather continued hot, water scarce as the thousands marched out of southwest Missouri; dusty roads fed clouds of dust churned by wagon wheels, hooves, and bare feet. Dr. Wyatt lamented the "weather is hot and dry, have had no rain for some time (weeks)."[627]

Sunday, September 5, 800 MSG soldiers under command of Gen. Alexander E. Steen neared Ft. Scott.[628] An advance party of 75 men under Hunter approached a federal camp. While James Montgomery delivered a sermon to the gathered Kansans, Hunter's men rushed in and made off with about 100 horses and mules that were grazing nearby. Montgomery's sermon came to an abrupt halt and his jayhawker congregation pursued. Opposing lines formed on the prairie and a temporary standoff began.

Steen reported the situation to Price who decided to move more men in Ft. Scott's direction. Monday morning September 6, Rains's cavalry moved into position on Big Drywood Creek. Hiram Bledsoe's artillery battery, following, supported them. "Rains' division with little caution, barely suspicious of an enemy in front, moved along the road without deploying, and the head of their column had penetrated through the road northward to the front of the house and beyond to the ford."[629] Lud's cavalry embedded in the advance.

Fighting began with a rush by the Kansans and their supporting artillery. Lud's cavalry absorbed the attack. This early artillery barrage from Moonlight's company severely injured Hiram Bledsoe and several men in his battery. Guibor's guns quickly joined the action supporting Bledsoe. For an hour and a half, in the August heat, fighting continued between the two sides. Peyton's 3rd Cavalry played a major role in the fighting. Companies "A" and "B" given the satisfaction of defending and defeating the Jayhawkers who had been decimating Missouri's border communities.

---

627 Eakins. *Diary of a Doctor, Missouri State Guards*. 1861. Page 12.
628 *History of Vernon County, Missouri*. Page 279.
629 *Southern Bivouac*. "The War in Missouri." May 1886. Page 747.

Outnumbered, Montgomery retreated back to Ft. Scott, leaving the field to the Missouri State Guard. Fearing a full-scale attack on Ft. Scott, Lane abandoned the town and moved his forces north to Ft. Lincoln. Lane, now convinced Price intended to invade Kansas pleaded for more troops and support.[630] Price's primary focus, however, remained steadily fixed on Missouri soil and Lexington.

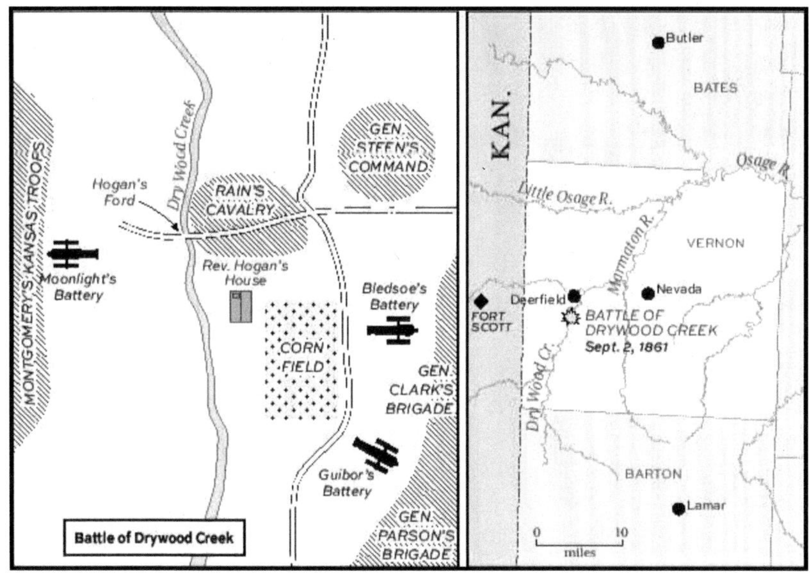

Battle of Drywood Creek
September 2, 1861

---------- Battle of Lexington ----------

Immediately following the battle at Drywood Creek, Price's Army rested in place for two days. Then September 5 the march north began as the troops retraced their steps to Nevada.

During the next 11 days, Peyton's 3rd Cavalry accompanied Price's command from Drywood Creek, in western Vernon County, to Lexington, the key to controlling the Missouri River. The army's strategic need for speed battled alternating sessions of inclement weather. The associated mud and water made for slow going, as

630 OR. Series I. Volume 3. Page 162.

roads became streams. The further north Price's army moved the more refugees interfered with and slowed progress. As the advance squads double-timed to Warrensburg and Lexington, the supply trains carrying ammunition and food fell further behind.

The army then turned north and moved through Bates County crossing the Grand River in the southeast corner of Cass County and the road flowed into Johnson County. Moving efficiently through Rose Hill, Price learned Federal troops were advancing on Warrensburg so he quickened the pace. The gap between the army and its supply train widened. Gov. Jackson addressed locals at Warrensburg and then it was on to Lexington. Price's army arrived within 2 ½ miles of Lexington on September 12.

Lud's cavalry, along with Price's entire army, battled the weather from Drywood Creek to Lexington. Immediately after the fight at Drywood Creek, the rain began. The rain fell "last night" and "this morning it is still cloudy and some rain. The ground is very muddy."[631] Lud's cavalry found themselves, "thoroughly drenched and completely surrounded by mud and water."[632] The weather cleared, the regiment continued slogging through muddy roads, "in a miserable condition."[633] Heavy rains returned, further delaying progress, when Lud's men reached Warrensburg. Despite the rain and mud, Lud's regiment remained in rapid pursuit.

Gen. Price, anxious to catch the retreating Federal troops, "pushed forward with his cavalry in pursuit: the order 'forward, double quick' was given and our horses were spurred into a lope."[634] The pace soon took its toll, as the "pace had been a hard gallop, and many of the horses gave out, forcing some of the men to a slower gait, or a halt."[635]

As the cavalry raced toward Lexington "women, children, and negroes gathering together along the roads begging us to take them

631 Eakins. *Diary of a Doctor, Missouri State Guards*. 1861. Page 19.
632 Anderson and Bearss. Page 59.
633 Anderson and Bearss. Page 61.
634 Anderson and Bearss. Page 62.
635 Anderson and Bearss. Page 62.

to safety. The Dutch burnt them out & left them and their sick out in the rain and cold."[636] Another cavalryman wrote, "Citizens joined us on the road at different points, who gave information that the retreating force was pressing every means of transportation – horses, mules and wagons; they were also taking along negro men they could get."[637]

Late in the evening, September 11, Price's cavalry arrived on Lexington's outskirts. Price's army and the Missouri River soon encircled the town. For the next nine days the Missouri State Guard tightened its squeeze. Bolivar's Dr. John F. Snyder wrote after the war, "Lexington was not captured by hard fighting, but by well-planned stratagem and well-maintained siege."[638] The siege culminated in three days of intense fighting, September 18 to 20.

By September 18, "General Rains and his Eighth Division, consisting of slightly more than three thousand men, reached downtown Lexington about the same time as Parsons and took up a position north and east of the college fort in a semicircular line about six to eight hundred yards away."[639] The fighting, on this first day of the siege, evolved into an artillery duel between the two forces. The next day, September 19, artillery ammunition running low, the attack fell to Southern sharpshooters who harassed the Federals throughout the day. Hemp bales from the surrounding countryside, as well as from local warehouses and steamboats, were to prove the decisive tool in a Southern victory.

The second element of a Southern victory surfaced the afternoon of the nineteenth – water had become very scarce inside the Federal fort. September 20 Price's men began rolling hemp bales toward the Federal lines, firing from behind the bales. Around 4:00 p.m. a white flag of surrender was raised and the Federal troops capitulated. Price demanded "unconditional surrender" and an oath from each Federal prisoner never to take up arms against Missouri

[636] Eakins. *Diary of a Doctor, Missouri State Guards*. 1861. Page 23.
[637] Anderson and Bearss. Page 62.
[638] Snyder. Page 4.
[639] Wood. Page 70.

or the Confederacy. September 20, Major Frederick Becker of the Union Home Guards raised a white flag.

The Missouri State Guards victory at Lexington resulted from several key factors. The Southern forces greatly outnumbered those of the Union, surrounded on three sides by Price's men and on the north by the Missouri River. Prior to the encirclement, Union leaders opted to keep their cavalry inside the fort. As the temperature rose so did the horses' thirst. Union officer R.T. Van Horn wrote, "It was those horses, the finest I ever saw together – owned by the men who rode them – that exhausted our water supply and weakened our lines of defense, necessarily extended to protect them."[640] On September 20 the Southern forces rolled hemp bales toward the Union lines. Protected by the hemp bales and firing from behind them, the Southern forces were able to overwhelm the surrounded Union Army.

The general circumstances dictating the Battle of Lexington negated any significant cavalry role. Artillery and infantry ruled the day. Lud's 3rd Cavalry, although present and participating at Lexington, did not play a significant individual role in the fighting. Neither Lud nor his officers or men received mention in official reports. They had however played a major role in the muddy pursuit of the Federals prior to the siege.

The evening of September 20, Lexington filled with civilians from the surrounding countryside. Southern soldiers celebrated their victory with the swelling civilian crowd. The following morning Gov. Claiborne F. Jackson addressed the Federal prisoners prior to their parole.

As Jackson spoke, Lud stood at the head of his 3rd Cavalry regiment. Against the background noise of jingling bridles, shuffling hooves, and low, intermittent chatter, he surveyed the scene. Lines of finely uniformed, defeated, Federal troops faced Jackson, who spoke beneath a wind whipped Confederate flag. Thousands of ragtag, poorly armed, now victorious, Missouri

---

640 *The Battle of Lexington*. Page 6.

farmers surrounded the central gathering. Lud and his border regiment watched and listened, absorbing the potent confidence that comes with of winning. In just three months, the army had won four major battles, all in western Missouri. A future, bright but still uncertain loomed.

THE REBEL EX-GOVERNOR JACKSON, OF MISSOURI, ADDRESSING COLONEL MULLIGAN'S TROOPS AFTER THE SURRENDER AT LEXINGTON.

Gov. Jackson addressing prisoners
Harper's Weekly

Chapter Nine
Jackson's "Extraordinary Legislative Session"

Price's army remained at Lexington another nine days but victory's euphoria quickly evaporated. Gov. Jackson, his advisory council, and Maj. Gen. Price recognized their tenuous position. Although the Missouri State Guard had achieved a significant victory, the command was not positioned to maintain its grip on either Lexington or western Missouri. Additionally, Jackson's state government floated in limbo.

The secessionist government, although divorced from the Union had not as yet joined the Confederate States of America. Missouri's Unionists had already appointed a state government challenging the legitimacy of Jackson's secessionists. Many Confederate officials remained dubious of Missouri's commitment to the Southern cause. Formalizing secession gaining acceptance into the Confederacy demanded the rebel leaders' immediate attention.

While still in Lexington, Gov. Jackson with his advisors, including Lud and David R. Atchison, outlined a political strategy. Formal relations with the Confederate States of America came first. Jackson appointed Edward C. Cabell and Thomas L. Snead "commissioners to negotiate an offensive-defensive treaty alliance with the Confederacy;" the two men hurriedly left Lexington, September 26, heading for Richmond, Va.[641] The same day, Jackson called a "Special Session" of Missouri's elected General Assembly to convene October 21 at the Masonic Lodge in Neosho, Newton County. Once at Neosho, Gov. Jackson and the other rebelling legislators planned to formally secede and provide for the state's military.

Three days later, September 29, Price issued orders for the army to begin moving south. September 30 the command left Lexington. The army, along with Gov. Jackson's entourage, retraced the basic route it had followed earlier in attacking Lexington. Federal troops

[641] Kirkpatrick. "The Admission of Missouri to the Confederacy." Page 376.

pursued hoping to trap the rebel army as it fled south. Peyton's 3rd Cavalry moved back through their home communities and farms.

Throughout the return march Price's command melted away. Many men, serving minimal 60-day enlistments, returned home. The fall harvest and approaching winter demanded their presence. Also, in the increasingly polarizing and dangerous environment, wives and children, unprotected, faced threats.

The day the Federals surrendered, Price's army contained around 18,000 men but within a week had shrunk to 11,000 as volunteers returned home. By the time the army reached the Osage River it had dropped to about 7,000, the same number of men as had started north earlier in September.[642]

The Extraordinary Prairie
October – November 1861

[642] Wood. Page 121.

October through December 1861, the nation's attention remained riveted upon western Missouri. *Harper's Weekly* continued a series of articles chronicling events. While Jackson's legislative assembly met at Neosho the national magazine reported Union troop movements and skirmishes. The November 2 issue contained an engraving, "Tipton, Missouri," the November 16 issue presented three engravings depicting events in southwest Missouri; Sigel Crossing the Osage," and two under the title the "War in Southwest Missouri" portrayed the drama. The *Harper's Weekly* cover for the November 23 issue featured Kansas jayhawker, James Lane and his infamous "Kansas Brigade" camped at Humansville, Mo. near Osceola.

Under the guise of pursuing and fighting rebel forces, Lane's Kansas Brigade devoted the period from October 2 to November 15 to applying a scorched earth policy in western Missouri, particularly to Peyton's senatorial district.

When Lane's Kansas Brigade arrived in Ft. Scott, November 15, 1861, the marauders had been in Missouri for 76 days. The command had scourged over 400 miles through western Missouri countryside. It had never confronted Confederate forces. Living off the countryside, the brigade, conservatively, had looted and plundered between 1,600 and 2,400 Missouri farms.[643]

Lane was censored by the Union command for the plundering and murdering associated with his Jayhawkers. His invasion and the atrocities associated with his Kansas unit did much to inflame and stir the rebels gathered at Neosho even as Union forces continued their pursuit.

General John C. Fremont, soon to be relieved, commanded the pursuing Union forces. Fremont had five separate divisions in Missouri, well equipped and trained; additionally Union troops led by Gen. Samuel Sturgis from Ft. Leavenworth joined the pursuit. After Price's troops settled into the hills around Neosho and while Jackson's government was meeting, Fremont's forces occupied

[643] Rafiner. *Cinders and Silence*. Page 146.

Springfield, just 75 miles from Neosho. November 2, all of the Union forces, including the plundering Kansans under Lane, were headquartered there.

---------- Neosho: Missouri's Capital ----------

Missouri's southwest corner again welcomed the rebel contingent. Neosho provided the optimal venue. The Newton County seat, centrally located within the county, sat roughly 25 miles from Arkansas and Gen. Ben McCulloch's Confederate Army. A possible consolidation with McCulloch threatened the Union command with a much stronger foe as well as another imminent Missouri invasion. If needed, Arkansas offered Price an obvious safe haven for his winter encampment. Also, Cowskin Prairie, where, in July, the MSG had first assembled and trained was just 24 miles southwest of Neosho.

MSG Brig. Gen. James Rains shared a long association with Neosho. In 1841 Newton County had granted Rains a merchant license to operate a grocery store in Neosho.[644] When Neosho's Mason Lodge No. 81 was originally chartered, October 14, 1846, Rains's carried the rank of Worshipful Master.[645] It was hardly a coincidence Neosho's Mason's Lodge housed Jackson's special assembly. In May 1861, Peyton and Rains had canvassed Neosho and the surrounding southwest Missouri communities recruiting for the Missouri State Guard. Although Rains had moved to Jasper County during the 1850s, Neosho, still a part of his constituency, retained primary rights to its native son.

Prior to the arrival of Gov. Jackson's procession of politicians, representatives, and military, Neosho claimed a population of 500 citizens, twice its 1850 size. By autumn, 1861, the population was entirely pro-south, "all the Union families had fled" or been driven

644 *History of Newton, Lawrence, Barry and McDonald Counties, Missouri*. Page 245.

645 *Neosho, A City of Springs*. Page 198.

out.[646] Southern locals "were painstaking in pointing out loyal families."[647] Later in the war, the Union army occupied Neosho and these same southern sympathizers fled for Arkansas and other safe harbors.

Four months before Jackson's arrival, Neosho's populace suffered the war's violence. Federal troops under Gen. Franz Sigel occupied the town just prior to the Battle of Carthage. When Sigel's main force left Neosho to engage Price's army at Carthage, a small Federal squad remained behind. Capt. Joseph Conrad was in command. Gen. Ben McCulloch's Confederate forces soon invaded Neosho from the south and west. Significantly outmanned, Capt. Conrad prudently surrendered. McCulloch's soldiers also captured "…100 rifles with saber bayonets, a quantity of ammunition, and a train of seven wagons loaded with provisions."[648]

Conrad's squad had been captured July 5. Three days later McCulloch granted them paroles. The paroled soldiers required a 30-man Confederate escort to safely escape. Conrad later reported, "'The people of Neosho and farmers of that vicinity … threatened to kill us in the streets.'"[649] Stripped of food and water, unarmed, the Union soldiers fled to Springfield, covering the 85 miles in fifty hours.[650] Four months later, in October 1861, Claiborne F. Jackson's fleeing, secessionist government, protected by Price's retreating army received a hearty welcome and reception from Neosho's locals.

Neosho rests in a basin ringed by high, wooded hills, a beautiful setting. The land surrounding Neosho was described by one soldier as "generally rocky and hilly, or undulating; there are, however some level bottoms on the streams."[651] As Price's army arrived, units were assigned protective encampments on the hill crests

[646] *History of Newton, Lawrence, Barry and McDonald Counties, Missouri*. Page 330.
[647] Britton. Page 110.
[648] Farnham and Hinze. Page 200.
[649] Farnham and Hinze. Page 201.
[650] Farnham and Hinze. Page 201.
[651] Anderson and Bearss. Page 95.

ringing the town. Artillery batteries occupied the highest, strategic points.

Many of the Southern soldiers arrived barefoot, an uncomfortable situation because as one soldier noted, "the frosts were beginning to fall."[652] The shoe crisis was so severe in one company that three pairs of shoes were distributed among five completely barefoot soldiers by drawing straws.[653] Neosho's two shoemakers, Andrew Tibbetts and Charles Elliott, struggled to handle the endless stream of barefoot soldiers.

Neosho's population swelled with the sudden influx. For a brief period the town became Missouri's southern capitol, although it lacked the hotels and boarding houses needed to fully accommodate the sudden flood of visitors. The largest hotel, the Armstrong House, capably handled Gov. Jackson and his entourage.[654] Hugh and Sarah Armstrong owned and operated the hotel. Other new arrivals boarded with private citizens if they could find room or camped near town. Those Senators and Representatives serving with the Missouri State Guard camped with their units. Although most officers had tents, the rank and file soldiers slept in the open.

Armstrong House circa 1880
Author's Collection

[652] Anderson and Bearss. Page 95.
[653] Anderson and Bearss.. Page 94.
[654] *History of Newton County*. Page 330.

Neosho Masonic Hall
Author's Collection

The 21st General Assembly conducted business in several venues under fluid circumstances. The "official sessions" as reflected in the minutes were held in the Neosho Masonic Lodge. Dr. John J. Barlow, a Neosho resident, attended the assembly's sessions, integrating himself with the legislators. Dr. Barlow later recorded "... the greater part of the business was done at the Armstrong House, rather than the Masonic Lodge." Barlow added, the assembly members arrived at Neosho well stocked with "a good supply of whiskey, brandy, and champagne."[655]

Neosho's public houses and streets filled with an eclectic montage of people. Officers and soldiers, most without uniforms, some without shoes, mixed with the locals. Many un-uniformed officers of the Missouri State Guard wore top hats. Civilian politicians and dignitaries, members of the varied entourages populated the streets. Interested local citizens like Dr. Barlow intermixed with the soldiers and politicians. Indians walked Neosho's streets as several regiments of Native Americans encamped outside town. Government business was conducted wherever involved parties congregated, the courthouse, city streets, the Armstrong Hotel, surrounding military camps, and private homes.

The assembly's debates and political process overflowed into the streets. For the ten days the assembly and army were in Neosho, discussions and negotiations were helped along by a constant flow "of champagne, brandy, and whiskey" although it was noted, "...but it cannot be said any of the members were drunk."[656] It appears from the minutes of both the House and the Senate that intense debate, negotiations, and decisions were made away from

655 *History of Newton County*. Page 330.
656 *History of Newton County*. Page 330.

the Masonic Lodge. Seemingly the Assembly Houses met in official session only to formally codify decisions.

Price's Missouri State Guard included many men, like Lud, who arrived at Neosho with the dual responsibilities of serving as elected officials as well as military officers. Gov. Jackson's entourage included advisors and staff, who were neither elected officials or military officers, but who attended and participated based on a commitment to secession. Joseph W. Tucker, a former St. Louis newspaper editor, accompanied Jackson. Tucker, an intense fire-eater, edited the MSG's *Missouri Army Argus*. Former U.S. Senator and Jackson confidant, David Rice Atchison also played an influential role at Neosho.

Although united by the common goal of secession, the rebels gathered at Neosho harbored differing views on a host of issues. Paramount among the pending decisions, were those regarding the movement's future leadership, political and military. Sterling Price, although commander of the Missouri State Guard, had already become a controversial lightning rod. Price faced opposition from both Atchison and Ben McCulloch. Gen. James S. Rains, although an early leader in the movement and a State Senator, suffered from sharp criticism of his inept military leadership and rumors of excessive drinking.

David R. Atchison
Courtesy Library of Congress

David Atchison actively guided and influenced the Neosho proceedings. Gov. Jackson relied heavily on Atchison's advice and counsel. "Although Atchison took no direct part in the formal proceedings, he counseled Jackson as to the procedure to follow in addressing the legislature."[657] Atchison's presence and influence at Neosho proved unsettling for Sterling Price. Just two months earlier, while in Richmond, Va. meeting with the Confederate

[657] Parrish. *Atchison: Border Politician.* Page 219.

government, Atchison had openly and severely criticized Price's military skills, planting seeds of doubt that festered throughout the war.[658] Lud's earlier misgivings about Price's commitment to the South cause remained.

---------- October 21, 1861 ----------

CSS Nashville
Courtesy Library of Congress

In a curious twist of fate, on Monday, October 21, 1861, two Peyton cousins launched vastly different voyages. John Lewis Peyton and his wife, Henrietta, prepared to board the *C.S.S. Nashville* at Charleston, South Carolina. They sailed for England and John's assignment as North Carolina's Ambassador to Europe. Although the *Nashville* had accommodations for "200 first class passengers," on this voyage, John and Henrietta were the only passengers.[659] On the stormy voyage the *Nashville* became the first Confederate ship to break through the Union blockade. Before landing at South Hampton the *Nashville's* crew boarded and sank a Union ship, the *Harvey Birch*.[660] Their historic crossing completed, John and Henrietta, landed in England not to return to the United States for 16 years.

While John and Henrietta waited to set sail for England, Lud, hundreds of miles to the west, prepared to lead Missouri into the Confederacy. Monday, October 21, 1861, the "Special Session" of the 21st General Assembly was called to order in Neosho.[661] Both the Senate and House of Representatives were called to business but neither House had a quorum.

658 Reynolds. Page 42.
659 Peyton. *Crisis*. Page 195.
660 Peyton. *Crisis*. Page 292.
661 *Journal of the Senate. Rebel Legislature*. Page 3.

The session's low attendance and biased agenda caused outside observers to dub this legislative assembly the "bogus legislature" and/or the "rebel legislature." Although this may be true relative to statewide attendance, the legislative delegation representing Peyton's senatorial district, Jackson, Cass, and Bates counties was in full attendance. These three counties, destined later in the war to become Missouri's "burnt district," were all three present and in active support of Gov. Jackson's government.

---------- Roll Call ----------

Senator Lud Peyton along with his district's representatives shared a sincere commitment to the South. Lud's rapid political rise from an obscure western Missouri attorney to Gov. Jackson's inner-circle, had from inception been propelled by deep, unwavering Southern beliefs. The other members of Peyton's delegation shared his ties:

- Dr. G.M.B. Maughs, Jackson County's junior Representative, was hardly a political novice. Dr. Maughs had been Mayor of Kansas City in 1859. Running for re-election in 1860, he was opposed by Robert T. Van Horn. Van Horn won the election in Jackson County's Union stronghold. Dr. Maughs became a member of the Missouri House of Representatives when Nathaniel C. Claiborne resigned in May 1861.[662]

Dr. Maughs- Author's Collection

[662] *Journal of the House of Representatives of the State of Missouri. Called Session of the Twenty-First General Assembly.* Page 21.

- Jackson County's senior Representative, James Porter, arrived at Neosho as a member of the Missouri State Guard.
- William M. Briscoe, Cass County's representative, serving his second term in the Missouri house, had long supported the South. Briscoe's political resume included membership in the American Party, whose statewide base was anchored in Cass County. Briscoe had fought alongside Peyton during the Kansas border troubles.
- Representative John E. Morgan of Bates County had a consistent history of Southern support.

Monday, October 21, 1861 both houses of the 21st Missouri State Assembly were called to order. The low number of senators and representatives in attendance that Monday created a quorum problem. As a result, from Monday, October 21 until the following Monday, October 28 little legislative business was conducted while considerable attention was directed toward rounding up the absent senators and representatives. On Wednesday, October 23 the frustration level peaked in both houses.

In the Senate, attendees directed the Senate President to send as many messengers as necessary to find and retrieve the missing members. The House took a different approach to "compel the attendance of the absent members." Rep. George G. Vest encouraged the House to begin business – the House declined. However when the House next convened on Thursday, it revisited Vest's recommendation and suddenly found itself ready to do business. The Senate resolved on Friday, October 25 to direct Gen. Price to send messengers to each of the absentee Senators and escort them to Neosho.

The legislature's inability to gather a quorum was public knowledge. The Missouri State Guard's traveling newspaper, the *Missouri Army Argus*, carried an article informing the soldiers "both branches met on the 21st ult, but there being no quorum present they adjourned from day to day without transacting business of importance."[663] Chariton County's Judge M.C. Hunt had been

[663] *St. Louis Missouri Republican*. November 14, 1861.

traveling with Sterling Price's army. When Judge Hunt left Price and returned home he reported "the legislature was in session at Neosho but lacked four of a quorum. They were expected."[664]

One barrier to the presence of quorums at Neosho and later at Cassville was a lack of delegate availability. Representative Ignatius Beall, of St. Francois County, had supported Jackson and "espoused the secession cause and in various ways" providing "aid and comfort to the Southern rebellion."[665] As the assembly met in southwest Missouri, Rep. Beall was a prisoner in St. Louis having been arrested and transported to the city by Union authorities. Beall's detainment was not the only arrest blocking attendance.

Sen. Sam Churchill, one of the Senate's strongest Southern advocates also found himself under arrest. Churchill had returned to St. Louis following his essential role in the Assembly's May session. He was particularly close to Gov. Jackson, having read Jackson's message to the Senate on May 3. Federal troops occupied Churchill's farm the first week in September and arrested him shortly thereafter.[666] Churchill remained incarcerated until banished from Missouri in 1863.

Another representative, Livingston County's A.J. Austin had been killed-in-action. Austin had been appointed Lt. Col. of the 1st Cavalry Regiment, MSG, June 21. Six weeks later Austin died during the Battle of Wilson's Creek.

William Shakespeare McConnell, Barry County's representative, presented a very unique challenge in the efforts to gather a quorum. McConnell, a man of strong southern belief, had nonetheless been a thorn in the side of Gov. Jackson. When proposals supporting a public referendum on secession circulated, McConnell publically supported a referendum – against Jackson's leadership.[667] When the Governor's "Special Assembly" met at Neosho, Rep.

---

[664] *St. Louis Daily Democrat.* November 2, 1861. Page 2.
[665] *St. Louis Missouri Republican.* November 6, 1861.
[666] Missouri Secretary of State. Archives. *Missouri's Union Provost Marshal Papers: 1861 – 1865.* Reel F-1237.
[667] Melton. Page 165.

McConnell refused to attend. Later, when the Assembly moved its meetings to Barry County and Cassville, McConnell's hometown, he attended the sessions but refused to vote.[668]

Both houses adjourned over the weekend, October 26-27. Federal military pressure continued to build and the business of secession, even for a government "in absentia" required action. The secessionist leaders decided, during discussions on Saturday and Sunday, both houses would move forward on the necessary legislation Monday, October 28. The leaders found themselves caught between the harsh reality of the situation and the legal, constitutional requirements for legislative action. Behind the scenes, discussions obviously acknowledged the realities, no quorum and the advancing Union armies, leading all to the decision to move forward with the talent and resources at hand.

The actual number of elected officials in attendance may never be known and the minutes of neither house contain a roll call. One account of the attendance reported that 39 members of the House of Representatives and 10 members of the Senate were present.[669] All of the representatives from those counties in Lud's senatorial district were present. Their attendance and participation spoke loudly of the inclinations of the citizens in Cass, Bates, and Jackson counties who had suffered the most during the previous six years.

---------- Down to Business ----------

October 28, Brig. Gen. James Rains began his day meeting with Indian delegations. Gen. Rains hosted a breakfast for several Indian leaders. Rains, a former Indian Agent, reputably spoke "their native dialect as fluently as if he were, himself, a painted brave."[670] For several months Rains had worked feverishly recruiting tribes to join the Southern cause. Several Indian regiments had enlisted, and one large regiment was present at Neosho. The *Missouri Army Argus* reported the Indians "are armed exclusively with bows and

[668] Melton. Page 166.
[669] *History of Newton, Lawrence, Barry and McDonald Counties, Mo.* Page 329.
[670] *Missouri's Army Argus*. October 28, 1861.

arrows, scalping knives, and tomahawks," ready to take Federal scalps.[671]

Following breakfast Rains made his way to the Masonic Lodge where both houses were called to order. Senator M.C. Goodlett, of Johnson County, rose, reading Gov. Jackson's address.[672] The message included a directive that the State Assembly approve five measures, deemed of extreme importance:[673]

- An ordinance dissolving all political connection between the State of Missouri and the United States of America.
- An act of provisional union with the Confederate States of America
- The appointment of three commissioners to the Provisional Congress of the Confederate States of America
- A law authorizing the Executive of the State to hold elections for Senators and Representatives to the Confederate States of America
- An act empowering the Chief Executive to issue bonds of the State of Missouri

Immediately following his reading of Jackson's address, Senator Goodlett "introduced a bill entitled 'An act to dissolve the political connection of the State of Missouri with the United States of America.'"[674] The bill was read three times and passed. The House addressed the same subject. Both houses adjourned after passing slightly different versions of the bill.

The Senate reconvened at 2:00 p.m. Lud rose and addressed the assembly. He made a motion that the House return the bill of secession. This was approved. Next, Sen. Peyton moved that the

[671] *Missouri's Army Argus*. October 28, 1861.

[672] **Michael C. Goodlett**: Goodlett survived the war and settled in Tennessee. May 27, 1865 he married Caroline Douglas Meriwether. Caroline founded the United Daughters of the Confederacy in 1894. Under her leadership the UDC had a profound impact crafting the "Lost Cause" narrative.

[673] *Journal of the Senate*. Page 8.

[674] *Journal of the Senate*. Page 8.

Senate reconsider the bill – which it did, making minor amendments. The revised bill returned to the House where it was promptly approved. By late afternoon, the General Assembly had passed the bill of secession as well as an act "ratifying the Constitution for the Provisional Government of the Confederate States of America." Both bills awaited signatures.

The lone dissenting secession vote had come from Audrain County's Sen. Charles Hardin. Hardin and Lud, associates since their collegiate days at Miami University, graduated together in 1841, later serving together in the Missouri Senate. The October 28 secession vote signaled a permanent separation – Hardin returned home, survived the war, becoming Missouri's Governor in 1874. Lud did not survive the war, disappearing from memory. But on this day, Lud's fire-eating leadership carried the moment and Missouri into the Confederacy.

Both houses adjourned until 7:00 p.m. that evening. All of the senators, and representatives, as well as Gov. Jackson, reassembled on the Newton County Courthouse steps where the secession declaration was read and speeches were made before an excited public.

Neosho's citizens, visiting dignitaries, and soldiers, had waited with heightened expectation for an announcement that Missouri had finally, officially seceded from the Union. As the government representatives paraded into the square, the celebration began. In the many decades since the proclamation, two vivid memories remain etched in Missouri history, the sounds of celebration and the free flow of alcohol.

Lud stood in Neosho's square surrounded by compatriots. He along with the multitude, stood transfixed by the sound.

> "The firing of cannon that sent their hoarse voices to the distance of forty-five miles, echoing and re-echoing among the thousand hills and valleys of the southwest. The shouts of the soldiers rent the heavens, and the volleys of small arms accompanying the roar of the cannon fully testified to the joy with which they

> received the glad news."[675] The sounds of the artillery were followed by "great speeches" given by all the "principal leaders."[676]

Ephraim Anderson remembered the secession declaration "was greeted with cheers, and salvos of artillery echoed and resounded through the valleys and over the hills. Gayety and rejoicing were the order of the day, and the success and glory of the cause were toasted "in reamin swats that drank divinely."[677]

A correspondent for the *Memphis Daily Appeal*, wrote that many present threw themselves "into the arms of Bacchus. The number was rather too great for the protector of the vine to accommodate, and not a few lingered around old houses and fields, and road-side ditches, as if they were charming places to them."[678]

No one present ever forgot the cannonade. The thunderous sound, so powerful, was thought to have echoed throughout the entire state. In the moment, Lud not only heard the explosions, he felt them to his very core – transformed and vindicated.

The next day, Tuesday, October 29, the Senate was informed that the Speaker of the House had signed the bill ratifying the "Constitution for the Provisional Government of the Confederate States of America." Rep. George Vest, representing the committee on Federal Relations, had introduced the bill to the House the preceding day where it was read three times and passed; DeKalb County's Rep. Isaac N. Shambaugh the sole dissenting vote.[679]

Military matters dictated a change of venue for the assembly. Having spent 10 days in Neosho, the Assembly, along with Price's army, abandoned the town for neighboring Barry County and its county seat, Cassville.

---

675 *Memphis Daily Appeal*. November 28, 1861.
676 Britton. Page 111.
677 Anderson and Bearss. Page 94.
678 *Memphis Daily Appeal*. November 28, 1861.
679 *House Minutes*. Page 17.

---------- Cassville ----------

Wednesday, October 30, the legislature and the army left Neosho and rambled 30 miles southeast to Cassville. The Cassville road overflowed with the military as well as the convoy and conveyances of the rebel politicians. Price's army, large but low on supplies lived off the land. Observers described the army as being almost destitute. "None of the men have uniforms, and their clothing is sadly rent and torn. They have but comparatively few tents. Their arms, so far as they observed, were chiefly rifles and heavy shot-guns, which the men preferred to the regulation musket with bayonet."[680] As the army moved, forage teams scoured for food while simultaneously routing local Union families. The roads heading north filled with fleeing Union refugees.[681]

Cassville, Barry County's county seat, had been chartered in 1845 and named for Lewis Cass. In the 1840s, (Lewis) "Cass had become the hero of Southern democrats," and his name adorned counties (including Lud's home county), towns, and villages.[682] The town's name was an accurate reflection its citizens' political allegiance. The "wire road," formerly the military road connecting St. Louis's Jefferson Barracks with Ft. Smith, Ark. passed through Cassville. The road's traffic fueled the local economy. Heavy alternating traffic between the Confederate and Union armies destroyed much of the town during the war.

A new Barry County courthouse greeted Gov. Jackson's "Special Assembly." The county had spent $5,000 to build the new stone courthouse. The two-story building opened for business in 1857 and its original lighting system, tallow candles, had been replaced with gas lamps.[683] When the rebel assembly reconvened, October 31, they did so on the courthouse's second floor.[684]

680 *St. Louis Daily Democrat*. November 19, 1861.
681 *St. Louis Daily Democrat*. November 15, 1861.
682 Tyler. Pamphlet. Last Page.
683 Melton. Page 53.
684 Melton. Page 123.

Cassville courthouse- Author's Collection

Cassville's public accommodations, normally able to handle travelers, were not up to the excessive requirements placed upon them by the arrival of Gov. Jackson's entourage and army. The town had two hotels. One was commonly known as "Widow Burton's Hotel," and the other owned and operated by the gadfly representative, William Shakespeare McConnell.[685] The arriving throng filled both hotels as well as private homes willing to take guests. Most however slept where they found shelter, those with the military slept in the open. For the next ten days Cassville assumed the prestige of being Missouri's Confederate Capital.

---------- Back to Business ----------

Once in Cassville, Rep. George Vest finalized Missouri's Act of Secession. Vest, working alone, sat upstairs in the courthouse's northeast corner. He rewrote and polished the original draft; Gov. Jackson signed the final proclamation and moved outside the courthouse.

685 *History of Barry County.* Page 674.

For a second time, the Governor declared secession. Just as in Neosho, days before, albeit without the cannonade, locals celebrated Missouri's new status. Jubilation erupted around the courthouse. Having proclaimed Missouri's exit from the Union, Jackson "raised the Stars and Bars above Cassville's new brick courthouse and Cassville became the State Capitol of Missouri."[686]

The Senate and the House resumed deliberations working to complete Jackson's requested legislation. Still pending were bills providing for financial bonds to fund the State, requests for commissioners to the Confederate government, and the scheduling of elections. A few miscellaneous bills were also proposed and addressed.

Of Gov. Jackson's five initial legislative requests, three bills, each addressing a single need, had been delivered in Neosho, October 29. These three bills, the secession proclamation, recognition of the Provisional Confederate government's constitution, and a bond-financing bill had been quickly passed and sent to the Governor. Gov. Jackson promptly signed the secession and the provisional constitution bills. He did not sign the financing bill; when the assembly met at Cassville this piece of legislation still pended.

The Senate, during its first morning session, reconsidered the bond financing legislation. Unable in full session to resolve issues, the bill was referred to a select committee of three senators, Lud, Goodlett, and J.T.V. Thompson. A fourth member, Henry Lyday was added before the committee adjourned to amend the legislation.[687] The four men failed to agree and resolve the issues. Friday morning they reported the impasse to the Senate.[688]

For three days, debate on the bond financing, "An Act to provide for the defense of Missouri" continued. When agreement was reached Gov. Jackson signed the legislation November 5. As approved, the bill provided $10 million in bonds funding the

686 *History of Cassville, Missouri.* Page 4.
687 *Senate Journal.* Page 12.
688 *Senate Journal.* Page 14.

rebellion, and granted the appointment of three administrative commissioners.[689]

Lud introduced legislation to amend the military bill enacted May 14, 1861. The original bill codified "the organization, support, and government of the military forces of the State of Missouri."[690] At Cassville, the original military organization changed. Gen. Price, Gov. Jackson and Lud, orchestrated the new structure.

Once the legislation had been introduced in the Senate, November 4, a "Select Committee of Three" reviewed and amended the bill. The three select committee members were Lud, Henry Lyday and J.T.V. Thompson.[691]

Lud reported the committee's recommendations back to the Senate the following morning. He then orchestrated the Senate deliberations. For the next two days both the House and Senate debated the Missouri State Guard's staffing levels, finally approving a bill. Jackson signed the legislation on Thursday, November 7. During the deliberations Sen. Goodlett introduced an amendment, eventually rejected, but nonetheless of significance.

---------- Sobriety and Influence ----------

Sen. Goodlett's amendment to the military bill demanded the immediate dismissal of any officer found drunk on duty.[692] The conflict between sobriety and drunkenness nagged throughout the Civil War haunting both Union and Confederate armies. In this specific instance, Goodlett's proposal probably was directed specifically at Gen. James S. Rains. Rains, Lud's close friend, confidant and immediate superior, had already earned an unsavory reputation for insobriety. Although the Senate rejected Goodlett's amendment, attempts to censure Rains remained.

[689] *Senate Journal.* Page 34.
[690] *Laws of Missouri. Volume 17. 1860 – 1861.* Pages 3 – 43.
[691] *Senate Journal.* Page 18.
[692] *Senate Journal.* Page 22.

Ray County's Rep. L.C. Bohannon introduced House Bill No. 11 to create a new Military District, a 10th District.[693] Bohannon's proposal recommended the new military district be carved from the existing 8th and 6th military districts; the proposed district would contain the following 10 counties: Jackson, Lafayette, Saline, Cass, Johnson, Pettis, Bates, Henry, Benton, and St. Clair. The proposed district was yet another direct attack on Gen. Rains.

Just five months into the war, Rains's perceived military ineptitude and character flaws had created a faction hostile to his leadership. Bohannon's bill would have stripped the eight most populous counties in Rains's Eighth Military District from his recruiting base. The bill passed the House on November 5 and was forwarded to the Senate. At his juncture, Gen. Price stepped into the fray convincing "them to drop the idea since the earlier divisions were hardly up to strength."[694] November 6, the Senate again debated the bill and it failed, but regardless, the damage to Rains had been done.

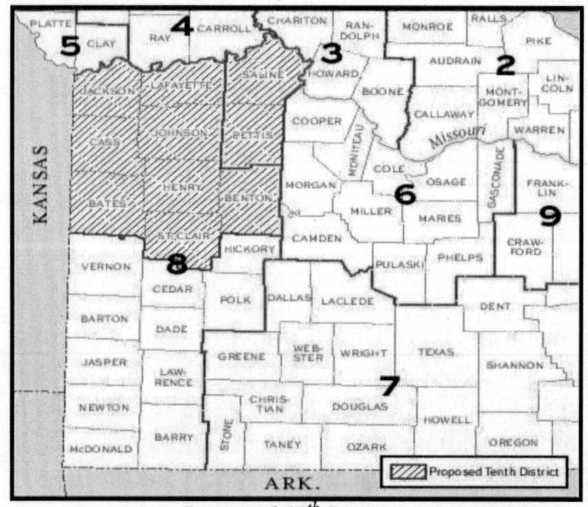

Proposed 10th Division

---

[693] State Historical Society of Missouri. Manuscript Collection. MSSS 2722. Folder 1.

[694] *Sterling Price's Lieutenants*. Page 23.

---------- Border Memorial ----------

Lud again took the Senate floor on Monday and Tuesday introducing and participating in two discussions of particular relevance to western Missouri. Missouri border counties had long suffered from Kansan jayhawking raids. The terror's ferocity and scorched earth nature reached new levels when Lane's Kansas Brigade leveled much of western Missouri from September through November 1861. At Cassville, the Missouri Senate addressed the atrocities. Although the Senate records and corresponding details have been lost, the devastating significance remains.

The first issue Lud introduced on Monday, November 4, was a memorial received from "certain citizens of Kansas."[695] Lud had received the Kansans' grievances and admitted them to the formal Senate proceedings. The Senate President referred the document to a Special Committee of Peyton, Henry Lyday, and M.C. Goodlett. Lud requested and received permission to add James Thompson and Charles Hardin to the committee. The Kansans' memorial has disappeared, but it is easy to approximate its contents based on Henry Lyday's proposal the next day.

Tuesday morning Senator Lyday requested and received approval to publish 2,000 copies of "the act of the Confederate Congress entitled 'an act to perpetuate testimony in case of slaves abducted or harbored by the enemy, and of other property seized, wasted and destroyed by them.'"[696] This act passed by the Provisional Confederate Government, August 30, 1861, addressed the need to record, locally and with the government at Richmond, each instance of Union troops stealing property from Confederate citizens. Lyday's resolution, addressing Peyton's border constituents was an obvious response to the looting and plundering inflicted upon Missourians, and former Missourians in Kansas, by James Montgomery and James Lane. The Special Committee's action

[695] *Senate Journal.* Page 20.
[696] *Senate Journal.* Page 21.

alerted Missouri citizens to the need to document each instance of theft.[697]

The Senate approved Lud's Special Committee recommendation to publish and distribute 2,000 copies of the Confederate law. The action acknowledged the horrific devastation unfolding in western Missouri.

---------- Confederate Representation ----------

November 6, the House brought to the floor and began debating a bill that transformed Lud's life. The bill, once passed and approved, elevated Peyton from the Missouri State Guard and the Missouri Senate into the Confederate Congress. Richmond, Virginia beckoned.

The House bill entitled "An Act to provide for holding an election for Representatives to the Congress of the Confederate States of America and for other purposes" exceeded Gov. Jackson's request that the assembly appoint three commissioners to the Confederate Congress and schedule elections. This proposal bypassed Commissioners and elections, naming and appointing seven Representatives to the Confederate House of Representatives and naming two Confederate Senators, "Robert L.Y. Peyton" and John B. Clark. The seven representatives were:

First District	Edward C. Cabell
Second District	Thomas A. Harris
Third District	Caspar W. Bell
Fourth District	Aaron H. Conrow
Fifth District	George G. Vest
Sixth District	Thomas W. Freeman
Seventh District	John Hyer

Discussions about the Confederate Congressional delegation continued behind the scenes, outside the "minutes" limelight. The

[697] **Note**: For a detailed discussion of Lane's Kansas Brigade in Missouri the fall of 1861, refer to Chapter Four in *Cinders and Silence: A Chronicle of Missouri's Burnt District*.

following day, November 7, Edward C. Cabell's name, on motion of Senator Parsons, was scratched from the bill and William M. Cooke replaced him.[698] Cabell, at the moment, was in Richmond conferring with the Confederate government. The most apparent reason for the change being that Gov. Jackson desired retaining Cabell's services as his Aide-de-Camp and advisor.

The naming of a full Confederate Congressional delegation was unusual and unconstitutional, but under the circumstances, necessary. Missouri was not, as yet, a fully, recognized member of the Confederacy. Appointing three commissioners while awaiting a formal election would have minimized Missouri's governmental presence and reduced its leverage with the Confederate government. It was also apparent, that with the Federal forces controlling the entire state, holding normal elections was an impossibility.

The decision to send a full delegation to the Confederate Congress had been made outside the public confines of the House and Senate. In addition, the individual delegation members were chosen behind the scenes. When the bill was introduced in the House it carried a full slate.

Surviving House minutes fail to provide debate or discussion about the candidates themselves. The delegation bill came to the floor during the evening session of November 6. There was obvious disagreement among the Representatives because six voted against the measure. W.C. Duvall (McDonald Co.), Henry Hardin (Audrain Co.), W.A. Gordon (Lafayette Co.), L.D. Wyatt (Gasconade Co.), Joseph L. Moore (Laclede Co.), and Isaac N. Shambaugh (DeKalb Co.) cast the six dissenting votes.[699]

The decision to send a full delegation to Richmond, in place of three commissioners, could not have been made and passed without Gov. Jackson's prior involvement and approval. Although Jackson, on November 8, published a letter of explanation, and had the letter

[698] *Senate Minutes*. Page 27.

[699] State Historical Society of Missouri. *Journal of the House of Representatives*. Page 46.

included in the assembly minutes, the fact he signed the bill, recognizing the precarious status of his government validates his total participation.[700] Jackson's letter of concern addressed the very issues the secessionists undoubtedly debated off stage. At the most basic level, the measure was unconstitutional. Missouri's Constitution required a popular election in order to send members to the national House of Representatives; sending a delegation to Richmond without a popular vote clearly broke the law.

The delegates themselves were undoubtedly "hand picked." David Atchison, Jackson's closest advisor during this period, and a close friend of Jefferson Davis played a part in delegate selection. Ultimately, the final decision would have been Jackson's.

---Missouri's Confederate Congressional Delegation ----

Missouri's youthful Confederate congressional delegation contained two senators and seven representatives. This nine member delegation contained just two men 40-years old or older. In addition to its youth, the group was diverse in background and experience. The men selected to serve in the Confederate House of Representatives brought an intense and focused commitment to their new responsibilities.

----- Representatives -----

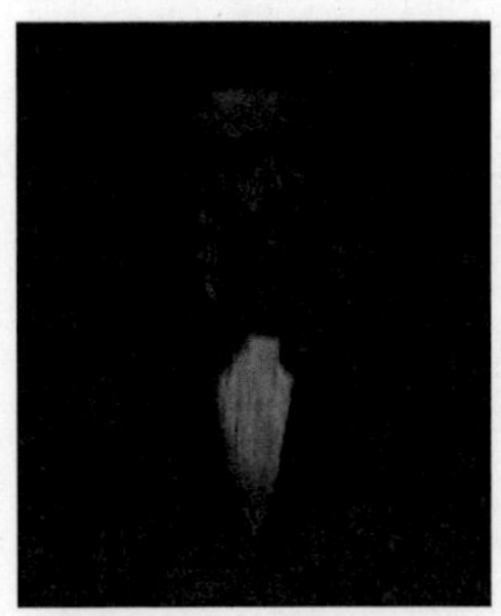

Casper W. Clark- Weekly Brunswicker, October 29, 1898

Caspar W. Bell, 41 years old, was like Lud, a native Virginian. Bell had attended William and Mary University. He studied law under Henry S. Foote in Mississippi before receiving his law degree from the University of Virginia. Under Foote's tutelage Bell acquired a deep distrust of Jefferson Davis. Bell moved to Missouri in 1843 and settled in Chariton County where he practiced law in the 11th Judicial District. In 1861 Bell

[700] **Note**: For a full text of Gov. C.F. Jackson's letter of November 18, 1861 see the Appendix.

enlisted in the Missouri State Guard, serving as Adjutant-General of John B. Clark, Sr.'s division.

Aaron H. Conrow, an Ohio native, moved to Ray County and began a law practice. Just 37 years old when elected to the Confederate House of Representatives, Conrow had been elected to the Missouri House of Representatives in 1860. Previously, in 1857, he had been elected the Circuit Attorney of the Fifth Judicial District. As hostilities neared, Gov. Jackson sent Conrow to Arkansas soliciting military assistance.[701] Conrow enlisted in the Missouri State Guard, appointed Colonel, he served as Adjutant-General in Brig. Gen. William Slack's Division. Unlike Lud and George Vest, Conrow was not known as an orator. His talents lay in other areas. Conrow survived the war but fled to Mexico where guerrillas murdered him in 1865.

William M. Cooke, arrived in Richmond having just turned 38. Cooke, like Lud and Bell, was a native Virginian and a graduate of the University of Virginia Law School. Cooke moved to St. Louis soon after graduation. He practiced law in Hannibal and St. Louis before the war. The spring of 1861, Gov. Jackson appointed Cooke "Commissioner from Missouri to the President of the Confederacy." Cooke's duties took him to Richmond in May where he first met fire-eater Edmund Ruffin. Cooke enlisted in the MSG serving as a volunteer aide-de-camp in Clark's Third Division. Gov. Jackson sent Clark and Cooke to Richmond in early September 1861. Cooke's fate, like Lud's, carried a premature 1863 death.

Representative Thomas W. Freeman, 37 years old, lived in southwest Missouri. Freeman, an attorney hailed from Bolivar in Polk County. Polk County's voters sent him to the Missouri House of Representatives in 1860. Like Lud, Freeman campaigned as a Breckinridge Elector in the 1860 Presidential election. As war approached, Gov. Jackson "sent him on a private commission to

[701] Castel. Page 22.

Texas and Louisiana."[702] Unlike his fellow congressmen, Freeman did not serve in the Missouri State Guard.

Representative Thomas A. Harris, 35 years old, was a Marion County attorney. Harris had attended West Point but left after two years. During the mid-1850s Harris played an instrumental role in the organization of Missouri's branch of the American (Know Nothing) Party. He was a member of the Missouri House of Representatives when hostilities began. Gov. Jackson appointed Harris Brig. Gen. of the Missouri State Guard's Second Division.[703]

Thirty-one year old Representative George Graham Vest hailed from Boonville, Cooper County. Vest had initially practiced law in Pettis County at Georgetown. In 1856 Vest relocated to Cooper County where, in 1860, he was elected to the Missouri House of Representatives. In 1860, Vest was a Presidential Elector for Stephen Douglas. When war erupted Vest enlisted in the Missouri State Guard near Johnstown, Missouri. Vest, along with Lud, entered the Confederate Congress with a well-established oratorical reputation.[704]

Of the seven men sent to the Confederate House of Representatives, one never served in Richmond. Dr. John Hyer's his seat remained open throughout the war. Although absent at Neosho, Hyer had been chosen "on the strength of his often-stated Southern sympathies."[705] His Neosho absence and later failure to serve in Richmond were due to circumstance and the Union Army. Hyer

[702] Bay. Page 341.
[703] **Thomas A. Harris**: Harris survived the Civil War. Captured in 1865 while trying to flee the United States, he was eventually pardoned. In the 1870s Harris reconnected with Samuel B. Churchill who was serving as Kentucky's Secretary of State. Churchill appointed him Assistant Secretary of State.
[704] **George G. Vest**: Vest survived the Civil War and returned to Missouri. He re-entered politics and was elected to the U.S. Senate in 1879. He served in the Senate until 1903 when he retired due to poor health. Vest died at Sweet Springs, Mo. in 1904.
[705] Kirkpatrick, Arthur R. "Missouri's Delegation to the Confederate Congress." MHR. Page 190.

received word of the Neosho convention too late to attend. Following his election to the CSA House of Representatives he began the trip to Richmond only to become ill, forced to return home. Back in Dent County he was arrested, spending the duration of the war in prison or under house arrest.

John B. Clark, Sr.
Courtesy Library of Congress

Missouri's two Confederate senators, John B. Clark, Sr. and Lud Peyton could not have been more different. Clark, from Fayette in Howard County, had long been a fixture on Missouri's political stage. Fifty-eight years old, the Howard County native brought the most experience to the Missouri delegation. A veteran of the Mormon, Black Hawk, and Mexican wars, Clark also sported an extensive political resume.

Clark had unsuccessfully run for Missouri governor in 1840 on the Whig ticket. When the Civil War started Clark was serving in the United States House of Representatives. In 1861 Clark joined the Missouri State Guard and served as a Brig. General under Sterling Price. He fought at Boonville, Carthage, Wilson's Creek, and Lexington.

Personally, Clark was loud, pompous and narcissistic. In Richmond his self-image far exceeded his contribution.

---------- Why Lud? ----------

On the surface, Lud's selection to represent Missouri in the Confederate Senate, seems surprising. In an era when an individual's age, by itself carried merit, Lud's youthful 37 years belied his credentials. Almost 20 years younger than Clark, Lud's shadow paled in comparison to Clark's experience. However, there were strong reasons why Peyton's presence, not only in Missouri's Congressional delegation, but also in the Confederacy's highest assembly made sense.

Lud represented those western Missouri border counties most threatened and damaged by the Kansas abolitionists. Lud had lived along the border ravaged by years of confrontation. He, along with William Briscoe, had led Home Militia companies in defense of western Missouri. Lud's section of Missouri had been the victim of John Brown's raids and the continuing threats of James Montgomery. During the Southwest Expedition of 1860 and 1861, Lud's presence and oratory had rallied the Missouri General Assembly to provide protection for those living along Missouri's western border.

Lud's presence and participation during the border conflict endowed the credentials to chronicle, first-hand, abolitionist aggression. This theatre of operation also tightly linked him to David R. Atchison, Missouri's pivotal border leader. Atchison's "Blue Lodge" network included Lud's district where many constituents were members and had fought with Atchison's "Army of Law and Order". Furthermore, both Lud and Atchison shared strong personal ties to Jefferson Davis.

Lud had championed the Southern cause, supporting Calhoun's states rights policy from the initial stages of the political debate. Lud, unlike others among the Missouri delegation had from the beginning been a hard-line supporter of the secession. His early, uncompromising stance on secession imbued him an unquestioned position in the Southern cause. Throughout 1861 Peyton had fervently supported Gov. Jackson's move to pull Missouri out of the Union and carry her to the Confederacy. A member of Jackson's "inner circle" the spring and summer of 1861, Lud's loyalty to Jackson's policy made him a suitable ambassador for the Governor.

Although the Missouri State Guard had been fighting for just five months, the number of engagements with Union troops was high. Lud had distinguished himself as a leader and fighter, albeit without any formal military training or experience. Beloved by his men, the 3rd Cavalry had fought successfully at the battles of Carthage, Dry Wood Creek, Wilson's Creek, and Lexington. His military service in the Missouri State Guard gained the support of both Sterling Price and James S. Rains.

Missouri's late exit from the Union, coupled to Gov. Jackson's shaky reputation and trust with the Provisional Confederate Government, created an opportunity to improve relations for which Lud was uniquely qualified. Lud was a friend and relation of Jefferson Davis's favorite nephew, Joseph R. Davis. Lud and Joe had been classmates at Miami University. Joe Davis had married Lud's sister, Fanny, in 1842.

As Gov. Jackson's government was meeting at Neosho and Cassville, Lud's brother-in-law, Joe Davis, was serving as an Aide-de-Camp to his uncle, now the Confederacy's President, Jefferson Davis. Lud's sister, Fanny, was a member of, Varina Davis's social circle. At a point in Missouri's tenuous relationship with the Confederacy, when access to President Davis was both essential and difficult, Lud would have ease of access.

The Peyton name was already known to the Confederate Government. As Lud had led the 3rd Cavalry south, from Lexington to Neosho, his cousin, John Lewis Peyton, journeyed, from America to England. October 15, 1861, the Confederacy's Acting Secretary of War, Judah Benjamin signed the appointment making John L. Peyton the North Carolina ambassador to Europe. John Lewis's responsibility defined as the acquisition of arms and ammunition for the North Carolina forces.[706]

In addition to a presence in the Confederate Government, Missouri also needed a voice. Lud's oratorical skills, so powerful in Missouri's Senate and so electric in the public forum, put him on a level above his contemporaries. Lud, described by some as Missouri's rising star, had earned the adulation by virtue of his electric oratory during an age when oratorical skills provided the primary medium of public debate and persuasion.

[706] *OR*. Page 692.

Lud's unique passion and qualifications elevated him to a position of public prominence few would have imagined just five years before. From Cassville, Peyton began a journey to the highest levels of the Confederate government.

---------- To Richmond ----------

Gov. C.F. Jackson's "Special Assembly" adjourned to reconvene at New Madrid in March 1862. The week following the adjournment the St. Louis *Daily Missouri Republican* published an article that contained brief minutes of the Assembly's early sessions; the article was sub-titled "Bogus Missouri Legislature."[707] History forever attached "bogus" to the men and proceedings of the Neosho assembly.

Members and participants of the legislature dispersed at the session's adjournment. Legislators not in the Missouri State Guard or appointed to the Confederate Congress returned home to their districts either to remain or gather families and move to safer climes. Those in the Missouri State Guard returned to their commands. The new members of the Confederate Congress packed and headed to Richmond, Va.

The legislators and advisors dispersed as individual agendas dictated. Many accompanied Sterling Price's army north, back toward the Osage River. General McCulloch led his forces back into Arkansas.

Several of those newly appointed to the Confederate Congress were also, like Lud, officers in the Missouri State Guard. These officers accompanied their former commands north, before departing for their new duties. When Price's army reached Sarcoxie in southern Jasper County, John B. Clark and Caspar W. Bell left to begin their new duties. The parting, at this early stage of the fighting, with rebel victories in hand was difficult.

[707] *St. Louis Daily Missouri Republican*. November 14, 1861. Front Page.

"At Sarcoxie, General Clark took his leave of us, and made a very appropriate farewell address to his command. Colonel Bell also left; they were both Representatives to the Confederate Congress. So strong were the emotions of the General on leaving, that he shed tears, betraying in his whole appearance marks of sincere regret, and exhibiting the most affectionate solicitude for the interest and welfare of the soldiers of his command."[708]

Lud's separation from the 3rd Cavalry was equally painful. The regiment's five-month history, though brief, was long in experience. The men had traveled from Lexington to the Battle of Carthage and then to Cowskin Prairie where, although battle tested, they were yet green and undisciplined. They then returned to Lexington, and victory, by way of the Battle of Wilson's Creek, and the Battle of Drywood Creek. Peyton's cavalry left Cassville as hardcore veterans. His men had known each other before enlistment, and their MSG service tightened the bond. Colonel Peyton left his regiment having earned both his rank and the respect of his men.

When the 3rd Cavalry, now under Lt. Col. Martin White's command, turned northeast to Osceola, Peyton said his good-byes and made his way back to Harrisonville. But Harrisonville, no longer a safe haven, did not openly welcome Lud; Andrew Newgent's Union Home Guard controlled the town and much of the county with an iron hand. A return home, no matter how short, was dangerous. Lud said his good-byes. "When taking leave of a near and dear friend on his departure for Richmond, soon after his election to the senate, he was heard to say, in response to an inquiry, that 'the man with a beard would be fortunate who lived to see its (the war's) end.'"[709]

Missouri's Congressional Delegation left Missouri traveling to Richmond. Gov. Jackson and his staff also left, initially, heading for Memphis. Most of the delegates were in Memphis at the end of November. They all stayed at Memphis's exclusive Gayoso Hotel.

708 Anderson and Bearss. Page 103.
709 *History of Cass and Bates Counties, Missouri*. Page 378.

Gov. Jackson arrived November 26. A partial group of Missouri's Congressional Delegation arrived two days later – Representatives Caspar Bell, Thomas Freeman, Wm. Cooke, Aaron Conrow and George Vest. The next day Senator John B. Clark, Sr. arrived.[710] Lud, Thomas Harris and Dr. John Hyer were not a part of the group.

Gayoso Hotel- Memphis, Tennessee

Lud's activities between Cassville and his arrival in Richmond are not known. His return to Harrisonville would have been brief and secretive because the town and most of the county were under the tight control of Andrew Newgent's Home Guards. It is possible he spent time with Price's army near Osceola. Lud may have traveled with Gov. Jackson as a member of his staff. The Governor, and his staff, met with Gen. M. Jeff Thompson at New Madrid in mid-December. Whatever his travels, Lud arrived in Richmond and assumed his responsibilities in January.[711]

---

[710] *Daily Memphis Appeal.* November 30, 1861.

[711] Kirkpatrick, Major Arthur. "Missouri's Delegation In the Confederate Congress." Page 190.

Chapter Ten
Senator Peyton: Confederate States of America

Lud served in the Confederate Senate from February 1862 until it recessed in May 1863. The Senate convened for three separate sessions during this sixteen-month period. As Lud began his first term the Southern cause faced a uniquely different challenge than it had just months earlier. It was now beyond the fire-eating justification for secession and independence. The Confederacy now faced the challenge of winning a war of independence while simultaneously building a sustainable government.

Lud's fiery oratory and diatribe, so powerful and incendiary in generating rebellion, had no place in current circumstances. Jefferson Davis had excluded fire-eaters from his administration. Lud's oratorical gifts and passion for the South needed redirection to the challenges at hand.

During his Senate service, Lud, dealt with several ongoing issues. Missouri's credibility as a full-fledged, contributing member of the Confederacy was constantly in question. A late member to the Confederacy and occupied by Union forces, Missouri was never able to contribute the resources to the war effort other Southern states could deliver.

As a member of the Trans-Mississippi Department, Missouri jointly suffered along with Arkansas, Louisiana, and Texas from a lack of general support from the Confederate Government. The government expected contributions of resources and men yet never reached a point of being able to provide the military aid needed to fend off the Union west of the Mississippi.

Sterling Price provided continual drama. Eventually the situation put Lud at odds with Price and his supporters. Price's inability to work with almost anybody, his oversized ego, and constant lobbying for promotion became a permanent distraction for Missouri's delegation. Price visited Richmond annually during Lud's Senate tenure, each trip sparking controversy.

Lud's personal connection to the Davis family although influential also created tension. Well liked and respected by President Davis, Lud's opinion carried weight when Missouri military leaders lobbied for promotion. When Davis came under attack from critics, especially in Missouri's congressional delegation, Lud found himself caught between peers and family.

When Lud arrived in Richmond his sister Fanny had been with the Jefferson Davis family since May. Her husband, Joe Davis, an aide-de-camp for President Davis, and later a General, was often away. Fanny's health was deteriorating. Lud devoted time and attention to her care.

---------- Richmond ----------

The trip from Cassville to Richmond the winter of 1861 – 62 was long but unencumbered by Federal troops. The Mississippi River remained open for travel and railroad lines ran on schedule. Missouri's Congressional delegation traveled through Arkansas to Memphis and at Memphis the party boarded a train for Richmond.

Memphis prided itself as a jewel on the Mississippi. The city prospered as a major Mississippi River port. The western terminus of the South's railroad network, it connected the Trans-Mississippi with all points east.[712] Its population of 23,000 enjoyed the benefits of gaslights along major streets.[713] The first telegraph arrived in 1857 and Little Rock joined the network in 1858.[714]

The largest hotel in Memphis, the Gayoso House, was already an icon in 1861. Missouri Gov. C.F. Jackson, Missouri's Congressional delegation and other dignitaries stayed at the Gayoso. During the Civil War the hotel also served as the military headquarters for both Union and Confederate officers.[715] Leaving

[712] **Memphis**: June 6, 1862 Memphis fell to Union forces, who occupied the city for the remainder of the war. The Union occupation terminated Memphis's role as a transportation hub for the Trans-Mississippi.
[713] Young, J.P., editor. Page 108.
[714] Young, J.P., editor. Page 95.
[715] Young, J.P., editor. Page 34.

Memphis, Missouri's Congressional delegation boarded the Memphis and Charleston Railroad beginning the trip to Richmond.

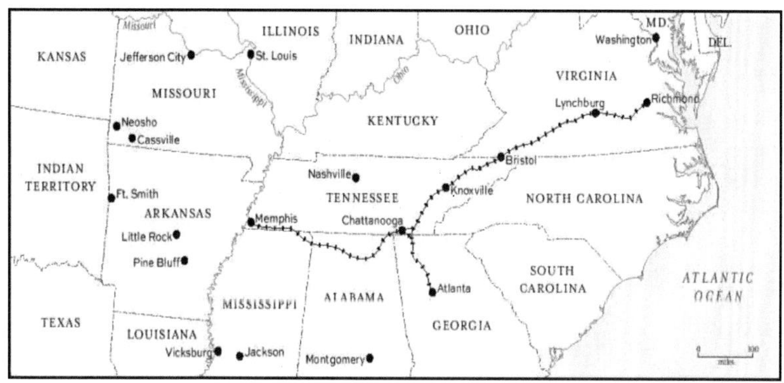

Road to Richmond - Circa 1861

When Missouri's Confederate Delegation arrived at Richmond, December 1861, the city had transitioned from state capitol to national capitol. Richmond's population had exploded with Confederate government employees and the Confederate army. Sitting just 110 miles southeast of Washington, D.C., Richmond faced off against the Union north.

When Lud stepped off the train in Richmond, he entered the Confederacy's political epicenter. Richmond prided, itself as being "The City of Seven Hills." Everywhere in the city movement is either uphill or downhill. Steep streets connect the James River quay to the city center. Richmond's population of 38,000 in 1861 included almost 12,000 slaves and 2,500 free-blacks.

Before Lud's arrival, Missouri's delegation stood on Richmond's railroad platform immediately immersed in a busy mass of humanity.

The city accommodations had already expanded beyond capacity. Missouri's contingent found permanent lodging in the few hotels and numerous boarding houses. Four of the Missouri Representatives, Thomas Harris, Caspar Bell, Aaron Conrow, and Thomas Freeman found lodging in Mrs. Nicholas' boarding house.[716] They shared small rooms. Mrs. Nicholas's place, located on Franklin Street between 1st and 2nd streets was a good nine-block walk to the capitol. The men did not enjoy walking the vertical ups and downs, especially in the deep, sloshy, mud during inclement weather.

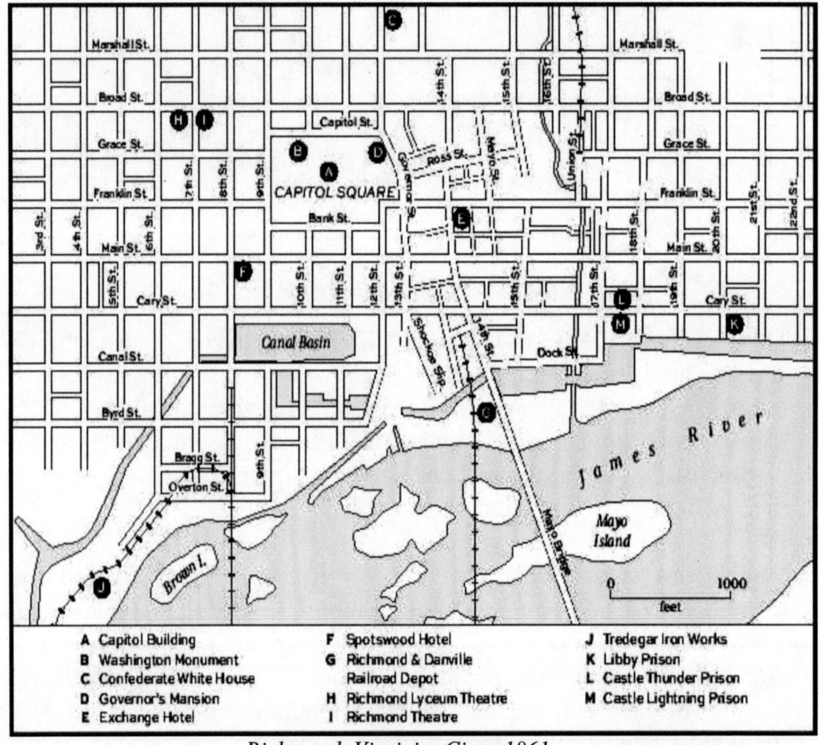

Richmond, Virginia- Circa 1861

The lucky Congressmen found lodging in either the Spotswood Hotel or the Exchange Hotel. Both hotels hummed with a constant flow of military and government dignitaries, and each was within a block of the capitol.

716 *The City Intelligencer or Stranger's Guide*. By V. & C. Macfarlane & Ferguson, Printers. 1862. Page 11.

Spotswood Hotel
Courtesy Library of Congress

Sen. John Clark and Rep. William Cooke found accommodations at the Spotswood. Jefferson Davis and his entourage had stayed at the Spotswood from May 29 until they moved into the Confederate White House in August. Lud's sister Fanny lived at the Spotswood with Jefferson and Varina Davis through the summer.[717] The Spotswood would later host Gen. Sterling Price and witness one of Missouri's most embarrassing episodes of the war.

Exchange Hotel- Courtesy Library of Congress

[717] Jefferson Davis Papers. *William Stanley Hoole Collection*. University of Alabama. Folder 6.

Lud and Rep. George Vest found rooms at the Exchange Hotel. Lud was in room 103 and Vest was in room 279. Four members of the Arkansas delegation also lived at the Exchange.[718] The Confederate Post Office operated out of the Exchange. At one point early in the government's transition to Richmond, the Exchange Hotel was available for purchase. The Davis government hoped to convert it into government offices but the deal fell through.

Virginia Capitol- Courtesy Library of Congress

The walk to the capitol building was a short, one block jaunt from both the Spotswood and the Exchange. The Confederate House of Representatives met in this building. The Confederate Senate briefly used small rooms on the upper floor but later often opted to meet away from the capitol in more accommodating space.

A native Virginian, George Washington's presence dominated the Confederate capitol and grounds. Inside the capitol a life size statue of Washington dominated the foyer. Outside, the Washington Monument commands the capitol's grounds. Jefferson Davis's inauguration on Washington's birthday, honored Washington's continuing influence and inspiration.

---

718 *The City Intelligencer or Stranger's Guide*. By V. & C. Macfarlane & Ferguson, Printers. 1862. Page 11.

The Missouri delegation arrived in time to experience Richmond's winter. The winter of 1861 – 1862 was especially difficult. "It was a singular fact, but from actual observance we assert the truth, that from the 1st day of January, 1862, until the middle of March, there were not two consecutive days of fine weather."[719] Cloudy skies, rain, sleet, snow and cold burdened Richmond and its residents.

---------- Price, Heth, and Davis ----------

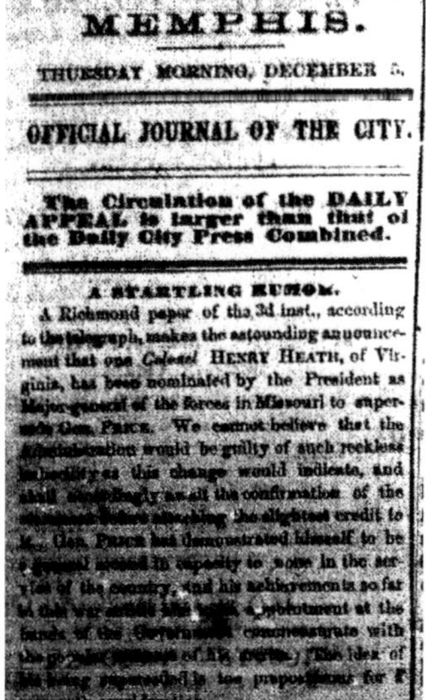

MEMPHIS.

THURSDAY MORNING, DECEMBER 5.

OFFICIAL JOURNAL OF THE CITY.

The Circulation of the DAILY APPEAL is larger than that of the Daily City Press Combined.

A STARTLING RUMOR.

A Richmond paper of the 3d inst., according to the telegraph, makes the astounding announcement that one *Colonel* HENRY HEATH, of Virginia, has been nominated by the President as Major-general of the forces in Missouri to supersede Gen. PRICE. We cannot believe that the Administration would be guilty of such reckless [illegible] as this change would indicate, and shall [illegible] await the confirmation of the [illegible] the slightest credit to [illegible]. Gen. PRICE has demonstrated himself to be a general second in capacity to none in the service of the country, and his achievements so far in this war entitle him to [illegible] appointment at the hands of the Government commensurate with the [illegible] of his merits. The idea of his being superseded is too preposterous for [illegible]

Henry Heth Rumor
Memphis Daily Appeal
December 5, 1861

Before unpacking their bags, the Missouri delegation waded into what was to become, throughout the war, a continuing diversion and drama. Sterling Price's inability to work effectively with other military commanders, politicians or leaders, coupled to his unbridled ego and push for self-advancement often muddled Missouri's situation. Price and Gen. Ben McCulloch had initiated a feud at the Battle of Wilson's Creek. By the end of autumn, 1861, Jefferson Davis had had enough of the infighting and determined to replace Price.

Davis's intention to remove Sterling Price soon dominated the political rumor mill. Edmund Ruffin, December 3, 1861, wrote in his diary, "Heard, as certain that the President has made Col. Heth, a young man of but 36 years old, a Major General, & will send him to Missouri, where by his higher rank, he will supersede Gen. Price, the most successful of our commanders. This act of the President is very unpleasing to his best friends & thorough supporters, & is strongly denounced by some others, who support and generally

719 Putnam. Page 92.

approve of President Davis, but who will not be silent on his errors, of which this is the very worst."[720]

Henry Heath Courtesy Library of Congress

The swirling rumor and controversy about Heth's replacing Sterling Price contained truth. Davis did in fact plan to promote Henry Heth to Major General replacing Price. In late November, Heth was called to Davis's office. Heth wrote in his memoirs after the war, Davis began the conversation by asking, "Young man how much rank can you stand?"[721] When Heth deferred the question Davis replied, "I will make you a Major General and send you to the Trans-Mississippi, Price and McCulloch are fighting each other over there harder than they are fighting the enemy."[722]

Unfortunately for Missouri and Price the debate continued. Price's ego, arrogance, and questionable military ability continually placed him in public dialogue. Albert Castel best summarized it:

> "But although Price had the ability to win the devotion of his troops, he had absolutely no talent for maintaining friendly relations with superiors and associates. Without exception he quarreled with, harbored resentments against, or was disliked by every commanding general he served under or with – McCulloch, McIntosh, Van Dorn, Pemberton, Marmaduke, Holmes, and Kirby Smith – not to mention his controversies with such civilian leaders as Davis, Seddon, and Reynolds. Although the fault in no case was exclusively his, and indeed in several cases he was the aggrieved party, such a record speaks for itself.[723]

In early December 1861, Price's replacement by Henry Heth was but the first public confrontation between Price and Confederate

[720] Ruffin. Page 181.
[721] Heth. Page 159.
[722] Heth. Page 159.
[723] Castel. Page 283.

authorities. The issue spread beyond Richmond into the Trans-Mississippi.

Davis's "announcement was anything but pleasant" for Heth.[724] The promotion and replacement of Gen. Price generated debate in the Provisional Senate. Opposed strongly by the Missouri delegation and others in Richmond the heated discussion created a stir. Heth, uncomfortable at being a focal point of the argument eventually visited Secretary of War, Mr. Benjamin and "declined the opportunity and the promotion."[725] The debate over

Sterling Price, so early in Missouri's effort to gain Confederate support, damaged the state's image and split the delegation.

The Price debacle created a lasting split in Missouri's Confederate government. When the congressional delegation arrived in Richmond, Lt. Gov. Reynolds awaited them. Led by John Clark, the delegation met with Pres. Davis before conferring with Reynolds. When Lt. Gov. Reynolds got involved in the Price affair, Clark informed him the delegation spoke for Missouri and Reynolds had no authority. In April 1862 Reynolds left Richmond, retiring "completely from public life."[726]

Clark and others in Missouri's delegation expanded the Price debate into an attack on President Davis. The controversy resulted in a widening gap between Price supporters and detractors. Lud and Rep. Thomas A. Harris came to lead the anti-Price faction.

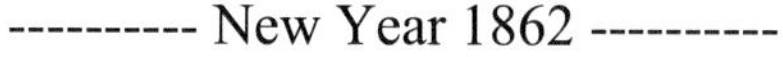

---------- New Year 1862 ----------

Jefferson Davis and Virginia Governor, John Letcher opened their homes, hosting New Year's receptions. "New Year's Day 1862 was bright and beautiful, although the breeze stirred up the dust considerably."[727] Invitees first attended President Davis's reception, from 1:00 to 3:00, then proceeded to the Governor's Mansion on

[724] Heth. Page 159.
[725] Heth. Page 159.
[726] Reynolds. Page 43.
[727] Kimmel. Page 98.

Capitol Square. The receptions were Lud's first formal, social occasions since arriving in Richmond.[728] To a large degree, his expected attendance marked entry into the Confederacy's social and political world.

From his lodging at the Exchange Hotel, the walk uphill to the President's Mansion, at the corner of 12th and Clay Street, covered five blocks. Lud joined other dignitaries and their wives as they converged. The Executive Mansion stood three stories with four pairs of columns on the front portico. "The rooms of the house were comparatively few, but very large, some of them more than forty feet square. The ceilings were high, the windows wide, and the stair wells turned in easy curves to the expansive hallways above."[729]

Lud arrived at the Executive Mansion and joined the line of awaiting invitees. "The officers; civil, naval, and military, the members of Congress and the State Legislature, and admiring crowds of less note, pressed forward to testify their admiration and esteem of the first President of the South."[730] Waiting and slowly advancing, the guests' spirits rose as they heard music pulsing out from the mansion. The Armory Band's play elevated moods and inspired smiles. Once inside the mansion's doorway, the music's volume increased and Lud absorbed the event. The line of attendees slowly inched forward, moving through the door of a large reception room. Standing in the reception room's doorway, Jefferson Davis stood welcoming his guests. "Mr. Davis received his guests, to all of whom he had something cheerful to say – some pleasant reminiscence to revive, and some graceful, genuine compliment to offer."[731]

---

[728] **Lud's Arrival**: The exact date Lud arrived in Richmond is not known. With the exception of Lud and Thomas Harris, the other members of the Missouri delegation arrived in early December.

[729] Kimmel. Page 74.

[730] Putnam. Page 91.

[731] Putnam. Page 91.

Confederate White House - Courtesy Library of Congress

Jefferson Davis's entourage included Lud's brother-in-law, Joe Davis. Joe worked as an aide-de-camp to President Davis. As Lud appeared at the doorway, Joe introduced him to Col. G.W. "Custis" Lee, also a President's aide, and the eldest son of Robert E. Lee. Both Col. Davis and Col. Lee wore their finest military uniforms. "Mrs. Davis was not visible in consequence of a recent interesting domestic occurrence, but the honors of the house were gracefully done by her sister, Miss Howell, Mrs. Jones and Mrs. Joseph Davis," Lud's sister.[732] On this day, moving through the reception line, Lud entered the Confederate social and political world, as a member of the Jefferson Davis family and a Senator from Missouri.

Greetings and reception complete, Lud moved into the loud, happy conversation and music of the reception itself. Those present were dressed for the occasion. The ladies wore their finest dresses and the men in their best uniforms and suits. Eggnog flowed; as well as other "compounds peculiar to winter festivities.'"[733] The sun, the music, the uniforms, and the occasion lifted the participants, optimism and confidence soaring.

[732] *Memphis Daily Appeal*. January 18, 1862.
[733] Kimmell. Page 98.

Lud, along with hundreds of guests, left the Executive Mansion transferring to Gov. Letcher's reception. Denied champagne by the Union blockade, Letcher's guests nonetheless enjoyed a "giant punchbowl…filled with the steaming beverage, the smell of roasted apples betrayed the characteristic toddy, and through the crystal cut-glass gleamed the golden hue of the egg-nog."[734] On this New Year's Day, 1862, "Bacchus asserted his triumph over Mars," Letcher's guests "oblivious, happily, to the sterner mandates of the God of War."[735] The happy mood from President Davis's and Gov. Letcher's receptions carried itself back to the Exchange Hotel's lobby and bar.

The New Year ceremoniously welcomed, Lud and associates turned to reality and the struggle to gain independence.

Nineteen days later, Lud again dressed in his more formal clothing, but for a sadder cause. John Tyler, "former President of the United States and late member of the Confederate Congress from Virginia," died in Richmond.[736] Tyler's body was taken to the Hall of Congress to lie in state. January 20, 1862 Tyler's funeral was conducted in the Hall; the Hall filled to overflowing. Lud listened as several congressmen offered their final respects. Later that day, Lud, and all other congressmen, attached a badge to his suit coat honoring Tyler's life and death – he wore the badge for the next 30 days.

---------- The Inauguration ----------

February 1862 proved a milestone month for the Southern Confederacy. The heretofore-Confederate, "provisional" government, was replaced by the permanent, elected government. The transition from provisional to permanent began with the Confederate Congress and concluded with the inauguration of Jefferson Davis as President of the Confederate States of America.

[734] Putnam. Page 90.
[735] Putnam. Page 91.
[736] Kimmell. Page 99.

Richmond's population swelled the second and third week of February as dignitaries, military leaders, relations, and spectators arrived for the government's transition from "provisional" to permanent. "The hospitable old town was crowded with the families of officers and members of the Government."[737] Confederate army officers, granted leave, arrived in Richmond, adding to the flood of people. The sidewalks filled with visitors.

Private homes opened their doors to accommodate the flood of people and ameliorate the financial pressures of living in Richmond and the South. Louise Wigfall, the daughter of Texas Senator Louis T. Wigfall, remembered later "private houses received boarders, as the reduction in the purchasing power of their incomes, through the depreciation of the currency, was already severely felt by the people."[738] Homes and hotels filled with arriving spectators.

As the official days of transition approached, a festive and celebratory atmosphere energized Richmond. The city filled with available young women and single military officers. Miss Wigfall and friends partied, enjoying the occasion. The war remained young and optimism prevailed. "Social pressures, however, were not neglected, and music and song and the dance made merry the hearts of the gallant soldier boys, who came from the wet, and mud, and discomfort of the camp."[739]

The Confederate provisional government officially dissolved in the capitol building, Tuesday, February 18, 1862. "A thousand people gathered at the Capitol" to participate in and witness the transition.[740] The galleries above the capitol's lower floor were packed elbow-to-elbow, ladies in the majority. "Long before the tap of the Speaker's gavel, the members-elect, the members of the Virginia Legislature, prominent citizens, several military officers, and many pretty ladies waited for the solemn and impressive ceremonies."

---

737 Harrison. Page 439.
738 Wright. Page 76.
739 Wright. Page 76.
740 Kimmel. Page 103.

Lud, so recently at Neosho and Cassville, stood amongst the South's highest leaders accepting the responsibilities conferred upon him. The ceremonies concluded, now officially a Senator, R.L.Y. Peyton took his seat in the Confederate Congress February 18.[741] Three days later, February 21, 1862, Senator Peyton's term in office was officially designated to be four years, expiring February 22, 1866.[742]

Jefferson Davis
Courtesy Library of Congress

The following Saturday, February 22, George Washington's Birthday had been designated the day of Jefferson Davis's inauguration. Washington's statue dominated Richmond's capitol square, the site of Davis's acceptance. Both the day and the setting seemed appropriate to those Virginians present; George Washington, a Virginian, and father of his country, would again be the foundation upon which a new nation began. On this cold, wet February Saturday, Davis's inauguration and Presidential reception marked the beginning of the legitimate, functioning government.

Lud arose early this Saturday. The Exchange Hotel already throbbed with the overcrowded conditions. The hallways and lobby filled with noisy activity. Conversation centered around the day's festivities and the worrying weather; it quickly became clear that staying warm and keeping dry were going to be challenging. The low, gray skies already were dropping an unending torrent of water. Lud dressed, donned his top hat and coat, and grabbed his umbrella. By 10:45 a.m. he left room 103, walked to the Exchange's lobby, and stepped out into the downpour, beginning a soggy walk to the Hall of the House of Delegates of Virginia. The mood on the streets was energetic and festive. "Although stormy clouds hovered above

741 *SHSP*. Vol. 44. Page 5.
742 *SHSP*. Vol. 44. Page 29.

the city and the air was damp and chilly, downtown sidewalks were crammed with pedestrians and shouting souvenir vendors. Streets were jammed with vehicles of all descriptions, flanked by men, women, and boys on horseback. Flags waved from government buildings, business places, and private homes. Stores were closed, soldiers paraded, and bands played."[743] Lud, on leaving the Exchange Hotel lobby, entered the day's happy albeit wet mayhem. On this momentous day, optimism and celebration trumped rain and cold.

Lud's wet walk to the Capitol, although a short three blocks, went slowly due to the crowds and vendors. He entered the Capitol building and slowly made his way through the crowd to the House of Delegates chamber. The entire Confederate congressional delegation gathered in advance of the procession back out into the inclement weather for the inauguration. By 11:30 a.m. the congressmen had assembled and ordered themselves.[744] Lud and fellow Missouri Senator, John B. Clark, visited and bemoaned the weather conditions along with the other dignitaries. At 12:30 p.m. the entire procession began to move slowly out of the capitol and into Washington Square.[745]

A scaffolding platform, constructed for the inauguration, faced Washington Square with the Confederate Capitol in the background. Although the occasion was both historic and monumental, the weather belied and dampened things. "Such a day! The heavens weep incessantly. Capitol Square is black with umbrellas."[746] Sallie Putnam described the scene in her diary:

> The square of the Capitol was crowded with a dense throng of old and young – men, women, and children – soldiers and citizens – mingled with carriages and umbrellas, dripping hats, and cloaks, and blankets, and oil clothes, and draggled skirts, and muddy boots, and all other accompaniments of mud and rain upon such a

[743] Kimmel. Page 103.
[744] Kimmel. Page 103.
[745] Kimmel. Page 103.
[746] Jones. Page 111.

> dense mass of human beings in the singular panorama of the occasion.[747]

Constance Harrison watched the inauguration from an upper window in the Capitol. Ms. Harrison watched the "pouring rain" and wrote, "the concourse of umbrellas in the square beneath us had the effect of an immense mushroom-bed."[748]

Lud, along with his fellow dignitaries, stood in deep mud, tightly packed and surrounded, enduring the rain and attempting to see the event through the forest of umbrellas. The Rt. Rev. John Johns opened the inauguration with "an eloquent and patriotic prayer."[749] Jefferson Davis moved to the front center of the platform and read his inauguration address. His speech lasted a short 20 minutes. Following Davis's speech, J.D. Halyburton administered the Presidential Oath.[750] When Davis completed the oath, he bent and kissed the Bible. As soon as Davis kissed the Bible, "a shout went up."[751] One of those shouting was John B. Jones, a government clerk, observed, "The permanent government had its birth in a storm, but it may yet flourish in sunshine."[752]

The happy but drenched crowd dispersed as quickly as the mud and mass allowed. Lud along with his fellow congressmen made his way back into the Capitol. Cold, soggy and muddy, Lud joined the other senators "in quickly adjourning" the session.[753] Individual senators made their way back to homes, boarding houses, and hotel rooms to prepare for the President's Reception. Returning to the Exchange Hotel, Lud changed into dry clothes and warmed himself in front of the hotel's massive fireplace."That night the President and Mrs. Davis held a Washington-style levee in the executive mansion."[754]

---

747 Putnam. Page 106.
748 Harrison. Page 439.
749 Kimmel. Page 103.
750 Kimmel. Page 104.
751 Harrison. Page 440.
752 Jones. Page 111.
753 Thomas. Page 79.
754 Thomas. Page 79.

Confederate White House
Courtesy Library of Congress

Guests and dignitaries patiently waited, in the continuing rain, to enter the Confederate White House. "It was a lugubrious reception but the President himself was calm, and Mrs. Davis seemed in spirits."[755]

Varina Davis
Courtesy Library of Congress

The President and Varina welcomed Lud as he entered the mansion. The house, filled with light and laughter, provided an antidote to the foul weather. Lud mixed with his sister, Fanny, and her husband Joe. A long way from distant Harrisonville and Missouri's western border, Lud, an eyewitness and participant to history, chatted, smiled and enjoyed the moment.

Walking back to the Exchange Hotel, Lud mentally prepared for

[755] Jones. Page 111.

the task ahead of him, while revisiting the year's whirlwind. With his arrival in Richmond, 60 days before, Lud had moved from western Missouri's battlefields to the Confederacy's epicenter. Davis's inauguration now complete the government's focus would now move to the monumental task of fighting a war, winning independence.

---------- The Elected Government ----------

The third week of February 1862, marked the Confederate government's formal transition from "provisional" to permanent. The regular Congress of the Confederate States replaced the provisional congress. Jefferson Davis and Alexander H. Stephens, formally elected in November 1861, were inaugurated and began duties as the regular President and Vice-President, each with a six-year term. The Provisional Confederate Congress met for its final secession on Monday, February 17, 1862.

Tuesday, February 18, the Senators-elect assembled at the Virginia State Capitol. Vice-President Stephens called the assembly to order, performed a roll call, and administered the oath of office. Missouri Senators, John B. Clark and R.L.Y. Peyton, received the oath of office and took their seats, now fully vested as Confederate congressmen, two among the twenty-six Southern senators.

Senator Hunter of Virginia announced Senate Standing Committee assignments on Tuesday, February 25. Committee assignments had been discussed and made the preceding day during an "informal meeting" of senators. Lud would be serving on the standing committees for Commerce, Indian Affairs, and Claims. Clark was appointed to Foreign Affairs, Public Lands, and Printing.[756] Neither of Missouri's senators served as a committee chairman.

Lud's Standing Committee work brought him into close contact with other Senators, The Commerce Committee, chaired by Clement C. Clay of Alabama, contained five members. Besides Lud, the other members were Augustus E. Maxwell of Florida,

[756] *Southern Historical Society Papers.* Vol. 44. Page 46.

North Carolina's William T Dortch and Kentucky's Henry C. Burnett.

Sen. Robert W. Johnson chaired the Committee on Indian Affairs. Supporting him on the committee, along with Lud, were Williamson S. Oldham, of Texas, W.E. Simms of Kentucky, and Clement C. Clay, Alabama. Sen. Johnson brought experience into the Chairmanship. While a member of the U.S. House of Representatives Johnson had chaired the House Committee on Indian Affairs. This standing committee was of particular importance to the Trans-Mississippi Department where Indian issues touched every state and territory.

R.W. Johnson Courtesy Library of Congress

Johnson wielded substantial power in1861; in addition to Indian Affairs, he also served on the Military Affairs and Naval standing committees.[757] Johnson came from "the Family," also known as "the Dynasty," that had controlled Arkansas politics from 1833 to 1860. An uncle, Richard Johnson, had been Vice President of the United States under Martin Van Buren. Robert had served in the U.S. House of Representatives, beginning in 1846, continuing through three congresses. In 1855 the Arkansas Legislature elected Johnson to the U.S. Senate where he served until March 1861.[758] He was the 7th wealthiest man ever to serve in Congress and at one time owned 193 slaves.[759] During his service in the Confederate Senate Johnson was a consistent supporter of Jefferson Davis. Following Lud's death in 1863, Johnson delivered a eulogy in the Confederate Senate.[760]

---

757 Woods. Page 236.
758 Woods. Page 229.
759 Woods. Page 229.
760 *Richmond Daily Examiner.* December 21, 1863.

Senator George Davis chaired the Claims Committee. This committee contained just three total members, the other two being Lud and Henry C. Burnett.

H.C. Burnett
Courtesy Library of Congress

Lud and Burnett served together on two standing committees, Claims and Commerce. Burnett, a 37 year-old firebrand from Kentucky, came to the Confederate Senate from a seat in the U.S. House of Representatives. The U.S. Congress expelled Burnett December 3, 1861. His relationship with, and support of, Jefferson Davis fluctuated. Normally a Davis supporter he split with the President on conscription. April 19, 1862, on the Senate floor, Burnett attacked Davis and his preference for West Point graduates. This public rebuke triggered such emotional support from the gallery that some were expelled.[761] Burnett and Lud's relationship developed, deepened and Burnett delivered a eulogy following Lud's death.

Clement C. Clay
Courtesy Library of Congress

Alabama Sen. Clement C. Clay and Peyton served on two committees, Commerce and Indian Affairs. Clay carried an impressive record into the Confederate Congress. From 1853 to 1861 Clay had served in the U.S. Senate; he resigned his Senate seat on January 11, 1861 and returned to Alabama.

The Alabama Confederate legislature elected Clay to the First Confederate Congress.

As February 1862 drew to a close, with the First Confederate Congress installed and committee assignments made, Lud and the Missouri delegation began its work. The waters this group would

761 Walther. Pages 339-340.

tread swirled with more than congressional protocol. Jefferson Davis's policies stirred debate and dissention. Missouri and the Trans-Mississippi carried unique burdens. Each member of the delegation would, by necessity, devote time and energy dealing with lobbying requests for military advancement. Sterling Price, by himself, generated ongoing and increasingly distracting annoyances for the entire group. Finally, the delegation itself, owing to a few members, began developing a reputation for boorish behavior.

Through time, Jefferson Davis's policies became a lightning rod for debate and dissension. As the war progressed, Congressional members became identified as being either "pro Davis" or "anti Davis." Lud, a member of Davis's family, remained a steadfast supporter, as did other members of Missouri's delegation. There were strong anti-Davis members in the delegation whose public criticism caused division. Paramount among the issues was Davis's preference for West Point graduates in filling the upper army ranks and the lack of sympathy and support for the Trans-Mississippi Department.

Missouri's support of, and place in the Confederacy, never left the political dialogue. Early in the Confederacy's establishment many southerners took exception to the wording of the agreement Jackson and Price reached with Union leaders in St. Louis. The document did not name the Union as an aggressor, and notably left open the possibility the South could be attacked.

Missouri's late application for entry into the Confederacy created a credibility issue. Certainly Missouri's State Convention, February 1861, voted almost unanimously to remain in the Union. Missouri was a border state, "completely in federal hands by mid-1863" and considered occupied by Southern politicians."[762]

The Trans-Mississippi Department throughout the war, suffered from a lack of government attention and military support. The Missouri, Arkansas, and Texas congressional delegations were united in continually seeking resources for their constituencies.

[762] Yearns. Page 57.

Local communities complained Trans-Mississippi soldiers were fighting east of the Mississippi River and not defending their home communities.

In February 1863 the Arkansas delegation sent a letter to President Davis officially complaining about the number of Arkansas soldiers fighting east of the Mississippi rather than west, defending their communities.[763] This issue also rang true to the Missouri delegation. From spring 1862, until the war's end, complaints mounted. Missouri's guerrilla groups were in large degree staffed by former Missouri State Guard or Confederate soldiers who had returned to Missouri to defend homes. Lud's home border counties mirrored the lack of Confederate military support.

John G. Walker
Courtesy Library of Congress

Military advancement depended upon political support, both Congressional and Presidential. Missouri military officers promoting themselves and lobbying for commands traveled to Richmond, many meeting with President Davis himself. The list included John S. Bowen, M. Jeff Thompson, John G. Walker, William Quantrill, and Sterling Price. These men lobbied for the support and political assistance of each member of the Missouri delegation.

Lud maintained an unshakeable loyalty to James Rains. Believing Rains was unfairly censored by rumors and that his military record surpassed that of many lobbying officers he resisted supporting others until Rains was recognized.

---------- Missouri's Congressional Delegation ----------

Quickly, the Missouri delegation's reputation deteriorated to a point that it became a central issue in the Confederate elections of 1863. Congressional delegations assumed group personalities and sadly

763 Woods. Page 238.

Missouri's reputation ranked among the lowest. Drinking, womanizing, and gambling tainted their reputation. This was especially true of Missouri's delegation to the First Confederate Congress who "...were so uninhibited that their escapades reverberated back across the Mississippi."[764]

Rep. Thomas Harris owned a well-earned reputation for heavy drinking and gambling. "Harris broke his leg in a gambling house so badly that he could not run for reelection in 1863."[765] Heavily inebriated he "walked over a veranda and fell a distance of 43 feet upon the brick pavement below."[766] Harris, in an obvious spoof on his own behavior, refused to "believe a word of the public rumors" regarding drunkenness in the Confederate army and voted against publishing laws against it.[767]

Senator John B. Clark, Peyton's partner in the Senate, developed a reputation for womanizing and drunkenness in addition to being considered crude and rude.[768] "John B. Clark treated Cabinet officials with crude familiarity, once climbing through a window into Secretary of War George W. Randolph's room for a talk; he drank heavily until the 'high price of liquor and fear for his health ... improved his habits;' and the gossip was that he tried to steal Albert Pike's mistress.[769] Clark's unsavory exploits, encouraged other candidates during the congressional elections of 1863 to run on platforms of "morality and sobriety."[770]

George G. Vest suffered public ridicule when a woman beat him with a cane on the assembly floor for immoral behavior. Vest's public philandering unfortunately fit the general image Richmond society carried for the Missourians.

---

764 Yearns. Page 19.
765 Yearns. Page 20.
766 *Columbia Missouri Herald.* November 4, 1880.
767 *Memphis Daily Appeal.* March 2, 1862.
768 Yearns. Page 20.
769 Yearns. Page 19.
770 Yearns. Page 57.

George G. Vest public cowhiding
Courtesy John Anderson Diary
December 8, 1864

In a Richmond society, priding itself on morality and culture, Missouri's delegation came off as uncouth.

Lud fit uncomfortably into the breech between his delegation's reputation and his place within the Davis's role.

------ New Madrid, Mo. & the Legislative Session ------

In November 1861, when the Claiborne F. Jackson's "Extraordinary Legislative Session" adjourned it scheduled its next session for March 3, 1862 at New Madrid, Mo. At the time, it had no way of anticipating the ill fated nature of the schedule. By March 1862 the struggle for control of the Mississippi River was well underway. The final outcome of this contest would be decisive for the Trans-Mississippi Department and each of the Confederate states west of the Mississippi River.

Even more unfortunate for Missouri's Confederate delegation and General Assembly, the contest for control of the upper Mississippi unfolded at the exact spot Missouri's Confederate legislature was to meet and at the precise time Union and Southern armies faced off at New Madrid and Island No. 10.

New Madrid and Island No. 10 Area- Circa 1862

The battle for control of the upper Mississippi occurred during the same period Missouri's Confederate government was to meet at New Madrid. Two days before Lud stood in the rain listening to Jefferson Davis's inaugural speech, Gen. Ulysses S. Grant had occupied Ft. Donelson, in western Tennessee; a result tightening Union control and shifting the military focus to New Madrid and Island No. 10.

Earlier in the war, the summer of 1861, Confederate military strategy called for a push beginning at New Madrid in southeast Missouri. "On July 28, 1861, eight Confederate steamers splashed up to the New Madrid levee, and amid the cheers of the local citizenry General (Gideon J.) Pillow's Army of Liberation tramped off the gangplanks onto Missouri soil."[771] General Pillow, William J. Hardee, and M. Jeff Thompson met with Governor Claiborne F. Jackson to plan a coordinated liberation of southeast Missouri and

[771] Mullen. Page 327.

eventually Rolla and St. Louis. "New Madrid was of prime military importance in this area. Besides serving as a base of operations for a Missouri Confederate offensive, it could also be a base for cutting communications of any force attempting an overland invasion of Arkansas."[772] But an even more important military location lay just eight miles north of New Madrid in the Mississippi River. "Island Number Ten, so named because it was the tenth island below the Ohio, was declared by a Confederate engineer, A.B. Gray, to have no superior above Memphis as a position for repelling the enemy and protecting the Mississippi Valley."[773]

Late in the summer of 1861 the hoped for Confederate offensive in southeast Missouri lost impetus and stalled. The failed initiative did not however eliminate the strategic importance of both New Madrid and Island Number Ten. Thus, early in 1862, as the scheduled session of the Confederate government approached, Union efforts to remove Confederate troops from the upper Mississippi gained steam. February 28 Union troops left Commerce, Mo., north of New Madrid and headed south toward New Madrid. Through "drizzling rain and snow" Gen. Pope's army dragged its artillery through the mud but maintained a steady approach. Pope's army arrived outside New Madrid on Monday, March 3 – the very day when Missouri's Confederate State Assembly was to convene.

M. Jeff Thompson Courtesy State Historical Society of Missouri

General M. Jeff Thompson carried the unfortunate burden of defending New Madrid from the Union troops while shepherding the Confederate legislative delegation, allowing them to meet and then escape safely. Only a portion of Missouri's Confederate Congressional delegation made the trip back to Missouri. Sen. Peyton, and Representatives George Vest, Thomas Harris, Aaron Conrow, and Thomas Freeman arrived in New Madrid ready to

772 Mullen. Page 328.
773 Mullen. Page 328.

conduct business.[774] It is not known how many, if any, of the Missouri Assembly members were present but neither Gov. Jackson or Lt. Gov. Reynolds arrived. Lt. Gov. Reynolds had remained in Richmond and he soon retired to South Carolina.

The Congressional delegation arrived in New Madrid following a nonstop journey from Richmond. The men had attended Jefferson Davis's rainy inauguration and Presidential Reception on Saturday, February 22. Seven days later they were in New Madrid, in the eye of the hurricane.

Traveling overland by train the group left Richmond and journeyed southwest toward Memphis through Bristol (Va.), Chattanooga (Tenn.), and Corinth (Ms.).[775] The railroad trip from Richmond to Memphis covered 850 miles. Railroads of the day did not provide high levels of comfort or follow reliable timetables. Southern railroads burned wood exclusively and traveling with the windows open exposed the travelers to nonstop smoke and wind. Long distance travelers slept in their seats; sleeping cars were not available. The trip from Richmond to Memphis required several different railroads and transfers because each railroad used a different rail gauge.[776] Most passenger trains moved at an average speed of 25 miles per hour.

Arriving at Memphis, the delegation transferred to a steamboat and headed north on the serpentine Mississippi River. The winding, up river trip to New Madrid covered 153 miles. The river, while held by the Confederacy, tied the Trans-Mississippi states and territories to the Confederacy. As the steamboat, against the current, wound its way north, Arkansas and Missouri desperately needed to remain fused to Tennessee, Mississippi, and the Confederacy. As Lud and the rest of the delegation moved north, they noticed how the shore's landscape had changed. Confederate military vessels, known as the "River Defense" protected Southern interests. Military fortifications along the river's banks controlled the flow of river traffic.

[774] Kirkpatrick. *MHR*. Vol. 55. No. 4. Page 382.
[775] Stover. Page 27.
[776] Black. Page 19.

Just 40 miles above Memphis the steamboat passed Ft. Pillow on the eastern, Tennessee shore. In 1861, the Confederates had constructed Ft. Pillow, and named it for Confederate Brig. Gen. Gideon J. Pillow. The fort sat on high bluffs, commanding the Mississippi River, defending Memphis and the southern stretch of the river from Union attack. From the steamboat's deck the fort's position on the bluffs with its protruding guns commanding the river, seemed impenetrable. The Mississippi River seemed secure.

Passing Ft. Pillow the delegation progressed north 73 miles to Caruthersville, located in Missouri's boot-heel. As the steamboat completed the last 39 miles from Caruthersville to New Madrid it left the calm for the storm. Union troops pushed south, nearing New Madrid as the steamboat carrying the Richmond delegation slowly approached northward. Lud's delegation docked at New Madrid just before Union troops arrived and began a siege.

It is doubtful the Richmond delegation arrived at New Madrid looking anything but bedraggled and exhausted. Additionally, Rep. Vest walked down the gangplank lugging a musket for Gen. Thompson. Thompson had been in Richmond earlier campaigning for promotion to Brig. General. During his brief Richmond visit he met Edmund Ruffin who offered Thompson a souvenir musket recovered from the Manassas battlefield. Thompson accepted the gift but had to leave Richmond before the musket could be delivered. Ruffin then asked Vest to make the delivery.[777] Vest carted the musket from Richmond to New Madrid and delivered it.[778]

Disembarking the steamboat, the congressmen entered a war zone, not the hoped for, protected and quiet atmosphere necessary for making essential government policy decisions. Gen. Thompson, anticipating the officials' arrival and meeting, "received permission to take some of my own men, who were then being organized for the Confederate service, and to (go) up to the Fords, and delay Pope until after Monday, when the Legislature would meet."[779]

[777] Ruffin. Page 242.
[778] Thompson. Page 137.
[779] Thompson. Page 140.

Thompson's attempt to slow the Union troops failed and the Federal advance continued.

Equally unsettling, the welcoming party did not include other top government officials. Gov. Jackson and Lt. Gov. Reynolds were absent as well as other State Assembly members. In fact, there were no other members of the assembly present. The day after arriving, the small delegation met with Gen. Thompson. Thompson memorialized the meeting thus: "Monday morning came but the Representatives that were expected to come up on a steamboat from Memphis did not appear and I had all the members of the Legislature that were about Madrid to assemble, and formally adjourn to Gayosa in Pemiscot County. The whole meeting and adjournment were unique, and my order in the premises, were decidedly Cromwellian! When we finished the business a Committee was sent down the River to meet Governor Jackson and the Legislature and stop them at Gayosa. However, they never left Memphis, and all of our Legislative strategy was thrown away. At noon we dispatched the boat and I now began to pay attention to the Military aspects."[780]

Fleeing New Madrid the congressional delegation escaped south retracing their route to Memphis; a route that would soon slam shut as Union forces grabbed control of the Mississippi. At the heels of the retreating delegation, within weeks, New Madrid, Island Number Ten, Ft. Pillow, and Memphis fell to Union control. The upper Mississippi, and water access to Missouri lost for the duration of the war.

---------- The First Confederate Congress ----------

First Session: February 18 to April 21, 1862

The First Confederate Congress met in the Virginia State House. The House of Representatives, the larger of the two bodies, met on the second floor of the state house. The assembly room was twelve yards by twenty-five yards. The room was cold! According to

[780] Thompson. Pages 145-146.

House members, the room, even when occupied was cold.[781] The Confederate Senate normally met on the third floor. Their accommodations were cramped and uncomfortable, so when the Virginia State Senate was not in session, the Confederate Senate moved down into their chambers. Overall, conditions were cramped and unsuitable for the Confederate Congress and attempts were made to find different facilities.

All attempts to relocate the congressional quarters proved unsuccessful. Richmond's building inventory and space capacity was pushed beyond its limits. Early in the war, the government made overtones hoping to purchase or rent the Exchange Hotel, the same hotel where Lud lodged, but the high cost involved killed the idea.[782] For the war's duration, Congress, especially the Senate, and its standing committees jockeyed for available, comfortable space.

As the Confederate Congress began the arduous journey of leading a new government, its members settled into the process representing a variety of different constituencies. Missouri's Congressional Delegation entered the legislative process in a complex position. The state of Missouri held a tenuous political position. Besides being occupied by federal troops, Missouri by geographic location and political identity was defined as a "border state" and a part of the Trans-Mississippi Department. Situated west of the Mississippi River, this geographic reality created problems.

Missouri entered the Confederacy late. In February 1861 Missouri's state convention had voted overwhelmingly to remain in the Union. Although Gov. C.F. Jackson stood for secession and the Confederacy, by the time Missouri was admitted to the Confederacy, November 1861, Gov. Jackson governed "in absentia." When the Missouri Confederate delegation arrived in Richmond, December 1861, Union troops had a stranglehold on the state. Additionally, an appointed Union state government also

781 Yearns. Page 13.
782 Yearns. Page 14.

claimed legitimacy. Thus occupied, Missouri could never be viewed as a resource of the Southern war effort or as a breadbasket.

Confederate Assembly- Author's Collection

As a border state other Confederate politicians questioned Missouri's commitment to the Confederacy. Missouri's value and contribution remained under constant scrutiny. Other Confederate congressional delegations harbored fear the Border States were diluting the Confederacy's war efforts.[783] During Congressional deliberation and decision-making, the border-states often united, the coalition supporting positions adverse to the Deep South. This was best exemplified in the debate over the military exemption of plantation overseers.[784]

The Trans-Mississippi Department, of which Missouri was a member, routinely faced challenges for recognition, men, and material throughout the war.[785] "Congressmen naturally spent

[783] Yearns. Page 39.
[784] Yearns. Page 72.
[785] **Note**: "The Trans-Mississippi Department, included within its limits, the states of Missouri, Arkansas, Texas, and that part of Louisiana west of the

much of their time championing local needs. The Trans-Mississippi states had a number of unique problems and kept a standing committee to work upon them."[786]

A missing Confederate military presence and support was foremost among the issues facing the Trans-Mississippi. Inadequate military protection against Union troops, guerrillas, and Indians only increased during the war. Commerce along the Mississippi River as well as trade from Texas into Mexico created constant irritation. Missouri congressmen fruitlessly championed the need for a military presence west of the Mississippi, dreaming of a military invasion to take the state back.

Although the foregoing issues and tensions emerged through time, when the Confederate Congress initially convened, they had yet to fully coalesce. February 18, at noon, Alexander H. Stephens, Vice President of the Provisional Congress, called the session to order in the Virginia Capitol's Senate Chamber. Georgia's A.R. Lamar, temporary Secretary, called the roll. The roll call followed the states alphabetical order.

Following John B. Clark, Mr. Lamar called the name, R.L.Y. Peyton. Lud stepped to the chair, presented his credentials, was duly certified and took his seat. Once all names had been called and all credentials accepted, the Senate moved to the election of officers.

The following day, both houses of congress met in joint session for the presentation of electoral ballots for President and Vice-President. Missouri, not having participated in the election process had no ballots in the Electoral College and thus, did not participate in the process. Jefferson Davis and Alexander H. Stephens were elected President and Vice President respectively for six-year terms. Senator Clark, of Missouri, along with South Carolina's Robert W.

Mississippi River, the Territories of New Mexico and Arizona and the Indian country south of Kansas and west of Arkansas." Oldham. Page 220.

[786] Yearns. Page 142.

Barnwell, was appointed to coordinate with the House in notifying President Jefferson Davis of the result.[787]

Friday, February 21, the Senate's primary order of business required the 'classification of senators." The classification process assigned each of the twenty-six senators a term limit. Senatorial terms were staggered, at two, four, and six years. The staggered senatorial terms ensured an orderly transition of leadership going forward as a portion of the Senate would be up for re-election in each election cycle.

Each senator's term of office was to be determined by two drawn ballots. The first ballots drawn, alphabetically by state, set the term limits for each state's two senators. The states would be divided into three classes: (1) one senate term of two years and one senate term of four years (2) one senate term of four years and one senate term of six years (3) one senate term of two years and one senate term of six years. A senator from each state, left his seat, walked to the front of the assembly and drew a class ballot.

The Senate's President Pro-Tempore drew the second ballot, again by state. This draw assigned senate terms to each state's two senators. The name drawn received the shorter of the designated terms, the remaining name received the longer term. The first ballot draw proceeded in alphabetical order by state. The ballots had all been placed in a box at the front of the Senate Chamber. Seven states had been called and ballots drawn before Missouri's turn. Then, "the state of Missouri being called, Mr. Peyton came forward and drew from the box on behalf of that State, a ballot having marked thereon, 'two years – four years.'"[788] It was thus determined that of Missouri's two senators, one would serve a two year term and one a four year term.

The President Pro-Tempore personally managed the second ballot process. For each state, in alphabetical order, he placed the two terms assigned by the first drawing. The President Pro-Tempore

---

787 *Journal of the Congress of the Confederate States of American, 1861-1865*, Vol. II. Page 11. Hereafter referenced as JCCSA. V2.
788 *JCCSA*. V 2. Page 13.

then drew the ballots assigning the individual senator terms. "The ballots for the State of Missouri having been placed in the box, properly marked, were drawn as follows: John B. Clark, two years; R.L.Y. Peyton, four years."[789] By the "luck of the draw," John B. Clark's term would end in 1864 necessitating his campaigning for re-election in 1863. Lud Peyton's term would expire in 1866, thus requiring campaigning and re-election in 1865.

The next day, Saturday, February 22, 1862, Lud attended the inauguration of Jefferson Davis. As Lud stood in the torrential downpour, listening to Davis's speech, he did so with the understanding he would be in Richmond, serving Missouri, for the next four years.

The following Monday, the Senate confirmed fifteen standing committees. Following adjournment the senators, through discussion outside the Senate chambers, appointed and agreed upon each standing committee's membership. Tuesday morning, as the first order of business, the Senate approved the committees. Missouri Sen. Clark's name appeared on the membership of the Foreign Affairs, Printing, and Public Lands committees and he was later made chairman of the Public Lands Committee. Later Sen. Clark was appointed to the Committee on Post-Offices and Post-Roads.[790] Lud joined the Claims, Commerce, and Indian Affairs standing committees.[791]

---------- Secret Sessions ----------

By way of preface, it is often extremely difficult to analyze an individual senator's role in Senate deliberations. All too often, when the Confederate Senate moved to debate specific bills and questions, the body moved into "Secret Session." Senate rules specified, "all matters relating to foreign affairs or public defense be considered in secret session."[792] In theory, the secrecy afforded

789 *JCCSA*. V 2. Page 13.
790 *JCCSA*. V 2. Page 26.
791 *JCCSA*. V 2. Page 19.
792 Yearns. Page 35.

"freer debate and a greater use of confidential information."[793] During the secret sessions the Senate galleries were cleared of all audience, including newspaper reporters. The debate flared behind closed doors. From February 18 to April 21, the Senate moved into "Secret Session" on thirty-five occasions in 46 daily sessions.
Overtime, this propensity for secrecy attracted intense criticism from the press and public at large. Although the Senate sought to minimize the number of secret sessions, more transparent discourse and reporting never occurred.

The excessive number of Senate secret sessions, makes determining Lud's debate participation and his political positions nearly impossible to ascertain. In Lud's case, the only windows, into his Senate , lies in the published vote results and limited newspaper accounts.

The First Session of the Confederate Congress, February 18 to April 21, faced a number of issues critical to the establishment of the new government, while simultaneously marshaling soldiers and war resources. The subjects had varying relevance to Missouri, the Trans-Mississippi Department, and Missouri's delegation. During this sixty-two day session, Lud was a regular participant and voter. The issues of greatest significance were:

- Military Conscription
- Conscription Exemptions
- Drunkenness in the Confederate Army
- Planters: Cotton and Tobacco
- Suspension of the Writ of Habeas Corpus
- Missouri's Military Funding
- Partisan Ranger Act
- Government and Military Appointments

Foremost among the issues facing the Confederacy in this first congressional session were those focused on its military, strength, size, effectiveness, and provisioning. Already by early 1862 the flood of volunteer recruits had dwindled. Maintaining military

[793] Yearns. Page 35.

staffing became critical, thrusting conscription into open debate. Linked tightly to conscription was the exemption issue. Who among the available recruits would be exempted due to the importance of their jobs? Drunkenness among officers and soldiers alike threatened to weaken and destroy the overall effectiveness of the Southern army. Congress addressed the issue. Lastly, provisioning the army, providing what was needed for full stomachs also entered the public debate. On all four of the above major challenges Lud attended debates and voted with the majority.

Jefferson Davis requested a Conscription Law and Texas Sen. Louis Wigfall introduced the Conscription Bill on April 1. Just fifteen days later the conscription bill became law. The new law applied to men between the ages of 18 and 35 who were not already exempt from military service. For those already in service, enlistments would be for three years from the original date of enlistment. Military units would be allowed to elect officers. The new law also allowed men drafted to "hire substitutes," a policy that sparked bitter criticism among the general populace.

Missouri's Senators, Peyton and Clark, voted with the majority, to enact the Conscription Law. The conscription policy had no direct impact on Missouri. Missouri, already occupied by federal forces, could not enforce the conscription law; also, strongly divided, the number of men available for the draft was low. The Conscription Law however did have a significant impact, not positive, on a Trans-Mississippi partner, Texas. The law created a rift between eastern and western congressmen. "Eastern congressmen claimed that conscription had been poorly applied in the border-states and that, since Congress was pledged to redeem these states, their manpower should be used."[794]

Five days after President Davis signed the Conscription Bill into law, the Congress sent a companion bill for his approval. This companion was designed "to exempt certain persons from enrollment for service in the armies of the Confederate States."[795]

[794] Yearns. Page 69.
[795] *JCCSA*. V. 2. Page 158.

The law "established the familiar system of 'class exemptions,' which conferred blanket freedom from military service upon men in certain occupations."[796] Among those exempted were clerks at all levels of government, members of the judicial and executive branches, educators, iron workers, textile workers, and employees for institutions for the indigent. Very soon after passage the ranks of teachers began to grow.

Senators Peyton and Clark both voted to table the exemption bill early in the deliberations. Although both Senators were on the same page, their votes were included among a small minority. The minority included the Missouri, Kentucky, and South Carolina senators.[797] Eventually both men supported the overall passage of the exemption bill and it moved to President Davis for approval.

Excessive alcohol consumption and drunkenness, a social challenge in both the north and south, became such a problem in the Southern armies that it threatened to undermine any possibility of success. Discussion and debate began April 14 and was signed into law April 19. Drunkenness as a subject was not foreign to Missouri's military. Sterling Price and James Rains were linked to insobriety and the discussion undoubtedly had an impact on their military advancement; certainly this was true of Rains, Lud's close friend and former superior.

Lud's stance on drunkenness mirrored the Senate as a whole. Of the eight individual votes taken on the bill Lud voted with the majority in seven. Both Lud and Clark, however, objected to officers being permanently barred from further advancement during the war following a conviction.[798] That said, both men supported the bill's final approval.

Provisioning the Southern armies by limiting the production of tobacco and cotton hit the Senate floor early in March 1862. The bill, first introduced in the House, generated considerable discussion because it touched soldiers' stomachs and the South's

[796] Yearns. Page 68.
[797] *JCCSA*. V. 2. Page 204.
[798] *JCCSA*. V. 2. Page 163.

economic and diplomatic success. "Southerners realized that large amounts of cotton and tobacco would soon glut the market and that food shortages were becoming critical."[799] After considerable deliberation, Congress decided not to take action on the issue allowing the states to address it.

Lud's votes on the issue were solidly with the cotton and tobacco states. He voted against limiting production of either crop. His stance was solidly aligned with Virginia, Texas, and Arkansas. Lud and Clark voted on opposite sides of this issue.

February 27, Texas Sen. Louis Wigfall, "from the Committee on Military Affairs reported a bill to authorize suspension of the writ of habeas corpus in certain cases."[800] President Davis had requested the ability to declare martial law in certain locations with the goal of providing safety, particularly in cities. The Senate went into secret session and passed the bill. The same day the House of Representatives, also in secret session, passed the bill. President Davis signed the legislation into law the same day.

While the Confederate houses rushed the legislation from draft bill to law, Lud and other members of the Missouri delegation had begun the race to New Madrid, Mo. and the scheduled meeting of Missouri's Confederate Assembly.

Although absent when Congress authorized the suspension of the writ of habeas corpus, Lud experienced the law's impact first hand on his return to Richmond the following week. President Davis had requested the power to suspend habeas corpus to address specific problems in the Norfolk and Portsmouth, battlefields.

However, in addition to these two towns, March 1, Davis declared Richmond and all areas with 10 miles of the city under martial law. By late February 1862, Richmond swirled chaotically with spies, liquor, gambling, prostitution, and spiraling prices. Davis's martial law edit sought to impose order to the chaos. "Martial law meant

[799] Yearns. Page 131.
[800] *JCCSA*. V. 2. Page 65.

placing the whole community under a military regime with the ordinary processes of justice suspended."[801]

Martial law's impact on Richmond's daily life, including the lives of Senators, was immediate. Liquor, its sale and availability, was the initial target. Upon Lud's return to Richmond he found liquor sales forbidden. Even apothecaries were forbidden to sell any product containing alcohol.[802] The railroads were not allowed to deliver liquor to Richmond.[803] A secondary element of martial law required private citizens to surrender personal firearms to the Provost Marshal.[804]

Obstacles were thrown up for to freedom of movement. Military passes were now required for private citizens traveling in and out of Richmond, including all members of Congress. Daily, hotels had to provide the Provost Marshal, with the names of new arrivals.[805] The restrictions imposed by martial law continued by degrees to the war's end. During marital law, passes were required in Richmond.

Lud and other members of Congress complained of carrying passes wherever they went.[806] Some issues confronting the Confederate Congress had minimal direct relevance to Missouri or to the congressional delegation. While Congressional debates on removing the writ of habeas corpus, the conscription law, and restrictions on the growth of tobacco and cotton had little direct impact on Missouri, the delegation's participation nonetheless provided leverage for support on local issues.

The state's delegation was also a member of the Trans-Mississippi coalition. The delegation viewed many issues through a common lens containing Arkansas, Texas, Missouri and parts of Louisiana. These state delegations cooperated on common issues.

---

[801] Yearns. Page 152.
[802] Thomas. Page 82.
[803] Thomas. Page 82.
[804] Thomas. Page 82.
[805] Thomas. Page 82.
[806] Yearns. Page 151.

The fall of 1861, the Provisional Confederate Congress had approved one million dollars in funding for Missouri's military. When April 1862 arrived the funds had not been distributed. The House sponsored funding request arrived in the Senate on April 9. Missouri's Senators Peyton, and Clark, championed payment before the Senate.

Lud, standing and addressing the Senate, "explained that the money was for the purpose of paying the soldiers of the State of Missouri prior to their being mustered in the Confederate Service."[807] The timing of the Senate debate corresponded to the period when the Missouri State Guard was being phased from existence and its troops transitioning to the regular Confederate Army. Arkansas's Sen. Johnson rose and supported Lud and Missouri's participation, advising the Senate, "Missouri had nobly sustained the cause of the South; her soldiers were now fighting our battles, and the appropriation was required to furnish them shoes and blankets to ensure their comfort."[808] Following Lud's speech and Johnson's strong support, the Senate approved the military funding.

The next week both Congressional houses debated the Partisan Ranger Act. This proposal carried particular significance to Border States. In many cases lacking the presence of regular Confederate troops, men fighting in guerrilla or bushwhacking units defended the Southern cause. Lacking a legitimate identity with the Confederate Army, captured southern fighters were not accorded the status of prisoners of war. They were thus liable to being shot on the spot. Some senators opposed the act. Texas Sen. Wigfall "feared that men would enlist in the Partisan Rangers to the detriment of enlistments in the regular army."[809]

The Partisan Ranger Act carried particular importance for Missouri. Missouri's battle theatre operated under a unique and brutal set of rules. James Lane's Kansas Brigade initially established a "black flag" order of battle. Autumn, 1861, the Kansas Brigade marched

[807] *Southern Historical Society Papers* (Hereafter *SHSP*). Vol. 45. Page 105.
[808] *SHSP*. V. 45. Page 105.
[809] Cooper. Page 104.

through western Missouri; as the brigade took prisoners, many were forced to dig their own graves, and were then summarily murdered. Missouri bushwhackers, accepting Lane's "take no prisoners" policy, reciprocated and by 1862 the black flag flew throughout Missouri.

Even given Missouri's violent, chaotic circumstance there was not complete support of the Partisan Ranger Act within Missouri's delegation. Missouri's Southern civilian population feared federal reprisals would worsen under the act. Missouri's large Southern population lived under federal occupation – easily accessible to federal troops in the aftermath of any conflict. Both Thomas Harris and Thomas Reynolds opposed the act fearing reprisals.[810] Rep. Harris "wrote the secretary of war in 1862 of his desire not to carry on or abet guerrilla war in Missouri. Loyal citizens already 'writhing under the yoke and oppression of the enemy' were subject to daily guerrilla 'acts of unprecedented oppression and barbarity, in violation of all principles of civilized warfare.'"[811]

In spite of opposition, the Partisan Ranger Act flew through both the House and Senate in a single day. April 19, both bodies approved the bill. Two days later, President Davis signed the act into Confederate Law.[812]

Lud and the Partisan Ranger Act, through fate and circumstance, had an unusual tie. In December 1862, Col. John S. Mosby, perhaps the Civil War's most famous partisan ranger received his commission on the same Loudoun County, Va. farm where Lud had been born 38 years before.[813] Mosby received his commission from Gen. J.E.B. Stuart in the Peyton family's former parlor.

The Confederate Senate regularly considered and approved appointments, both military and governmental. The approval process, during this First Session, allowed Lud to renew, via his supporting vote, association with two friends, Albert T. Bledsoe

---

810 Fellman. Page 100.
811 Fellman. Page 100.
812 *JCCSP*. V. 2. Pages 195-220.
813 *Mosby's War Reminiscences: Stuart's Cavalry Campaigns*. Page 29.

and John S. Bowen. With Prof. A.T. Bledsoe, Lud renewed an old Miami University association. Bledsoe had taught at Miami University during Lud's early years there. John S. Bowen and Lud had become close associates during Bowen's tour of duty with the Southwest Expedition's presence along Missouri's western border the winter of 1860 – '61.

Although not personally present in Richmond, March 18, Bowen's name was placed in nomination, for the rank of Brigadier General. The nomination granted Lud the opportunity to champion a former western Missouri veteran.

April 1, the Senate received President Davis's nomination of A.T. Bledsoe to serve as Assistant Secretary of War. Lud and Bledsoe first met in Oxford, Ohio where Bledsoe held the Mathematics Chair at Miami University – Bledsoe the professor and Lud the student. Prior to teaching at Miami University Bledsoe had "graduated at West Point in 1830. He was there with both Jefferson Davis and Robert E. Lee, though not a classmate of either."[814] Bledsoe left Ohio for Springfield, Illinois. While at Springfield he became friends with Abraham Lincoln and once agreed to serve as Lincoln's "second" in a scheduled but later cancelled duel with James Shields. Bledsoe and Jefferson Davis reconnected when Bledsoe taught at the University of Mississippi. The friendship between Davis and Bledsoe continued at Richmond, where Lud joined the pair. April 2 the Senate approved Bledsoe's nomination as Assistant Secretary of War.[815]

---------- Recess, Siege, & Price ----------

Tuesday, April 22 the Confederate Congress adjourned its first session and began recess until August. During the recess, congressmen served in other capacities.[816] At this early stage of the war, Union armies had not, as yet, taken control of any southern territory; as a result congressmen were able to travel freely within the Confederate states. Some congressmen served as aides to

[814] Bledsoe. Explanatory Preface.
[815] *JCCSA*. Page 120.
[816] Yearns. Page 17.

general officers with whom they had a close relationship. Other congressmen publically known took advantage of the time to embark on speaking tours in other states. They spoke in support of the war and generally aimed to uplift spirits. Still, some congressmen returned to their home constituencies.[817]

Many families of the Missouri delegation had resettled outside Missouri in Arkansas or Texas where the congressmen reunited with loved ones. A few congressmen stayed in Richmond but "the city soon became thoroughly congested, however, and hotels began to pack even the parlors and halls with beds and to serve wretched meals."[818]

Richmond fell under Federal attack. Throughout May and June the city suffered through its near loss to the Federals at Seven Pines and the horrific aftermath of the Seven Days Battle. May 31 Union troops advanced "within sight of the spires and the sound of church bells of Richmond," but were driven back by Gen. Joe Johnston's troops.[819] Robert E. Lee later replaced Gen. Johnston, who had been severely wounded. The Federal attack on Richmond culminated in the Seven Days Battle the end of June. Defense of the capitol took precedence, "every state in the Confederacy was represented."[820] Lud, and all men with military experience, were called to duty.

Sterling Price arrived in Richmond during the Federal attack. Price's motivation for leaving the Trans-Mississippi was to lobby, in person, for command of the Missouri – Arkansas theatre of operations. Missouri's congressional delegation drawn into Price's drama fell further into disrepute. Price, and an aide, Thomas Snead, met with President Davis. Although Davis promised to eventually transfer Price's command to the west, but offered no promotion. The General became infuriated. "Certain that he was supported by public opinion, Price declared that if Davis did not want his services

817 Yearns. Page 18.
818 Yearns. Page 18.
819 Kimmel. Page 117.
820 Kimmel. Page 118.

he would resign and return to Missouri."[821] Davis seemed inclined to accept the resignation.

Price and Snead stormed back to the Spotswood Hotel where Snead ripped "off his Confederate insignia" declaring he too "would no longer fight for the Confederacy, but for Missouri."[822] The following day Price and Davis resolved the argument and by July 2 Price was again back at the front.

The Missouri delegation suffered heavy fallout from Price's Richmond visit. Sen. Clark and Rep. William Cooke, Price's strongest supporters, began publically circulating rumors Price should replace Jefferson Davis as President of the Confederacy. Lud, a member of the Davis household, as well as having been always skeptical of Price's commitment to the Southern cause, became an adversary.

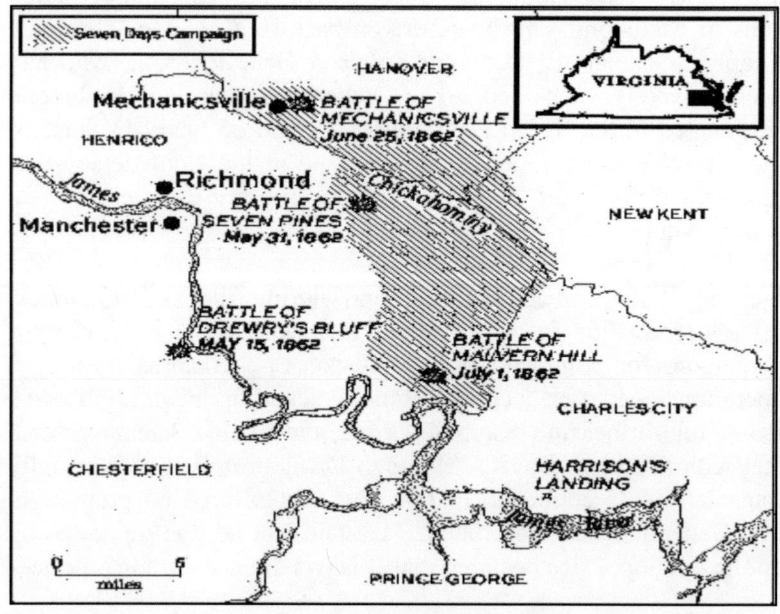

The Richmond Seige May – July 1862

[821] Castel. Page 214.
[822] Castel. Page 215.

When Price arrived in Richmond Lud was asked if he intended to call on Price at the Spotswood Hotel. Lud responded, "'Why should I? I have had enough of that humbug!'"[823] Clark approached Lud directly about Price commanding in the west. Lud not only refused to support the scheme but advised Clark to drop the effort.[824]

---------- The First Confederate Congress ----------

Second Session: August 18 to October 13, 1862

The Confederate Senate's second session debated and amended several central issues, carried over from the first session. Military staffing continued a nagging problem throughout the Confederate armies; conscription and military service exemptions continued foremost among the challenges. The unit assignment of recruits also surfaced as an important point. The Partisan Rangers, although passed into law in the first session, returned to the Senate docket. Suspending the writ of habeas corpus resurfaced. Military appointments proved a point of contention between the Senate and Davis's government.

---------- Nepotism: Joseph R. Davis ----------

Near the end of Congress's second session, Lud, as a Senator and Davis family member, was caught in a contentious debate between Jefferson Davis and members of Congress. Throughout Davis's administration frequent charges of nepotism were leveled at the President. Appointments, both of family members and West Point contacts, fueled the allegations. Years after the fact, Henry S. Foote revisited Davis's nepotism. Foote wrote, "I assert that the grossest and most shameless acts of nepotism that the world has ever seen were constantly occurring during the short and stormy reign of Jefferson the First in Richmond. I do not think that there was a single male relative, either of Mr. Davis or his wife, to be found in any part of the Confederate States, that was not given official

[823] Reynolds. Page 62.
[824] Reynolds. Page 62.

advancement of some kind or other."[825] Lud found himself squarely caught in the nepotism controversy in October 1862.

Joseph R. Davis
Author's Collection

President Davis nominated Joseph R. Davis for promotion to Brigadier General. Joe Davis, the President's nephew, was known widely as the "favorite" nephew. Joe was Lud's brother-in-law, married to Lud's sister, Fanny. Their 1842 marriage had brought Lud into the Davis family. Joe Davis, in addition to being Peyton's brother-in-law, had also been Peyton's classmate at Miami University.

Prior to his Brig. General nomination, Joe had served as one of several aide-de-camps to President Davis. When Jefferson Davis nominated his nephew for the rank of Brig. General, nepotism exploded center stage in the Confederate Senate. Lud, a member of the Davis family, the nominee's friend, and a voting Senator, found himself caught squarely in the middle of the crossfire.

Secretary of War G.W. Randolph included Joe Davis's nomination with a list of others sent to the Senate, September 26. The nominations were referred to the Committee on Military Affairs. The nominations arrived back in the Senate on Friday, October 3. Prior to the Senate's vote, the nominations of Francis S .Shoup and Joseph R. Davis were pulled from the last of nominees and "placed on the table."[826] South Carolina Senator James Orr made the motion to have Davis's nomination lie on the table. The Senate approved the other Brig. Gen. nominations, less Shoup and Davis.

Senator Orr then motioned that the nomination of Joe Davis be brought before the Senate for discussion and debate. After a considerable debate, the details of which are not known, the

[825] Foote, Henry S. *Casket of Reminiscences*. Page 393.
[826] *JCCSA*. V. 2. Page 414.

Senate rejected Davis's nomination by a vote of six in favor of the nomination against eleven against. Lud's presence is not recorded either in debate or vote. Missouri Sen. John Clark was present and voted against Joe Davis's appointment. This did not sit well with Lud.

The Senate's rejection did not end the discussion because the following Wednesday, October 8, Davis's nomination again surfaced. Georgia Sen. Benjamin Hill, who had initially voted against Joe, brought his name back to the Senate floor. Lud, absent for the first vote, was present and participating. After debate the nomination was brought to a vote. Joe was confirmed to the rank of Brig. General by a final tally, 13 for and 6 against. The final approval included three senators who switched positions and four senators, Lud included, who had not voted on October 3.

---------- William C. Quantrill ----------

About a month following the adjournment of the Second Session of Congress, William C. Quantrill arrived in Richmond. Quantrill had come to Richmond from winter camp in Texas. When winter approached and all the leaves fell, Missouri's guerrillas headed south. This seasonal rhythm dictated the ebb and flow of violence; rivers of blood in warm weather and a return to icy calm in winter. Although brief, Quantrill's trip to Richmond underscored the difference between the code of conduct followed in the eastern theatres and the black flag flying in Missouri.

Quantrill, seeking a Partisan Ranger commission, arrived in Richmond after Congress adjourned. It is not known if Quantrill made attempts to meet with members of Missouri's congressional delegation or if they were even in Richmond at the time. Lud would have been a logical contact. He had lived and represented the very area of western Missouri in which Quantrill now operated. If indeed they met, it would have been an interesting conversation. Lud had represented western Missouri during the time, when Quantrill, before his conversion to the South, had been jayhawking Lud's constituency. Regardless, we know that neither, Lud or another member of the Missouri delegation accompanied Quantrill when he met with Secretary of War, Seddon.

Texas Sen. Wigfall joined Quantrill in the meeting with Seddon. All we know of the meeting was supplied by William E. Connelley, through John N. Edwards, from Wigfall after the war. Evidently, Quantrill forcibly and openly advocated the cold application of the black flag code of war to all theatres, as the basic mode of operation. Seddon rejected the suggestion as "barbarism," and well outside the accepted boundaries of modern warfare. The discussion ended with neither party having swayed the other.[827]

Quantrill left Richmond without commission or sanction. The cold reality of Missouri's brutal Civil War, personified in William Quantrill, exceeded Seddon's, and the Confederate government's blood conscience.

---------- Lud and J.E.B. Stuart ----------

J.E.B. Stuart
Courtesy Library of Congress

Thirty years after Lud's death his memory and legend continued when Chicago's *Sunday Chronicle* published a lengthy story about his exploits. Frank Brooks, a former Harrisonville resident, wrote the article. Brooks wrote, "This same man Peyton put himself in the saddle and under the command of 'Jeb' Stuart, who gave him a body guard and had reconnoitered the position of one of the divisions of the army of the Potomac 'to see for himself.'"[828]

As yet undocumented, it remains very probable Lud actually rode with a company of Stuart's cavalry. Jeb Stuart's command,

[827] Connelley. Page 279.
[828] *The Sunday Chronicle, Chicago*. Volume I, No. 209. December 22, 1895. Page 15.

November and December 1862, fought along the Potomac River in Loudoun County. Stuart's command drew large numbers of dignitaries from Richmond and it was not uncommon for the visitors to ride with patrols, sometimes along with Stuart.[829]

Shortly after the Battle of Fredericksburg members of the government visited the Confederate army, and it is highly possible Lud accompanied them. December 16 Jefferson Davis arrived with an entourage to see the battlefield.[830] Five days later Custis Lee, one of Davis's aide-de-camps, visited for the same purpose.[831] On Congressional recess, Lud had the time and the right connections with the Davis family to leave Richmond and visit Jeb Stuart's command. As a former cavalry officer himself, the temptation would have been too great to pass up.

December 29 Stuart was not only in Loudoun County, but stayed on the former Peyton Plantation where Lud had been born.[832] John Mosby, of Partisan Ranger fame, received his commission from Stuart in the Peyton's former parlor.[833]

---------- The First Confederate Congress ----------
Third Session: January 12 to May 1, 1863

Governor Claiborne F. Jackson died of stomach cancer December 6, 1862 at Little Rock, Arkansas. Jackson's death triggered the return of Lt. Gov. Thomas C. Reynolds, from his self-imposed political exile, to assume leadership of Missouri's Confederate government. Lud and the Missouri Congressional delegation dealt with the transition of leadership.

The New Year 1863 brought with it old issues, particularly those tied to the ambition and self-promotion of some of Missouri's military leaders. Sterling Price was back in Richmond and M. Jeff Thompson was pushing and campaigning for a promotion.

---

[829] Akers. Page 173.
[830] Borcke. Page 331.
[831] Borcke. Page 336.
[832] Akers. Page 196.
[833] Akers. Page 196.

Gen. Thompson, early in 1863, aggressively was lobbying for a promotion. Because military advancement required the approval of President Davis and the strong support of Missouri's political delegation, Gen. Thompson reached out to Gov. Reynolds for advice and support. Gov. Reynolds's response to Thompson vividly defines the complexities of military advancement. The response also highlights Lud's loyalty to James Rains, his close ties to Jefferson Davis, and his role in the Missouri delegation.

Gen. Thompson and Lud had been together at New Madrid, a year before. Although Thompson knew Lud, he requested that Reynolds provide advice on how to advance his case. Reynolds's response, dated March 13, 1863, speaks for itself:

> "The reports about your sprees are obstacles to your promotion. Senator Peyton spoke to me in favor of your appointment but he has the opinion that General Rains has been badly treated and he told me that he 'would oppose any appointment of a brigadier from Missouri until Rains was appointed.' I spoke to the President about Rains with every disposition to have him appointed but I think this impossible; and if Senator Peyton insists on the course he indicated to me, he may obstruct the appointment of yourself and others, as he stands high in the President's opinion. His sister is the wife of the President's nephew, General Davis, and this tie very justly would give his recommendation the weight of coming from one not only politically but personally interested in the success of the administration. Without alluding to what I write about Senator Peyton you should urge him to sustain your claims. He can, if he is inclined, do more than anyone else to advance the claims of yourself and other Missourians, and I imagine that his inactivity in such matters may have arisen from his felling slighted by the neglect more frequently to ask his interposition."[834]

---

[834] *Papers of Thomas Coute Reynolds*, 1862-1866. Shelf 13,777.000264.

---------- Recess ----------

When the Confederate Congress adjourned its third session beginning its recess, the overall situation inside the South had changed. Union troops had occupied significant territory in the Confederacy and areas not actually controlled were under dire threat. Vicksburg had become a primary Union objective. Mississippi and Louisiana had become insecure and volatile. For congressmen from the western states, journeys back to either home constituencies or family were problematic. Many found "that by 1863 trips home were always hazardous and often impossible."

Missouri's congressional delegation scattered to multiple destinations. Lud left Richmond and headed for Mississippi. Missouri's First Brigade, with whom Lud had former comrades and allegiances, was fighting in Mississippi and Louisiana. Brig. Gen. John S. Bowen, Lud's friend since the border fighting, commanded Missouri troops facing Grant's Union army. Lud's Senate term would not expire until 1866, so he avoided re-election campaigning while many of his peers returned to the stump.

Missouri Rep. Thomas Freeman headed to Texas and reunited with his family. Sen. Clark and Rep. George Vest headed to Arkansas. Both men, up for re-election, spent much of the summer campaigning. Because Union troops occupied Missouri, civilian voters and a legitimate election process were out of the question. The majority of Missouri's electorate were either refugees or in the army. The greatest concentration of available voters served in Missouri military units, so that is where the men campaigned. Campaigning followed no formal rules and personal connections carried great influence. "Governor Reynolds of Missouri accused John B. Clark of posting friends around balloting places."[835]
Following the Congressional adjournment Lud's thoughts and energy turned to Mississippi and Vicksburg. As other members of Missouri's delegation headed toward the Trans-Mississippi region to campaign or reunite with family, Lud sought a reunion with the Missourians fighting at Vicksburg. While he headed west to fight,

[835] Yearns. Page 53.

Gov. Reynolds begged Lud's attention and action in the Confederate Senate. Reynold's, frustrated by Lud's silence on the Senate floor encouraged him to take a more forceful and public stance in behalf of Missouri. Reynold's letter speaks to the urgency he holds:

> Hon. R.L.Y. Peyton
> C.S. Senate
> Richmond, Va.
>
> Dear Sir,
>
> Intending my letter to any of our Congressional delegation, for the perusal of all, I presume my previous communications will have apprised you of my movements. I met the Arkansas Senator, Dr. Mitchell, at his place about ten days ago, and was much gratified to learn from him that in your remarks in the C.S. Senate, on the death of our friend, Hon. Wm. M. Cooke, you had reflected great credit on yourself and our state, and attained an enviable reputation for eloquence and ability.[836]
>
> Let me urge you to overcome the delicacy which has heretofore prompted you, and to use actively in the proceedings of the Senate, that eloquence and ability in promoting the common cause. It is time that the peculiar circumstances, and disputed position of our unfortunate State, should inspire our members with tact and modesty in discussing matters concerning those sections which are the main military and financial supports of the Confederacy.
>
> But still, as soon as a Senator acquires an influential personal position, he would be justified in using it to shape general policy, so as to advance our Special State interests, in harmony with the common good. Excuse these suggestions; they are prompted by my high estimate of your talents, and my anxiety that everything

[836] **Note**: Gov. Reynolds's letter did not contain distinct paragraphs. The author has added paragraphs to enable easier reading.

should be brought to bear which can contribute to the liberation of our suffering State.

Hon. Thos. W. Freeman passed through this place about a week ago on his way to Texas to visit his family. He and Hon. A.H. Conrow crossed the Mississippi River near Gaine's Landing. The latter proceeding on to Little Rock. They were both in good health and spirits. Mr. Freeman informed me that the rest of our members in Congress proposed passing the vacation east of the Mississippi, unless a favorable opportunity should occur for crossing that river, a feat now both hazardous and difficult. Should you come over I trust you will not fail to visit my headquarters.

Lt. General E.K. Smith observes entire secrecy, concerning intended army movements and civilians cannot judge when we will re-enter Missouri. Have the greatest confidence on his enterprise and ability, I calmly await events; satisfied that our military interests are in safekeeping.

I hope to hear from you often on all public affairs you deem of interest. I enable you to know whether you receive my letters in regular order. I number them in succession; please afford me the same facility by numbering yours.

I remain dear Sir, very Truly Yours,
Thos. C. Reynolds

P.S. Please address me at Little Rock, Ark.
(Given to Hon. W. Hough, Camden, 3rd June 1863 to send by private hand across Mississippi)[837]

Lud departed Richmond for the last time in May. The South continued to wage war but independence remained very much in doubt.

[837] *Papers of Thomas Coute Reynolds, 1862 – 1866*. Shelf 13,777.000294. No. 1.

Chapter Eleven
Gone

The approaching summer, 1863, triggered mounting anxiety, both in the north and the south. Each saw the next few months as pivotal in the war's final outcome. The country braced for more blood and an unknown future. In Richmond, the Confederate Congress recessed for the summer. Missouri's congressional delegation, Lud among them, left Richmond, most heading toward the Trans-Mississippi theatre.

Robert E. Lee prepared to carry the war to the north, hopefully into Washington, D.C. Ulysses S. Grant positioned his armies to cutoff the Mississippi River. If successful, Grant would halve the Confederacy strangling the South's lifeblood.

Spurred by stunning victories at Fredericksburg (December 13, 1862) and Chancellorsville (April 30 to May 6, 1863), General Lee prepared to push the fight north. In June, Lee's Army of Northern Virginia crossed the Potomac River, marching into Pennsylvania toward Gettysburg. As Lud traveled through Alabama and Mississippi toward Vicksburg, his brother-in-law, Brig. Gen. Joe Davis, accompanied Lee to Gettysburg. Davis's command would play an active role at Gettysburg on the battle's first and third day.

Vicksburg, Mississippi remained the target of Gen. Grant's Trans-Mississippi strategy. This Vicksburg Campaign, hoping to finally succeed, began March 29, 1863. Lt. Gen. John C. Pemberton commanded the opposing Confederate Army. Pemberton's command included Missouri regiments, remnants of Lud's former Missouri State Guard.

In western Missouri, the horrific guerrilla war rapidly spun to historic disaster. Along the Kansas border, aiming to eradicate William Quantrill's unrelenting guerrilla attacks, federal authorities prepared to establish the District of the Border, placing it under the command of Thomas Ewing, Jr. On June 9, Ewing assumed command of the new military district but skirmishes and battles continued to increase in frequency and ferocity. By mid-summer rumors began to circulate that Quantrill planned a retaliatory attack on Lawrence, Kansas. Simultaneously the federal military began planning the total evacuation of Missouri's western border counties hoping to eliminate civilian aid for the guerrillas.

Although Lud was hundreds of miles from Harrisonville his memory was not forgotten. Local Unionists remembered, decrying his previous role.

> "I wonder what the gentry who only two short years ago dominated this county with such insolence and swagger would think, on knowing that this scene was enacted in their old home. What would R.L.Y. Payton say if, in his Richmond home, word should be brought to him that the niggers were parading the streets of his old home in military array? Rather a descent. Lud Payton pouring forth his fiery treason and fanaticism to a Harrisonville audience un-rebuked, then in high dignity, gathering up his senatorial robes and marching to the capital of the C.S.A. He now a fugitive, and a Company of 'niggers' occupying his residence – Pahaw! Maybe Payton will yet lead a conquering army into this region and drive out the white and black abolition soldiers. I suppose he will repossess Vicksburg on the way."[838]

The diatribe, written from Harrisonville and published in Kansas City, echoed the deep hate and wide chasm in western Missouri's populace.

In Virginia, Lud's birthplace and home community felt the war's devastation. June 17, federal cavalry led by Gen. Alfred Pleasanton attacked Fitz Lee's cavalry brigade of James Longstreet's command at Aldie. The old Peyton plantation filled with troops as the battle raged around the Aldie Mill, the site of many boyhood memories.

Many of Missouri's congressional delegation left Richmond heading west to the Trans-Mississippi. The massing of federal

[838] *Journal of Commerce*. June 2, 1863.

military forces around Vicksburg made the journey across the Mississippi River into Texas, Arkansas, and Missouri dangerous. By the end of May, Missouri Gov. Thomas C. Reynolds arrived in Camden, Arkansas. Reynolds's presence in Camden allowed him to legitimize the exiled Missouri government. It also provided access to Sterling Price who had arrived in Ark. on March 18. Representatives Thomas W. Freeman and Aaron H. Conrow briefly met with Gov. Reynolds at Camden. Freeman then left heading to Texas and a reunion with his family. Conrow moved to Little Rock, Ark.

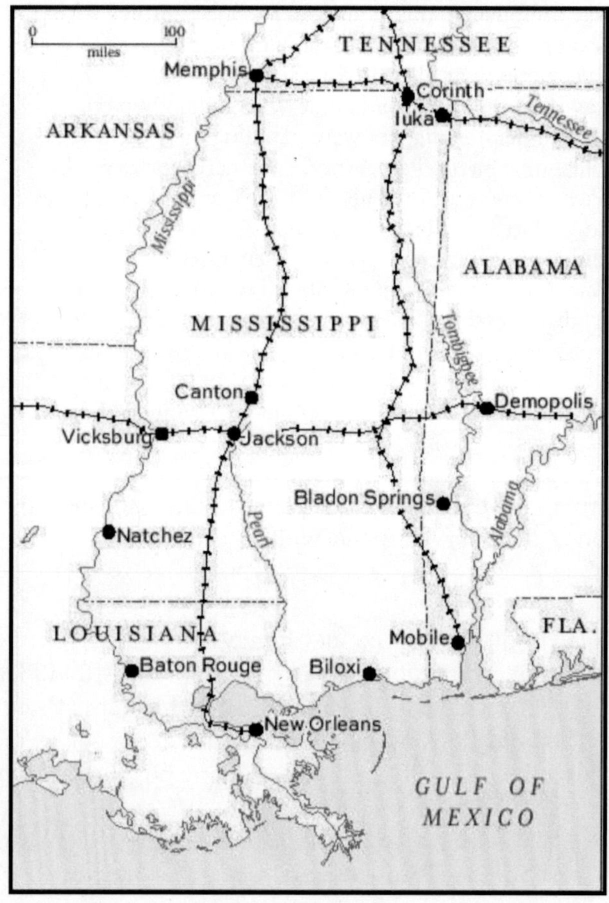

Vicksburg and Bladon Springs - Summer 1863

Lud made for Vicksburg, drawn by the fighting, his Missouri comrades, and the Trans-Mississippi.[839] He was just 39 years old, and he left Richmond much changed from the man who had arrived at the Capitol just 18 months earlier. The pressure of family, politics, and the war had taken a toll. John Maloy, Lud's personal secretary remembered, "I had noticed a marked change in him, he had aged perceptibly; in his full black beard some streaks of grey intruded; he wore an anxious look. He was still kindly and genial, but his thoughts seemed to have become somber. He may have sighted far off the coming of some event that would crush his heart."[840]

Lud's fellow Missourians, many of whom he had known in the Missouri State Guards, were now fighting in Mississippi, defending Vicksburg. Gen. John S. Bowen, who had commanded the Southwest Expedition Battalion along the Mo. – K.T. border in Bates and Vernon counties the winter of 1860-61, now commanded Missouri forces in southwest Mississippi. In late April, Bowen had been elevated to divisional command. In his diary Ephraim Anderson wrote, "General Bowen was in command of our division, and controlled operations at this point; and Colonel Cockrell was placed in command of the brigade."[841] Lud had known Francis Marion Cockrell in the pre-war days when both practiced law in Johnson County, Mo. Unknown to Lud, Tarlton Railey a close friend from Harrisonville, was also among those surrounded at Vicksburg.

The Missouri troops entered Vicksburg the evening of May 17, 1863.[842] They had, over a period of weeks, fought their way into the Mississippi town. They had participated in the Battle of Port Gibson in late April and early May. Under Pemberton, the Missourians had battled at Baker's Creek and the Black River. As

[839] **Note**: Peyton's exact movements, May through mid-August are unknown. It is highly probable he united with Missouri military units in Alabama and Mississippi before contracting malaria.
[840] Sloan. Page 416.
[841] Anderson and Bearss. Page 290.
[842] Anderson and Bearss. Page 319.

the siege tightened around Vicksburg, the Missouri troops fought brilliantly until the Confederate surrender, July 4, 1863.

As Lud and his Missouri comrades fought the heat, mosquitos, and federal troops in Mississippi, the Army of Northern Virginia continued its march to Gettysburg, Pa. July 1, Gen. Joe Davis, approached Gettysburg along the Chambersburg Pike. Davis's brigade was a part of Henry Heth's division; the same Henry Heth Jefferson Davis had put forward as a replacement for Sterling Price in December 1861.

Davis's soldiers were the first to shed blood at Gettysburg. As firing erupted along the Chambersburg Pike, the brigade "followed in strength under its inexperienced, pleasant and unpretending Brigadier."[843] He hastily pushed his men into the fight. "Davis's advancing line overlapped that of the Federals, who quickly retreated. From lack of experience, he permitted two of his regiments, pursuing the enemy to enter a railroad cut, where their files were at right angles to the front of attack. There they were captured by a reserve regiment of the Iron Brigade, brought over to the Federal left."[844] Davis survived the fight but his command, decimated by the engagement, was moved to the rear of Lee's army.

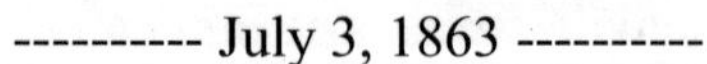
---------- July 3, 1863 ----------

July 3 proved fatal for the South and Lud's world. At Vicksburg, shortly before 9:00 a.m. "a flag of truce was sent out by General Pemberton and the firing ceased."[845] Negotiations began between Pemberton and Union General Grant. The initial "parleying was principally between Bowen and McPherson; Grant and Pemberton talked but little." The initial terms of the Vicksburg surrender failed, fighting resumed but ceased in the afternoon. At 3:00 p.m. "another truce occurred, during which the terms of surrender were settled."[846]

843 Freeman. Page 78.
844 Freeman. Page 80.
845 Anderson and Bearss. Page 357.
846 Anderson and Bearss. Page 357.

Simultaneous with the surrender at Vicksburg, day three of the Battle of Gettysburg neared a bloody conclusion. At 1:07 p.m. southern artillery began the barrage of Seminary Ridge.[847] Following the bombardment, Pickett's Charge raced forward. "Joe Davis's shattered, inexperienced troops, almost without field officers, were to be on the extreme left."[848] Devastating fire leveled his regiment. "Most of the troops under Mayo and Davis started back to their own lines before they reached the ridge."[849] Davis himself was slightly wounded in the charge.[850] Before nightfall both Vicksburg and Gettysburg became monumental Confederate defeats.

Although Bowen, Davis, and Lud survived the first week of July, fate had yet one cruel card to play. Joe Davis, although just slightly wounded at Gettysburg, ended up fighting for his life against disease not injury. Davis returned to Richmond gravely ill. July 21, Jefferson Davis, in a letter to Robert E. Lee related Joe was fighting typhoid fever.

In Mississippi, John Bowen, while negotiating Vicksburg's surrender, became ill. He fell violently sick the day after the surrender, July 4; Bowen battled "dysentery and exhaustion. Following his capture and parole at Vicksburg, he was moved in an ambulance as far as Raymond, Mississippi. After the onset of his illness, Bowen's wife, who had been residing outside Vicksburg, joined him before his death on July 13, 1863."[851]

During this period, as Joe Davis slowly recovered and John Bowen died, a mosquito landed on Lud – malaria soon began draining his energy and life. When the disease gained the upper hand, Lud retreated to Bladon Springs, Choctaw County, Alabama.

As Lud fought for his life in Mississippi and Alabama, a brother-in-law, Rev. Henry F. Luckett argued for his life at Memphis,

---

847 Freeman. Page 154.
848 Freeman. Page 148.
849 Freeman. Page 187.
850 Welch. *Medical*. Page 52.
851 Welch. *Medical*. Page 22.

Tennessee. Rev. Luckett was the husband of Lud's sister, Maria. July 9, 1863 a detachment of federal cavalry arrested Luckett on Pigeon Roost Road, just outside Memphis. He was attempting to smuggle percussion caps, medicine, and handkerchiefs through the Memphis picket lines to Confederate troops. Luckett was hauled to the headquarters of Major Gen. Stephen Hurlbut. Following a thorough search of his wagon, the prisoner was moved to Irving Prison.[852]

Henry F. Luckett's trial began in Memphis on July 21. A three member military commission, headed by Lt. Col. Richard Ritter, reviewed the charges, examining witnesses. Luckett submitted a lengthy written defense to the commission. His spring wagon contained a false bottom that he had installed himself. Throwing himself on the mercy of the court he begged leniency; he was an old man trying to provide for his family. The argument carried little weight. July 24, the military commission sentenced Luckett to death by hanging.[853] Luckett's family carried his case all the way to Abraham Lincoln whom Luckett had known in Springfield, Illinois in the 1840s.[854]

---------- Choctaw County, Alabama ----------

Vicksburg's fall threw Mississippi and Alabama into chaos. Refugees flooded roads as armies repositioned for the next phase of fighting. Joseph Davis, Jefferson's older brother, with family, was swept up in the refugee flood. Joseph's party found a temporary safe haven in Choctaw County not far from Bladon Springs.

One of Davis's granddaughters wrote, we were finally "… forced to pitch our tents on the Tombigbee river, our tired stock could go no

[852] NARA. RG 153. Records of the Judge Advocate General (Army). E18 Court Martial Files.
[853] NARA. RG 153. Records of the Judge Advocate General (Army). E18 Court Martial Files.
[854] **Rev. Henry F. Luckett**: December 17, 1863 President Abraham Lincoln issued a stay of execution and Rev. Luckett was released. April 30, 1864 Luckett wrote a letter to Lincoln thanking him for sparing his life.

further."[855] The spot selected "… was not the most inviting, but there was a little deserted cabin of three rooms situated on the top of a little sand hill with a clear running stream at its foot and pasture nearby for our exhausted stock."[856] The Davis's remained in Choctaw County for three or four weeks before finding a safe haven elsewhere. A few miles south, at Bladon Springs, Lud fought for his life.

Bladon Springs, Alabama had become a recognized and established haven for rest, recovery, and rehabilitation long before the Civil War. The Bladon Springs's grounds and hotel were known throughout the United States. The healing springs, in Choctaw County, were within three miles of the Tombigbee River. "In the old romantic steamboat days, the boats on the line of the Alabama Central went leisurely back and forth between Mobile and Demopolis, carrying merry parties to their haven of rest and pleasure."[857] The trip from the river to the hotel moved through a "leafy and winding road."[858]

The hotel "with its colonnade, great white pillars, spacious rooms, large ballroom, beautiful stairways and mullioned windows was constructed and ready for occupancy the summer season of 1846. It was a two-story structure, with a useful basement. A front veranda extended the length of the building on the first and second floors.

The accommodations of the hotel were sufficient for two hundred guests."[859] During the 1850s the hotel contained a skating rink, billiard rooms, croquet grounds, and swings hanging from the oak trees surrounding the hotel.

The springs contained six fountains of water. "The virtues of the waters were fully attested for many years and were confidently

---

[855] William Stanley Hoole Special Collections Library. Jefferson Davis Papers. Box 126, Folder 6.
[856] William Stanley Hoole Special Collections Library. Jefferson Davis Papers. Box 126, Folder 6.
[857] Sulzby. Page 53.
[858] Sulzby. Page 53.
[859] Sulzby. Page 53.

recommended for the 'cure of gout, rheumatics, scrofula, skin disease, dyspepsia, diseases incident to females, dropsy, and general debility.'"[860] One local physician, Dr. Wm. H. Anderson, attested, he had "the highest opinion of the water, and do not hesitate to recommend it to invalids who are suffering with diseases of the skin, liver, the digestive and the urinary organs."[861]

Business at Bladon Springs dropped with the beginning of the Civil War. The hotel remained open throughout the war, becoming a safe haven for soldiers and civilians requiring rest and recuperation. A year before Lud arrived at Bladon Springs, June 1862, Confederate General P.G.T. Beauregard spent time at the hotel recovering from a chronic throat problem.[862] Several months after Lud's death, a Missouri Confederate soldier, Ephraim Anderson, recuperated at the springs early in 1864.[863]

Lud arrived at Bladon Springs in mid-August 1863. Hoping to regain strength and recover to full activity, he slid, and began to succumb. The lack of available quinine handcuffed Peyton's physician.

Bladon Springs Hotel- Author's Collection

860 Sulzby. Page 53.
861 Sulzby. Page 55.
862 Welch. Page 19.
863 Anderson and Bearss. Page 385.

Quinine, although a known and effective malarial treatment, was unavailable. When Lud passed through Memphis in late 1861 a local druggist advertised that he had 1,000 ounces (62 pounds) of quinine available.[864] By the time Lud needed quinine none was available. "The Union blockade then caused an acute shortage of quinine in the South."[865] "Without quinine, 'no man alive could have counteracted the effects of that climate.'"[866] "For the first time in history, quinine helped decide the outcome of the war."[867]

Secondary treatments included "external applications of turpentine as well as concoctions of whiskey and dogwood, poplar, and willow bark."[868] None of these rustic treatments worked. Lud lapsed into a coma.

---------- September 3, 1863 ----------

In a cruel twist of fate, Lud's beloved western Missouri, the community he had represented and loved, disappeared in a firestorm of destruction as he lay dying. August 21, 1863, William Quantrill's raiders devastated Lawrence, Kansas triggering General Thomas Ewing, Jr. to issue General Orders No. 11. When Lud died at Bladon Springs on September 3, 1863 thousands of refugees fled western Missouri as Union troops applied a scorched earth policy to 2,200 square miles. Within one fifteen day period, Lud's neighbors, Lud's friends, Lud's communities, and Lud himself, just short of his 40th birthday, disappeared forever.

---------- To the Ages ----------

A week after Lud's death *The Memphis Appeal* published a short, one line death announcement. No details were given.[869]

The Confederate Congress honored Lud December 19, 1863.

---

[864] *Memphis Daily Appeal*. November 16, 1861.
[865] Winegard. Page 327.
[866] Winegard. Page 323.
[867] Winegard. Page 326.
[868] *Library of Congress, Civil War Desk Reference*. Page 646.
[869] *Memphis Appeal*. September 10, 1863.

Richmond's *Daily Examiner* noted Lud's passing and the Senate's recognition on December 19, 1863. John B. Clark, Sr. "announced the death of his colleague, the late Robert L.Y. Peyton of Missouri and submitted the following resolutions, which were unanimously agreed to:

> *Resolved*, That we have heard, with deep regret, of the death of the Hon. Robert L.Y. Peyton, a Senator from the State of Missouri.
>
> *Resolved*, That the secretary communicate to the House of Representatives a copy of these resolutions.
>
> *Resolved*, As a further mark of respect to the memory of the deceased, that the Senate now adjourn.

Messrs. Caperton of Virginia, Maxwell of Florida, and Johnson of Arkansas delivered eulogies on the deceased.

Eulogies were also delivered in the House of Representatives by Caspar W. Bell of Missouri, Thomas W. Freeman of Missouri, Lewis M. Ayer of South Carolina and H.C. Burnett of Kentucky.

Caspar Bell's eulogy honored Lud while healing a rift with the Davis family. Bell, in partnership with Henry Foote, had long been a critic of Jefferson Davis but his eulogy opened reconciliation. Bell often told the story that "…Mr. Peyton, one of his colleagues and a relative to Mrs. Davis died" and he "was selected to make the announcement to the House which he did in such a way as to win Mrs. Davis and ultimately her husband, after which their former relationship was reestablished."[870]

News of Lud's death slowly drifted back to Missouri. St. Louis's *Missouri Republican* did not carry an announcement until December 19, 1863. Unamplified it merely reported, "Peyton, R.L.Y. 'bogus Senator' from Missouri in the Confederate Congress,

[870] *Salisbury Press – Spectator*. November 4, 1898.

3 Sept. at Bladen Springs, Alabama." The *Liberty Tribune* did not announce his death until its January 8, 1864. The paper notified its readers "R.L.Y. Peyton, formerly of Cass Co., and a member of the rebel congress, died in Mississippi last fall." The same day, Columbia's *Missouri Statesman* carried the following:

> "**Death of R.L.Y. Peyton** – The *Lexington Union* learns from a reliable source that R.L.Y. Peyton, formerly from Harrisonville, and a member of the rebel Congress from this State, died in Mississippi last fall".

Lud's death, occurring during the turbulent summer of 1863, quickly fell into the war's abyss. Many Missouri refugees and former comrades in arms would not learn of it for decades. Forty years after Lud's passing, in 1903, Gibson Garwood, a member of Peyton's 3rd Cavalry Regiment, searched for Lud, hoping "to hear from his old Colonel R.L.Y. Peyton."[871]

Although the war continued for two years, the summer of 1863 signaled the South's death knell. The war's outcome, the South's defeat, would have been complete devastation for Lud. Perhaps his early death was a blessing.

"It is believed by those who knew him best, to have been fortunate for him that he did not survive the down-fall of the Confederacy. He was so devoted to the 'Lost Cause' that he would have readily have offered his life a willing sacrifice to its success. Far-seeing as he evidently was, it is believed he never doubted ultimate success. It is doubtful if he could have survived ultimate failure."[872]

John Maloy, who knew Peyton best during the last months of life, wrote, "Whether right or wrong his was a great soul; whether in failure or success he was a great man."[873]

---

[871] *Confederate Veteran*. Vol. II, No. 9. September 1903. Page 424.
[872] *History of Cass and Bates Counties, Mo*. Page 379.
[873] Sloan. Page 416.

Appendix

Item No. 1
Lands in Logan County, Illinois

From Townshend Peyton's "Last Will and Testament" dated March 19, 1849:

"Second, I give and devise to my son, Robert L.Y. Peyton, my Illinois farm of six hundred acres described as follows to wit: the south half of section twenty-nine (29) in township nineteen north of range four west of the third principal meridian containing three hundred and twenty acres (320) and the west half of the southwest quarter of section twenty (20) in township nineteen north of range four, west of the third principle meridian containing eighty (80) acres, and the northeast quarter of the northeast quarter in section thirty (30) township and range as aforesaid containing forty (40) acres and also the north quarter section of section twenty (20) in township and range as aforesaid, all of said several tracts, being subject to entry at Springfield, Illinois, also a good feather bed and furniture to him and to his heirs forever."

Townshend Peyton sold land to Alfred Peyton on June 8, 1850 and Recorded on November 14, 1850 as recorded in Book E Page 416. Alfred Peyton then sold the land to Cooley Knapp on May 24, 1851 and recorded May 28, 1851 as recorded in Book F, Page 87.

Deed Books "E" and "F" were destroyed in a fire.

Description from my notes:

- All in Township 19 and Range 4 west
- N ½ of Section 29
- W ½ of NE ¼ of Section 20
- SE ½ of NE ¼ of Section 30
- W ½ of N ¼ of Section 20
- ?? E ½ of NW ¼

T.D. Peyton was listed among "individuals entering land in Logan County, from the time of the first settlement, as shown by the government records, with the year when the claim was filed and the fee paid." T.D.'s land was listed in Corwin Township in 1835.

History of Logan County, Illinois. Stringer, Lawrence B. Chicago, Illinois, Pioneer Publishing. Page 122.

Item No. 2
Lands in Butler County, Ohio

Townshend Peyton from Richard F. Peyton
Deed Book One, Page 293
October 1835 to March 1837

Received and recorded November 23, 1836 from sale on July 22, 1836 for the amount of $2,800.00

"...the Lot or tract of land known and designated on the Plat of the Miami University lands according to the sub-division thereof by lot numbered five in section numbered nine in the fifth township of the first range of townships east of the meridian line drawn from the mouth of the great Miami River said lot containing one hundred and fifteen acres and 6/100th subject to a quit rent of $21.74 to be paid annually to the treasurer of Miami University on the 24th day of March. Also, the undivided north half of the lot numbered one in section numbered nine in the fifth township of the first range of townships east of the meridian line drawn from the mouth of the great Miami River containing forty-nine acres and 85/100 ... quit rent of $10.76 due 3rd of February every year."

Townshend Peyton from John and Sarah Woods
Deed Book Two, Page 185
November 1835 to August 1836

Received and recorded February 15, 1836
"... in consideration of $600.00 to John and Sarah Woods of Hamilton described lot and tract of land lying in the town of Oxford ... being the in lot numbered 21 on the plat of inlots ... said lot being 4 poles wide by 10 poles in length containing 40 square poles ... said lot being held by a deed lease from the Miami University for the term of 99 years for $3.00 per year."

Item No. 3
Miami University Graduates: 1841
Bachelor of Arts

Andrew, George L.-Rossville, Ohio
Branham, John L.-Frankfort, Kentucky
Bishop, John M.-Oxford, Ohio
Calhoun, P.B.-Wilson County, Tennessee
Goudy, George W.-Xenia, Ohio
Gilchrist, John -Franklin County, Indiana
Hardin, Charles H.-Columbia, Missouri
Junkin, John M.-Oxford, Ohio
Long, James Union County, Indiana
Lowes, James A.I.-Oxford, Ohio
Moore, Samuel L.-Bourbon County, Kentucky
Moore, William H.-Rising Sun, Indiana
Martin, William S.-Paris, Kentucky
Mack, David- Preble County, Ohio
Mills, Benjamin- Frankfort, Kentucky
Mills, John M. -Frankfort, Kentucky
Naylor, Arthur R.-Warren County, Ohio
Ogle, John-Butler County, Ohio
Paddack, Alexander-Cincinnati, Ohio
Peyton, R.L.Y.- Oxford, Ohio
Shellabarger, Samuel -Clark County, Ohio
Scott, John J. - Fairfield County, Ohio
Vance, Calvin F.-Urbana, Ohio

Item No. 4
The Cass County Excitement

We publish to-day a letter addressed to us by the Rev. Wm. H. Wiley, giving a statement of the treatment he received recently in Cass county, Mo. We know nothing of the facts further than what is contained in the communication itself and in the subjoined extract from the Cass county Gazette. As we desire and design to give a fair hearing to both sides in all these border difficulties in Missouri, we open our columns both to those who feel their personal rights infringed by the acts of the citizens of Missouri, and to our citizens themselves in explaining the motives which induced their conduct. *The Gazette*, in noticing the affair, says: "A preacher of the Northern Methodist church, Rev. Mr. Wiley, was accused of having promulgated publicly, abolitionist sentiments, and his case became the case of our citizens who assembled in a public meeting at the court house on 27th July, and appointed committees to investigate the charges. After protracted and careful deliberation, it was considered that Rev. Mr. Wiley's sentiments savored too thoroughly of abolitionism, and that in a public capacity he had made himself obnoxious to the serious charges alleged against him, and that it was necessary for the peace and harmony of our county, that he leave the State. and therefore it was resolved, that Rev. Mr. Wiley be required to leave the State within seven days, with the injunction not to go into the adjoining territory".

Afterwards, on motion, a fund was raised to assist in defraying his traveling expenses; whereupon Mr. Wiley, who was present, consented to leave immediately. Mr. Wiley had a public hearing, and was treated with gentlemanly politeness – he acquiesced without a murmur in the wishes of the large concourse present.

Daily Missouri Democrat, August 11, 1855, Page 2

Item No. 5
Mob Law in Western Missouri

Mr. Editor – I wish to present to the public through the columns of the Democrat, a plain statement of an affair which recently took place in Cass county, Mo. In the providence of God, and the arrangement of the Methodist Episcopal Church I was called to preach the gospel in Cass county, Mo., in the Harrisonville circuit. I endeavored to discharge my duty as a Christian minister, to the best of my ability, teaching nothing but those truths which make wise unto salvation, and having nothing to do with any of the vexing questions of the day. I had labored thus on the above circuit for a period of seven months, and up to about three weeks ago, the blessings of God attending my labors, and nothing occurring to mar the peace and harmony between me and my people. About the tie named an article appeared in the Cass County Gazette, written by one John A. Tuggle, a member of the M.E. Church, South, in which the was an attempt to excite public opposition against me, by alleging that I had said certain things to him, in a *private conversation*, respecting the decision of the question of slavery or no slavery in Kansas, and styling me a northern abolitionist. About a week after the appearance of this article, two negroes attempted to escape from Harrisonville, and a report was immediately circulated that I, together with other residents of the town and county, had instigated them to make the attempt – than which nothing could be more false, as I had not even once spoken to a single negro while resident in Cass county; and the other persons were citizens long standing, whose characters were above suspicion, one of whom had been a resident in the State *forty-seven years*.

On Thursday, July 26th, while peaceably pursuing my way along the public road, I was overtaken by two men – one of them known as Col. Worley – who addressed me some impudent questions respecting where I was going &c., and finally informed me that I had been accused of inciting slaves to escape, and of preaching abolition doctrine, and that I must return with them to Harrisonville and have the charges investigated. This conversation they interlaided with the most profane oaths that could fall from mortal lips. I protested against their right thus to stop me on the public highway, when the afore-named Col. W. leaped from his horse, and began fumbling about his person, as if feeling for a pistol. After some further parley, I informed them that, inasmuch as I was entirely innocent of the charges alleged, and did not fear a fair investigation, I would accompany them to Harrisonville for that purpose. Just as we turned to go back, sixteen more men, mounted, made their appearance. We stopped at a cabin in the prairie for supper, where the bottle was freely passed, and I received the most insulting treatment, being asked to drink, and made the subject of obscene jests and horrid oaths.

We reached Harrisonville about 12 o'clock at night, and I was taken to a hotel, and a guard of three men placed over me during the night, as if I had been the greatest criminal. Next morning I was waited upon by three men, who informed me that they were appointed a committee to search my effects, in order to ascertain if I had any abolition documents. This committee was composed of a Rev. Mr. Allen, Baptist preacher, Mr. Bailey, and the proprietor of the hotel where I was confined. They searched everything I had, examined my bible and hymn book, and ready my private letters carefully; but could find nothing to substantiate their charges. While this examination was in progress, a meeting was called at the Court House, and I could hear some person delivering what seemed to be a very inflammatory speech. After a while a committee composed of a Dr. Hansbrough, Col. Worley, and Rev. Mr. Allen, came to inform me that I was wanted at the Court House. I accompanied them, and found about two hundred men, the most of whom were of a low class, for I will do that community justice to say that very few respectable persons participated in these outrages. A certain Dr. Maxwel sat as chairman of the meeting. After a call to order, Dr. Hansbrough rose and said that I had been accused of aiding some negroes in running off, and had been preaching abolition doctrines and circulating abolition documents, and that it had resolved as the sense of that meeting that I should leave the State in seven days.

I replied briefly that I protested against their entire proceedings; that with a fair investigation I could prove all their charges false, and challenged them to such investigation; that if I had one anything contrary to law, I help myself amenable to it, and was willing to suffer its penalties to the full. I was told by one of the foremost in the matter, that the law was not strict enough, and they intended *to take it in their own hands*, and that if I did not leave, the consequences would be upon my own head.

This, sir, is but a brief statement of the manner in which I have been treated on American soil, by persons calling themselves American citizens. How long these things are to continue, I cannot tell, but I think it is high time that something was done to put a stop to them. The fair fame of Missouri is thus disgraced by bands of outlaws – for certainly men thus acting can be termed nothing else, and as yet no effort has been made by the officers of the law or the executive of the State, to relieve her from the stain. What a contrast do such proceedings form to the genius of our institutions and the spirit of '76. Can this be called the land of liberty if such a state of affairs is allowed to continue? I, sir, am a Southern man by birth, and came here from a Southern city, but if Southern institutions are to be protected by such men as have maltreated me, I think I shall seek some spot where, at least, my dearest rights shall be free from lawless invasions. Let the citizens of Missouri think upon the circumstance which I have endeavored dispassionately to describe – one only of several similar ones which have recently occurred – and let them decide what they will do. Whether they will let these fire-eating politicians ride over them rough-shot any longer, disgrace the State, and bring contempt upon themselves and their children?

Hoping that wise and prudent councils may obtain,

I am Yours, &c.,

W.II. Wiley

St. Louis, August 8, 1855

Daily Missouri Democrat, August 11, 1855 ,Page 2

Item No. 6
To His Excellency Sterling Price
Gov. of Missouri

Whereas a large party of abolitionists under the Command of J.H. Lane have recently invaded the Territory of Kansas have sacked, plundered and burnt several of the Principal Towns of that Territory and are now savaging that whole country murdering, butchering, robbing, and driving did, in the most brutal manner without discrimination of age or sex, all the citizens of that Territory who refuse to take up arms and aid in their insurrectionary designs: And whereas the said party of abolitionists have threatened repeatedly and are still threatening to attack and destroy by fire or otherwise, Kansas City, West Port, New Santa Fe and the other principal towns and villages in the border counties of this state; And whereas they have also threatened and are still threatening to invade, rob, plunder and lay waste in several counties of this State which border upon the Territory of Kansas; Now Therefore, We the undersigned memorialists, Citizens of the County of Cass, do most respectfully ask and petition the Governor of this state to order out the militia of this State of Missouri in sufficient numbers to insure safety to the persons and property of the citizens of said border counties, as in duty bound &c Cass County. August 20th 1856

Sq Allen
AB Sloan
Achilles Easley
C.F. Payne
L.P. Scroggins
Thos. W. Hart
J.B. Turgeson
Thos. E. Trent
John Farmer
J.L. Maxwell
M. O'Neal
R.J. Hiser
E.J. Clark
Nelson Millington
James W. Barnard
J.F. White
Charles Ha.???
Henry Tarrant
A.T. Sloane
J.W. Briscoe

AAG Stayton
W.B. Payne
HC Spears
G.A. Wade
A.C. Patton
C.T. Worley
Thos. W. Ament
Darling Williams
Robert Lewis
M. Woods
E.C. Heiskell
Wm. A. Ryan
H.G. Glenn
John L. Jackson
J.M. Cooper
Wm. G. Durfey
Jas.H.Callaway
G.M.L. Wright
J.G. Martin
J.N. Willett

Jonathan Crist	G.W. Zion
Alfred K.	Thos. Smith James
S.E. Rowden	J.B. Hook
Silas Price	T. Railey
John Cummins	W.T. Harris
R.A. Brown	R.W. Massey
R. Smith	M.H. Wilson
J.D. Armstrong	David Brookhart
J.E. Wilmott	E.P. West
Harvey Myers	A. Cassell
J.V. Sherman	David Williams
E.W. Fox	D.D. Martin
Wm. Moffatt	J.W. Blakely
L.W. Frazier	Owen Moffatt
G. Yebunk (old Indian Fighter)	
James Thomas	R. Burney
J.H. Henne	Wm. Pebworth
Y.S. Parsons	L.H. Williams
W. Payne	?? Christian
C.D. Palmer	A.J. Hooper
John K. Simpson	Bryan M. Wright
Richard Horn	F. Royantier
L.B. Ellis	***R.L.Y. Peyton***
Robert Sloan	W.L. Austin
A.J. Coots	Mas. N. Magers
H.R. Samuels	Samuel Wright
H.M. Welden	John D. Williams
C.D. Millis	M.W. Garrison
J.L. Millen	Thos. J. Milam
R.O. Boggess	Wm. Franklin

Source: Missouri Militia Collection, Missouri History Museum, St. Louis, Missouri

Item No. 7
Speech of Mr. Peyton

On calling out volunteers to protect our border:

Mr. Peyton offered the report of the Committee on Federal Relations, recommending the passage of the bill calling on the Executive to protect the border counties against the marauders from Kansas.
The rules were suspended and the bill read for the third time. It authorized the Governor to call out one or more companies, and station them on the frontier, to protect the border, and $30,000 were appropriated for the purpose.

Mr. Peyton: The Senate will bear witness that I have hitherto borne myself modestly in this body, and taken little, or no part, in its discussions. But outrages of an unparalleled nature compel me now to raise my voice. No language can adequately describe the outrages to which my constituents are subjected. Fire and sword, murder and rapine, are devastating the border counties of Missouri. Some of my constituents have been massacred – their houses burned – their property driven off – war of the most savage kind is waged against them. They are a brave, high-minded, honorable people, equal to any in the world – and they have been most grievously wronged. And the same band of thieves, midnight assassins and robbers, have devastated and wronged the constituents of the Senator from Jasper.

We can submit no longer. Our altars, our hearthstones, and our fire-sides must be protected. Our wives and children must be shielded and our wrongs avenged by the strong hand. We must be protected at all hazards – at any cost. Nor were these outrages of recent origin; I will say nothing which I do not know of my own knowledge. But in a neighboring Territory outrages have for a long time been committed, at which human nature shudders and most of these upon those who had gone from my own section of the country. From the extreme southern border of Kansas up to Ossawottomie, an Abolition den of the vilest kind, and westwardly to the extreme settlement, an organized band of outlaws had for a year past been in the constant commission of those outrages.

Every pro-slavery man they could discover was attacked, his property taken away or destroyed, and his family driven out of the Territory. It was an organized band of thieves, robbers, cutthroats and lawless miscreants. Their crimes have been innumerable and unparalleled. It was a regular Black Republican army, organized, armed and equipped, provided with artillery and arms of every description – furnished, doubtless by the Abolition fanatics of the North. All law had been set at defiance. The courts had been insulted, the juries outraged, and all the legal authorities despised.

These vile cohorts called themselves **Crusaders of Freedom**. The whole Union should anathematize them; a ban should be placed upon them, and the united South should demand retribution. It makes the blood boil to think of their enormities. Every pro-slavery family have been driven out of Linn and Bourbon counties. The base ??? of abolitionism were the authors of these hideous deeds. The Black Republicans showed themselves in their true colors, and unveiled the true nature of their abominable doctrines. Drove off three hundred persons and robbed them of their property. "Get Off," they would say; "you are for Lecompton." I witnessed a party of the lamentable exodus: a large portion of the sufferers had gone off from my own county, and I would be false to every dictate of duty, to every sentiment which becomes a man, if I did not lift up my voice in their behalf. If there is no help for us, I have done my duty; I have shown you what Black Republicans have done to my constituents. In 1851 they began the work of emigration. They came to war upon our institutions, and to drive Missourians out of the Territory. But what better could be expected from the Cadmus crop of fanatics, marching under the banner of a higher law, setting their feet upon the Constitution, and with pirates' devices upon their arms, can we wonder that this hungry brood of massacre and crime had swarmed to so congenial soil; we know by whom they are hounded on; at the very sanctuary of the constitution, at the very shrine whence Washington and Jefferson and Wright, and Buchanan, had drawn their inspiration, the instigators of all these crimes gathered, they were the Sewards, the Hales, the Wilsons, and their Black Republican compeers: the name of Cataline was execrated, yet he was a bold conspirator and exposed a drawn dagger in the Senate, and perished fighting at the head of an armed host; but these conspirators against the constitution steal down Pennsylvania avenue, sneaking from dark and dingy caucus rooms, where they have hatched their vile plots; for thirty years they have been at work; for thirty years they have defiled the sanctuary of the constitution; they are the incarnation of everything that disgraces and degrades humanity.

Hypocrites in religion, leprous with political corruption, reeking with infidelity and every abominable ism, they are a blot upon the fair fame of our country. There they stand, Garrison with the Bible, and Seward with the Constitution under his foot, and Beecher standing between them, under the garb of religion, preaching murder and war. Such are the real authors of all these crimes. They have hounded on the Abolition cohorts who have driven us out of Kansas. They have been successful, and now emboldened by impunity in crime, they dare invade the sacred soil of Missouri, and assail the sovereignty over which waves our proud banner. But they will find the infant Hercules strong enough in its cradle to strangle these vipers. Never will Abolitionism get a foothold upon the soil of Missouri. Our people have suffered aggression enough, and it must be stopped, long suffering and forbearance have been of no avail. Our endurance has been misunderstood, and only increased our sufferings; it has only brought upon us the burning and sacking of our houses, and other outrages I have described.

In one instance these bandits crossed over into our territory, seized one of our innocent citizens and held him in chains at their county seat for three months. Families have been ruined, and there was no redress for them. Though his constituents were a law-abiding people, they could not stand quietly by and endure these enormities in folded arms. The frontier of Missouri must be rendered as safe as the interior. These thieves must be pursued at every cost; the invaders must be repelled and punished. Missouri owes it to her sons to demand full reparation and to inflict condign punishment upon the marauders. We shall never obtain peace by submission. We scorn, spit upon and reject so disgraceful a proposition: our own strong arms will protect us. This bill is a prudent one; the State owes us protection; untie the hands of the Executive. The sum proposed may not be enough. We can increase it. The sanctity of Missouri's soil has been invaded and must be avenged. I thank you, gentlemen, for your attention.

The Liberty Tribune, January 21, 1859

Item No. 8
Special Message
(From Governor Stewart)

Sometime in May last the Executive Department received information that an armed and lawless force, numbering several hundred men, was quartered in Kansas Territory, near the Missouri line, and threatening to invade the state; and indeed had made incursions into the counties of Cass and Bates, committing acts of personal violence, and plundering and robbing our citizens. People in these counties became greatly alarmed, and many of them along the line abandoned their homes. Even some of the towns had been visited by the bandits, and it was stated, had been threatened with destruction.

Under these circumstances, an appeal was made to the Executive for mean of protection. Adjutant General Parsons was accordingly dispatched to the border, under instructions to there learn the actual state of facts, the causes of the difficulties, and the probability of their recurrence; also to ascertain what steps were necessary to provide our citizens with adequate protection, and if it became necessary to at once enroll a sufficient volunteer force to accomplish that purpose. He was also instructed, if he deemed it necessary, to organize military companies in the counties most convenient to the scene of difficulties, taking care to direct that none of the force thus called into service be allowed to cross the line into Kansas, or to do any other act of an aggressive character.

General Parsons having satisfied himself that numerous overt acts had already been committed, and that there was cause to apprehend further incursions into the State, organized several companies in the counties mentioned, and they were furnished with arms by the Quartermaster General Hackney, who accompanied Adjutant General Parsons for that purpose.

These measures served, for a time, to prevent the threatened invasions, but the people along the line who had been driven from their homes, were, by the presence of the same armed force in the vicinity, deterred from returning, and it was urged that they could not cultivate their farms and protect themselves, and therefore, were entitled to aid from other sources.
In consequence of these representations, I, on August 7th, wrote to Gov. Denver, then the Executive in Kansas, informing him that it might become necessary to station an armed force along the border, in Missouri for purposes of protection, at the same time soliciting his earnest cooperation with the authorities of this State in their efforts to preserve peace. And

regarding it the duty of the Federal Government to suppress bands of outlaws organized within the limits of Territories under its immediate control. I, on the 9th of the same month, addressed the President of the United States, (document marked "A") soliciting the aid of the General Government in the protection of our citizens, and in the preservation of the peace so necessary to the prosperity of our people.

An answer from the War Department (document marked "B") informed me that no available troops were known to said Department and could then be so employed. Doubts were also intimated of the "expediency of employing United States troops against bands of civil marauders."

Gov. Denver, in response to my letter, expressed regrets that the course I had indicated should be thought necessary, and the hope that the necessity might be obviated, assuring me he would do all in his power to suppress the evil complained of.

For a time the difficulties seemed to subside, consequently no further efforts were made on the part of the authorities of this State. Recently, however, a smaller party, led, it is stated, by the same chief, has made an incursion into the State, committing murder, robbery, and, as stated in affidavits herewith submitted, (documents marked, "C," and "D") and a petition signed by sundry citizens of Vernon county (document marked "E") driving off ten negroes belonging to citizens of the county mentioned. And within a day or two additional advices have been received, in which it is stated (see document marked "F") that a regularly organized band of thieves, robbers and midnight assassins have congregated in Kansas, immediately upon the western border of Bates county, who are making incursions into the State, taking the lives of our citizens, committing to the flames their houses, and robbing them of their property.

Again the Executive of the State is appealed to for military aid, to protect the border from a repetition of the evils complained of, and which they seem to have cause to apprehend. But the Governor, as Commander-in-Chief, has power under existing laws to call the militia into active service only in cases of "rebellion, invasions or insurrection." If the bandits referred to are to be regarded merely as "civilian marauders," only the sheriffs of the respective counties have authority, under our present military code, to call upon the militia to aid the legally constituted civil authorities in preserving order and enforcing the laws.

Unwilling to do any act that shall involve the State, or the country at large, in undue sectional or party strife, and yet anxious that the border counties should enjoy the protection of life and property to which, in common with other portions of the State, they are entitled, I submit these facts for your consideration, and bespeak for them your immediate attention, hoping that whatever is possible for the General Assembly to do constitutionally, it will be done at once.

R.M. Stewart

The Liberty Tribune, January 21, 1859

Item No. 9
Hon. R.L.Y. Peyton

The Democratic Elector for this district will close his list of appointments today at Clinton in Henry county and we venture this assertion that his is the most brilliant canvas ever made in this district. Private letters and the press give the most flattering account of his speeches at every point he has visited; and all concur in opinion that he has triumphantly borne the Democratic banner over the head of the entire opposition. A correspondent of the *St. Louis Bulletin*, writing from Boonville pays Mr. Peyton the following compliment:

My object in forcing these lines upon the attention of the public, was to notice briefly through your columns, as the only tribute I could pay it, the speech delivered here on yesterday by the Democratic elector, R.L.Y. Peyton. From the little we have heard of Mr. Peyton, we had been led to anticipate a fair Democratic address from a tolerably fair Missouri orator. But shades of Webster! Never before have I listened to anything in the way of a political effort even approaching to it, in this State; and this was in substance the language of nearly everyone who heard it. I *heard* a half dozen of the most rabid Douglas men in this city, and Bell me *ad infinitum*, use the expression on the street afterwards, and when they had had time to cool down from the magic effects of it, that it was the strongest political speech they had ever heard, without *any* exception, and it was unanswerable. For three long hours did he expose the treachery and corruption of, and hurl his crushing denunciations and anathemas at that traitor to the South, Stephen Douglas; for three long hours did her pour the hot shot of his burning indignation and wrath into the two arch enemies of our beloved South, and appealed to her sons – to all they held sacred and dear and to their Revolutionary blood, to rally, *united*, to her rescue. But it were like attempting to paint the rainbow, for me to attempt even the faintest report of the outlines of this master speech. I could not but deplore in my heart the fact that neither "the talented Vest" nor "the invincible Douglas" were there to "pitch in." Mr. Peyton was urgently solicited to address the citizens again at night, and a house *full* of ladies alone promised him; but his strength was exhausted, and he was forced to refuse. From tea until ten o'clock, his room at the hotel was so crowded with proud and admiring friends, (even politically differing from him) anxious to do him their just tribute of congratulation, that "Pierce's" seemed about to be taken by storm. At that hour a band of Music was heard approaching in the distance, and soon a splendid serenade contributing to charm those present and enliven the scene, to which Col.

Peyton responded in a short speech, enthusiastically received. He left us this morning for Jefferson City.

Should he, in his travels stumble upon "the talented Vest," or "the invincible Douglas," or they upon him; I warn them in all spirit of old friendship and personal kindness, and with all the earnestness of parental solicitude, to *stand from under*.

En Passant

Harrisonville's *Western Democrat,* October 27, 1860

Item No. 10
Cassville, Barry County, Missouri
November 8, 1861

To the Speaker of the
House of Representatives,

Sir –

A House Bill entitled "An Act to provide for holding an election for Representation to the Confederate State of America and for other purposes" has been presented to me for my approval. In yielding my assent to this bill it is due to myself that I should state the grounds upon which it is given. This most extraordinary bill, in the history of legislation, has undertaken to elect Senators and Representatives to the Confederate Congress, & my approval of such election is required. It is known to everyone that the Executive of the State, under the Constitution, has nothing whatever to do with the election, either of Senators or Representatives. It is equally well known that the two Houses of the General Assembly, in making an election of Senators, must together, in joint session, and hold the election as the Constitution requires, and when it is so made the approval or the objection of the Executive, having no earthly bearing upon the subject; and is, is therefore, simply an absurdity to call upon the Executive for his approval of a measure over which the Constitution has given him no power whatever. It is also equally well known that the election of Representatives to the Confederate Congress belongs exclusively to the people in their respective Congressional district, and when made by the people in accordance with the Constitution and laws of the State, neither the legislative nor the Executive branch of the government can set it aside or give it any additional force by their approval. So far as this bill undertakes, by mere ordinary enactment – each house acting separated and independent, of the other – to elect Senators and Representatives to the Confederate Congress, it is, in my judgment, a mere nullity, having no force or effect, except to place the state in a false & ludicrous position before the world. In this respect this bill is highly objectionable in my estimation, while at the same time it constitutionality, touching those provisions, may well be questioned.

But with all my objections to these provisions of the bill there are others in it of a character so important to the best interests of the state, that I have affixed my signature to it. The provision of the bill relating to the appointment of Commissioners or Deputies to the Provisional Congress, and to the election of representatives to the Confederate Congress by the people, have my hearty assent, and are, of themselves so important that I have deemed it my duty, and in all the circumstances surrounding us, to give the bill my approval.

Had time allowed for a reconsideration of the bill I should most certainly have withheld my assent. I ask that this document be spread upon your journal.

Respectfully,
C.F. Jackson

Source: Missouri Confederate Archives, Manuscripts 2722, Folder 1, State Historical Society of Missouri

Item No. 11
An Act to perpetuate testimony in cases of slaves abducted or harbored by the enemy, and of other property seized, wasted or destroyed by them.

August 30, 1861

Perpetuation of testimony in case of abduction or harboring slaves by the enemy

Proceedings

Evidence to be filed and preserved by the State Department

Copies to be furnished

The Congress of the Confederate States of America do enact, That when any slave or slaves owned by a citizen of the Confederate States, or an inhabitant thereof, shall be, or may have been abducted or harbored by the enemy, or by any person or persons acting under the authority or color of authority of the United States Government, or engaged in the military or naval service thereof, during the existing war, it shall be lawful for the owner or his attorney to appear before any Judge of the Confederate States, or a commissioner of any court thereof, or any notary public, or in case of there being no such officer within the county, city or corporation, where the proceedings are instituted, before any justice of the peace or alderman, consenting to act in the premises, and adduce proof, oral or written, of the fact of such ownership and abduction or harboring. If the owner of such slave or slaves is laboring under the legal disability of infancy, insanity, or coverture, the evidence tending to establish such ownership, and abduction or harboring, may be adduced by the proper legal representative of the owner, in all cases such owner, attorney, or representative shall make affidavit of the loss. Such affidavit shall not be taken as evidence of the fact of loss, unless it shall appear to the satisfaction of the officer, and it shall be the duty of the judicial officer taking cognizance of the case, to reduce to writing the oral evidence, and to retain the written evidence in support of the alleged ownership and loss, and within thirty days after the hearing, to transmit the same to the Secretary of State of the Confederate States, to be filed and preserved among the archives of the State Department, accompanied by a certificate from the said judicial officer, authenticating the report so made by him. And the said judicial officer shall also state in his certificate of authentication, whether in his opinion, the evidence so heard and transmitted, is, or is not, entitled to credit. It shall be the duty of the

Secretary of State to receive and file in his Department, the report so transmitted, and to furnish to the owners, attorney, or representative a duly certified copy thereof, whenever the same shall be demanded.

Perpetuation of testimony where property, other than slaves, shall be seized, wasted or destroyed by the enemy

SEC. 2. *And be it further enacted*, That whenever any property, other than slaves, real or personal, belonging to any citizen of the Confederate States, or any inhabitant thereof, shall be seized, wasted or destroyed by the enemy during the existing war, or by any person or persons acting under the authority, or color of authority of the United States Government, or engaged in the military or naval service thereof, the mode of taking and preserving proof thereof, shall conform in all respects to that prescribed in the above section, and have like effect.

Act not to be construed as implying that the C.S. will make compensation

SEC. 3. *And be it further enacted*, That the provisions of this act shall not be construed as implying that the Confederate States are in any way liable to make compensation to any of the property to which it refers.

The Statutes at Large of the Provisional Government of the Confederate States of America from the Institution of the Government, February 8, 1861, to its termination, February 18, 1862, Inclusive.

Arranged in Chronological Order, Together with the Constitution for the Provisional Government, and the Permanent Constitution of the Confederate States, and the Treaties Concluded by the Confederate States with Indian Tribes.

Confederate States of America

Matthews, James M. (James Muscoe), b. 1822. Ed.
Source: *Documenting the American South*
(docsouth.unc.edu/imls/19conf/19conf.html)

Item No. 12
Died Cursing Jeff Davis

A Christmas Offering to the Confederate Administration

Col. Peyton's Deep Malice

Urged Lee to Disobey Executive Orders and Invade Northern Territory, But Peace was Declared

Somewhere in the archives of the "lost cause" there is the name of Peyton. There were no stenographic reports of the debates of the Richmond Congress which watched the toppling and the final overthrow of the Confederacy. If there had been the present generation could read some of the fervid oratory that fell from the lips of this man Peyton in those days says the *Chicago Chronicle*.

Peyton was one of the Confederate Senators from Missouri. He died one Christmas morning when the bells of peace and good will were ringing in the ears of most of the people of the earth. But not in his. Embittered at what he called the pa?? of the Richmond government, he had fought its policy as a Senator and had stood face to face with Jefferson Davis in the executive office of the latter and denounced and defied him. He had sat in the wilderness and the thickets of Virginia and told Lee what he had told Davis, and he urged Lee to expose Davis by disregarding the latter's orders and issue a call for an invasion of the North. This same man put himself in the saddle and under the command of "Jeb" Stuart, who gave him a body guard and had reconnoitered the position of one of the divisions of the army of the Potomac ?? to see for himself.

In the town where he had practiced law years before the war, he was known to man, woman and child in the county as Lud Peyton. He went to Harrisonville, Cass County, Mo., as a young lawyer in 1840. It is not known to the writer what books were necessary in those days in the practice of law, but for years after in that town events were reckoned "from the day Lud Peyton came to town with his fiddle."

Peyton was long and gangly in his gait; his hair was like a brush heap; his arms were always in the way, and his nose was like that which sculptors and artists give to Julius Caesar. A good for nothing boy in the community or a balky horse was likened to Lud Peyton. He was laziness personified. The courthouse stood in the center of a square and the town, what there was of it, was built around the square. Peyton's office – for it seemed he had a place where he could be found, occasionally – was a room in the courthouse, perhaps having table room with one of the county officials. Often when the summer heat sizzled on the prairie town, and grasshoppers and gallanippers filled the air, and the dog fennel weeds grew thick to the very doorway of the courthouse, and merchants stretched themselves out on their counters and went to sleep, Lud Peyton was seen and heard playing his fiddle in the window of the room which was his office. "Napoleon's retreat from Moscow," and "Brian Boru" and "Yankee Doodle" constituted his stock of airs, except when he would create some out of his brain, for he was what people in those days called "a natural musician."

There was a society, even in those days, in that new country. It had no receptions; there was no such thing as "pouring," and the charity ball had not been dreamed of. In the winter there was a dance somewhere in the country. During the summer the mothers and their sons and daughters, where there were any, went "plumming" – for wild plums, or for grapes, which fruit also grew wild in the woods. Sometime during the outing there would be a Virginia reel under the trees.

This apparent digression is for the purpose of introducing Lud Peyton as the fiddler. He was the only one to be had, and as he was a gallant sort of fellow in spite of his laziness he was always ready to accommodate.

Court was held at least once a year at the county seat, and all classes of litigation came before "his honor." Once in a long run there was a murder trial, and it always drew. Farmers came in with their families and camped out in order to hear the trial. It was the only diversion they had. On one of these occasions Peyton defended a young man whose life was at stake. The testimony was against the client, and so was public sentiment. The judge was thought to be on the side of the State's Attorney. Peyton, however, had surprised all who knew of his case, and became famous as an examiner. When he "spoke" to the jury the Sheriff removed the sash and doors from the court-room so that the people without could hear Peyton. It must have been an argument of force, and convincing, for, twenty-five years ago, when the writer was a visitor to Harrisonville, he heard people who had come upon earth long after the effort in question talking about the great speech of Lud Peyton, which their grand-fathers had heard.

The arguments in the court and officials left the room to the jury and the Sheriff having put in the windows and doors stood guard while the jury deliberated. Many of the farmers, having cooked their dinners on the square, grew tired of waiting for the verdict, and stretched themselves on the ground and slept, the understanding being that, if the jury "decided any way at all" the Sheriff was to blow a horn and thus arouse the sleepers. It may be a slander that has traveled down the lane of years, but it is a part of this story that the court, having divested "herself" of surplus clothing, was having a game of "sold sledge" in the Sheriff's house – the only tavern in town – with the State's Attorney and some of the States' witnesses in the case just closed.

The night wore on and there had been no token from the jury. Only the Sheriff and his deputy were awake without, as was supposed. Then the sound of a fiddle was heard. It was soothing and restful, as all music is when it comes in the night. Then one of the sashes in the court-room was raised, and the jury assembled about the opening and listened. The Sheriff was a conscientious man and went over to the wagon from which the music emanated and found Lud Peyton sitting on the pole of the wagon fiddling. The Sheriff ordered Mr. Peyton to stop playing, as it was liable to influence the jury. Peyton spoke of his constitutional rights as all men in those days did when they were ordered to stop anything, even horse-stealing. The Sheriff said the Constitution did not cover the case, and Peyton asked him what he was going to do about it – a question which afterward became famous in this country – when asked by another.

The Sheriff made no reply, but went over to his house and notified the Court that Peyton was trying to tamper with the jury by playing his fiddle. The State's attorney and the State's witnesses in the game wanted the Court to interfere, but the jurist, who afterward helped form the Constitution of Missouri, declined to interfere, except to tell the Sheriff that the window sash at which the jury was listening was to be pulled down.

Sometime after the Court was notified that the jury had agreed and the game was stopped temporarily while the Court and attendants went to the Court-house. Then the Sheriff blew the horn and the farmers, aroused from their sleep, walked in. The jury stood up and the Court asked if an agreement had been reached. It had. "Before the verdict is read," said the Court, "I want to ask the jury, one question. It has been reported to this court, that during the deliberations of this jury, someone, unknown to this Court, thought to influence the jury," in other words to tamper with it, by means of a Stradivarius, or violin, or fiddle, in reaching a verdict in the case you have been deliberating upon?"

The foreman disclaimed having been influenced by anything, save the testimony and the instructions of the court, and each member of the jury said the same thing for himself.

The verdict was then read, first ___ence by the court, and before it was read aloud the court said "I don't want any ???? or demonstration in this court-room after the verdict is read. If you people will want to cut up any capers about it you must go out of doors and do it."

The verdict was "not guilty," and from that time Lud Peyton was known as Col. Peyton, and his reputation as a pleader traveled as rapidly as the news conveyances of those days would permit.

He declined honors in the way of office, but he never declined the invitation of the ladies to "fiddle." Children in the country were named Lud Peyton, and some of the good old colored folks named theirs "Kunnel Peyton."

The war cloud shadowed the land. Claiborne F. Jackson was Governor of Missouri when Lincoln called for volunteers. Jackson replied for Missouri that his State would not furnish a man to fight against the South. The result showed Jackson's lack of foresight. Missouri furnished more men for the Union army than it did for the other side, in spite of its reputation as a rebel State. Sometime after Jackson's reply to Lincoln, he was in flight, with his Legislature, seeking the protection of Sterling Price's army. The Legislature, as it called itself, gathered in a town in the southwest corner of the State, and elected two Senators to go to Richmond. One was George Vest, now in the United States Senate from Missouri. The other was Lud Peyton – Col. Peyton.

The war had been carried on, until, in the West, it was a struggle between guerrilla and jayhawker. Quantrell led the former, Jennison was the chief of the latter. The flag was black; the motto "No quarter." It was pillage and rapine and merciless murder.

One Christmas eve a tall, quiet man called on Senator Peyton in Richmond, and the two sat down to talk. The quiet man was Quantrell. He had traveled, necessarily, by a circuitous route, to the confederate capital. He came to make some suggestions. In brief, this guerrilla chief proposed to hold Missouri so that it would require an army from the North to watch it; thus the force on the Potomac and elsewhere would be weakened. All Quantrell asked was gold. There was gold in the confederate treasury. Perhaps not literally, but it is well known that the confederate treasury had gold in foreign capitals and that by reason of the financial policy of Davis and his followers it remained there.

Senator Peyton went with Quantrell to see Davis. The guerrilla submitted his plan. Senator Peyton urged its adoption. Peyton denounced the Confederate president, and if Quantrell had been as impetuous as the Missouri Senator the assassination would have occurred in Richmond instead of Washington.

Quantrell returned to Missouri, disheartened with his mission, but his followers were never any wiser for it. The war on the border went on with more ferocity than ever.

Peyton died later, and that was when the bells of Richmond were trying to ring out Christmas tidings. Peyton sent his curse as a Christmas offering to the Davis administration and foreshadowed just what occurred afterward.

Christmas 1864, found Quantrell and some of his followers heading for Arkansas, leaving Missouri forever, where there was neither food, nor rent nor guide, nor fire. The game of the forests had disappeared, and the people on both sides were weary and willing to die. There had not been a Christmas since Quantrell had become a leader that he had not given his men what he called a jollification of some character. It had been a surprise for Federals, or the burning of a town, or the capture of a train or the closing of a bank. This Christmas, 1864, he "went calling" on his way out of Missouri into Kentucky. At King's Mountain he called upon a federal colonel named McWilliams, dined with him, and as he was leaving he told the astonished colonel who he was. There were 400 federal soldiers camped around the house at the time. Quantrell rode away on his swift steed and joined his men, as many as were left, and they all galloped across the line to Arkansas. At Pocahontas, Ark., there was a detachment of eighty Illinois infantry. Quantrell introduced himself to the colonel as another in the Government's employ; was entertained that night, Christmas, at dinner, and remained in the town several days, recruiting in the way of food, ammunition, and some clothing, all at the expense of Uncle Sam.

Quantrell crossed the Mississippi at Memphis; went into Tennessee, and from there into Kentucky, where he was shot, from the effects of which he died in 1865.

It had been his intention, as he expressed it to one of his confidential companions, of whom he had few, to rest in Kentucky quietly if he could, during 1865, until late in the fall. Then with some of his trusted men and such others recruit and upon whom he could rely, he was going with his command to Washington, and on Christmas morning 1865, he was going to make Uncle Sam such a Christmas gift as he had never had before.

Beyond that he did not unfold his plans. It would have been in keeping with the man's character. He was "through" in Missouri; and there was nothing for him to do in Kentucky.

But against the wild vagary and plan of the guerrilla, there was written, "Appomattox, April 9, 1865, Grant – Lee." But for that, who knows?

St. Louis Post-Dispatch, January 5, 1896, Sunday

Item No. 13

Trio of Great Orators

A Reminiscence of Peyton, Philips, and Vest

The Memorable Campaign of 1860 – The Parts Played by Prominent Missourians in that Stirring Period

General B.G. Boone, in the *Clinton Democrat.*

"Thence to the famous orators repair,
Those ancients whose resistless eloquence
Wielded at will that Serce domocratis."
-Milton

The political campaign of `1860 is the most memorable and far reaching in its results in the annuals of this country. It is not the purpose of this article to attempt an analysis of the result of that campaign. Or to impress philosophical consideration on the issues involved and discussed in that transcendent political contest, but in a brief way to sketch the personalities of three great orators who addressed the people of this county at the court house in Clinton in the fall of 1860, now nearly forty years ago, and to give my yet vivid recollections of their charming and persuasive eloquence – Peyton, Philips and Vest; names imperishably linked with that stirring and epoch-making period of American political history.

There were four presidential candidates in the field – Lincoln, Douglas, Breckinridge and Bell.

The contrast in this district, as far as public speaking was concerned, was triangular, the Lincoln elector not participating in the discussion. Robert L.Y. Peyton, then of Harrisonville, Cass County, was the Breckenridge elector; George G. Vest, then of Boonville, Cooper County, the Douglas elector, and John F. Philips, then of Georgetown, Pettis County, the Bell elector. Douglas was the regular nominee of the Democracy, Breckenridge of the Southern wing of that party, and Bell the candidate of the 'Constitutional Union' party. There was no joint debate between these electors in this county, each speaking on separate occasions to unusually large audiences of deeply and earnestly interested citizens of every political creed. They were each in the prime and vigor of young manhood – Peyton, 33; Vest, 30, and Philips 26. They were lawyers by profession, and had already attained distinction as legal advocates, were collegiate graduates, and equipped with a thorough classical and collegiate education. Peyton, a Virginian, Vest, a Kentuckian and Philips, 'native here' and to the manner born.

Daniel Webster defined eloquence as follows: "It does not consist in speeches. It must exist in the man; in the subject; in the occasion. It comes like the out-breaking of a fountain from the earth, or the bursting with spontaneous natural force of volcanic fire." Therein Webster described Peyton, Philips and Vest, as they electrified and swayed their hearers in Henry county by their matchless and charming eloquence in the long ago of 1860.

During the campaign of 1860 the whole country was aflame with forensic eloquence, and the political forum was resonant with oratory.

In Virginia, Henry A. Wise, William L. Goggins, Thomas S. Flournoy, and Alexander H. Stuart.

In Kentucky, John J. Crittenden, John C. Breckenridge, Joshua F. Bell, Beriah MaGoffin and Charles S. Morehead.

In Tennessee, Thomas R. Nelson, Andrew Johnson, Emerson Etheridge and Meredith P. Gentry.

In Maryland, Reverdy Johnson and Henry Winter Davis.

In Indiana, Daniel W. Voorhees, Henry S. Lane, Thomas A. Hendricks, Albert G. Porter, and Oliver P. Morton.

In Ohio, George H. Pendleton, James A. Garfield, Allen G. Thurman, Rutherford B. Hayes, John A. Bingham, George E. Pugh, Samuel S. Cox, and Clement L. Vallandigham.

In Illinois, Richard Yates, James C. Robinson, William A. Richardson, John R. Eden, John A. Logan, Murray McConnell and James C. Allen.

In Pennsylvania, Andrew G. Curtin, William A. Wallace, Charles A. Buckalew and Galusha A. Grow.

In New England, Edward Everett, Charles Sumner, William P. Fessenden and James G. Blaine.

In the Northwest, Matthew H. Carpentr, Zack Chandler and James R. Doolittle.

In the South, William L. Yancey, Thomas H. Watts, Judah P. Benjamin, Alexander H. Stephens, John B. Gordon, Howell Cobb, and Robert Toombs, and in Missouri James S. Rollins, John B. Henderson, Thomas L. Anderson, James S. Green, Uriel Wright, Thomas P. Akers, Frank T. Mitchell, Frank P. Blair, B. Gratz Brown, Silas Woodson, William F. Switzler, Thomas W. Freeman, Robert L.Y. Peyton, George G. Vest, and John F. Philips were each in their respective states, swaying the multitudes by the irresistible power and effect of their marvelous and masterly oratory; and it is safe to say that they were not surpassed in the palmist days of Athenian and Roman eloquence, which has come to us gilded with the halo of ages; and among this resplendent galaxy of intellectual stars that decorated and bedecked the political forum of 1860, there may have been some more eminent and dazzling, but none more brave, or truer, or brighter than this trio of whom I am writing.

Peyton was born in Loudon County, Va.; was closely related to the celebrated John Randolph, of that state, and a cousin of Bailie Peyton, the famous orator of Tennessee. He was over six feet in height, rather slender in person, with large dark gray eyes, large mouth, heavy dark hair and a high broad forehead. His voice was extremely musical in tone and full of the sweetest melody. His gesticulation was faultless and his diction a model of purity. At times his sentences were lengthy, after the style of William M. Evarts, the great New York statesman and orator, though always free of ambiguity or confusion, or expressed with a graceful fascination, and came from his lips with persuasive and convincing power, like the 'out breaking of a fountain from earth.' His power of analysis was truly wonderful and his fervid impassioned appeals were indeed 'resistless.' He stood as the champion and defender of the ultra-Southern wing of the Democratic Party, and boldly affirmed the constitutional right of state secession with a plausibility of reasoning not excelled by Calhoun, Haynes, or McDuffie. He made no effort at witticism or anecdote, but employed the most profound aphorisms to enforce and impress his argument. His style was dignified and impressive, displaying great mental power and earnestness.

At that time – 1860 – he was state senator from the Cass County district, and was the conceded leader of the Democratic party in the Senate. He was a regular attendant at our circuit court, and was often employed in the most important cases in this county.

In 1861 he espoused the Southern cause; raised a regiment of which he was the colonel, and went into the Confederate Army. He was chosen one of the Confederate States senators from Missouri, and served in the Confederate congress at Richmond, Va., until the late summer of 1863, when on account of declining health, he retired to Bladen Springs, Ala. where on the 3rd of October, 1863, far away from the scenes of his early triumphs and honors and the friends of his early manhood, his brilliant career terminated, and his noble, generous and elevated spirit passed from its earthly existence. It may be truly said of him that earth never pillowed on its bosom a manlier form, or heaven threw wide its enduring gates to receive a nobler spirit than that of Robert L.Y. Peyton.

George G. Vest was born in Frankfort, Ky., on the last day of the year 1830. I shall not attempt a resume of his long and distinguished career in the public service. I am not writing of the great senator and statesman of 1899, but of the brilliant and gifted young orator of 1860.

In personal appearance and carriage he was entirely dissimilar to either Peyton or Philips. He was ruddy in complexion, rotund in form, below medium height, with a facial expression indicating every variety of mental activity. He was endowed with conceptive and creative faculties of the rarest order; with invention 'bold, vigorous, fertile and discriminating;' with a power of analysis and fervor of passion that deeply impressed his hearers. He was graceful and impassioned, tender and profound, humorous and sarcastic by turns, yet logical and convincing by the force and power of his reasoning. His voice was as sweet and musical as the notes of an Aeolian harp. His witticisms were frequent and pungent, his anecdotes risible, and his illustrations pointed and appropriate, and enwreathed his speech with the choicest flowers of rhetorical metaphor, and never failed to win unrestrained applause of his delighted audience. He stood then, has ever since stood and now stands for the formal and regular edict of his party without questioning its fallibility.

I shall never forget his splendid panegyric of Thomas Jefferson, and his grand, patriotic and soul-stirring appeal in behalf of the Union which this Douglas elector made in 1860. I have heard Rollins, Anderson, Akers, Uriel Wright and many other eminent orators plead for the perpetuity and integrity of the Union, and warn their countrymen against the folly of disunion, but none of them ever surpassed George G. Vest in logic, in eloquence, in pathos and in genuine patriotism in his touching and patriotic appeal for the Union, as he held aloft the banner of his party in that memorable campaign. His noble and manly appeals were unavailing, the fearful separation came and he followed the fateful star of the South to its final and eternal setting. He was chosen as Confederate States Senator from Missouri, and ranked in the Confederate congress as one of the most brilliant and gifted of its orators. After the close of the war between the states, he returned to the scene of his early achievements, and with undaunted courage and unfaltering faith he entered again upon that illustrious and commanding career which he has been so grandly and gloriously crowned with enduring and fadeless fame.

For twenty long and eventful years he has stood as a great senator of the West; a faithful and fearless sentinel on the out walls of the citadel of free government; guarding it against the insidious approach of centralization; defending the ancient landmarks of the fathers, and pleading eloquently for the rights of the citizen under the calm and regnant shield of the constitution. Senator Vest is now in the meridian of his faculties, "time fame," and as the dawn was bright and full of promise, and the noon-tide illumined by the splendors of performance, the evening will catch the accumulated radiance and plant among the fixed lights the constellation that glitters to his genius.

John F. Philips, the youngest of this "trio of great orators," was born in Boone County, Mo., December 31, 1834, just four years to a day later than the birth of his "companion in greatness" George G. Vest. At the May term, 1860, of circuit court, he was enrolled at our bar and resisted the first case, which was the foreclosure of a mortgage, that I had brought in the circuit court. He knocked me out on demurrer. I amended and knocked him on the trial.

In the late fall of the same year he addressed the people of this county at the court house as the Bell and Everett elector of this district. At that time he was strikingly handsome in personal appearance, and age, with its iconoclastic hand, had not displaced, only dignified and improved the magnetic fascination of his elegant and charming personality. His elocutionary powers were of the highest and rarest order; his sentiments were broad, liberal, elevated and patriotic, revealing a genuine love of country and an unyielding devotion to the constitution, and the enforcement of the laws within the Union. His style was a harmonious and happy combination of purity of thought, sincerity of purpose and profound reasoning. His voice was clear and distinct, with a pleasing and attractable intonation, and his speech was adorned and enriched with classical and historical illusions and illustrations with felicitous diction and scholastic beauty. It is not the purpose here to write of the accomplished and sagacious statesman in his representative capacity in the convention and congress, or of the great and profound jurist in 1899, but of the native Missouri orator as I listened to and was fascinated and enchanted by his charming and matchless eloquence forty years ago. Since that time he has won unfading laurels in the domain of statesmanship and imperishable renown in the still difficult and exacting domain of jurisprudence.

Both in the state and federal judiciary, this Missouri orator of 1860 has given to his native state as bright and as enduring a record as can be found in the ample pages of judicial history. In youth he was a great orator, in early manhood a sagacious statesman, and in the evening of life a profound and accomplished jurist, and at all times a great man.

He is now in the far West in quest of health, and may the vitalizing air of the majestic mountains speedily restore him to his great old-time vigor. Vest, the Kentuckian, the great senator of the West; Philips the Missourian, the great jurist of the West – may a kind Providence preserve each many years of yet of their useful and splendid lives. A salutation and a cheer for Philips and Vest; a sincere tear to the memory of the noble and brilliant Peyton, and a genuine pride in the illustrious career of this trio of great orators of 1860.

The Kansas City Journal, Sunday, June 4, 1899

Item No. 14

R.L.Y. Peyton

"R.L.Y. Peyton was born in Loudon Co., Va. His education was classical and polished. He was bred to the Law. He came to Missouri and settled in Harrisonville, from which he practiced law in the neighboring counties. He was kind and seemed pure in thought. He did have the ways of the politician. As habit of his was to put off until tomorrow what might be done today, but he never forgot to prepare for business. In 1858 he was elected State Senator. In 1861 he was Colonel of a regiment of State Guards, and soon after elected to a Senator tó the Southern Congress. As the war drew to a close and all looked dark for the Confederacy Peyton arose from a sick bed and went to Davis and begged him to turn all over to Lee and let him take entire charge. With other suggestions he had a stormy time with Davis. He returned to his room and the next morning was found dead in his bed. He was devoted to the Lost Cause and it is believed that he could not have survived its failure. He died in Alabama in 1863."

Garland C. Broadhead
Missouri Historical Society – Library, Broadhead Papers, Garland (Folder 3),"Virginians in Missouri", Pages 62 – 63.

Bibliography

Books

Abrahamson, James L. *The Men of Secession and Civil War: 1859 – 1861*. Scholarly Resources, Inc. Wilmington, Delaware. 2000.

Ainsworth, Elizabeth and Robert G. *A Pictorial History of Wheeling*. Donning Publishing Co. 1977.

Akers, Monte. *Year of Glory: The Life and Battles of Jeb Stuart and his Cavalry, June 1862 – June 1863*. Casemate Publishers. Havertown, Pennsylvania. 2012.

Alexander, Thomas B. and Beringer, Richard E. *The Anatomy of the Confederate Congress. Vanderbilt University Press*. Nashville, Tennessee. 1972.

Allmendinger, David F., Jr. *Nat Turner and the Rising in Southampton County*. John Hopkins University Press. Baltimore, Maryland. 2014.

Anderson, Ephraim and Bearss, Edwin C. *Memoirs: Historical and Persona: Including the Campaigns of the First Missouri Confederate Brigade*. Times Printing Company. St. Louis, Missouri. 1868. (Reprint by Morningside Bookshop, 1972.

Andrist, Ralph K. *The Long Death: The Last Days of the Plains Indian*. MacMillen Publishing Company. New York, New York. 1964.

Applegate, Debby. *The Most Famous Man in America: The Biography of Henry Ward Beecher*. Random House Publishing. New York, New York. 2006.

Barnes, Chancy R., editor. *The Commonwealth of Missouri*. Bryan, Breand, & Co. St. Louis, Missouri. 1877.

Bay, W.V.N. *Reminiscences of the Bench and Bar of Missouri*. F.H. Thomas and Company. St. Louis, Missouri. 1878.

Biographical Cyclopaedia of Butler County, Ohio. 1882.

Black, Robert C., III. *The Railroads of the Confederacy*. The University of North Carolina Press. Chapel Hill, North Carolina. 1998.

Blair, Edward. *History of Johnson County, Kansas*. Standard Publishing Company. Lawrence, Kansas. 1915.

Bledsoe, Albert T. *The War Between the States or Was Secession a Constitutional Right Previous to the War of 1861 -65?* J.P. Bell Company, Inc. Lynchburg, Virginia. 1915.

Bleeding Kansas, Bleeding Missouri: The Long Civil War on the Border. Burke, Diane Mutti and Earle, Jonathan, Editors. University Press of Kansas. Lawrence, Kansas. 2013.

Blincoe, Don Sr. *Loudoun County, Virginia, Militia Journals: 1793 – 1829*. Iberian Publishing Company. Athens, Georgia.

Borcke, Heros von. *Memoirs of the Confederate War for Independence*. W. Blackwood and Sons. Edinburgh, Scotland. 1866. Reprint J.S. Sanders and Company, 1999.

Bowen, Elbert R. *Theatrical Entertainments in Rural Missouri Before the Civil War*. University of Missouri Press. Columbia, Missouri. 1959.

Brewerton, G. Douglas. *The War in Kansas*. Derby & Jackson Publishers. New York, New York. 1856.

Britton, Wiley. *Memoirs of the Rebellion on the Border – 1863.* University of Nebraska Press. Lincoln, Nebraska. 1993. (Reprint)

Cass County, Missouri, Families. Cass County Historical Society. Cass County, Missouri. 1976.

Castel, Albert. *General Sterling Price and the Civil War in the West*. Louisiana State University Press. Baton Rouge, Louisiana.

Cohen, Stan. *John Brown: The Thundering Voice of Jehoval.* Pictorial Publishing *Company. Missoula, Montana. 1999.*

Connelley, William E. *Quantrill and the Border Wars*. Pageant Book Company. New York, New York. 1909.

Conrad, Howard L. *Encyclopedia of the History of Missouri*. The Southern History Company. St. Louis, Missouri. 1901.

Cooper, Edward S. *Louis Trezevant Wigfall: The Disintegration of the Union and Collapse of the Confederacy*. Fairleigh Dickinson University Press.

Day, Reed B. *The Cumberland Road: A History of the National Road*. Closson Press. Apollo, Pennsylvania. 1996.

Deane, Abner H. *Reminiscences of Half a Century*. Jackson County (Mo.) Historical Society Archives.

The Diary of Edmund Ruffin, Volume II: The Years of Hope, April 1861 – June, 1863. Edited by Scarborough, William Kauffman. Louisiana State University Press. Baton Rouge, Louisiana. 1976.

Duke, Basil W. *Reminiscences of Basil W. Duke, C.S.A*.

Durham, Walter T. *Balie Peyton of Tennessee: Nineteenth Century Politics and Thoroughbreds*. Hillsboro Press. Franklin, Tennessee. 2004.

Eakin, Joanne Chiles. *The Battle of Lexington: From the Confederate Field Reports*. Independence, Missouri. 1994.

Eakin, Joanne Chiles. *Diary of a Doctor, Missouri State Guards, 1861*. Two Trails Publishing. Independence, Missouri. 1999.

English, William Francis. *The Pioneer Lawyer and Jurist in Missouri*. University of Missouri Press. Columbia, Missouri. 1947.

Farquhar, Roger B. *Historic Montgomery County, Maryland: Old Homes and History*. Monumental Printing Co. Baltimore, Maryland. 1952.

Fischer, David Hackett. *Albion's Seed: Four British Folkways in America*. Oxford University Press. New York, New York. 1989.

Fellman, Michael. *Inside War: The Guerrilla Conflict in Missouri During the American Civil War*. Oxford University Press. New York, New York. 1989.

Fischer, David Hackett and Kelly, James C. *Bound Away: Virginia and the Westward Movemen*t. University of Virginia Press. Charlottesville, Virginia. 2000.

Foote, Henry. *Casket of Reminiscences.* Chronicle Publishing Company. Washington, D.C. 1874.

Freeman, Douglas Southall. *Lee's Lieutenants. Volume III, Gettysburg to Appomattox.* Charles Scribner's Sons. New York, New York. 1944.

The General Statutes of the State of Missouri. Emory S. Foster, Public Printer. City of Jefferson, Missouri. 1866.

Gillespie, Michael. *Come Hell or High Water: A Lively History of Steamboating on the Mississippi and Ohio Rivers.* Great River Publishing. Stoddard, Wisconsin. 2001.

The Great Valley Road of Virginia. Hofstra, Warren R. and Raitz, Karl, editors. University of Virginia Press. Charlottesville, Virginia. 2010.

Havighurst, Walter. *The Miami Years: 1809 – 1959.* G.P. Putnam's Sons. New York, New York. 1958.

Hedrick, Joan D. *Harriet Beecher Stowe: A Life.* Oxford University Press. New York, New York. 1994.

Heth, Henry. *The Memoirs of Henry Heth.* Greenwood Press. Westport, Connecticut. 1974. (edited by James L. Morrison)

Himmel, Stanley. *Mr. Davis's Richmond.* Coward-McCann Publishers. New York, New York. 1958.

Hinze, David C. and Farnham, Karen. *The Battle of Carthage: Border War in Southwest Missouri, July 5, 1861.* Pelican Publishing Company. Gretna, Louisiana. 1997.

Historic Houses of Staunton, Virginia. Gibbs, Marney and Nutt, Joe. Mid-Valley Press. Verona, Virginia. 2008.

A History and Biographical Cyclopaedia of Butler County, Ohio.

History of Newton, Lawrence, Barry and McDonald Counties, Missouri. Goodspeed Publishing Co. Chicago, Illinois. 1888.

History of Butler County, Ohio. Western Biographical Publishing Co. Cincinnati, Ohio. 1882.

History of Cass and Bates Counties, Missouri. National Historical Company. St. Joseph, Missouri. 1883.

History of Cassville, Missouri.

History of Clark County, Ohio. W.H. Beers & Company. Chicago, Illinois. 1881.

History of Jackson County, Missouri. Union Historical Company, Birdsall, Williams & Co. Kansas City, Missouri. 1881.

History of Lafayette County, Missouri. Missouri Historical Company. St. Louis, Missouri. 1881.

History of Memphis, Tennessee. Editor, Young, Judge J.P. H.W. Crew and Co. Publishers. Knoxville, Tennessee. 1912.

History of Newton, Barry, Lawrence, and McDonald Counties, Missouri. John Marvis Publishing Co. Chicago, Illinois. 1888.

History of Saline County, Missouri. Missouri Historical Company. St. Louis, Missouri. 1881.

History of Vernon County, Missouri. Brown and Company. St. Louis, Missouri. 1887. (Reprint by The Printery, 1974)

Howe, Henry. *History of Butler County, Ohio: 1803 – 1889.* The Bookmark. Knightstown, Indiana. Reprint, 1977.

Elliott, Valerie Edwards. *Images of America: Oxford.* Arcadia Publishing. Chicago, Illinois. 2004.

Journal of the Confederate States of America, 1861-1865, Volume II. Government Printing Office. Washington, D.C. 1904.

Journal of the Senate, Extra Session of the Rebel Legislature. Jefferson City, Missouri. Emory S. Foster, Public Printer. 1865 Reprint by University of Michigan.

Junkin, D.X. *The Reverend George Junkin: A Historical Biography.* J.B. Lippincott & Co. Philadelphia, Pennsylvania. 1871. (Reprint, by University of Michigan).

Kimmel, Stanley. *Mr. Davis's Richmond.* Coward-McCann, Inc. Publishers. New York, New York. 1958.

Leftwich, William M. *Martyrdom in Missouri: A History of Religious Proscription, the Seizure of Churches, and the Persecution of Ministers of the Gospel, in the State of Missouri During the Late Civil War, and Under the 'Test Oath' of the New Constitution, Vol. 2."* S.W. Book & Publishers. St. Louis, Missouri. 1870.

Library of Congress: Civil War Desk Reference. Editors, Wagner, Margaret E., Gallagher, Gary W., and Finkelman, Paul. Grand Central Press, Publishers. New York, New York. 2002.

McCandless, Perry. *A History of Missouri: Volume II, 1820 to 1860.* University of Missouri Press. Columbia, Missouri. 1971.

McLaurin, Melton A. *Celia, A Slave: A True Story*. University of Georgia Press. Athen, Georgia. 1991.

McPherson, James M. (Editor) *To the Best of My Ability: The American Presidents*. The Society of American Historians. Dorling Kindersley. New York, New York. 2000.

Marriage and Death Notices from Alexandria, Va. Newspapers. Vol. I. 1784 to 1838.

Marshall, Howard Wight. *Play Me Something Quick and Devilish: Old-Time Fiddlers in Missouri*. University of Missouri Press. Columbia, Missouri. 2012.

Melton, Emory. *The First 150 Years in Cassville, Missouri: 1845 – 1995.* Litho Printers & Bindery. Cassville, Missouri. 1995.

Mildfelt, Todd. *The Secret Danites: Kansas' First Jayhawkers*. Todd Mildfelt Publishing. Richmond, Kansas. 2003.

Monaco, Ralph A., II. *Scattered to the Four Winds: General Order No. 11 and Martial Law in Jackson County, Missouri, 1863*. Monaco Publishing, LLC. Kansas City, Missouri. 2013.

Monaghan, Jay. *Civil War on the Western Border, 1854 – 1865.* University of Nebraska Press. Lincoln, Nebraska. 1955.

Mosby, John Singleton. *Mosby's War Reminiscences*. Dodd, Mead and Company. New York, New York. 1898.

The National Cyclopaedia of American Biography. Vol. 1 – 13. 1898.

Neosho, City of Fountains.

O'Brien, William Patrick. *Merchants of Independence*. Truman State University Press. Kirksville, Missouri. 2014.

Old Settlers History of Bates County, Missouri. Tathwell & Moore Publishers. Amsterdam, Missouri. 1897.

Oldham, Williamson S. *The Memoir of Senator Williamson S. Oldham, CSA: Rise and Fall of the Confederacy*. Edited by Jewett, Clayton E. University of Missouri Press. Columbia, Missouri. 2006.

Parkman, Francis. *The Oregon Trail.* Doubleday & Company, Inc. Garden City, New York. 1946.

Parrish, William E. *David Rice Atchison of Missouri: Border Politician*. University of Missouri Press. Columbia, Missouri. 1961.

Parrish, William E. *A History of Missouri, Volume III, 1860 to 1875*. University of Missouri Press. Columbia, Missouri. 1973.

Peckham, James. *General Nathaniel Lyon, and Missouri in 1861*. American News Company Publishers. New York, New York. 1866.

Peterson, Richard C., McGhee, James E., Lindberg, Kip A., and Daleen, Keith I. *Sterling Price's Lieutenants, Revised Edition*. Two Trails Publishing. Independence, Missouri. 2007.

Peyton, John Lewis. *The American Crisis, Volume* I. Saunders, Otley and Co. London, England. 1867.

Peyton, John Lewis. *Over the Alleghanies and Across the Prairies: Personal Recollections of the Far West, One and Twenty Years Ago*. London, England. A Schulze, Printer. UL1869. (Reprint by ULAN Press)

Peyton, John Lewis. *Memoir of John Howe Peyton*. A.B. Blackburn & Co. Staunton, Virginia *Peyton's of Virginia, II.* Vol. I. Page 18.

Phillips, Christopher. *Missouri's Confederate: Claiborne Fox Jackson and the Creation of Southern Identity in the Border West*. University of Missouri Press. Columbia, Missouri. 2000.

The Pioneer Lawyer and Jurist in Missouri. English, William Francis, PhD. The University of Missouri Studies. Volume XXI. Columbia, Missouri. 1947.

Piston, William Garrett & Hatcher, Richard W., III. *Wilson's Creek: The Second Battle of the Civil War and the Men Who Fought It*. University of North Carolina Press. Chapel Hill, North Carolina. 2000.

Public Laws of the Confederate States of America. R.M. Smith, Printer to Congress. Richmond, Virginia. 1862. (Reprint by Scholar Select, 2017)

Putnam, Sallie Brock. *Richmond During the War: Four Years of Personal Observation*. University of Nebraska Press. Lincoln, Nebraska. 1996.

Rafiner, Tom A. *Cinders and Silence: A Chronicle of Missouri's Burnt District, 1854 – 1870.* Burnt District Press. Harrisonville, Missouri. 2013.

The Revised Statutes of the State of Missouri. 2nd Edition. Chambers, Knapp & Co.. Saint Louis, Missouri. 1840.

The Revised Statutes of the State of Missouri. Chambers & Knapp. St. Louis, Missouri. 1845.

The Revised Statutes of the State of Missouri, Volume I. James Lusk, Public Printer. Jefferson City, Missouri. 1856.

Reynolds, David S. *Mightier Than the Sword: Uncle Tom's Cabin and the Battle for America*. W.W. Norton & Company. New York, New York. 2011.

Reynolds, Thomas C. *General Sterling Price and the Confederacy*. Missouri History Museum. St. Louis, Missouri. 1904. (Edited by Robert G. Schultz)

Rodabaugh, James H.. *History of Miami University. Worthington, Ohio. 1949.*

Rusk, Ralph Leslie. *The Literature of the Middle Western Frontier.* Columbia University Press. New York, New York. 1926.

Schroeder, Walter A. *Presettlement Prairie of Missouri.* Missouri Department of Conservation. Second Edition, Revised, 1982.

Shalhope, Robert E. *Sterling Price: Portrait of a Southerner.* University of Missouri Press. Columbia, Missouri.

Sheel, Eugene M. *The History of Middleburg and Vicinity.* Piedmont Press. Warrenton, Virginia, 1987.

Sheel, Eugene M. *Loudoun Discovered: Communities, Corners, and Crossroads, Vol. 2.*

Snead, Thomas L. *The Fight for Missouri: From the Election of Lincoln to the Death of Lyon.* Charles Scribner's Sons. New York, New York. 1886.

Southern Historical Society Papers, Volumes 44 – 50. 1923. Kraus Reprint Company. Millwood, New York. 1977.

Stephens, Walter B. *The Centennial History of Missouri: 1821- 1921.* Volume I.

Stewart, A.J.D. *The History of the Bench and Bar of Missouri.* Legal Publishing Company. St. Louis, Missouri. 1898.

Stover, John F. *The Routledge Historical Atlas of the American Railroads.* Routledge Publishing. New York, New York. 1999.

Sulzby, James F., Jr. *Historic Alabama Hotels and Resorts.* University of Alabama Press. Tuscaloosa, Alabama. 1960.

Thomas, Emory M. *The Confederate State of Richmond: A Biography of the Capital.* University of Texas Press. Austin, Texas. 1971.

Thompson, M. Jeff. *The Civil War Reminiscences of General M. Jeff Thompson.* Berquist, Goodwin F., Bowers, Paul C. and Stanton, Donal J., editors. Morningside Publishing. 1988.

Tixier, Victor. *Tixier's Travels on the Osage Prairies.* Editor, McDermott, John Francis. University of Oklahoma Press. Norman, Oklahoma. 1940.

Tucker, Phillip Thomas. *The Forgotten "Stonewall of the West:" Major General John Stevens Bowen. Mercer University Press*. Macon, Georgia. 1997.

Tyler Family History.

Upham, Alfred H. *Old Miami: The Yale of the Early West*. The Republican Publishing Company. Hamilton, Ohio. 1909.

Wakelyn, Jon L. *Biographical Dictionary of the Confederacy*. Greenwood Press. Westport, Connecticut. 1977.

Walther, Eric H. *The Fire-Eaters.* Louisiana State University Press. Baton Rouge, Louisiana. 1992.

Walther, Eric H. *William Lowndes Yancey and the Coming of the Civil War*. Chapel Hill University of North Carolina Press.

Ware, E.F. *The Lyon Campaign in Missouri: A History of the First Iowa Infantry*. Crane and Company. Topeka, Kansas. 1907. (Reprint by Camp Pope Bookshop)

Webb, W.L. *Centennial History of Independence*. 1927.

Welch, G. Murlin. *Border Warfare "In Southeastern Kansas: 1856 – 1859*. Linn County Publishing, Co. Inc. Pleasanton, Kansas. 1977.

Welch, Jack D. *The Medical Histories of Confederate Generals*. Kent State University Press. Kent, Ohio. 1995.

Wilcox, Pearl. *Jackson County Pioneers*. Jackson County Historical Society. 1990. (Reprint)

Williams, Harrison. *Legends of Loudoun*. Garrett & Massie Publishers. Richmond, Virginia. 1938.

Winegard, Timothy C. *The Mosquito*. Penguin Random House LLC. New York, New York. 2019.

Wood, Larry. *The Siege of Lexington, Missouri: The Battle of the Hemp Bales*. The History Press. Charleston, South Carolina. 2014.

Yearns, Wilfred B. *The Confederate Congress.* University of Georgia Press. Athens, Georgia. 1960.

Pamphlets & Booklets

The Battle of Lexington: Fought in and About the City of Lexington, Missouri on September 18th, 19th and 20th 1861, Recollections of Participants, Official Records, Maps and Cuts. The Intelligencer Printing Company. 1903. (1999 Reprint)

The City Intelligencer or Stranger's Guide. By V. & C. Macfarlane & Ferguson, Printers. 1862. (*Note*: Richmond, Virginia)

Lexington, Missouri: 1822 – 1972. Official Commemorative Book.

Neosho, A City of Springs.

Presettlement Prairie of Missouri. Schroeder, Walter A. Missouri Department of Conservation. 1982.

Proceedings and Speeches on the Announcement of the Death of Hon. R.L.Y. Peyton of Missouri. Sentinel Job Office. 1864.

Tyler, L.H. *Cassville: Pioneer Missourians and the Early Wars.* Barry County Historical Society. 1981. (Pamphlet)

Thesis

Harcourt, Verna. *Pioneer Days of Oxford Through 1859: A Thesis Submitted to Faculty of Miami University.* 1953.

Magazines

Confederate Veteran. Volume XI. 1903.

The Green Bag: An Entertaining Magazine for Lawyers. The Boston Book Company. Boston, Massachusetts. Volume X. 1898.

Newspapers

Bolivar Pilot. 1859.

Border Star. 1860.
Cass County Gazette. July 1855 and October 1856.
Chicago Chronicle. December 22, 1895.
Columbia Missouri Herald. 1880.
Daily Missouri Democrat. 1855 through 1860.
Daily Journal of Commerce. Kansas City, Missouri. June 2, 1863.
Glasgow Times. 1860.
Hamilton Intelligencer. Hamilton, Ohio. 1838 to 1844.
Jackson County Democrat. 1861.
Jefferson Examiner. 1856
Lexington Express. 1852.
Liberty Tribune. Liberty, Missouri. January 8, 1864.
Memphis Daily Appeal. 1859 to 1863.
Missouri's Army Argus. 1861.
The Missouri Republican. December 19, 1863.
The Montgomery Standard. Montgomery County, Missouri. August 26, 1904.
Richmond Examiner. Richmond, Virginia. 1863.
St. Charles Banner – News. St. Charles, Missouri. 1902.
St. Louis Post-Dispatch. January 5, 1896.
Salisbury Press – Spectator. 1898.
Weekly Missouri Statesman. 1855 – 1860.
Western Democrat. Harrisonville, Missouri.

Articles

Boone, B.G. "A Trio of Great Orators: The Campaign of1860 – Peyton, Philips, and Vest." *Cass County Democrat*. June 8, 1899.

Bowen, Nancy Bunker. "An Uncivil Warrior: Missouri's Col. James J. Clarkson."

Brooks, Frank H. "Harrisonville Back Numbers." *Cass County Democrat*. 1916.

Brooks, Frank H. "Missouri Bygones." A Series. *Cass County Democrat*. 1917.

Crittenden, T.T. "Selections from the Autobiography of Governor T.T. Crittenden, Part I." *Missouri Historical Review*. Vol. 26, No. 1.
Dyer, Thomas G. "A Most Unexampled Exhibition of Madness and Brutality: Judge Lynch in Saline County, Mo., 1859." *Missouri Historical Review*. Vol. 89. Nos. 3 & 4. July 1995.

Easley, Virginia, Editor. "Journal of the Civil War in Missouri: 1861, Henry Martyn Cheavens." *Missouri History Review*. October 1861.

Harrison, Constance Carry. "Richmond Scenes in '62." *Battles and Leaders of the Civil War. The Struggle Intensifies, Vol. II*. Reprint Castle Publishing.

Heiser, Alta. "A Printer's Troubles, Oxford, Ohio, During the Eighteen-Thirties. *Ohio History Journal*. Volume 47. No. 1. PP. 40 – 58.

Horton, Laurel. "History: The Parlor." *Southern Spaces*. 2006.

Hulbert, Archer B. "The Old National Road." Hulbert, Archer B. *Ohio History Journal*. Volume 9, No. 3. January 1901.

Kuhr, Manuel Irwin. "How George Vest Came to Missouri." *Missouri Historical Review*. Vol. LIX, No. 4. July 1965.

Kirkpatrick, Arthur Roy. "The Admission of Missouri to the Confederacy." *Missouri Historical Review*. Volume 55, No. 4. July 1961.

Kirkpatrick, Arthur R. "Missouri's Delegation to the Confederate Congress." *Missouri Historical Review*.

Lewis, Warner. "Senator Robert L.Y. Peyton." *The Montgomery Standard*. Montgomery County, Missouri. August 26, 1904.

McCurdy, Frances. "Courtroom Oratory of the Pioneer Period." *Missouri History Review*. Vol. 56. October 1861.

Malin, James. "The Identification of the Stranger at the Pottawatomie Massacre." K*ansas Historical Review*. Vol. 9, No. 1.

"Memorial Monuments and Tablets in Kansas." *Kansas Historical Collection*. Volume XI. 1909- 1910.

"Montgomery Hall: A Plantation and a Park." *Augusta Historical Bulletin*. Volume 53. 2017. (From "The National Register Nomination submitted by Frazier & Associates to the Virginia Department of Historic Resources for inclusion of the park on the National Register of Historic Places.)

Mullen, Jay Carlton. "Pope's New Madrid and Island Number 10 Campaigns." *Missouri Historical Review*. Volume LIX, No. 3. April 1965.

Musser, Richard H. "The War in Missouri." *Southern Bivouac*. April 1886.

Organ, Minnie. "History of the County Press." *Missouri Historical Review*. Vol. 4, No. 4. July 1910.

Pantle, Alberta, Editor. "The Story of a Kansas Freedman." *Kansas Historical Quarterly*. Vol. XI, No. 4. November 1942.

"The Parlor." *American Heritage*. Vol. 14, No. 6. October 1963.

Peyton, John Lewis. "Sketch of Hon. Robert L. Y. Peyton of Missouri: 1825 – 1863." *The Magazine of American History*. Volume XVI. July – December 1886.

"Price Farm Home Burns." *Crossroads*. Cass County Historical Society. Winter 2004.

Robbins, Eloise Frisbie. "The Original Military Post Road Between Fort Leavenworth and Fort Scott." *Kansas History*.

Rodabaugh, James H. "Miami University, Calvinism, and the Anti-Slavery Movement." *Ohio History Journal*. Volume 48. No. 1. PP. 66 – 73.

Ryle, Walter Harrington, PhD. "Missouri: Union or Secession." George Peabody College for Teachers. Nashville, Tennessee. 1931.

Ryle, Walter H. "Slavery and Party Realignment in the State Election." *The Missouri Historical Review*.

Schneider, Norris F. "The National Road: Main Street of America." *Ohio History Journal*. Volume 83.

Sloan, Charles W. "Robert Ludwell Yates Peyton." *The Green Bag*. Volume X, No. 10. October, 1898.

Smith, Ophia D. "Gold Rush Days." Alice Phelan Sullivan Library. The Society of California Pioneers. San Francisco, California.

Snyder, Dr. John F. "The Capture of Lexington." *Missouri Historical Review*. Vol. 7, No. 1. October 1912.

Snyder, Dr. John F. "The Democratic State Convention of Missouri in 1860." *Missouri Historical Review*. Vol. II, No. 2. January 1908.

Sparlin, Estal E. "The Jefferson Inquirer." *Missouri Historical Review*. Vol. 32, No. 2. January 1938.
Warren, Harris Gaylord. "Vignettes of Culture of Old Clairborne." *The Journal of Mississippi History. Volume XX.*

Woods, James M. "Devotees and Dissenters: Arkansans in the Confederate Congress, 1861 – 1865." *Arkansas Historical Quarterly*. 1978.

Interviews

Stuckey, Janice. Special Collections Librarian. King Library, Miami University. February 23, 2011.

Family Histories, Personal Diaries and Letters

"Aunt Lizzies Story." *Glimpses of the Past, Vol. I-III*. St. Louis Historical Society. 1933-1936.

Bourne, Ezra Diary. Alice Phelan Sullivan Library at the Society of California Pioneers. San Francisco, California.

Brown, Elizabeth Daniel. "Autobiographical Sketches – Elizabeth Daniel Brown." Tennessee Historical Society.

Dean, Abner H. *Reminiscences of Half a Century*. Jackson County, Missouri, Archives. Jackson County Historical Society.

Eakin, Joanne Chiles. *Diary of a Doctor, Missouri State Guards, 1861*. Two Trails Publishing. Independence, Missouri. 1999. (*Note*: Diary of John Wiatt)
Donovan, Ethel. *The White Family*.

Jones, John B. *A Rebel War Clerk's Diary*. J.B. Lippincott & Co. Philadelphia, Pennsylvania. 1866. Reprinted 1982.

Harding, Samuel Bannister, Ph. D. *Life of George R. Smith*. Privately Published. Sedalia, Missouri. 1904.

Magoffin, Susan S. *Down the Santa Fe Trail and Into Mexico: The Diary of Susan Shelby Magoffin*.

Overdyke, W. Darrell. "A Southern Family on the Missouri Frontier: Letters from Independence, 1843 – 1855." *The Journal of Southern History*. Volume XVII (May 1951), pages 216 – 237. *The Letters of Samuel Ralston*. Located in the Missouri Valley Collections of the Kansas City Public Library.

Price Genealogy: Silas and Mary Ellen Price of Cass County, Mo. Price, Dr. William E. 1996.

Reese, Dr. Alexander W. *Personal Recollections*. Kansas State Historical Society.

Ruffin, Edmund. *The Diary of Edmund Ruffin, Volume II: the Years of Hope, April, 1861 – June, 1863*. Edited by Scarborough, William Kauffman. Louisiana State University Press. Baton Rouge, Louisiana. 1976.

Smith, A.B. "A.B. Smith Letters." Manuscripts Collection. Missouri History Museum and Archives. St. Louis, Missouri.

Stephen Douglas Papers. Special Collections. University of Chicago. Box 32.

Walker Diary. Manuscripts Collection. State Historical Society of Missouri.

Wright, Louise Wigfall. *As Southern Girl in '61: The War-time Memories of a Confederate Senator's Daughter, 1861-1865*. 1905. Reprint by Corner House Historical Publications. Gansevoort, New York. 2000.

Government Records

NARA. Record Group: 153. Records of the Judge Advocate General (Army). Court Martial Files.

Oakham Farm. National Register of Historic Places. United States Department of the Interior. National Park Service. Middleburg, Loudoun County, Virginia.

The War of the Rebellion: A Compilation of the Official Records of the Union and Confederate Armies. 128 Volumes and Atlas. Government Printing Office. Washington, D.C. 1881 to 1901. *(Note*: cited as *OR)*

Report of the Special Committee appointed to Investigate the Troubles in Kansas; with The Views of the Minority of Said Committee. Cornelius Wendell Printer. Washington, D.C. 1856.

Official Records of the State of Missouri

Journal of the House of Representatives of the State of Missouri. First Session. 20th General Assembly. C.J.Corwin, Public Printer. Jefferson City, Missouri. 1859.

Journal of the House of Representatives of Missouri. Called Session of the Twenty-First General Assembly.

Journal of the Senate of Missouri. First Session. 20th General Assembly. C.J.Corwin, Public Printer. Jefferson City, Missouri. 1859.

Journal of the Senate of Missouri. First Session, Twenty-First General Assembly.

Journal of the Senate of the State of Missouri, Called Session.

Journal of the Senate. Rebel Legislature.

Laws of Missouri. Volume 17. 1860-1861.

Missouri State Archives. Cass County Case Files. Jefferson City, Missouri.

Missouri State Archives. Election Returns. Boxes 4 & 5.

Missouri Secretary of State. Missouri State Archives. Missouri's Union Provost Marshal Papers: 1861 – 1865.

Missouri State Archives. Record Group 5: Pardons. Jefferson City, Missouri.

Missouri State Archives. Special Collections. “Missouri-Kansas Border War, 1858 to 1860.” Jefferson City. Missouri.

Missouri Supreme Court Records. Missouri State Archives. Jefferson City, Missouri.

Butler County, Ohio, Records

Butler County, Ohio. Marriage Records Index.

Butler County, Ohio. Probate Court Records.

Cass County, Missouri, Records

Cass County Circuit Court Records. Book C.

Cass County Circuit Court Records. Court Minutes. Book 275-9.

Cass County Circuit Court Records. Minute Book. Book 275-14.

Cass County Circuit Court Records. Book 80-8. November 1849 to September 1858.

Cass County Circuit Court Records. Special Session. May 25, 1854.

Cass County. Record of Transcripts.1848 to 1861.Book 313 – 1.

Cass County Trial Docket. September 1849 to September 1856. Book 275 – 10.

Circuit Court. Van Buren County. Minute Book. March 1842 to March 1851.

County Court Minutes. 1836 to 1845. Book 317 – 1.

County Court Minutes. September 1846 – September 1856. Book 275 – 9.

Cass County. Executive Docket: Fee Book. 1837 to 1849. Book 275 – 5.
Cass County Probate Files.

King George County, Virginia, Records

King George County, Va. Deed Book 8.

King George County, Va. Deed Book 14.

Lafayette County, Missouri

Lafayette County Circuit Court Records. Box 27.

General Archives

"An Address Delivered Before the Graduates of the Erodelphian Society of Miami University, August 10, 1841." Millikan, Thomas. Miami University Archives.

"Faculty Minutes – 1844." Special Collections. Miami University Archives.

Jefferson Davis Papers. William Stanley Hoole Collection. University of Alabama.

Papers of Thomas Coute Reynolds, 1862-1866.

Record Group: Student Lives. Sub-Group: Literary Societies. Box 1. Miami University Archives.

INDEX

A

B

C

D

E

F

G

H

I

J

K

L

M

N

O

P

Q

R

S

T

U

V

W

Y